The Coolie's
Great War

RADHIKA SINGHA

The Coolie's Great War

Indian Labour in a Global Conflict 1914-1921

HarperCollins *Publishers* India

First published in the UK in 2020 by
C. Hurst & Co. (Publishers) Ltd.,
41 Great Russell Street, London, WC1B 3PL

First published in India in 2020 by
HarperCollins *Publishers*
A-75, Sector 57, Noida, Uttar Pradesh 201301, India
www.harpercollins.co.in

2 4 6 8 10 9 7 5 3 1

P-ISBN: 978-93-5357-985-2
E-ISBN: 978-93-5357-986-9

Printed and bound at
Thomson Press (India) Ltd.

For Ravi

CONTENTS

GLOSSARY

arkatia	labour contractor
beldar	navvy
bhangis	those who cleaned out human excrement, a derogatory term
bhent and *begar*	forced supplies, forced labour
bhisti	water-carrier
boi	sometimes translated as slave, a very dependent stratum of Lushai (Mizo) society
chungi	top-knot
coolie utar	compulsory porterage
daffadar	cavalry NCO; also a title for jail-recruited warder or overseer
dhobi	washerman
drabi	mule-driver
ganthia	knot (here, a knot on a rope)
ghadar	insurgency, rebellion
gurgas	utensil-washers
hakim	official, person in authority
jangi inam	a war reward in the form of a monthly payment
jehazi	seamen
kafir	infidel
kahar	palanquin- or stretcher-bearers
kamin	village artisan and labourer, not belonging to the coparcenary land-holding community
khalasi	labour employed by the Ordnance Department, for loading and unloading stores (also labour used for pitching tents)

GLOSSARY

langri	cook for Indian regiments
lascar	'coloured' merchant seaman, engaged on a distinct contract
likapui	high platform outside a Lushai (Mizo) home
lohar	ironsmith
mahayudh	great war
meli	rebellious gathering
mochi	cobbler, leather-worker
muharrir	clerk, accountant
padhan	head man
pakhal	water-carrier
pugri	turban
punkah	fan
sahayak	assistant
sardar	chief
sarkar	government
syce	groom and grass-cutter
tamasha	performance, spectacle
thlangra	winnowing tray (Mizo)
zamindar	landowner

LIST OF ILLUSTRATIONS

1. Map, 'Mohammedans' in the British, Turkish and French empires, in G. A. Natesan (ed.), *All About the War: The Indian Review War Book*, Madras: Natesan and Co., 1915, p. 208, https://archive.org/details/ in.ernet.dli.2015.144570. Out of copyright.
2. Maintenance train on the Bolan Pass line, 1890.
   Photograph by William Edge. Reproduced by kind permission of David Edge, grandson of William Edge, and acknowledgements to Ravindra Bhalerao's blog 'Railways of the Raj', http://railwaysofraj.blogspot. com/2010/01.
3. Indian mule cart train embarks from Alexandria for Gallipoli, April 1915. Reproduced by kind permission of Centre for Armed Forces Historical Research, United Services Institution, Delhi.
4. At the horse pond, Indian muleteers, France (n.d., 1914–15).
   Reproduced by kind permission of In Flanders Field Museum, Ieper, Belgium.
5. Stretcher bearers carrying a patient along a track, Gallipoli, 1915.
   A. D. Hood collection, Australian War Museum, P0116.055.
6. Washerman *dhobis*, Swat campaign, 1915.
   Reproduced by kind permission of Robert Clark.
7. Pumping up water for the *bhistis*, Swat campaign, 1915.
   Reproduced by kind permission of Robert Clark.
8. Indian camp followers, Marseilles, 1914.
   Reproduced by kind permission of In Flanders Field Museum, Ieper, Belgium.

LIST OF ACRONYMS

AD	Army Department, Government of India
ADG	Adjutant General, India
AR	Army Regulation
ASA	Assam State Archives, Guwahati
CC	Chief Commissioner
C-in-C	Commander-in-Chief
CLC	Chinese Labour Corps
CO	Commanding Officer
DGIMS	Director General, Indian Medical Service
GOC	General Officer Commanding
GOI	Government of India
IAA	Indian Army Act
ILC	Indian Labour Corps
IOR	India Office Records and Library
IPC	Indian Porter Corps
JAG	Judge Advocate General
KSA	Karnataka State Archives
MD	Military Department, Government of India
MSA	Maharashtra State Archives
NAI	National Archives of India, Delhi
QMG	Quartermaster General
QMTS	Queen Mary's Technical School
SANLC	South African Native Labour Contingent
SSI	Secretary of State for India
S&T	Supply and Transport
TNA	The National Archives, Kew Gardens, London
TNSA	Tamil Nadu State Archives

ACKNOWLEDGEMENTS

This book is dedicated to Ravi, my steady source of happiness since we met at Jawaharlal Nehru University, Delhi, some forty years ago. Without his support, companionship and decisive interventions this book would not have seen the light of day. His ability to sum up an argument with sharpness and clarity has left its mark on every chapter. He has reason to feel immensely relieved that he doesn't have to suffer through any further revisions of the manuscript.

In the crucial finishing stages of this book I benefitted hugely from the comments and suggestions of Hari Vasudevan, Ravi Ahuja, Santanu Das, Peter Anatol Lieven, Prabhu Mohapatra, Janaki Nair, Aditya Sarkar, Chitra Joshi and Marcel van der Linden. Others who, as editors, scholars, colleagues and friends, have gone through previous articles and drafts are Nandini Sundar, George Morton-Jack, James Kitchen, Anupama Rao, David Akin, Ian Kerr, Heike Liebau, Jan Lucassen, Renisa Mawani, Thomas Metcalf, Sumit Sarkar, Tanika Sarkar, Dominiek Dendooven and Prasannan Parthasarathi.

I owe a lot to the generosity of fellow historians, some of whom, such as John Starling, I have never even met. John shared his notes from war diaries and gifted me a copy of *No Labour, No Battle: Military Labour During the First World War*, the pioneering monograph he wrote with Ivor Lee. Joy Pachuau allowed me to use her translation of Sainghinga Sailo's memoir *Indopui* as well as extracts from the periodical *Mizo leh Vai*. Rinku Arda Pegu and Lipokmar Dzuvichu introduced me to Assam and the hill districts of the North-East Frontier, a region I knew very little about. A conversation with Tanika Sarkar made all the difference between finishing this project and seeing it collapse. Professor K. C. Yadav, Director of the Haryana Academy of History and Culture, has done sterling work putting together material on World War One and making it available to scholars. He also organised a lovely outing to Bhondsi village in

ACKNOWLEDGEMENTS

Haryana to see a war memorial and meet with descendants of World War One servicemen. Squadron Leader Rana T. S. Chhina, Secretary for the Centre for Armed Forces Historical Research at the United Service Institution in Delhi, patiently scrutinised certain sections to weed out factual errors, gave me crucial help with images, and invited me to conferences on World War One where diverse opinions were freely aired. These are the liberal traditions of the Indian Army which I remember from my father and my uncles' generation of service families. Santanu Das, who has done path-breaking work on the cultural history of World War One, was someone with whom I could laugh, gossip and exchange ideas over the internet and at conferences. I cherish the memory of my brilliant, kind and supportive Ph.D supervisor, Chris Bayly, who put South Asia centrally in the field of global history. My conversations with Harald Fischer-Tiné, Mrinalini Sinha, Luisa Passerini, Jane Caplan, Douglas Peers, Mark Brown and Gopalan Balachandran contributed to my learning curve in transnational history. At Hurst, Michael Dwyer understood that I wasn't going to make it for the centenary of the end of the war and let it ride, and Farhaana Arefin has been a very supportive editor. I thank Erin Cunningham for her alert and empathetic copy editing and I am grateful to the two reviewers who gave me their comments on the manuscript submitted to Hurst. My thanks also to Siddhesh Inamdar and HarperCollins India for handling the Indian edition of this book.

My first opportunity to read widely on World War One and to pick out the threads which wove South Asia into this conjuncture came with a five-month fellowship in 2011 at the Lichtenberg-Kolleg, the Göttingen Institute for Advanced Study. Professor Dr Dagmar Coester-Waltjen was the scholarly, gracious and highly focused director of this Institute, who did everything possible to create a collegial environment. The weekly seminars were of a high quality, but what remains in my memory is the berry pie served with coffee at our more informal gatherings, as well as the soothing ease of being able to cycle around everywhere instead of the arduous experience of negotiating traffic in Delhi.

The other, equally serene interlude which allowed me to explore both the European theatre of war and to absorb some of the new writing on demobilisation came about through a three-month fellowship at the Institute for Advanced Study in Nantes in 2016. My grateful thanks to Professor Samuel Jubé, the Director of the IAS-Nantes, and to Aspasia Nanaki, the Secretary General, for sustaining such a pleasant and productive environment—I was able to start working literally from day one. Among those who enlivened mealtimes were Babacar Fall, José Emilio Burucua, Sudhir Chandra and Geetanjali Pandey.

ACKNOWLEDGEMENTS

The Nehru Memorial Museum and Library has been for years the one substantial resource which historians of modern and contemporary India can count on, and a two-year fellowship there gave me the sustained time I needed to wind up this project. I thank the two directors of this institute, Professor Mahesh Rangarajan and Shri Shakti Sinha, for their support.

Among the conferences which helped me to shape various chapters of this book were one held in 2007 at the Zentrum Moderner Orient in Berlin, which made a serious effort to bring 'the global south' into the history of the two world wars; another titled 'Asia, the Great War and the Continuum of Violence' at University College Dublin in 2012; and 'The World During the First World War', a symposium organised by the Volkswagen Foundation at Hanover in 2013. An absorbing seminar, 'Iterations of the Law', put together by Bhavani Raman, Rashmi Pant and Aparna Balachandran at the Nehru Memorial Museum and Library the same year, enthused me to get a grip on military law. The Centre for Armed Forces Historical Research organised an important international seminar titled 'India and the Great War' in Delhi in March 2014, and one in collaboration with the In Flanders Fields Museum and King's College London in October 2014 focusing on 'Indians at the Western Front'. The conferences held by the Association of Indian Labour Historians at the V. V. Giri Labour Institute, Noida, provided a regular platform for interaction. I am grateful to the Nehru Memorial Museum and Library, the National Archives of India and the Odisha State Archives at Bhubaneshwar for inviting me to give public lectures on World War One. It was also a privilege to deliver the inaugural lecture in the *Itineraries of Empire* series at the Centre for India and South Asia Research, a part of the Institute of Asian Research at the University of British Columbia, Vancouver, in February 2014. My struggle to understand something of war finance was helped along by a paper presented at the Kerala History Congress in December 2016, thereafter revised and presented at Wellington in April 2017 for 'The Myriad Faces of War: 1917 and its Legacy'. Professor Sekhar Bandyopadhyay kindly arranged for my participation in this event under the aegis of the New Zealand India Research Institute. The first time I ever participated in an arts event was through an invitation extended by the Raqs Media Collective to give a public lecture at their exhibition at Colchester titled 'Not Yet At Ease' in 2018. The weary closing stages of writing were enlivened by a conference titled 'Masters of Their Own Destiny: Asians in the First World War and its Aftermath', organised by the History Department of Chulalongkorn University and the Institute of Research on Contemporary

Southeast Asia (IRASEC—CNRS), in Bangkok in November 2018, and by an invitation to talk on 'The North East in World War One' by the North-Eastern Student Collective 'Mosaic' at the Tata Institute of Social Sciences in Mumbai in January 2019. The last chapter of my book was aired in its final form at a public seminar organised by the Global History and Culture Centre at Warwick University in February 2019.

I am indebted to the staff of the National Archives of India in Delhi for their help, especially Jaya Ravindran. The canteen workers there and I have grown old together. The dust of its files has entered my DNA and the tea served there runs in my veins. Opening up a digitised file is a soulless experience by comparison. The Delhi Archives and the United Service Institution have been the other spaces which have provided resources for this book. Duster in hand, Father George Gispert Sauch introduced me to the periodicals and books of the Vidyajyoti College of Theology Library, Delhi, and trusted me enough to let me work late there on my own. My memory of places is filtered through encounters at various archives—the Maharashtra State Archives housed in Elphinstone College, the Tamil Nadu Archives in Chennai, the Odisha State Archives in Bhubaneshwar, the Karnataka State Archives in Bengaluru, and the Jharkhand State Archives in Ranchi. I thank Father Alexius Ekka, the director of the Xavier Institute of Social Service in Ranchi, for research support and Professor Krityanand Bhagat for his generous help with all arrangements. Research interludes in Mumbai and Bengaluru gave me the additional pleasure of one-on-one sibling time with my brothers. Some of these trips have been sponsored by grants from the Centre of Advanced Studies programme administered by the Centre for Historical Studies, Jawaharlal Nehru University. My colleague Radha Gayathri not only helps with advice in this matter, but gives me fragrant tea in beautiful cups.

The staff of the Oriental and India Office Collections Reading Room dispense the treasures of the British Library to visitors from all over the world with pleasant professionalism. The National Archives at Kew and the Imperial War Museum provided valuable material. The Cambridge South Asian Archive offered a cosy niche, one in which tea and biscuits were also on offer, and for this I thank Chris Bayly, who was Director at the time, and Kevin Greenbank, Barbara Roe and Rachel Rowe.

Chapters Two, Three, Four and Five of this book had previous incarnations in the following publications: 'Finding Labor from India for the War in Iraq: The Jail Porter and Labour Corps, 1916–1920', *Comparative Studies in Society and History*, vol. 49, no. 2 (2007), pp. 412–45; 'Front Lines and Status Lines:

Sepoy and "Menial" in the Great War, 1916–1920', in Heike Liebau et al. (eds), *The World in World Wars: Experiences, Perceptions and Perspectives from Africa and Asia*, Leiden: Brill, 2010, pp. 55–106; 'The Recruiter's Eye on "The Primitive": To France—and Back—in the Indian Labour Corps, 1917–18', in James E. Kitchen, Alisa Miller and Laura Rowe (eds), *Other Combatants, Other Fronts: Competing Histories of the First World War*, Newcastle upon Tyne: Cambridge Scholars Publishing, 2011, pp. 199–224; and 'The Short Career of the Indian Labour Corps in France, 1917–1919', *International Labor and Working-Class History*, 87 (2015), pp. 27–62.

I acquired my love for history from my father, 'Eno', and miss him so much and so often. I remember with deep gratitude the loving care of Basantu Ram Chacha, and of Kaushaliya Masi who allowed me to think of her home as my home for decades. My mother Daya taught me to value aspiration and hard work and my sister Anjali Rani gives me life-lessons in fortitude. Rani has kept me happy despite the troubling times we live in, as have Karan, Sanjeev, Neeta and Hema. Chand Ahooja has been the nicest, most supportive cousin possible, even if Ganga Ram Hospital is the only place we manage to have a cup of coffee together. I thank Seema Alavi, Ben and Rana Behal, Neeladri Bhattacharya, Budhi Singh Bisht, Jim Cook, Rachel Dwyer, Suvrita Khatri, Mukul Mangalik, Prabhu Mohapatra, Fareda Nariman Abrar, Anne Ninan, Kumkum Roy, Rukun Advani, Anuradha Roy, Anju Singh, Nandini Sundar, Brij and Kamini Tankha, Siddharth Varadarajan, Ulrike Siegelohr and Susan Vishwanathan for their presence in my world. The warmth and generosity of Isabelle and Robert Tombs made every research interlude in the UK really very wonderful for Ravi and I.

Those who have not spent long years in undergraduate teaching would not understand the sense of creative freedom I felt when a late-in-life appointment at the Centre for Historical Studies at Jawaharlal Nehru University gave me room to formulate my own courses and time to do my own research. Up to the fateful year 2016 it was a joyous experience, and my students continue to leave their questioning impress on every theme I explore. Agendas have changed, and turning out docile technocrats and managers rather than thoughtful and humane citizens is now the priority of the powers that be. This beloved public university, this verdant space in India's capital city, is now ritualistically defamed by anyone setting himself or herself up as a super-patriot. I wish I could find words to express the full measure of my admiration for those students, teachers and staff of JNU who, in the face of sustained intimidation, defend liberal values and keep visible those being abandoned as citizens.

INTRODUCTION

I didn't know it at the time, but a few lines that I put in print in 2004 would slowly materialise as this book.[1] The newspaper article in question expressed the revulsion many then felt about the possibility that Indian troops might be sent in support of the U.S. occupation of Iraq. In the ineffectual way of historians I found myself in the National Archives at Delhi, going through the records of that fateful conjuncture in World War One when Indian soldiers sailed into the Persian Gulf at the behest of another superpower. What intrigued me was a confidential letter from Mesopotamia in March 1916 calling urgently for latrine sweepers from India. Clearly, trouble was piling up in more ways than one for Indian Expeditionary Force D. But why was this correspondence marked 'confidential'? It turned out that cholera had broken out at Basra and sweepers were going to be placed in jeopardy at that epidemic front. Later, Indian washermen, *dhobis*, were also demanded in large numbers, with a glancing admission that their work in the disinfection sections of military hospitals would expose them to special risk.

I began to dip into the archives to find out more about the war experiences of the follower or non-combatant ranks of the Indian Army, sometimes harvesting only a line or two. What emerged was a story of back-breaking work by construction workers, porters, mule-drivers, stretcher-bearers, cooks, sweepers and grooms, a story barely mentioned in the official literature on 'India's Contribution to the Great War'. Friends at the Association of Indian

---

[1] Radhika Singha, 'Iraq: on duty once again?', *The Hindu*, 21 March 2004, https://www.thehindu.com/todays-paper/tp-features/tp-sundaymagazine/iraq-on-duty-once-again/article28526093.ece, last accessed 26 September 2019.

Labour Historians encouraged me to present the occasional paper on the follower ranks of the Indian Army. A lively legal history seminar in 2013 prompted me to move away from my comfort zone, that of colonial criminal law, and to take in military law as well.[2] The other field in which I have long had an interest is the history of movement and migration, and its necessary constituent, the history of colonial border-making. The geopolitical ambitions of empire rested not only upon the ability to tap into the labour and productive resources of millions of smallholder farms in India, but also upon the manipulation of patterns of movement across India's land and sea frontiers to imperial ends.[3] I have drawn upon this proposition to explore various themes in this book, enjoying the connections it created between the files of the military, commerce and emigration, finance, foreign and legislative departments.

The use of India's demographic resources for imperial military purposes also spoke to my growing interest in the buoyant field of transnational or 'connected' history, a history which moves between local, national and global spaces and between different timeframes to explore a particular event.[4] The centenary of the war came along and I missed the tide which took many manuscripts past the finishing line. However, I found myself in the spirited company of World War One historians, engaged in a mind-boggling range of new themes, and they were hospitable to a rank newcomer in the field. If I have any excuse at all for this meandering path, it is a love for dawdling in the

---

[2] Radhika Singha, 'The "Rare Infliction": The Abolition of Flogging in the Indian Army, circa 1835–1920', *Law and History Review*, vol. 34, no. 3 (2016), pp. 783–818.

[3] See Radhika Singha, 'India's Silver Bullets: War Loans and War Propaganda, 1917–18', in Maartje Abbenhuis, Neill Atkinson, Kingsley Baird and Gail Romano (eds), *The Myriad Legacies of 1917: A Year of War and Revolution*, Cham: Palgrave Macmillan, 2018, pp. 77–102; and 'The Great War and a "Proper" Passport for the Colony: Border-Crossing in British India, c. 1882–1922', *Indian Economic and Social History Review*, vol. 50, no. 3 (2013), pp. 289–315. For an excellent exploration of Indian military and police circulation around the Indian Ocean, see Thomas R. Metcalf, *Imperial Connections: India in the Indian Ocean Arena, 1860–1920*, Ranikhet: Permanent Black, 2007, pp. 68–101.

[4] Santanu Das moves deftly between imperial, national and local frames to give us a beautifully textured account of the multiplicity of Indian experiences of World War One. See Santanu Das, *India, Empire, and First World War Culture: Writing, Images, and Songs*, Cambridge: Cambridge University Press, 2018.

archives, working at more than one project at a time, and teaching and supervising students.

I have used the word 'coolie' in the title of the book to denote a category of labour consigned to the lowest rung of the global market in the nineteenth century, one presumed to be unskilled and infinitely replaceable.[5] My aim was to open a conversation between military history and labour history, and to shine some light on actors consigned to the sidelines of the story of India in World War One. Of the 1.4 million Indians recruited to the war up to 31 December 1919, some 563,369 were followers or non-combatants.[6] For different reasons, both the colonial regime and the Indian intelligentsia preferred to foreground the 'martial classes', and to let 'coolies' and 'menial followers' simply swell the total of India's manpower contribution. The Government of India wanted to throw a military cloak over the 'coolie', to bypass controversies around indentured migration as well as the formalities of the Indian Emigration Act. Educated Indians preferred to dwell on the figure of the valorous sepoy to advance their political claims, rather than on the subjugated figure of the coolie or the regimental 'menial'.

However, the aim of this book is not only to rescue the coolie and 'the menial' in military employment from their condition of historical obscurity. It is also to find vantage points for developing a less Eurocentric, more transnational account of World War One.[7] How can we position India 'in' the

---

[5] I draw here upon Jan Breman and E. Valentine Daniel, 'Conclusion: The Making of a Coolie', *The Journal of Peasant Studies*, vol. 19, nos 3–4 (1992), pp. 268–95.

[6] *War Office: Statistics of the Military Effort of the British Empire During the Great War, 1914–1920*, London: HMSO, 1922, p. 777. The proportion of non-combatants to combatants went up during the war from 1:3 to 3:5. This is based on the prewar figure of 159,134 serving Indian combatants and 45,660 non-combatants, versus 877,068 combatants and 563,369 non-combatants for the war period up to 31 December 1919 (ibid., p. 777). The high proportion of non-combatants may account for the relatively low figure of mortality for the Indian Army in World War One, that is 53,486 dead and 64,350 wounded (ibid., p. 778). However, qualitative evidence suggests that morbidity was very high for non-combatants.

[7] For other such exercises, see Heike Liebau, Katrin Bromber, Dyala Hamza, Katharina Lange and Ravi Ahuja (eds), *The World in World Wars: Experiences, Perceptions and Perspectives from Africa and Asia*, Leiden: Brill, 2010; Dominiek Dendooven and Piet Chielens (eds), *World War I: Five Continents in Flanders*, Tielt: Lannoo, 2008; Das, *India, Empire, and First World War Culture*.

Great War instead of viewing the latter only as an external conflict to which the nation 'contributed'? How can we do so while nevertheless retaining a sense of the 'lumpiness' of this worldwide conflict, the differences in timeline, form, scale and intensity through which its impact was felt?[8]

Jane Burbank and Frederick Cooper suggest that World War One should be evaluated not just as a conflict between different European nation states, but as an interimperial conflict, with empires understood as 'multiplex polities'.[9] The declaration of war was the signal for an escalation of ongoing struggles for strategic advantage, territory and resources in Africa, the Middle and Near East, and the South China Sea. The outcome of these contests would have a deep impact on the nature of the postwar international order.[10] Chapter

---

[8] Frederick Cooper underlines the importance of staying alert to variations in the depth or thinness of transborder connections and to the nature of their connecting mechanisms. Frederick Cooper, 'What Is the Concept of Globalization Good For? An African Historian's Perspective', *African Affairs*, vol. 100, no. 399 (2001), pp. 189–213. One striking illustration of differences in scales of loss is the figure of 53,486 dead and 64,350 wounded from the 1.4 million Indians recruited for the army, and the death toll exacted by the influenza epidemic of 1918–19, which, by modified estimates, amounted to 13.88 million. War Office, *Statistics*, p. 778; Siddharth Chandra, Goran Kuljanin and Jennifer Wray, 'Mortality from the Influenza Pandemic of 1918–1919: The Case of India', *Demography*, vol. 49, no. 3 (2012), pp. 857–65. The effect of the wartime movement of men and grain stocks on the spread of plague, cholera and relapsing fever remains to be investigated.

[9] Jane Burbank and Frederick Cooper, *Empires in World History: Power and the Politics of Difference*, Princeton: Princeton University Press, 2010, p. 371. For the importance of history made at interweaving imperial frameworks, see A. G. Hopkins, 'Back to the Future: From National History to Imperial History', *Past and Present*, vol. 164, no. 1 (1999), pp. 198–243; and Selim Deringil, '"They Live in a State of Nomadism and Savagery": The Late Ottoman Empire and the Post-Colonial Debate', *Comparative Studies in Society and History*, vol. 45, no. 2 (2003), pp. 311–42.

[10] Michelle Moyd, 'Extra-European Theatres of War', in *1914–1918-online, International Encyclopedia of the First World War*, eds Ute Daniel, Peter Gatrell, Oliver Janz, Heather Jones, Jennifer Keene, Alan Kramer, and Bill Nasson, Freie Universität Berlin, https://encyclopedia.1914–1918-online.net/article/extra-european_theatres_of_war, last accessed 10 November 2019; Brian Digre, *Imperialism's New Clothes: The Repartition of Tropical Africa, 1914–1919,* New York: Peter Lang, 1990; and Melvin E. Page and Andy McKinlay (eds), *Africa and the First World War*, London: Palgrave Macmillan, 1987.

One steps back to locate World War One in the longer history of the deployment of Indian manpower in arenas stretching out across the land and sea frontiers of India.[11] These arenas were constituted by overarching imperial geopolitics, but also by regionally driven ambitions. As the opening chapter shows, one of the 'sub-imperial' drives emanating from India was a contest for influence along the Arabian frontiers of the Ottoman Empire. The Government of India therefore had to stay ever attentive to diverse Muslim publics within India and across her borders.[12] This imperative had to be worked out even more elaborately in World War One, given that the Ottoman Sultan was allied with Germany, and one-third of the Indian Army was made up of Muslims. The Russian Revolution of November 1917 and the signing of the Treaty of Brest-Litovsk on 3 March 1918 likewise prompted engagement with transnational Muslim publics. 'German-Turco-Bolshevik intrigue' in Central Asia, Persia and Afghanistan seemed to bring war closer to the borders of India, and covert and overt operations by the Indian Army were deployed to throw up a barrier.[13]

Chapters One and Four engage with one of the key themes of this book—that is, the labour regimes and ecologies of work which sustained the colonial military infrastructure in India. India's role as an imperial garrison east of the Suez meant that a third of the colony's pre-World War One annual budget was spent on the army. This does not take account of roads and railways built for strategic, rather than commercial, imperatives.[14] The proportion would have

---

[11] By going into the pre-World War One deployment of the Indian Army, Morton-Jack sharpens our understanding of its operational performance in World War One. At the point of their arrival in France, he notes crisply, Indian soldiers were professionals who were 'more travelled, more politically aware and more militarily skilled' than some evaluations of their achievements in World War One suggest. George Morton-Jack, *The Indian Empire at War: From Jihad to Victory, The Untold Story of the Indian Army in the First World War*, London: Little, Brown and Company, 2018, pp. 38–50. See also George Morton-Jack, *The Indian Army on the Western Front: India's Expeditionary Force to France and Belgium in the First World War*, Cambridge: Cambridge University Press, 2014, chapters 3 and 4.

[12] See Chapter 1.

[13] Hari Vasudevan drew my attention to the importance of this shift, but it was difficult to engage with this complex story in a book focusing on non-combatant manpower.

[14] P. J. Thomas, *The Growth of Federal Finance in India: Being a Survey of India's Public*

been even higher but for arrangements which allowed the military and military police columns to draw not only upon waged labour, but also upon labour obtained through tributary arrangements with frontier chiefs and through corvée or 'labour tax', mobilised by subordinate revenue agencies.[15] Militarised border-making also involved arrangements to secure supplies and draught cattle.[16]

Between 1914 and 1920, the colonial border-making complex was repurposed for global war. Men, material and information began to move between existing zones of conflict and new arenas of imperial ambition. This had a loopback effect, concluding in implosions along India's borders in 1918–19. Chapters Four and Six argue that the so-called 'minor frontier operations' of 1917–20 were not disconnected from the battles of worldwide significance taking place elsewhere.

A long-term and transnational perspective gives us a full sense of the factors which complicated the deployment of Indian manpower to theatres of war. The army's manpower needs had to be constantly weighed against other imperatives equally crucial to an empire at war: the generation of material resources, the creation of export surpluses, and the maintenance of transport infrastructures. The circulation of Indian labour around the Bay of Bengal was allowed to continue throughout the war, if on a reduced scale, because it sustained docks, mines, plantations, and oil works in Ceylon, Malaya, the Straits and Burma.[17] On the eve of World War One, 17.5 per cent of sailors on British merchant ships were lascars (seamen) from the Indian subcontinent, and the percentage increased as British seamen were drafted into the navy.[18]

Finances from 1833 to 1939, London: Oxford University Press, 1939, p. 497, table 3. See Chapter 6.

[15] See Chapter 4; also Lipokmar Dzuvichu, 'Empire on their Backs: Coolies in the Eastern Borderlands of the British Raj', *International Review of Social History*, vol. 59, no. 22 (2014), pp. 89–112.

[16] For the impact of the prodigious military demand for animal transport upon rural life and upon irrigation projects in the Punjab, see James Louis Hevia, *Animal Labor and Colonial Warfare*, Chicago: Chicago University Press, 2018, chapter 6.

[17] F&P, Secret, General, August 1917, pp. 10–99.

[18] Conrad Dixon, 'Lascars: The Forgotten Sea-Men', in R. Ommer and G. Panting (eds), *Working Men Who Got Wet*, St John's: Memorial University of Newfoundland, 1980, pp. 265–81, 265.

Chapter Two profiles the protagonists of this book: the follower ranks of the Indian Army, permanent and temporary. It assesses the service distinctions between combatants and followers, arguing that the follower's work of 'care' bolstered both the race standing of the British soldier and the status superiority of the 'martial castes'. It analyses the condition of 'menial' standing which structured the service milieu for attached followers—those such as the cook, sweeper, horse-groom, water-carrier, and cobbler. It was an institutional position shaped by the equation made between their work and that of domestic servants. This naturalised the assumption that they should be permanently 'on call', and subject to a regime of highly discretionary discipline. The presence among the attached followers of so-called 'untouchable' castes who were assigned to stigmatising work also kept them at the bottom of the status scale. This chapter goes into the specifics of contracts, wages, kit and allowances, and how these distinguished soldiers from followers, and different followers from one another. It also tracks the unsettling of these differences from 1916 onwards due to the acute difficulty of maintaining follower strength. This led to an improvement in wages and service conditions, particularly for the 'higher followers'—those who made up the transport, medical and ordnance departments. However, some room had to be made for the acknowledgement of 'war service' even amongst 'menial' followers.

Interestingly, a modern managerial discourse about manpower efficiency also found freer expression in the discussion about follower ranks than it did in considerations of combatants.[19] Chapter Two points out that from the turn of the century, military officers who pressed for better wages and service conditions for the follower ranks argued that if 'raw coolies' were to be turned into cooks and sweepers who understood the rudiments of sanitation, drilled stretcher-bearers, and mule-drivers who would not bolt under fire, then train-

---

[19] From the late nineteenth century, the word 'efficiency' was used as a shorthand in Britain for the belief that the application of scientific, technical and business expertise would make the best use of human energy, time, and natural resources, thereby arresting the decline of empire. A linked proposition was that only a much more interventionist state, acting over and above party politics, could bring this about. See Geoffrey Searle, 'The Politics of National Efficiency and of War, 1900–1918' in Chris Wrigley (ed.), *A Companion to Early Twentieth-Century Britain*, Malden, MA:, Wiley-Blackwell, 2003, pp. 56–71. For a tentative exploration of the discussion about 'labour efficiency' inside and outside the Indian Army during the same period, see 'Afterword'.

ing needed to intensify.[20] This had to be backed up by higher wages, food, kit and medical care to 'stimulate recruiting, reduce desertion and produce greater efficiency.'[21] The crowning argument was that the efficiency of the combatant ranks, British and Indian, depended crucially on an improvement of the auxiliary services. The epilogue to this book comments briefly on the stimulus which World War One gave to such discussions about labour efficiency, both in the realm of military service and in relation to Indian mill-hands.

Chapter Three focuses on the Mesopotamian campaign, beginning with the conjuncture at which there was a crisis in the supply of every sort of follower category. This problem emerged at a time when there was a full-scale movement underway to bring an end to the system of indentured contract by which Indian labour was sent overseas to sustain imperial sugar plantations. There followed intense debates as to the legal form through which Indian labour might be sent for 'military work overseas' without recourse to the pilloried system of indentured migration. Allegations over force and fraud in indentured migration also made it necessary for the Government of India to keep declaring that recruitment for the army was entirely 'voluntary', even when it was sourcing labour from jails or deploying the authority structures of corvée to complete recruitment for the Labour and Porter Corps. One way to reconcile this contradiction was to offer an emancipation from certain forms of labour servitude as the reward for 'war service'. For instance, the raising of Jail Porter and Labour Corps for Mesopotamia was presented as an interesting experiment in allowing prisoners to earn their way to an earlier release. The Government of India could thereby situate itself within international discussions about 'scientific penology'. In reality, some unreconstructed and regularly critiqued features of the Indian jail regime, such as the reliance on warders recruited from among convicts, turned out to be eminently suitable to the deployment of prison labour for war purposes.

Some of the new writing on the 'sideshows' of World War One— Mesopotamia, Palestine, and East Africa—has given us a fuller picture of

---

[20] For a good illustration see A. E. Milner, 'The Army Bearer Corps', *Journal of the Royal Army Medical Corps*, vol. 6, no. 6 (1906), pp. 685–89.

[21] Telegram from Viceroy to Secretary of State for India (SSI), 9 November 1917, explaining the decision to reduce the gap in service conditions between the Army Bearer Corps and the Indian soldier. Army Department, Adjutant General's Branch (AD, ADG), Medical, A, May 1919, nos 2238–46, National Archives of India, Delhi. All manuscript references are from this archive unless otherwise stated.

Britain's reliance upon human, animal and material resources from her dependent colonies.[22] Chapters Three and Four show that to maximise recruitment, the boundaries between different methods of bringing labour to the worksite were often overthrown. Existing forms of labour servitude were shaped to new ends. But officials were also compelled to take some account of structured patterns of off-farm waged work. Advance wages had to be paid to placate families and creditors, and sometimes fixed terms of a year or two years had to be offered in place of the 'duration of war' agreements which were compulsory for combatants and permanent followers. This book shows that repatriation at the end of a fixed term did not just happen. Temporary followers, such as the men in the Labour and Porter Corps, often had to struggle to bring it about. Chapters Three and Five deal with such incidents. Nevertheless, the army's need to replenish labour supply meant that it could not use force alone to keep manpower in place. It also had to persuade followers to renew their agreements, and this gave workers some bargaining power at the point of termination.

The fourth chapter highlights India's long history of drawing upon 'tribal populations' from Bihar, Orissa and the Assam-Burma hill districts for border-making along the North-East Frontier. In 1917, these labour regimes were intensified to raise Labour and Porter Corps for France. The deployment of 'primitive' subjects in the most industrialised theatre of the war was an exercise which spoke to a variety of different agendas—those of local chiefs, missionaries, paternalist administrator-ethnographers and first generation 'tribal' literati. The chapter discusses the reasons recruitment evoked more resistance in some instances than in others, highlighting the far-reaching impact of the war on seemingly remote areas such as the Assam-Burma border.

---

[22] Drawing productively upon Avner Offer's thesis that Britain's agrarian hinterland in the Dominions and the USA gave her the ability to outlast Germany, Kristian Coates Ulrichsen highlights the huge manpower and animal-power demand exerted upon Egypt and India by industrial warfare in the backward tracts of Ottoman Arabia. Kristian Coates Ulrichsen, *The Logistics and Politics of the British Campaigns in the Middle East, 1914–22*, Basingstoke: Palgrave Macmillan, 2011. See also David Killingray and James Matthews, 'Beasts of Burden: British West African Carriers in the First World War', *Canadian Journal of African Studies*, vol. 13, nos 1–2 (1979), pp. 5–23; and James Kitchen, 'The Indianization of the Egyptian Expeditionary Force: Palestine 1918', in Kaushik Roy (ed.), *The Indian Army in the Two World Wars*, Leiden: Brill, 2012, pp. 165–90.

Chapter Five adds the story of the Indian Labour Corps (ILC) to the now multiplying accounts of the various 'coloured' units brought into France to deal with the manpower crisis which overtook the western theatre of war by 1916. The labels of 'coloured' and 'native' labour justified inferior care and a harsher work and disciplinary regime than that which white labourers experienced. However, official reports and newspaper coverage also expose a dense play of ethnographic comparison between 'coloured corps'. The prevailing notion was that in order to 'work' natives properly, the supervisory regimes peculiar to them also had to be imported into the metropolis. The register of comparison was also shaped by specific political and social agendas which gave some 'coloured units' more room than others to negotiate acknowledgement of their services.

This chapter also explores the war experience of Indian labourers in France. What was their experience of the journey to this front, and of the social, institutional and material landscapes through which they moved? At one level they were being made over into military property, but at another there are intimations of their own efforts to reframe the environments, object worlds, and orders of time within which they were positioned. By creating suggestive equivalences between themselves and other military personnel, they sought to lift themselves from the status of coolies to that of participants in a common project of war service. At the same time, they indicated that they had not put themselves at the disposal of the state in exactly the same way as the Indian soldier had.

The concluding chapter draws upon approaches to demobilisation which assess it as a back-and-forth process, one whose morphology was defined by many interventions. As underlined earlier, different terms of engagement for different categories of follower meant that a very variegated timeline marked the termination of military service. There was a flow of men back to India throughout the war, made up of non-combatants who had completed their engagement, those granted furlough, invalided or discharged, and those who deserted. Using multiple timelines, Chapter Six explores the return from military service as a significant part of the war experience of Indian combatants and non-combatants—one which they tried to shape. Institutional hierarchies determined the distribution of war rewards, but due to a paucity of sources, soldiers and non-combatants are often dealt with together in this chapter.

Most histories of demobilisation have searched for links between returning soldiers and labourers and the seething political unrest of 1919–21. This chapter points out that for many Indian soldiers and followers, the period was one marked by continued deployment and deferment of leave as much as by the halting process of demobilisation. In a context in which British and Dominion troops were being demobilised, the extended post-Armistice deployment of Indian troops and followers amplified everyday challenges to race and status hierarchy. In the process, 'the veteran' was added to the hectic proliferation of political constituencies encouraged by the demands of war on the colony and the promise in 1917 of constitutional change. Throughout 1919–21, Punjab was still treated as an imperial 'home front', one which had to be kept secure for the empire through the extension of wartime executive authoritarianism. What emerged was a multisited political effort in India to arrest this slippage from wartime state of emergency to postwar imperial militarism. To a long-standing campaign to 'nationalise' the use of Indian 'coolies', there was added a demand for a 'national' say in the use of India's military manpower.

1

INDIAN LABOUR AND THE GEOGRAPHIES
OF THE GREAT WAR

In 1919, English journalist Edmund Candler wrote that:

> The Labour Corps in Mesopotamia introduced the nearest thing to Babel since
> the original confusion of tongues. Coolies and artisans came in from China
> and Egypt, and from the East and West Indies, the aboriginal Santals and
> Paharias from Bengal, Moplahs, Thyas and Nayars from the West Coast,
> Nepalese quarrymen, Indians of all races and creeds, as well as the Arabs and
> Chaldeans of the country.[1]

War journalists delighted in such descriptions of the wild ethnographic mix
brought together at worksites of World War One. Such spectacles seemed to
illustrate both the 'belonging' of diverse people within empire and the ability
of the ruling race to bring order and productivity out of chaos.[2]

The follower ranks of the Indian Army provided ample occasion for such
self-gratifying reflections. Dizzyingly diverse, they included the departmental
followers who made up the medical, transport and ordnance services, and the
attached followers, who were assigned to regiments or other formations as
cooks, sweepers, water-carriers, grass-cutters and grooms, laundrymen, blacksmiths, and cobblers. In addition there were the 'Coolie Corps' for porterage

---

[1] Edmund Candler, *The Sepoy*, John Murray: London, 1919, p. 217.
[2] '[A] man in Khaki Kit, who could handle men a bit', Rudyard Kipling, 'Pharoah and
the Sergeant', 1897.

and road-building or other construction work, who were a familiar feature of militaristic border-making in India. At some frontier stations there were virtually permanent Coolie Corps, but these units were not regarded as part of the army establishment.[3] The Coolie Corps give us a sense of the importance of the non-combatant element to that long history of mobile imperial militarism which preceded World War One. Coolie units accompanied many expeditionary forces sent from India: for instance, to Abyssinia (1868), China (1900), and Somaliland (1902–4). Indian Expeditionary Force B, sent to German East Africa in November 1914, had two Coolie Corps of 300 men each attached to the 25th and 26th Railway Companies.[4] Other units sent overseas in World War One were given the politically more acceptable label of the Indian Porter and Labour Corps to distance them from the system of indentured coolie migration, which was stigmatised by that time.

In 1915, Porter Corps from Madras Presidency and two Labour Corps from Punjab were raised for Gallipoli but diverted to Mesopotamia, where the Indian Expeditionary Force was facing an acute logistical crisis. Starting in 1916, the jails of India were also trawled for this theatre and some 16,000 prisoners were enrolled, the bulk in seven Jail Porter and Labour Corps, but 1,602 as sweepers or in miscellaneous units such as a Jail Gardener Corps.[5] A total of nineteen Indian Labour Corps (ILC) and twelve Indian Porter Corps (IPC) were sent to Mesopotamia.[6] Some, such as the Indian Labour and Porter Corps positioned at Bushire, South Persia, and along the Baghdad-

---

[3] After the Abor punitive expedition of 1911–12 along the route from upper Assam to Tibet, a standing Coolie Corps was maintained at Sadiya. Foreign, External, B, September 1914, no. 64.

[4] Harry Fecitt, April 2015. 'The Indian Railway Corps, East African Expeditionary Force 1914–1919', http://gweaa.com/wp-content/uploads/2012/02/The-Indian-Railway-Corps-East-African-Expeditionary-Force_1.pdf, last accessed 10 November 2019.

[5] Radhika Singha, 'Finding Labor from India for the War in Iraq: The Jail Porter and Labor Corps, 1916–1920', *Comparative Studies in Society and History*, vol. 49, no. 2 (2007), pp. 412–45.

[6] *India's Contribution to the Great War*, Calcutta: Superintendent Government Printing Press, 1923, p. 92 (henceforth *ICGW*). The strength of a Labour Corps sent to Mesopotamia was 1,000 men, later raised to 1,250; that of a Porter Corps was 800, but both often rose much higher. The strength of Labour Corps sent to France was 2,000 men, but these were divided into companies of 500.

Khanikin-Hamadan route, went on to play a role in the undeclared war in Persia. In February 1917, the Government of India undertook to provide 50,000 labourers for France as well, but an official report states that it was eventually decided to raise 30,000.[7] Sent as Labour Corps of 2,000 men, they were reorganised in France as units of 500, making up the 21st through to the 85th Indian labour companies. And finally, in October 1918, two agricultural units were dispatched to Salonika.[8] The signing of the Armistice on 11 November 1918 did not reduce the demand for labour in Mesopotamia and Persia, and drafts continued to be raised between 1919 and 1921 to replace the companies that were being repatriated.

Table 1: Distribution of Indian non-combatants across theatres of war.[9]

Mesopotamia	336,890
France	48,537
Egypt	25,512
Persian Gulf	25,301
East Africa	12,699
Gallipoli and Salonika	6,416
Aden	5,050

A complete table would include the large number of non-combatants required when war circled inwards to India's own borders in the form of the

---

[7] 'Recruiting in India Before and During the War of 1914–18', IOR/L/MIL/17/5/2152, p. 39 (IOR: India Office Library and Records). George Morton-Jack points out that the total number of non-combatants sent to the western front was 49,278, so the number for those in the ILC is probably the lower figure of 28,000, the balance being made up by attached followers. He draws upon the following sources: *War Office: Statistics of the Military Effort of the British Empire During the Great War, 1914–1920*, London: HMSO, 1922, p. 777; *Fourth Supplement to London Gazette*, 25 July 1919, p. 9541, and *ICGW*, p. 96. I am persuaded by his argument, but I would accept the somewhat higher figure of 30,000 to take account of later drafts.

[8] The 99th Indian labour company and the 102nd ILC, 'Recruiting in India', appendix XV, p. 77. Indian mule transport units pulling Punjabi and Greek ploughs grew crops and vegetables in Macedonia. 'Indian Military Transport Units in Macedonia', The Soldier's Burden, http://www.kaiserscross.com/304501/534401.html, last accessed 16 March 2019.

[9] Statement in Indian Legislative Council, 1 March 1919, Legislative, B, May 1919, nos 199–201.

Kuki-Chin operations of 1917–19 along the Assam-Burma border and, on the other side, the Third Afghan War, which trailed into the Waziristan campaign (1919–20).

The follower ranks of the Indian Army: new spatial and social frames

In tracking the localities from which followers originated, and the networks through which they were recruited, we move from conventional depictions of the composition of the Indian Army to a more complex social and political narrative. There is already an excellent body of work on the 'martial caste' construct, critically analysing the contention that in India, in contrast to Europe, soldiers could only come from a select list of 'martial castes and tribes'.[10] In World War One, this stereotype would be elaborated through ever more tense contrasts with the 'effeminate' educated Indian. I examine how the 'martial caste' status of the Indian sepoy and the race superiority of the white soldier were also anchored in the 'menial' status assigned to the attached followers, those charged with 'the care of the fighting man'. The notion that Indian soldiers were drawn from a superior 'yeomanry' and the follower ranks from the low-caste labouring and artisanal stratum, the *kamin* of Punjab villages, fed smoothly into depictions of the Indian Army as an idyllic extension of rural society, with the Raj as the benevolent *jajman*, or patron, receiving from each according to social standing and rewarding each accordingly.[11]

However, the figure of the follower could also disturb this idyllic vision, associated as it was with the disturbing erosion of 'traditional' occupations

---

[10] David Omissi, *The Sepoy and the Raj: The Indian Army, 1860–1940*, London: Macmillan, 1994; Heather Streets, *Martial Races: The Military, Race and Masculinity in British Imperial Culture, 1857–1914*, Manchester: Manchester University Press, 2004; Lionel Caplan, *Warrior Gentlemen, 'Gurkhas' in the Western Imagination*, Oxford: Berghahn, 1995.

[11] In India, wrote MacMunn, there was no exodus to the city and it was the landowner and the grazier who did the soldiering. This 'yeoman' recruit was 'a wellborn man, distinct from the mere helot of low birth who in some parts helps on the land.' MacMunn also sailed into a blithe description of the contrast between this figure and that of the British soldier, dragged into service he said, from the dregs of society. George F. MacMunn, *The Armies of India*, London: Adam and Charles Black, 1911, pp. 130–31, 189. *Kamin* was sometimes translated as 'village menial'.

and with rural migration to towns and construction sites. The regimental follower seemed to draw elements of the 'bazaar' and the market into the healthful space of the cantonment or military station, making it permeable to disease, contaminated liquor, and unsettling news.[12]

These idealised oppositions between 'yeoman' and 'village menial', between the countryside and the bazaar, found expression in institutional and symbolic distinctions between service conditions for sepoys and those for the follower ranks. The Government of India was readier to make a long-term financial commitment to family reproduction when it involved the sepoy as opposed to the follower, hoping thereby to strengthen its ties with dominant peasant communities. Yet if one appraises migrant streams pooling around road and railway heads, lumber camps, cantonments, garrisons, and hill stations along India's frontiers, one discovers significant overlaps between the recruiting base for combatant and non-combatant units of the Indian Army.[13]

When we bring follower labour into the frame, 'untouchable' and 'tribal' communities edge their way into the story of India in the Great War—so too do jail populations and those categorised as 'criminal tribes', the latter recruited for an extraordinarily wide spectrum of war work within India as well. We can also factor in, however notionally, the labour of women and children, whose role in sustaining the infrastructure of military stations and maintaining continuity of work at construction sites became more visible as men left for the war.[14] Most importantly, the non-waged work of women on

---

[12] One of the stories which circulated about the 1857 mutiny was that a low-caste *khalasi* (labourer) of the arsenal at Dum-Dum had taunted a Brahmin sepoy saying his caste pretensions would soon be shattered when he had to bite cartridges soaked in beef and pig fat. Noah Alfred Chick, *Annals of the Indian Rebellion 1857–58*, Calcutta: Sanders, Cones and Company, 1859, p. 30. See also Neema Cherian, 'Spaces for Races: Ordering of Camp Followers in the Military Cantonments, Madras Presidency, c. 1800–64', *Social Scientist*, vol. 32, nos 5/6 (2004), pp. 32–50; and Erica Wald, 'Health, Discipline and Appropriate Behavior: The Body of the Soldier and the Shape of the Cantonment', *Modern Asian Studies*, vol. 46, no. 4 (2012), pp. 815–56.

[13] See Chapter 2.

[14] From Kashmir eastwards to Assam, women were present in work gangs and porter columns attached to frontier expeditions. There were 600 Sikkimese women in the 10,000-strong Coolie Corps which accompanied Francis Younghusband's military expedition to Tibet in 1903. Patrick French, *Younghusband: The Last Great Imperial*

family farms allowed men to seek waged work in the army. One report stated confidently that recruitment had not disrupted agriculture in Gurgaon district because women of most castes worked in the field.[15] However, reporting from the adjoining tract of Delhi, Chief Commissioner Malcolm Hailey said that Jat women were obstructing recruitment, because with so many men being taken they were being sent into the fields, 'and quite apart from any marital or maternal feelings, they resent the enforced labour'.[16] An article explaining the impact of war upon rubber plantations in southern India uses the illustration of a woman tapper to describe the profitable extraction of Ceara rubber.[17] A British war documentary on tea, highlighting the far-flung resources of empire, shows happy women labourers on Assam plantations.[18] European women and some upper-class Indian women organised medical care, got socks knit and shirts tailored, packaged troop 'comforts' and pushed up war loan subscriptions. The list of honours and awards in India gives us a glimpse of this activity. Women doctors were inducted into military hospitals in India, an indication of the drain upon the civilian medical infrastructure, rudimentary as it was, for military use.[19] News of British women making their

---

Adventurer, London: Harper Collins, 1994, pp. 201, 217. Women were also among those impressed as porters during the 1911–12 Abor expedition from upper Assam. A. Bentinck, IOR Mss, Eur. D 1024/3. Long lines of women walked up planks to empty head-loads of coal into the ships carrying men and material from Bombay and Colombo to theatres of war. Boy followers, and 'boy' recruits and buglers, were a regular feature of prewar military life. In World War One there were constant complaints about men who were too old and boys who were far too young being recruited as followers and labourers.

[15] *Record of War Work in the Gurgaon District*, Poona: Scottish Mission Industries, 1923, p. 26.

[16] Chief Commissioner, Delhi, 31 July 1917, in Home, Political, Deposit, August 1917, no. 3. For the burden imposed on women in over-recruited villages of Nepal see Candler, *The Sepoy*, p. 21. Nevertheless, the official publication, *India's Contribution to the Great War*, points out apologetically that Indian women were 'far less able than their European sisters to replace men required for military service.' *ICGW*, p. 225.

[17] Arnold Wright, *Southern India: Its History, People, Commerce and Industrial Resources*, London: The Foreign and Colonial Compiling and Publishing Co., 1914–15, p. 226.

[18] 'The Story of India Tea 1917–1918', British Pathé, https://www.youtube.com/watch?v=v5merLaAw4A, last accessed 10 November 2019.

[19] Women doctors and surgeons ran the Freeman Thomas War Hospital in Bombay.

entry into new spheres of work and employment captured the imagination of educated Indian women.[20] A fourteen-year-old Parsi girl pointed out that one of the good things emerging from the war was that women had proved they could do all the work of a man, and fight too.[21] More broadly, the paucity of work on the extraction of material resources from India has obscured the wartime role of millions of small producers on farms and rubber and tea plantations, and in textile factories and mines. In April 1919, acute pressure on the supply of silver for minting rupee coins brought this contribution forcefully home. The Government of India was faced with the prospect that millions of small producers might stop bringing services and agricultural products to the market if there were not enough rupee coins in circulation. This 'secession' would have strangled the war effort.[22] The silver crisis of 1917–18 did much to disrupt the notion that India was at the periphery of the war.[23]

A focus on non-combatants also corrects too Punjab-centered a narrative of World War One. Moving into the Gangetic valley, we find that the United Provinces supplied the largest number of non-combatants, and came second in terms of combatants.[24] Further eastwards, the largely 'tribal' tracts of Chota

---

The Tribune, 12 December 1917; Sir George Barrow, *The Life of General Sir Charles Carmichael Monro*, London: Hutchinson, 1931, p. 145.

[20] Indian soldiers and labourers were not only intrigued but also remarkably appreciative of this development. In contrast, there were sometimes shockingly violent views in the Indian press about the suffragette movement.

[21] Dinoo S. Bastavala, *Stray Thoughts on the War*, Bombay: Commercial Press, 1918.

[22] Radhika Singha, 'India's Silver Bullets: War Loans and War Propaganda 1917–1918', in Maartje Abbenhuis, Neill Atkinson, Kingsley Baird, and Gail Romano (eds), *The Myriad Legacies of 1917: A Year of War and Revolution*, Cham: Palgrave Macmillan, 2018, pp. 77–102.

[23] This was the wartime 'romance' of the Finance Department of India—the story of how Finance Member William Meyer 'held the gate' against declaring that paper currency was now inconvertible to coin, and James Brunyate, formerly of the Indian Civil Service, fought the battle in Washington to secure American silver for India under the Pittman Act. *Financial Statement of the Government of India for 1919–20*, Bombay: Government Central Press, p. 52. I thank Alastair McClure for the suggestion that the connected nature of the war occasionally challenged the idea of a world divided into metropolitan centres and colonial peripheries.

[24] *ICGW*, p. 277. In the period July 1918 to October 1918, the United Provinces outstripped Punjab in the aggregate number of combatants and non-combatants. 'Recruiting in India', p. 25, IOR/L/MIL/17/5/2152.

Nagpur and the Santhal Parganas provided military labour for Mesopotamia, France, and the North-West Frontier. Along the sweep of the Himalayan ranges the recruiter's eye turned to Hazara, Pashtun, and Kumaoni labourers, who had become adept at rock-cutting, lime-burning, and laying roads and railway tracks, and to the hill-men of Assam and Burma, long incorporated into border porterage and road construction. Turning to Bengal, we see that it was the first province to have a Technical Recruiting Office, and its seafarers worked on the inland waterways and constructed railways in Mesopotamia.[25] Moving south, the Madras Presidency supplied the first Porter Corps as well as railway construction labour for Mesopotamia.

Table 2: Share of each province in obtaining combatant and non-combatant recruits up to the Armistice.[26]

Provinces	Non-combatants	Combatants	Total
Punjab	97,288	349,688	446,976
United Provinces	117,565	163,578	281,143
Madras	41,117	51,223	92,340
Bombay	30,211	41,272	71,483
Bengal	51,935	7,117	59,052
Bihar and Orissa	32,976	8,576	41,552
North West Frontier Province	13,050	32,181	45,231
Burma	4,579	14,094	18,673
Assam	14,182	942	15,124
Central Provinces	9,631	5,376	15,007
Ajmer-Merwara	1,632	7,341	8,973
Baluchistan	327	1,761	2,088
Total	414,493	683,149	1,097,642

Sub-imperial drives and the globalisation of war

Let it be known to all that from of old the British Government has had many millions of Muhammadan subjects, more than any other Power in the world, more even than Turkey.[27]

---

[25] 'Recruiting in India', p. 50.

[26] *ICGW*, p. 277. Adding 58,904 recruits from Nepal and 115,891 from the Indian princely states, the total up to the Armistice was 445,582 non-combatants and 826,855 combatants. Ibid. The War Office statistics take the totals up to 31 December 1919, so they are higher.

[27] 'Proclamation issued on behalf of the General Officer Commanding the British

Hew Strachan points out that terms such as 'the Great War' or 'the European Great War', commonly used at the time in England and France, reflected the belief that World War One was a fratricidal war waged largely between civilised and Christian powers of Europe.[28] The Hindi press in India also used the phrase *European Mahayudh*, the European Great War, and sometimes *German Yudh*, the German War. Both these labels captured the sense that these events were in some way external, implying that it was the struggle between European powers which had set off the conflagration and that its outcome would be decided there.[29] In Indian autobiographies, World War One is remembered pre-eminently as a clash between Britain and Germany, even though the greater proportion of South Asian troops fought in Ottoman domains.[30] In part this was because, keeping the sensitivities of Muslim soldiers and publics in mind, the Government of India avoided any extreme vilification of the Ottoman Sultan. In its war propaganda Turkey was cast as the dupe of Germany, or was portrayed in thrall to the 'atheist' Committee of Union and Progress.[31]

Forces in Occupation of Basra', 22 November 1914, in Arnold Wilson, *Loyalties; Mesopotamia, 1914–1917: A Personal and Historical Record*, London: Oxford University Press, 1930, p. 311.

[28] Hew Strachan, 'The First World War as a Global War', *First World War Studies*, vol. 1, no. 1 (2010), pp. 3–14.

[29] The Urdu newspaper *Zamindar*, published from Lahore, held that the tolling of war bells in Europe was just retribution for the violence European imperialism had long inflicted on Asia: 'If war is declared it won't be confined to Austria and Serbia, it will be a universal war in which all the great empires of Europe will be involved. The giant which has so far been ruining Asia will now be engaged in ruining himself; the materials of war which have so far been used to destroy Orientals will now be employed in the destruction of Europeans.' *Zamindar*, 30 July 1914, in *Selections from the Native Newspapers for Punjab*, no. 31, 1 August 1914. This statement was made before the Ottoman Empire threw its lot in with Germany.

[30] See, for example, Govind Ram Kala, *Memoir of the Raj*, New Delhi: Mukul Prakashan, 1974; Harivansh Rai Bachchan, *In the Afternoon of Time: An Autobiography*, trans. and ed. Rupert Snell, Delhi: Penguin, 2001; and Kali Ghosh, *The Autobiography of a Revolutionary in British India*, New Delhi: Social Science Press, 2013.

[31] Chandrika Kaul, *Reporting the Raj: The British Press and India, c. 1880–1920*, Manchester: Manchester University Press, 2003, p. 128. A pamphlet for Indian schoolboys said that England and Turkey had no real enmity; that it was Germany which had forced Turkey to declare war; that the deserts of Mesopotamia had been

However, in the opening phase of the war, what the label *European Mahayudh* also captured was the sense of wonder, both in India and in Britain, about an extraordinary departure from the spatial pattern in which Indian military manpower was typically deployed: namely, the sailing on 25 August 1914 of the first division of the Indian Corps for France. If the future of the world was going to be decided on the battlefields of France and Belgium, remarkably enough India had been allowed to register her presence there. In the official history, *India's Contribution to the Great War* (1923), one learns only a few pages later that India also sent an infantry brigade to the Persian Gulf, an Imperial Service Cavalry Brigade to Egypt and a mixed force to East Africa.[32] This followed, after all, the familiar arc of imperial power, one put in place not only through South Asian military and police units, but also through the circulation of artisanal and labour gangs, merchants, and pilgrims.[33] The pink colouration of empire oozed out from India not only along oceanic highways but also across her land borders towards Afghanistan and southern Persia on the one side and towards Chinese Central Asia, Tibet, and Yunan on the other.

Against this background, we can expand upon Hew Strachan's explanation for the rapid spread of conflict from the European centre to the periphery in 1914. The states of Europe were imperial powers, so war for Europe meant war for the world. However, Germany's enthusiasm for expanding the conflict, Strachan argues, 'was not primarily a form of covert imperialism. It was a way of fighting the war.'[34] Britain correspondingly had a pressing need to bring the war to an end. Its principal task outside Europe was defensive—to

---

made green and fertile; that in Palestine an English general had entered Jerusalem on foot and said every sacred place would be respected; and that Punjabi Muslims were given the honour of guarding the great mosque of Omar. P. Charlier, *The Empire at War 1914–18: A Short History for Indian Students*, Bombay: Oxford University Press, 1920, p. 21. Describing the capture of Baghdad, an Indian cavalryman commented: 'It is a matter of the greatest joy to us Muslims that this sacred place has escaped out of the hands of the evil Germans'. Risaldar Malik Mahomed Latif Khan PM, 28th Light Cavalry, Seistan, Persia, to Jemadar Usuf Ali Khan, 19th Lancers, France, 15 April 1917, IOR/L/MIL/5/827/2 letter 507, p. 286.

[32] *ICGW*, 1923, pp. 61, 75.

[33] By the 1880s, army officers felt they could pick up transport coolies for British expeditionary forces from around the Indian Ocean, choosing between Chinese, Indian and African carriers. Major G. Salis Schwabe, 'Carrier Corps and Coolies on Active Service in China, India, and Africa, 1860–1879', in *Journal of the Royal United Services Institution*, vol. 24, no. 108 (1881), pp. 815–48.

secure British sea routes against German attack. But while British imperialism was dormant between 1914 and 1918, argues Strachan, the sub-imperialism of her Dominions and her Entente partners flourished, and extended the terrain of conflict.[35]

In fact, sub-imperial drives from India contributed significantly to this momentum.[36] At the Arabian frontiers of the Ottoman Empire, from the Persian Gulf down to the Hijaz, the declaration of war impinged upon a long-running contest for influence and legitimacy between the Sublime Porte and the Government of India.[37] In a context in which waxing and waning multiethnic empires dominated the imagination, 'Muslim worlds' could be conceptualised around Delhi and Cairo as much as around Istanbul.[38] As Viceroy Lord Charles Hardinge and many officials in India often pointed out, going by the number of Muslim subjects in its fold, the British Empire was the 'largest Muhammadan empire' in the world.[39] This kind of demographic comparison was of crucial

---

[34] Hew Strachan, *The First World War*, New York: Viking, 2003, pp. 69–70.

[35] Ibid., p. 71.

[36] Metcalf, *Imperial Connections*; Briton Cooper Busch, *Britain, India, and the Arabs, 1914–1921*, Berkeley: University of California Press, 1971; Robert J. Blyth, *Empire of the Raj: India, Eastern Africa and the Middle East, 1858–1947*, New York: Palgrave Macmillan, 2003; Priya Satia, 'Developing Iraq: Britain, India and the Redemption of Empire and Technology in the First World War', *Past and Present*, vol. 197, no. 1 (2007), pp. 211–55. However, I would qualify Satia and Metcalf's contention that Indian nationalists shared in the subimperial ambitions of the Government of India. See Chapters 3 and 6.

[37] James Onley, *The Arabian Frontier of the British Raj: Merchants, Rulers and the British in the Nineteenth-Century Gulf*, Oxford: Oxford University Press, 2007; Busch, *Britain, India, and the Arabs*.

[38] Singha, 'Finding Labor from India for the War in Iraq'. For the imprint which the Government of India left on war aims in the earlier phase of the Mesopotamian campaign, see V. H. Rothwell, 'Mesopotamia in British War Aims, 1914–1918', *The Historical Journal*, vol. 13, no. 2 (1970), pp. 273–94.

[39] Hardinge, correspondence, vol. 3, 1915–16, Hardinge Mss, Cambridge University Library. In 1914, of the 270 million Muslims in the world some 100 million were British subjects, 20 million were under French rule, and 20 million were in the Russian Empire. Strachan, *The First World War*, p. 99. There were about 15 million Muslims in the Ottoman Empire. See illustration 1 comparing 'Mohammedans' in the British, Turkish and French empires'. G. A. Natesan (ed.), *All About the War: The Indian Review War Book*, Madras: Natesan and Co., 1915, p 208.

importance in World War One, given that about a third of the Indian Army was made up of Muslims who were being asked to stay loyal to the empire while fighting in Ottoman domains.[40] The Government of India had long congratulated itself on the quality of the 'assistance and protection' it extended to Muslim subjects on the pilgrim trek to the Hijaz, comparing it to the incompetence of the Ottomans or the conditions which Dutch, French, and Russian empires imposed on pilgrims.[41] When Muslims raised issues of concern to their community, they themselves called upon the British Empire to intervene in its capacity as 'the greatest Moslem Power upon earth'.[42]

In 1898, Kaiser Wilhelm intervened in this sphere, hailing Abdul Hamid II, the Ottoman sultan, as leader of the Muslim world. If the British press ridiculed 'Haji Wilhelm', it was because his 'soft diplomacy' was yielding dividends.[43] In World War One, to counter this challenge, the Government of India drew upon Muslim princes such as the Nizam of Hyderabad and the Begum of Bhopal, and spiritual figures such as the Aga Khan, to convince Muslims that Britain had gone to war with Turkey only because of its alliance with Germany, and to reassure them that the holy places of Islam would be safe from destruction.[44] Indian audiences were reminded in propaganda lectures that, starting with battles between the Mughals and the Portuguese, the Persian Gulf had long been regarded as the outer frontier of India. The archaeologist Gertrude Bell favoured an Arab over an Indian future for the admin-

---

[40] Of the 739,938 combatants recruited from 1 August 1914 to 30 November 1918, 240,783—that is, 32.5 per cent—were Muslims. Of these, Punjabi Muslims made up 136,126. See table, *ICGW*, appendix C, p. 276.

[41] Radhika Singha, 'Passport, Ticket, and India-Rubber Stamp: "The Problem of the Pauper Pilgrim" in Colonial India, c. 1882–1925', in Harald Fischer-Tiné and Ashwini Tambe (eds), *The Limits of British Colonial Control in South Asia: Spaces of Disorder in the Indian Ocean Region*, New York: Routledge, 2009, pp. 49–83.

[42] Ibid.

[43] Hew Strachan's magisterial work echoes this strain of thought: 'His [the Kaiser's] love of uniforms and military ceremonial, which looked faintly ridiculous to the cynics of the liberal West, struck a chord in the East. He was dubbed "Haji" Wilhelm'. Strachan, *The First World War*, p. 100.

[44] Margrit Pernau, *The Passing of Patrimonialism: Politics and Political Culture in Hyderabad 1911–1948*, Delhi: Manohar, 2000, pp. 96–97; 'Indian Mussalmans and the War' in G. A. Natesan (ed.), *All About the War: The Indian Review War Book*, Madras: G. A. Natesan, 1915.

istration of Iraq. Nevertheless, her claim of a longstanding British connection with the iconic Shia sites of Najaf and Karbala rested on a pious bequest made in 1827 by the Indian ruler, Ghazi-ud-din Haider, and dispensed annually by the Government of India.[45]

Finally, stakes in the Persian Gulf had risen sharply for the British Empire with the shift of the British Navy in 1912–13 from coal to oil, and the acquisition of a majority stake for the British government in the Anglo-Persian Oil Company (APOC).[46] By 1914 some 1,000 Indian labourers and artisans had accumulated at the APOC's works at Abadan, some drawn from the Rangoon refinery and oil fields in Burma.[47] Arguably, the success with which Indian work gangs had been moved around the Indian Ocean, from oil fields to harbour works and railway construction sites, added a 'developmentalist' vista to the strategic ambitions of the Government of India in Mesopotamia.[48]

Border perspectives

With the declaration of war, sub-imperial drives from contested tracts along the land frontiers of India were also reframed in a more internationalised context. From the 1880s, along India's North-West Frontier, construction took place on a road and railway network from Quetta to the Khyber Pass, which ensured that troops could be rushed up from Bombay and Calcutta. The same pattern of militaristic road-making was repeated on a smaller scale along stretches of India's North-East Frontier, where border-making had to be conducted on the cheap.

When India entered the war in August 1914, this militaristic construction complex along its land frontiers was tapped more intensively to raise non-combatant and combatant manpower for theatres of war overseas.[49] Skills in porterage, earth-work, rock-cutting, lime-burning, plate-laying, brick-making and lumbering, drawn upon and developed in the fold of Military Works, the Public Works Department and the Railway Board, were put at the disposal of

---

[45] 'Disposal of Conquered Territories (Mesopotamia and German East Africa)'. Note by India Office, 3 November 1918, IOR/L/PS/18/B294.

[46] Touraj Atabaki, 'Far from Home, but at Home: Indian Migrant Workers in the Iranian Oil Industry', in *Studies in History*, vol. 31, no. 1 (2015), pp. 85–114, 92.

[47] Ibid.

[48] See also Satia, 'Developing Iraq'.

[49] See Chapter 4.

empire in Mesopotamia, Persia, East Africa and France.[50] This movement of military construction practices also took place in the opposite direction; the lessons of the French theatre were increasingly applied to the Mohmand border on the North-West Frontier, where in the winter of 1916–17 a blockade was enforced by the construction of a 17-mile-wide trench system marked by 'high parapets, searchlights, machine gun blockhouses and continuous electrified barbed wire'.[51] Letters written by Indian soldiers positioned along this conflict zone reveal their perception that a worldwide circulation of military techniques was taking place. 'All along we have dug trenches just like you have in France', wrote Ahmad Khan, of the 6th Signalling Company, at Shabkadr. 'We have had no fighting yet but we are making the same sort of *bandobast* (arrangements) that you are.'[52]

Colonial satraps in Indian border provinces began to give an imperial cast to regional frontier ambitions. Along the unadministered tracts separating the formal borders of Assam and Burma, some frontier chiefs and headmen seized the opportunity to increase their influence with the colonial administration, and others felt the threat of dispossession more sharply. By the close of 1918, the tribal 'Alsatias' between the North-West Frontier Province and Afghanistan and between Assam and Burma had been enfolded into the global conflict for influence and territory.[53] Civilian populations in Waziristan (1919–20) and in the Kuki-Chin tracts (1917–19) experienced the same destruction of villages, livestock and crops as those caught up in the German retreat from northern France in 1917.[54] Yet if some link was acknowledged

war came home against local pop.

---

[50] See image no. 2: 'Maintenance train on the Bolan Pass line, 1890'. Also Public Works Department (PWD), 1918–21, no. 1066, MSA. Craft-training schools set up by the government and by missionaries were also tapped by the army. *The Wesleyan Methodist Church: The Twenty-Sixth Report of the South India Provincial Synod*, Madras, 1919, p. 62.

[51] George Morton-Jack, *The Indian Empire at War: From Jihad to Victory, The Untold Story of the Indian Army in the First World War*, London: Little, Brown and Company, 2018, p. 331

[52] Ahmad Khan to Jamadar Mahomed Khan, 9th Hodson's Horse, Urdu, 4 July 1917, IOR/L/MIL/5/827, part 3, p. 614.

[53] Ibid.

[54] See Chapter 4, and photograph titled 'Attack and burning of Longyin village' published, entirely without embarrassment, in Colonel L. W. Shakespear, *History of the Assam Rifles*, 1929, Aizawl: Tribal Research Institute, 1977, p. 217.

between an epochal conjuncture and these 'frontier uprisings', it was because British civilian and military personnel who had endured these arduous campaigns expected to get war medals and remembrance for the dead.[55] The inscription on Edwin Lutyens's war memorial arch at New Delhi, 'India Gate', acknowledged the conflict along the North-West Frontier, if almost as an afterthought:

> TO THE DEAD OF THE INDIAN ARMIES WHO FELL AND ARE HONOURED IN FRANCE AND FLANDERS MESOPOTAMIA AND PERSIA EAST AFRICA GALLIPOLI AND ELSEWHERE IN THE NEAR AND THE FAR EAST AND IN SACRED MEMORY ALSO OF THOSE WHOSE NAMES ARE HERE RECORDED AND WHO FELL IN INDIA OR THE NORTH WEST FRONTIER AND DURING THE THIRD AFGHAN WAR.[56]

The overseas deployment of the Indian Army

In August 1914, when Indian Expeditionary Force A left for Europe, there were some who recalled the earlier occasion in 1878 when the switch, so to speak, had been flipped.[57] The Conservative Prime Minister Disraeli had, without consulting Parliament, ordered the dispatch of 70,000 Indian soldiers to Malta to discourage Russian ambitions in Turkey.[58] What next, asked his critics in Parliament—could Indian troops even be ordered into England? Others revelled in the idea that India's seemingly unlimited supply of 'martial

---

[55] After considerable discussion, the British General Service and Victory Medals and the clasp for the North-East Frontier were awarded to military personnel involved in the Kuki-Chin campaign. Shakespear, *History of the Assam Rifles*, pp. 235–37. The colours of Indian Mountain Batteries pointedly linked frontier campaigns with the Great War—for instance, '7th Bengal: *The Great War*—Afghanistan 1919' in General C. A. L. Graham, *The History of the Indian Mountain Artillery*, Aldershot: Gale and Polden Ltd, 1957, p. 210 (italics in text).

[56] The foundation stone of the memorial arch was laid by the Duke of Connaught on 10 February 1921, and it was completed in 1931.

[57] Claude Hill, a member of the Viceroy's Council, remarked that the scene which Disraeli had enacted in 1878, in the spirit of a stage manager arranging cardboard scenery, was staged in grim reality in 1914. Sir Claude H. Hill, *India-Stepmother*, Edinburgh: William Blackwood and Sons Ltd, 1929, p. 209.

[58] Garnet I. Wolseley, 'The Native Army of India', *The North American Review*, vol. 127, no. 263 (1878), pp. 132–56.

races' could give Britain the demographic heft she needed to match Russia's Cossack hordes. General Garnet Wolseley pointed out proudly that with India's 240 million people Britain had three times Russia's population, and praised Lord Beaconsfield for being the first statesman to utilise the 'Native Army' in a European crisis.[59]

By the end of the century, however, there were public figures in Britain who were critical of an over-reliance on 'native' soldiers and demanded some form of universal military training for British citizens. The unexpected difficulty of bringing the South African War (1899–1902) to a conclusion affirmed their forebodings of national military enervation.[60] In striking contrast to this pessimistic strain of thought, we have the buoyant assessments of British officers of the Indian Army who had led the contingent, largely Indian in composition, which was sent to China in 1900 to crush the Boxer Rebellion.[61] France and Russia, they exulted, had expected Britain to be so tied down by the South African War that it would not be able to register a presence in the congregation of great powers assembled in North China. Extended training in Burma and along the North-West Frontier, wrote a correspondent for the *Times of India*, meant that British transport arrangements, which included mule units and a Punjabi Coolie Corps, were superior to any other. He described 'muscular Punjabis' transferring stores to lighters at the Chinese port of Taku Bar with

---

[59] Ibid, pp. 133–35.

[60] Aaron L. Friedberg, *The Weary Titan: Britain and the Experience of Relative Decline, 1895–1905*, Princeton: Princeton University Press, 1989. Although the Boer conflict was cast as a 'white man's war', nearly 10,000 Indians were sent to South Africa as military auxiliaries under the command of the War Office: horse-grooms, water-carriers, washermen, smiths, carpenters, cooks, butchers, bakers, sweepers, servants, doctors, ambulance workers and stretcher-bearers. Indians manned field hospitals and two veterinary establishments. E. S. Reddy, 'India and the Anglo-Boer War', 29 July 1999, http://www.mkgandhi.org/articles/boer_war.htm, last accessed 10 November 2019.

[61] Lieutenant Colonel H. B. Vaughan, *St George and the Chinese Dragon*, 1902, Dartford, Kent: The Alexius Press, 2000. 'In organisation, training and equipment our Indian Army was unsurpassed', wrote Captain Gordon Casserly. He also noted presciently that European armies had not fully absorbed the increased range and destructive power of modern weapons. 'Close formations are still the rule, and the history of the first few battles in the next European war will be a record of terrible slaughter.' Gordon Casserly, *The Land of the Boxers: Or, China under the Allies*, New York; Bombay: Longmans, Green and Co., 1903, pp. 34–35.

'energy and rapidity'.[62] Good news from China was, of course, particularly welcome given the bad news from South Africa. What both theatres illustrated was the importance to empire of the flexible deployment of combatant and non-combatant detachments of the Indian Army, in combination with units of the British Army and under officers reporting to the Army Council in Britain rather than to the Commander-in-Chief in India.[63] The prewar reluctance of the Dominions to commit themselves in advance to providing any expeditionary forces underlined the importance of this imperative.

The juridical frame: the Indian Army Act

The commitment of India's military resources to the maintenance of imperial power in interregional arenas emerges very clearly in discussions about the consolidation of Indian military law. A key concern was to deal with the new legal issues created by the posting of Indian Army detachments overseas. Since 1899, noted the Judge Advocate General, Indian military personnel had been

---

[62] 'Indian Contingent in China', *TOI*, 2 October 1900, p. 5. See also George Morton-Jack, *The Indian Army on the Western Front: India's Expeditionary Force to France and Belgium in the First World War*, Cambridge: Cambridge University Press, 2014, pp. 110–11.

[63] See Radhika Singha, 'The "Rare Infliction": The Abolition of Flogging in the Indian Army, circa 1835–1920', *Law and History Review*, vol. 34, no. 3 (2016), pp. 783–818; also Military Department, 2 October 1903, IOR/L/MIL/7/13733. By the turn of the century, select Indian princely state military units were being trained for deployment in combination with Indian and British Army units overseas. 'High-caste' regiments of the Indian Army were being persuaded to subordinate 'long established prejudices' to 'the exigencies of service'. The experiment of posting a class regiment of Brahmins to two years' garrison duty in Mauritius (1898–1910) in order to overcome caste scruples about crossing the sea was pronounced a success. 'Digest of Services of HM 1st Regiment Native Infantry 1871–1917', Mss, National Archives of India. Officials ensured that each Rajput company was recruited solely from the sub-division of one Rajput clan, and made the tactical and administrative unit also the cooking unit; Rajputs of the North-Western Provinces and Oudh were therefore induced to accept common messing on active service. A. H. Bingley, 'Rajputs, A Brief Account of their Origin, Religious Customs, and History, with Notes Regarding their Fitness for Modern Military Service', *United Services Institute Journal*, vol. XXIV, (1895), pp. 135–61, 149–50. My thanks to Salma Wasi for this reference.

sent to the South African War; as garrison troops to Crown colonies such as Ceylon, Hong Kong and Mauritius; to Uganda and Nyasaland 'under conditions which ... could hardly be distinguished from active service'; and 'in armed though peaceful occupation of territory belonging to a friendly power, as is the case in Tientsin'.[64] Scarcely a month passed by, he noted, without some difficulty created by the fact that the General Officer at one of these foreign stations was not the General Officer of a Command as defined in the Indian Articles of War, or was serving under the Army Council in Britain and not under the Commander-in-Chief in India.[65]

When the first consolidated Indian Army Act (Act VIII of 1911) was presented to the Indian Legislative Council on 21 January 1911, it was hailed as a modernising enactment which took account of the new role that had been assumed by the Indian Army. The 'Statement of Objects and Reasons' declared that the old Indian Articles of War were out of date and unsuited to an Indian Army which was 'now one Imperial Force serving not only in India but also in other parts of the Empire'.[66]

However, the literature on the reconstruction of the Indian Army in the early twentieth century has focused largely on Kitchener's determination to ensure that military resources were properly deprovincialised so that all units could be massed in strength against any substantial Russo-Afghan threat.[67] A related proposition is that the Indian Army was not really considered for use outside India until 1912, and then only to a very limited extent.[68] In 1919, reviewing India's services, Charles Monro, then Commander-in-Chief, said the magnitude of India's contribution in the early stages of the war could be appreciated only if one understood that the Army in India 'was in no sense

---

[64] Judge Advocate General, Notes, 8 January 1908, Legislative, March 1911, nos 158–78.

[65] Ibid. In 1903, field service in Somaliland revealed there was no procedure for correcting irregularities in courts-martial held for Indians serving in a force not under the command of the C-in-C, India. Military Department, 2 October 1903, IOR/L/MIL/7/13733.

[66] Legislative, March 1911, nos 158–78.

[67] For example, see T. A. Heathcote, *The Military in British India: The Development of British Land Forces in South Asia, 1600–1947*, Manchester: Manchester University Press, 1995.

[68] For a recent restatement, see Kaushik Roy, *Indian Army and the First World War: 1914–18*, Delhi: Oxford University Press, 2018.

maintained for meeting external obligations of an imperial character'.[69] Provision for a field army beyond the border was only 'for purposes of defence against external aggression'.[70] This statement was repeated in *India's Contribution to the Great War* (1923), in another official compilation, *The Empire at War* (1926), and in many subsequent military histories.[71]

This was a political contention, not a self-evident fact, and it was contested from budget to budget by Indian leaders who insisted that 'forward defence' was much too forward, and that imperial militarism, rather than India's security, was responsible for the skewed pattern of spending.[72] In 1912 Viceroy Lord Hardinge balked at the further undefined commitment of India's manpower and finances to a potential European war as well.[73] On this issue, we may also note Hew Strachan's observation that until 1914 Britain herself did not envisage any large-scale commitment of land forces on the continent, proposing to back her European allies primarily with naval and financial support.[74]

Encountering the colour bar: the coolie shadow over the sepoy

The other factor which filtered into discussions about imperial use of the Indian Army was the rising colour bar in the 'white' Dominions. At the 1911

---

[69] Despatch, C-in-C, India, 19 March 1919, printed in *The London Gazette*, 25 July 1919, https://www.thegazette.co.uk/London/issue/31476/supplement/9537, last accessed 11 November 2019.

[70] Ibid.

[71] *ICGW*, p. 73; Sir Charles Lucas (ed.), *The Empire at War*, vol. 5, London: Oxford University Press, 1926, pp. 175–76.

[72] Lala Lajpat Rai, *England's Debt to India: A Historical Narrative of England's Fiscal Policy Towards India*, New York: B. W. Huebsch, 1917. On 28 October 1911, the *Panjabee* asserted that Britain, not India, ought to pay for the Abor expedition, arguing that the expedition's real objective was to counter transfrontier Chinese influence. It also critiqued the killing of 1,000 Abors (Adis) for the death of one Englishman. *Selections from the Native Newspapers for Punjab*, no. 42, 21 October 1911, p. 1126, para. 26.

[73] Douglas E. Delaney, *The Imperial Army Project: Britain and the Land Forces of the Dominions and India, 1902–1945*, Oxford: Oxford University Press, 2018, pp. 67–68, 103.

[74] Hew Strachan, *1914–1918-online: International Encyclopedia of the First World War*, 'Pre-War Military Planning (Great Britain)', https://encyclopedia.1914–1918-on-line.net/article/pre-war_military_planning_great_britain, last accessed 10 November 2019.

Imperial Conference, the Secretary of State for India called upon the Dominions to show some responsibility on this issue:

> It is difficult to convey to those who do not know India the intense and natural resentment felt by veterans of the Indian Army, who have seen active service and won medals under the British flag ... when (as has actually happened) they find themselves described as 'coolies' and treated with contemptuous severity in parts of the British Empire.[75]

A significant number of Pashtun and Punjabi ex-sepoys had hoped that their service to the empire would assist them in migration to Canada, Australia and South Africa. They perceived themselves to be different from the pitiable indentured coolie because they could put together their own passage, and therefore felt they were of a superior social stamp.[76] Soldiers sent to garrison posts in Rangoon, Singapore, Malaya, Shanghai and Hong Kong were a significant element in nodes of Indian settlement along the migration corridor from Punjab towards the prosperous Pacific Rim.[77] The diasporic groups which debated the justice of entry restrictions in South Africa, Canada and Australia, and strategised to overcome them, also contained many soldiers and ex-soldiers.[78] In British Columbia in 1909, when Indian settlers lost their

---

[75] On the immigration issue, he added that there was a unanimity of opinion between 'seditious agitators' and loyal, politically moderate Indians. S. P. Sinha cites the SSI's memorandum of 1911 in Sinha, 7 August 1918, IOR/L/PJ/6/1519.

[76] Khushwant Singh and Satindar Singh, *Ghadar, 1915*, New Delhi: R and K Publishing House, 1966; Hugh Johnston, 'Group Identity in an Emigrant Worker Community: The Example of Sikhs in Twentieth-Century British Columbia', *British Columbia Studies*, no. 148 (2005/6), pp. 1–21.

[77] The fear of seditious propaganda flowing along the path from Punjab to Calcutta and South-East Asia emerges in the 1918 Rowlatt Committee Report. Recommending the postwar extension of powers for summary detention, it referred to *Ghadar* activists trying to contact Punjabi railway-construction workers in Northern Siam and Indian troops and military police in Rangoon. *Sedition Committee Report*, Calcutta: Government Press, 1918, p. 171. For an exploration of *Ghadar* radicalism see Maia Ramnath, *Haj to Utopia: How the Ghadar Movement Charted Global Radicalism and Attempted to Overthrow the British Empire*, Berkeley: University of California Press, 2011.

[78] For a fine exploration of these transnational debates see Renisa Mawani, *Across Oceans of Law: The Komagata Maru and Jurisdiction in the Time of Empire*, London: Duke University Press, 2018.

voting rights, the Sikh temple at Vancouver resolved that ex-soldiers would not wear their uniforms, insignia or medals, because these were now marks of slavery.[79] In South Africa, some former Indian viceroy's commissioned officers (VCOs) and sepoys joined Indian settler protests against the Asiatic Law Amendment Act of 1907, which required them to register by submitting ten fingerprints or face deportation.[80] Four Pashtun and Punjabi Muslim soldiers sent a dramatic petition to the Colonial Secretary, asking that instead of being subjected to the degradation of deportation they be taken and shot on one of the battlefields of South Africa where they had served their King Emperor. They submitted that 'their uniforms and their discharge papers should be a sufficient passport in any part of the British empire and constitute their complete identification.'[81] Boers who had felt the edge of the imperial harrow provocatively reduced the social standing of the sepoy to that of the coolie, as did Britain's continental rivals, in implied critique of her dependence on coloured and colonial manpower.[82] Of the 1902 assemblage of great powers in China to crush the Boxer rebellion, Henry Vaughan, an officer of the 7th Rajputs, recalled that many foreigners 'used to mistake, or possibly pretended to mistake, the followers for Sepoys and thus got the idea that they were an

---

[79] Ramnath, *Haj to Utopia*, p. 245, n. 41. However, some Sikh veterans still took pride in their medals. Hugh J. M. Johnston, *The Voyage of the Komagata Maru: The Sikh Challenge to Canada's Colour Bar* (revised and expanded 2nd edition), Vancouver: University of British Columbia Press, 2014, p. 11.

[80] See 'Trial of Ex-Soldiers', 3 January 1908, *The Collected Works of Mahatma Gandhi*, vol. 8, pp. 1–3, www.gandhiashramsevagram.org/gandhi-literature/mahatma-gandhi-collected-works-volume-8.pdf, last accessed 11 September 2019; and 'Petition to Secretary of State for Colonies', 14 September 1908, *The Collected Works of Mahatma Gandhi*, vol. 9, pp. 37–39, https://www.gandhiservefoundation.org/about-mahatma-gandhi/collected-works-of-mahatma-gandhi/009–19080901–19091112/, last accessed 11 September 2019.

[81] Gandhi, 'Petition to Secretary of State for Colonies'. Gandhi drew upon the services of Indian soldiers to challenge the contention that the Indian in South Africa could not be given the franchise because 'he represents the lowest-class Indian; in fact, he is the scum of India.' See 'The Indian Franchise', 16 December 1895, pp. 266–90, https://www.gandhiservefoundation.org/about-mahatma-gandhi/collected-works-of-mahatma-gandhi/001–18845050–18960604/, last accessed 11 November 2019.

[82] In World War One, Boer soldiers taunted Indian soldiers serving in East Africa, calling them coolies. Major R. S. Waters, *History of the 5th Battalion (Pathans) 14th Punjab Regiment*, London: James Bain, 1936, p. 174.

untidy and unsoldierly lot.'[83] He attributed the mistake to the fact that Indian followers were issued the same pattern of winter clothing as the sepoys. Followers ought to be clothed differently, the more so, he added, 'as united action by the European power against offenders of international law will probably be more frequent in the future, and the Indian Army will be taking its share in them.'[84]

World War One and the nationalisation of labour

The Indian press regularly critiqued the fiscal burden of imperial militarism and the exclusion of educated Indians from the commissioned ranks, but when war was declared in August 1914 there was an outpouring of loyal declarations.[85] Indian leaders hailed the decision to rush Indian soldiers to Europe in November 1914 as a sign that race barriers had been lowered. Yet autobiographies and memoirs reveal a sly satisfaction that German victories were denting the arrogance of the ruling race.[86] An ironic couplet was doing the rounds in Punjab:

Kadam German ka badhta hai
Fateh English ki hoti hai.[87]

---

[83] Vaughan, *St George and the Chinese Dragon*, p. 117. Major General L. C. Dunsterville said that the French 'affected to believe' that the British had dressed up coolies as soldiers. L. C. Dunsterville, *Stalky's Reminiscences*, London: Jonathan Cape, 1928, pp. 178–79. Amar Singh, officer in the Jodhpur Lancers, a princely state cavalry unit sent with the China expedition, commented privately that the epithet 'coolie' was appropriate because of the shabby treatment meted out to the VCOs (Indian officers). S. H. Rudolph and L. I. Rudolph with Mohan Singh Kanota, *Reversing the Gaze: Amar Singh's Diary. A Colonial Subject's Narrative of Imperial India*, Oxford: Westminster Press, 2002, p. 159.

[84] Vaughan, *St George and the Chinese Dragon*, p. 121.

[85] G. A. Natesan (ed.), *All About the War: The Indian Review War Book*, Madras: G. A. Natesan, 1915.

[86] Kala, *Memoir of the Raj*, p. 18. A famous poet recalled that as a schoolboy in Allahabad, as a 'result of who-knows-what subtle propaganda or self-gratifying leap of imagination, one felt the Germans were the bravest people in the world and that the British would never be able to defeat them'. Bachchan, *In the Afternoon of Time*, p. 107. See also Ghosh, *The Autobiography of a Revolutionary in British India*, p. 20.

[87] 'The Germans advance but the British claim victories'. B. K. Kapur, *Yester Years,*

Open criticism of the 'mercenary' use of the Indian Army was expressed only in anti-colonial networks within the Indian diaspora, made up of Indian literati, many of them from Bengal, as well as Punjabi labourers and ex-soldiers.[88] The concluding chapter of this book assesses the dramatic shift in mood after the Armistice. Repressive wartime ordinances were being made permanent, military spending still took a huge share of postwar annual budgets, and Indian military personnel were still spread out over the Near and Middle East. Figures at the more radical end of the political spectrum contended that Indian manpower should not be used to crush aspirations to self-government in dependent colonies, or in those Muslim-majority areas of the Ottoman empire which were being brought under mandatory forms of imperialism.

The assertion of a nationalist claim to control over the mobility of India's labouring masses had a longer timeline.[89] A broad political consensus had emerged that the migration of Indian labour under indentured contract should be abolished. This was a labour regime structured by five-year contracts which bound the emigrant to one employer, at remarkably stagnant wages, and used a grid of penal provisions to enforce work and punish desertion.[90] However, the mistreatment of Indian labourers was just one of the concerns which shaped the campaign to abolish indentured migration. The subjugated figure of the 'coolie' was also held to compromise the standing of respectable Indians in

Ramblings and Reflections of a Former Indian Ambassador, New Delhi: Siddharth Publications, 1994, p. 21.

[88] The headlines of the August 1914 issue of the newspaper *Ghadar* ('insurgency'), published from San Francisco, relocated the theatre of war: 'Wanted ... courageous soldiers for spreading *ghadar* in India. Salary: death. Reward: martyrdom. Pension: freedom. Place: the field of India.' See Maia Ramnath, 'Two Revolutions: The Ghadar Movement and India's Radical Diaspora, 1913–1918', *Radical History Review*, vol. 92 (2005), pp. 7–30.

[89] For a comprehensive account, see Hugh Tinker, *A New System of Slavery: The Export of Indian Labour Overseas, 1830–1920*, Oxford: Oxford University Press, 1974.

[90] For an insightful assessment, see Prabhu P. Mohapatra, 'Assam and the West Indies, 1860–1920: Immobilising Plantation Labour', in Douglas Hay and Paul Craven (eds), *Masters, Servants and Magistrates in Britain and Empire, 1562–1955*, Chapel Hill: University of North Carolina Press, 2004, pp. 455–80.

indentured labour repackaged as 'followers'

empire. The allegation was that norms of caste hierarchy and female chastity were being scandalously overthrown in the 'creole' communities emerging from coolie populations overseas.[91] With prospects of industrial and commercial expansion brightening for India due to the war, labour was also increasingly spoken of as a factor of production, and as a resource which the nation state was entitled to conserve for its own needs.[92] The dilemma which therefore confronted government was how to distance the sending of labour 'for military work overseas' from this now stigmatised system of migration.[93] The formal enrolment of labour under the Indian Army Act and the label of 'war service' not only served this purpose, but also facilitated the imposition of a blanket of censorship over conditions of work and treatment in Mesopotamia.

India's nationalists wanted India's coolies for themselves

The flow of Indian labour into Mesopotamia had the potential to become politically controversial for another reason as well. The British Foreign Office wanted to dispel any speculation by Arab notables that this wartime exercise would broaden into a move to settle Indians in Mesopotamia, and to incorporate the *vilayats* of Basra and Baghdad into the Empire of India. Sending labour in a specifically military frame helped to contain these fears. However, after the Armistice the question of how to continue using Indian labour in Mesopotamia without allowing the emergence of an Indian settler population loomed large again.[94]

Another migration issue emerged in the European theatre. The manpower crisis of 1916 provoked several questions: should Britain follow the example of France and call a 'million-strong Black Army' into existence in Europe? Would this lead to the destruction of the white races, or as some stoutly argued, prevent the decimation of the finest of such races? The solution chosen was to send in 'coloured' non-combatants to release British men for the combatant ranks. The arrival on 16 June 1917 of the first batches of the Indian Labour Corps by the SS Aragon inaugurated this second, almost unnoticed, flow of South Asian manpower to France.

---

[91] C. F. Andrews, *Report on Indentured Labour in Fiji: An Independent Enquiry*, Allahabad: C. Y. Chintamani, 1917.

[92] Radhika Singha, 'The Great War and a "Proper" Passport for the Colony: Border-Crossing in British India, c. 1882–1922', *Indian Economic and Social History Review*, vol. 50, no. 3 (2013), pp. 289–315.

[93] See Chapter 3.

[94] Ibid.

There was another similar turn which could have been taken and was not—that of sending Indian labour to England to free British labourers for combatant roles. On 29 June 1917 the British War Cabinet had noted that '[i]t was undesirable in principle to employ Indian Labour in this country, having regard to labour objection.'[95] The journalist Nihal Singh, whose articles dwelt ecstatically on India's martial races, acknowledged in passing that India could also contribute a large mass of labour for work behind the lines. However, he warned that Indians should not conclude thereby 'that Britons consider them good enough to work as coolies, but not fit to be soldiers and leaders of men.'[96] Care also had to be taken to avoid conflict with British labour unions 'because educated Indians believe in the good intentions of British labour towards Indian aspirations for self-government.'[97]

The Indian Labour Corps in France: the different colours of obscurity

Reviewing the literature on the various 'coloured' forces sent to Europe from dependent colonies and from China, two issues stand out: the constant 'confusion' which seemed to surround their contracts and the historical obscurity to which they were consigned. Why was it possible to dematerialise such large bodies of labour, even in the most publicised theatre of the Great War?

It is only very recently that the British Labour Battalions too have been rescued from their obscurity.[98] The wartime code of hyper-masculinity meant that tribute to non-combatants had to be tempered by gesturing simultaneously to the higher order of sacrifice offered by combatant units. There was also less of an institutional investment in writing the history of units conceived as temporary formations. Richard Holmes comments that not only

---

[95] 29 June 1917, CAB/23/3, The National Archives, UK (henceforth TNA). For the postwar backlash in Britain against 'coloured alien seamen', which affected Indian lascars even though they were not legally 'aliens', see Laura Tabili, 'The Construction of Racial Difference in Twentieth Century Britain: The Special Restriction (Coloured Alien Seamen) Order, 1925', *Journal of British Studies*, vol. 33, no. 1 (1994), pp. 54–98.

[96] St Nihal Singh, 'India's Man-Power', *The Contemporary Review*, vol. CXIII (1918), pp. 665–70.

[97] Ibid.

[98] John Starling and Ivor Lee, *No Labour, No Battle: Military Labour during the First World War*, Stroud: Spellmount, 2009.

were British Labour Battalions less glamorous, but that their organisation was 'fluid, often eccentric, and its wartime structures soon withered in the pale sub-light of peace.'[99] Labour Battalions were also the form in which war work was exacted not only from physically less fit citizens, but also from politically suspect or stigmatised subjects; in the British case these were conscientious objectors, 'aliens', and prisoners of war.[100]

 However, a man enrolled in a British Labour Battalion in France had the status of an enlisted soldier and would receive one of the 6.4 million British war medals cast in silver.[101] The issuing of 110,000 British war medals in the inferior metal of bronze to acknowledge the 'Native Labour Units' in France illustrates that their services were placed on a symbolically lower footing.[102] One bald but serviceable explanation for this distinction is that white labourers with citizenship status could demand recognition for 'war service'. The motivation of men in British Labour Battalions, even after the introduction of conscription, had to be acknowledged as of a higher order than that of coloured labourers, from dependent and white settler-dominated colonies or from China, who were low down in the international pecking order. The men of these units tended to be relegated to the status of coolies, who, attracted by better food and wages, had simply transferred their site of work to Europe.

The induction of coloured manpower into the European theatre, where it might be working or fighting side by side with white personnel, raised all

---

[99] Richard Holmes, foreword to Starling and Lee, *No Labour, No Battle*, p. 15.

[100] Indian labour units sent to Mesopotamia included recruits from jails and 'criminal tribes'. Transfrontier Pashtuns, excluded from combatant service from November 1915, were recruited for the Labour Corps for France but returned under a cloud of suspicion. See Chapters 4 and 5.

[101] 'A Guide to British Campaign Medals of WW1', The Great War 1914–1918, http://www.greatwar.co.uk/medals/ww1-campaign-medals.htm, last accessed 11 November 2019.

[102] Ibid. The British War Medal in bronze was awarded to the Chinese, Maltese, and Indian Labour Corps. The Dominion of South Africa refused to let the South African Native Labour Contingent (SANLC) receive any medals at all, to discourage political claims made on the strength of war service. Men recruited to the SANLC from the British Protectorates of Swaziland, Bechuanaland and Basutoland received the bronze medal. Albert Grundlingh, *War and Society: Participation and Remembrance: South African Black and Coloured Troops in the First World War, 1914–18*, Stellenbosch: SUN Media, 2014, p. 101.

kinds of troubling possibilities. Scenarios of disturbing intimacy had to be forestalled, as when the War Office declared that it was 'not desirable to employ British tailors on fitting and repairing the clothing of Indian personnel'.[103] As pointed out earlier, one way to assuage such anxieties was to place all coloured manpower, combatant and non-combatant, conceptually 'behind the lines'. Non-white soldiers in the Bermuda Royal Garrison Artillery, the British West Indian Regiments and the Cape Coloured Battalion would be confined in Europe to the non-combatant work of 'humping' ammunition and supplies, building roads, and salvage work.[104]

There was a second way in which coloured manpower was cast in an auxiliary role, and that was through the representation of it as inherently unskilled labour, which would free white non-combatants for skilled work. Brigadier General Evan Gibb, then Director of Labour in France, recalled that not only had the intensification of trench warfare created 'a labour problem, on a scale never known in any previous war', but that increased specialisation in warfare had created a greater need for personnel who would 'bear the burden of unskilled work and ... free the skilled men ... for their purely technical duties.'[105] Manpower shortages made it necessary to start scrutinising coloured labour more carefully for nodes of craft skill and literacy, but postwar assessments swung back to stereotypes about the unskilled coolie masses.[106]

Recent work on 'coloured labour' in the Great War makes it clear that in each case there were specific political factors which also contributed to this

---

[103] The War Office demanded an Indian tailor for the lowly Indian horse- and mule-drivers of the supply and ammunition columns: IOR/L/Mil/7/1835. S. K. Datta, an Indian YMCA worker, recalled that it was indeed a novel experience for Indian soldiers to get their hair cut or their shoes blackened by a member of the ruling race, tasks associated with low-caste work in India. Margarita Barnes, typescript, 'S. K. Datta and his People', IOR Mss Eur C.576/89/74.

[104] Glenford Deroy Howe, *Race, War and Nationalism: A Social History of West Indians in the First World War*, Oxford: James Currey, 2002, pp. 103, 111. In September 1915, a temporary Labour Battalion was also formed from the Indian Corps in France, and in January 1916, 1,000 dismounted men from the Indian Cavalry Corps replaced a British Labour Battalion handling stores in Marseilles. Starling and Lee, *No Labour, No Battle*, p. 257.

[105] Evan Gibb, 'The Organisation of Labour in the Great War', *Royal Army Service Corps Quarterly*.

[106] Francis Younghusband, 'India', in Sir Charles Lucas (ed.), *The Empire at War*, vol. 5, London: Oxford University Press, 1926, pp. 151–352.

obscurity. The Chinese Labour Corps (CLC), made up of 138,000 men, was the largest such contingent in Europe, with the men serving on three-year contracts in the British, French and American sectors. Xu Guoqi explains that China permitted this exodus to win a presence in Allied war councils, but did so surreptitiously to avoid alerting Japan, and to deflect accusations from Germany that she had violated her neutrality.[107] Due to the hostility of white labour to Chinese immigration, the CLC was routed through Canada with great secrecy, and the British War Office kept information to a minimum.[108]

While the number of Egyptian labourers who came to France is put at around 10,240, estimates for the total number of Egyptians mobilised in different theatres of war are both staggering and uncertain. Lee and Starling state there were 'at least 250,000 and could have been in excess of 500,000'.[109] The extensive use of Egyptian labour had to be played down, as Britain had promised that Egyptians would not be asked to fight against the Ottoman Sultan.[110] The Dominion of South Africa sent 21,000 men in the South African Native Labour Contingent (SANLC) but was determined to prevent them from making any political claims on the grounds of war service.[111] It therefore insisted that the SANLC be housed in segregated camps, and refused to let them receive any war medals.[112]

Homecoming?

The landscape of conflict did not contract for India in November 1918, and the Armistice led to no relaxation in the demand for non-combatant labour in the Mesopotamian theatre. New ILC companies were raised to replace those being repatriated, even as fresh demand built up along the North-West Frontier.[113] However, over this period of 1919–21, public figures in India

---

[107] Xu Guoqi, *Strangers on the Western Front: Chinese Workers in the Great War*, Cambridge, MA: Harvard University Press, 2011.

[108] Ibid. See also Nicholas J. Griffin, 'Britain's Chinese Labour Corps in World War I', *Military Affairs*, vol. 40, no. 3 (1976), pp. 102–8.

[109] Starling and Lee, *No Labour, No Battle*, p. 270.

[110] Kristian Coates Ulrichsen, *The Logistics and Politics of the British Campaigns in the Middle East, 1914–22*, Basingstoke: Palgrave Macmillan, 2011, p. 116.

[111] Alfred Grundlingh, *War and Society*, pp. 52, 73.

[112] Ibid., p. 101

[113] See Chapters 3 and 6.

began to call for the return home of Indian troops and labourers, and to demand that India's finances and manpower be limited to the defence of her own frontiers.] At the militant end of the spectrum this demand took an internationalist form. The principle of self-determination, it was argued, had to be carried across the threshold of the Christian-majority areas of the Ottoman Empire and recognised as valid for 'Asia' as well. This was an 'Asia' of Muslim-majority territories, stretching from Syria across Iraq, Persia, Egypt and Afghanistan, which shared a common aspiration to self-determination and felt the oppressive weight not of German militarism, but of the postwar ambitions of French and British empire. In the final chapter of this book, I will show how the segueing of global conflict into imperial geopolitics over 1919–21 meant that 'the end of the war' was a very protracted event for Indian soldiers and followers.[114]

---

[114] Gerwarth and Manela point out that the period 1911–23 gives a better sense of 'the Greater War' outside the European core than 1914–18. Robert Gerwarth and Erez Manela (eds), *Empires at War, 1911–1923*, Oxford: Oxford University Press, 2014.

2

FRONT LINES AND STATUS LINES

THE FOLLOWER RANKS OF THE INDIAN ARMY

Inspecting the Lady Hardinge Hospital at Brockenhurst, which treated Indians from the Expeditionary Force in France, Sir Walter Lawrence noted an act of local kindness. A burial plot had to be found

> for a sweeper belonging to a peculiar sect which never cremates. We asked the Woking Muhammadan Burial ground to allow us to bury him there, but they flatly declined. We then had recourse to the Rev. Mr. Chambers, the Vicar of Brockenburst. He came forward and kindly allowed us to bury him in his Churchyard.[1]

Lieutenant General George F. MacMunn embroidered this incident into a story about untouchable life, seeking to strike 'a mingled vein of sorrow and glory'.[2] Bigha, the latrine sweeper in MacMunn's account, is from the Lalbeghi community, whom MacMunn describes as 'nominal' Muslims, though 'untouchables'. They therefore bury their dead instead of cremating them, so that they 'might face the recording angels like any other follower of the

---

[1] Walter Roper Lawrence to Lord Kitchener, 15 February 1915, India Office Records, British Library, London, IOR Lawrence Mss Eur. F143/165, negative.

[2] George F. MacMunn, *The Underworld of India*, London: Jarrolds, 1933, pp. 44–45. In Anglo-Indian literature, the broom-wielding latrine sweeper was a figure of pathos, as well as the subject of an all-too-familiar line of humour about the fanciful hierarchies of the servant compound.

prophet.'[3] The Imam refuses to bury the outcaste in his 'cleanly plot', but the other hospital sweepers insist he has to be buried. Learning of the dilemma, the vicar declares, 'Surely Bigha Khan has died for England, I will bury him in the churchyard.'[4] 'And so Bigha, outcaste Lalbeghi, lies close to a crusader's tomb' by the end of the story, 'in the churchyard of St Agnes Without ... Lalbeghi and Norman, the alpha and the omega of social status.'[5]

There is no real churchyard of St Agnes Without, but the grave of one Sukha Kalloo, a sweeper, lies beside some New Zealand graves in the church-yard of St Nicholas at Brockenhurst.[6] Sukha was probably the sweeper of Lawrence's report and the 'Bigha' of MacMunn's fictional account, as his gravestone is indeed subscribed by the parishioners of Brockenhurst, and it has an Islamic arch instead of the cross which marks the grave of an Indian Christian sapper nearby.[7] MacMunn added a second such tale of 'pathos and glory', modelled, he claimed, on another real-life incident. In this, the regi-mental latrine cleaner Buldoo, inspired by his childhood play at soldiers with a golden-haired English boy, assumes the identity of a Rajput sepoy and dies leading a heroic counter-attack from a trench in Mesopotamia.[8] Clearly MacMunn was suggesting that it was in empire alone, in such spaces as the British home and regiment, that the 'untouchable' found succour, not, as he crudely put it, in 'Gandhi and his blather'.[9] But the war's hunger for manpower

---

[3] Ibid., p. 44.

[4] Ibid., p. 45.

[5] Ibid.

[6] 'New Zealand Memorial Brockenhurst', https://www.ypressalient.co.uk/New%20 Zealand%20Memorial%20brockenhurst.htm, last accessed 10 November 2019.

[7] Ibid.

[8] 'The War Story of an Outcaste Sweeper', in MacMunn, *The Underworld of India*, pp. 261–77.

[9] Ibid. Transferred from a Rajput regiment to a British one where he can breathe more freely, Buldoo is befriended by a British private who teaches him how to handle a rifle. Bakha, the protagonist of Mulk Raj Anand's novel *Untouchable*, is, like MacMunn's hero, a regimental latrine-cleaner, who models himself on the Tommies who 'had treated him like a human being'. Mulk Raj Anand, *Untouchable*, 1935, London: Penguin, 1940, p. 9. European households, regiments or hospitals could keep 'untouchables' at a distance, citing sanitary reasons or the sensitivities of other servants, but there was room for manoeuvre. The author, Hazari, recalls that his grand-father and father longed for service with a European household where they would be treated 'not as Untouchables but as servants'. Hazari, *I was an Outcaste: The*

had also allowed the unimaginable to be imagined—the sweeper to be cast as a war hero.[10]

'Not work at all!'

In recruitment propaganda, service as a sepoy or an Indian cavalryman was cast as the only form of off-farm work which did not demean a respectable agriculturalist:

> Jat ki kamai, kahan-kahan kis kaam mein aati hai
> Karen kheti hai zamindara, fauji kaam hamaara
> Aur jitne hain ahalkaar, yeh kamai nek kehti hai.
> Jat ki
> [Of all the different forms of work it is only cultivation or military service which is honourable for the Jat].[11]

Some propaganda pamphlets described sepoy service as 'not work at all!'[12] The peasant had to be induced to believe that when he put on his military boots, he distanced himself from an existence shaped by backbreaking labour and the vagaries of the weather. He also acquired, propaganda materials suggested, some immunity against the rough handling of his person by the policeman, the creditor and the revenue official. A World War One recruiting song contrasted the plight of the man outside army life with his position inside: 'Here you get tattered shoes, out there you get full boots ... Here you get

---

Autobiography of an 'Untouchable' in India, New Delhi: The Hindustan Times, 1951, pp. 10, 45, 61.

[10] The war journalist Candler refers to an incident in Mesopotamia where 'a sweeper of the —th Rifles took an unauthorised part in an assault on the Turkish lines, picked up the rifle of a dead sepoy, and went on firing till he was shot in the head.' Edmund Candler, *The Sepoy*, London: John Murray, 1919, p. 233. In a slightly different version, sweeper Itarsi, of the 125th Napier's Rifles, snatches up a rifle and fights in the Battle of Sannaiyat in 1916, after which the other sweepers appoint him 'to be their officer'. T. A. Heathcote, *The Indian Army: The Garrison of British Imperial India, 1822–1922*, West Vancouver: David and Charles, 1974, p. 114.

[11] However, the poet concedes that cultivation requires immense toil, and that military service means the risk of death. Ishwar Singh Gehlot, '*Nek Kamai*', from *Baldev Bhent*, issue 26–27, n.d., in 'World War One Folk Songs', unpublished collection, Haryana Academy of History and Culture, Kurukshetra. My gratitude to Professor K. C. Yadav for access to the resources of this institute.

[12] *How Gul Mahomed Joined the King's Army*, Simla: G. M. Press, n.d. (c. 1918); and *Teja Singh Khalsa Joins the Army*, 1918 (British Library pamphlets).

shoved around, out there you get a salute.'[13] Such immunities prioritised the army's own claims to the person of the sepoy, but they were cast as status-enhancing privileges acquired by service to the state.[14]

The world of work was still an insistent reality for the follower ranks. However, they were told that their uniform and fixed monthly wage gave them the prestige of government service. Medical and transport officers who wanted a better deal for their follower personnel had to contend with the hyper-masculine code of combatant service. The rhetoric they used was that the devotion of the follower ranks gave a higher gloss to the valour of the fighting races, rather than dimming it. At the same time, they pointed out that this duty of care exposed stretcher-bearers and mule-drivers to battlefield risk. They also drew upon contemporary ideas about labour efficiency to argue that better food and kit for followers would allow them to train more intensively and would prevent desertion and invaliding in field service.[15]

To track the improvement which took place over 1916–17 in the institutional position of the 'higher followers', this chapter focuses on the stretcher-bearers, or *kahars*, and the mule-drivers, or *drabis*. It also picks out the cook, *bhisti* (water-carrier), sweeper and *syce* (groom and grass-cutter) in order to explore the service milieu of the attached followers, often referred to as the 'menial ranks'.

Sepoy, coolie and menial: village bazaar and construction site

The distinction between combatant and non-combatant work within a military formation is, of course, never a given, but varies with combat situations, technologies of warfare, and modes of training.[16] Article 27 of the Indian

---

[13] Pandit Deepchand, '*Bharti hole re, kyun bahar khade rangroot*', in Rajaram Shastri, *Haryana ka Lok Manch*, no. 15, Haryana Academy of History and Culture, Gurgaon, n.d.

[14] No person subject to the Indian Army Act could be arrested for debt by any process of Civil or Revenue Court. Indian Army Act (Act VIII of 1911), section 119 (henceforth IAA). He could be arrested in a criminal case, but a sympathetic CO could obstruct police investigations. See Major General D. K. Palit, *Major General A. A. Rudra: His Service in Three Armies and Two World Wars*, New Delhi: Reliance Publishing House, 1997, p. 6.

[15] For further discussion, see Afterword.

[16] Erik-Jan Zürcher (ed.), *Fighting for a Living: A Comparative History of Military Labour, 1500–2000*, Amsterdam: Amsterdam University Press, 2013.

Articles of War, formulated in 1847, specified that 'on actual service' Indian officers and soldiers were bound to assist in the construction of field-works, a requirement that the British Articles of War did not have to underline.[17] Conditions of warfare for the Indian Army in frontier and overseas theatres were such that at the outbreak of the war it had no less than twelve Pioneer Battalions, whereas the British Army had none.[18] The men of these units, many recruited from experienced railway and construction labour gangs, had combatant status, but were trained both to fight and to construct roads, embankments and bridges.[19] As MacMunn pointed out: 'India alone of the British Empire has pioneer corps, since India alone expects campaigns by way of goat-tracks and mountain watercourses.'[20]

However, soldiers of other regiments could also be put on 'fatigue' work, building their own huts and reconstructing military stations. Lansdowne, the headquarters of the Garhwal Regiment in the central Himalayas, was made by literally carving away a mountain top, involving sepoys in intensive fatigues on and off for twenty years.[21] In 1916–17 the Indian cavalry in France was employed in trench-digging and road construction, and in the Mesopotamian theatre both Indian and British soldiers spent stretches of time building roads and railways along the lines of communication.

In frontier tracts, there was a considerable overlap in the recruiting pools for soldiers, departmental followers, and temporary 'Coolie Corps'. This was

---

[17] W. Hough, *Precedents in military law: including the practice of courts martial, the mode of conducting trials, the duties of officers at military courts of inquests, courts of inquiry, courts of requests, etc. etc.*, London: W. H. Allen, 1855, p. 470.

[18] George F. MacMunn, *The Armies of India*, London: Adam and Charles Black, 1911, p. 186.

[19] W. B. P. Tugwell, *History of the Bombay Pioneers*, London; Bedford: Sidney Press, 1938.

[20] MacMunn, *The Armies of India*, p. 186. By the later stages of the war, the Pioneers were too valuable to be used as assault battalions. Ian Sumner, *The Indian Army, 1914–1947*, Oxford: Osprey, 2001, p. 46.

[21] The regimental history admitted that the principle of making the men contribute labour for their accommodation had been 'carried to extremes'. J. T. Evatt, *Historical Record of the 39ᵗʰ Royal Garhwal Rifles*, vol. 1, 1887–1922, Aldershott: Gale and Polden, 1923, p. 213. From 1904, the Burma Military Police received extra pay for the construction and repair of roads and barracks, termed 'pioneer work'. Despatch, GOI to Secretary of State for India (SSI), Finance Dept, no. 11, 19 January 1919.

partly because transport officers preferred to select mule-drivers and other personnel from those who had been rejected for combatant service in the Punjab and the North West Frontier Provinces, rather than to turn to other regions.[22] It was also because, from the 1880s, military recruitment had to compete with other avenues of non-agricultural employment, such as railway-laying, bridge-building, lumber extraction, dock work and seafaring. Along the North-West Frontier, some of these work nodes had emerged as a consequence of F. S. Robert's policy of 'defence in depth'—that is, a communications structure from Quetta upwards which would allow rapid troop movement across the border and towards Afghanistan.[23] The same structure widened the circulation of transfrontier populations in border provinces, and drew men down to seek work in Bombay and Karachi.

An important objective of colonial policies of pacification was to expand the dependency of frontier communities on cross-border wage work and trade so that blockades could be used more effectively to punish recalcitrance. Tribal chiefs were often co-opted as overseers and labour contractors on frontier public works. For instance, in 1912 the famine-stricken Mahsuds of Waziristan were enlisted in the army, and their *maliks* (chiefs) were given petty contracts to bring labour to the Lakki-Pezu railway line, in a bid to prevent them from raiding in British territory.[24] Ethnic balancing acts could bring a transfrontier community such as the Hazaras, tapped for quarry and construction work, into consideration for a Pioneer Battalion.[25] Combatant service meant status, a regular wage, medical care and the prospect of a gratuity or pension. Construction work outside the army offered more flexibility at roughly comparable wages.[26] Many frontier communities chose one of these two labour

---

[22] Military Department (MD), A, November 1888, nos 190–92. Thus, in March 1915, the GOC of the Quetta Division reported that practically all of the mule-drivers were from Punjab, the Sindhis being 'naturally non-combatant'. Complaining about the difficulty of recruiting Punjabi Muslims, the GOC of the Poona Division held that the local 'Parwari caste [depressed classes] ... are not the best material' for transport units. AD, War, 1914–15, nos 13706–711, pp. 459–61; IOR/L/Mil/7/6712.

[23] R. A. Johnson, '"Russians at the Gates of India"? Planning the Defence of India, 1885–1900', *Journal of Military History*, vol. 67, no. 3 (2003), pp. 697–743. Frederick Sleigh Roberts was Commander-in-Chief, India, 1885–93.

[24] Railway Board, Railway Construction, A, August 1912, nos 330–31.

[25] Military Department, Native Army, A, January 1904, nos 230–38. The 106th Hazara Pioneers were raised at Quetta in 1904.

[26] The wage for male porters and construction workers along the frontier hovered at

regimes or even combined them. Edmund Candler wrote of some Pashtun sepoys who used their three-and-a-half-month military leave to enlist in the 'Coolie Corps' on the Bolan Pass because wages were high there and they were free to gamble: 'the place had become a kind of tribal Monte Carlo'.[27]

As World War One lurched on, the overlap between the recruiting pools for combatants and for non-combatants increased.[28] The list of communities in whom the Indian Army discovered martial qualities grew longer. For instance, the Gurkha recruiting depot at Gorakhpur was supposed to reserve Magars and Limbus for army units, permitting the Assam and Burma military police to recruit only from other Gurkha communities.[29] But when the demand for combatants spiked, or preferred communities veered away to other worksites in India, then the army embraced a wider range of Gurkhas.[30] On the other side, the improvements taking place in the wages and service conditions for department followers began to affect combatant recruitment, with lower casualty rates adding to the appeal of non-combatant work.[31] In March 1917, the service package for the Labour Corps for France was attractive enough to prompt a forceful intervention to preserve the combatant pool.

---

around eight annas (half a rupee) a day. One estimate put the monthly wage in 1915 for coolies at Kohat and Bannu, two military stations on the North-West Frontier, at Rs. 15/– and Rs. 11–4 annas respectively, and at eight annas a day for Peshawar. AD, War, 1916–17, III, appendix, nos 73290–93; AD, War, 1916–17, I, no. 11205, p. 282. A 1907 estimate put the daily wage for coolies on government construction in the Khasi hills on the North-East Frontier at eight annas. P. R. T. Gurdon, *The Khasis*, 1907, London: Macmillan, 1914. Assuming the (unlikely) situation of full employment, eight annas a day adds up to Rs. 15/– a month, which compares well with the sepoy's Rs. 11/–.

[27] Candler, *The Sepoy*, p. 80.

[28] However, recruitment for those follower services which were regarded as 'polluting' took place within a more socially restricted frame.

[29] Home, Police, B, December 1890, 32–33; Home, Police, June 1895, nos 137–41. Rinku Arda Pegu kindly supplied these references.

[30] By January 1915, the British resident in Nepal wanted access to Khas Gurkhas as well. F&P, External B, April 1915, nos 171–203; Alban Wilson, *Sport and Service in Assam and Elsewhere*, London: Hutchinson and Co., 1924, p. 30.

[31] Between 1914 and 1919, over 60,000 Gurkhas were recruited into the combat regiments, and about twice that number were recruited into non-combatant units such as the Army Bearer Corps and the Indian Labour Corps.

The Army Department prohibited recruitment for the follower ranks from 'Punjabis of all classes, Garhwalis, Rajputs, Nepalese, cis-Frontier Pathans.'[32]

Higher followers and attached followers

Frontier campaigns, notably the Tirah Campaign of 1897–98, had made it clear that transport and medical followers would have to be trained and placed on a permanent footing.[33] Over 1902–5, they were organised into standing departments: the Supply and Transport Corps and the Army Bearer Corps.[34] The Army in India Committee (1912) could therefore conceptualise the Army Bearer Corps as a permanent part of the establishment, whose institutional standing was confirmed by a uniform, training, the performance of work in squads under military command, and a promotional and benefits structure.[35] To offset the rise in cost, the Committee accepted that in peacetime stretcher-bearers could be employed as lower office staff, but emphasised that their work should 'not take the form of cooly labour. *Private employment of any kind is prohibited*.'[36]

The mule-, bullock- and camel-drivers in standing transport and the Army Bearer Corps came under the category of 'higher followers', listed under Rule 8 of the Indian Army Act (Act VIII of 1911).[37] Following the protocol for the combatant ranks, the higher followers were both enrolled and attested: that is, they took an oath of fidelity.[38] Attestation conferred certain privileges—for instance, promotion to a non-commissioned rank. Followers who

---

[32] Foreign and Political (F&P), Internal, B, August 1917, nos 110–15.

[33] The stretcher-bearers were described as 'wretched, untrained coolies, caught up from the nearest bazaar'. Colonel H. D. Hutchinson, *The Campaign in Tirah 1897–1898: An Account of the Expedition Against the Orakzais & Afridis under Gen. Sir. William Lockhart*, London: Macmillan, 1898, p. 243.

[34] For a good account of the transformation, see A. E. Milner, 'The Army Bearer Corps', *Journal of the Royal Army Medical Corps*, vol. 6, no. 6 (1906), pp. 685–89; and 'Re-organisation of the Supply and Transport Corps', Military, A, 1908.

[35] IOR/L/Mil/7/6700; IOR/L/Mil/7/6730.

[36] Ibid., p. 136 (emphasis added); Secy AD, to Director, Medical Services, 22 August 1914, AD War, 1914–15, no. 3623, p. 127.

[37] Also on this list were the Transport veterinary *dafadars*, and the lascars of the Arsenals and Depots of the Ordnance Department.

[38] *Manual of Indian Military Law*, Calcutta: Government Printing, 1922, p. 111.

were only enrolled could be dismissed by the simple order of a Commanding Officer, but the dismissal of those who were attested had to be confirmed by a higher authority.

The attached followers were those assigned to regiments, but also to departmental units as cooks, sweepers, grass-cutters, water-carriers, and leather-workers. They were made up of a public and a private element. The 'public' followers were those paid from the central treasury because they were held to be essential to the mobilisation of a certain unit as a fighting formation. So, for instance, the public follower establishment for an Indian cavalry regiment was made up of a cook, a water-carrier, a sweeper and a *mochi* (leather-worker), whereas just one sweeper was considered sufficient for a transport unit of ninety-six mules.[39]

However, infantry and cavalry units could not manage with their authorised public followers alone. Through mess funds, subscriptions and small deductions in the wages of British privates and non-commissioned officers (NCOs), money was raised for 'private' followers—barbers, *dhobis* (washermen), mess waiters, tailors, and blacksmiths.[40] The British officer in the Indian service received an extra allowance because he was expected to keep his own horse and *syce*. When he went into active service he took along his *syce* and his personal bearer (valet), who were then added to the list of 'private' followers and received rations from the regiment, but on payment.[41] In a regiment on service, therefore, one might find in the follower ranks a mix of public followers, regimental private followers, and officers' servants.[42]

---

[39] *Langri*: the cook for Indian regiments, who was paid less than the Indian cook hired for British troops. *Mochi*: a leather-worker for saddles, harnesses, shoes, etc.

[40] The Adjutant General, India (ADG) pointed out that, while government undertook to provide public followers, the entertainment of regimental *kahars*, barbers, *gurgas* (utensil-washers) and washermen was 'a purely private and regimental matter.' ADG to General Officer Commanding (GOC), 8th (Lucknow) Division, 28 September 1915, Army Department Proceedings (AD), War, 1916–17, I, no. 3386, p. 119.

[41] One letter from an officer's servant in France illustrates his pride in this semi-official status: 'We are not working like servants, but like real servants of Government ... such is the fidelity we have shown that ... not a single Sahib has so much as been displeased with us.' Pathan ... to Fida Anjuman, Jullunder, 23 August 1915, IOR Walter Lawrence Mss F 143/92–97.

[42] Regiments prided themselves on the smartness of their mess servants as much as on their silver. One K. Mahmood Shah, military outfitter in Ludhiana, regularly adver-

Such arrangements reveal the prewar Indian Army's considerable reliance upon regimental housekeeping to provide servants, mounts, and kit.[43] Reviewing the supply position of Indian troops in France, an officer of the British Ordnance Services was astonished at the degree to which India 'furnished its native troops with only a bare quota of essential fighting equipment, leaving them to provide for their own domestic wants.'[44] Some of these thrifty and decentralised arrangements had to be abandoned in World War One, as demands for manpower and equipment stepped up and training schedules intensified.

Public followers were enrolled under the terms of the Indian Army Act, which committed them to general service, but they were not considered worthy of attestation. 'Private' followers were often simply 'entertained'—that is, they were hired but not formally enrolled. However, the declaration of war in August 1914 was followed by efforts to enrol private followers, so that they too could be court-martialed if they refused to move with the regiment, or deserted.

The sheer variety of artisanal, service and construction work required from followers meant that the lines of caste and wage in the Indian Army did not always fall smoothly along the sepoy-follower status divide. Among the attached followers, there were Brahmin cooks on the one hand and, on the other, skilled artisans such as carpenters and smiths who although of low caste earned more than the sepoy. However, the official stance was that the follower ranks had to be kept distinct from the combatant ranks precisely because recruitment was

---

tised the sale of 'Servants bands and crest in your Regd. Colour, waist and pugri bands, plated buckle and runner', *TOI*, 27 April 1918. Pugri: turban.

[43] In the *sillahdar* (cavalry), the recruit used to contribute some money towards his horse and equipment and his regiment would advance him the rest from its loan fund, to be repaid in installments. Yeats-Brown mourned the passing away after World War One of this individualistic arrangement, declaring that it had attracted yeoman of substance, who enlisted for *izzat* (honour). Francis C. C. Yeats-Brown, *The Lives of a Bengal Lancer*, New York: The Viking Press, 1930, p. 23. In another such arrangement, sepoys were given a 'hutting' allowance and constructed their own lines. The allowance was withdrawn in 1919, and Military Works took responsibility for barracks and essential buildings. Brigadier E. V. R. Bellers, *The History of the 1ˢᵗ King George the V's Own Gurkha Rifles*, vol. II, 1920–47, Aldershot: The Wellington Press, 1956, p. 2.

[44] Major General A. Forbes, *A History of the Army Ordnance Services*, vol. 3, London: The Medici Society, Ltd., 1929, pp. 273, 32–33.

socially mixed.[45] The valency of the martial caste label was maintained by the emphasis on selective recruitment and the institutional investment in upholding sepoy respectability. A perception that these issues were not of the same institutional importance for the follower ranks could tinge all of them with 'menial' status.[46] The Dogra sepoys of Mulk Raj Anand's novel *Across the Black Waters* can bully Santu, their high-caste Brahmin cook, because he is a follower:

> it was the prestige of rank and higher pay which was the proper measure of authority created by the Sarkar ... And to Santu ... every sepoy was a man of higher species.[47]

The sepoy-follower distinction was upheld through wages, pension benefits, kit, rations and fuel allowance—and even through what was put into the Christmas boxes distributed to the Indian contingent in France in 1914:

> The Gurkhas were to receive the same gift as the British troops; Sikhs the box filled with sugar candy, a tin box of spices and the Christmas card; all other Indian troops, the box with a packet of cigarettes and sugar candy, a tin box of spices and the card. Authorised camp followers, grouped under the title of 'Bhistis' were to receive a tin box of spices and the card.[48]

In colonial civil offices, 'menial establishment' was the formal categorisation for the lowest rung of employees, from the peons (messengers) down to file-suppliers, *bhistis* and sweepers. There wasn't a similar list for the army, probably because the number of attached followers varied with the season and the station, and between peacetime and active service.[49] However, the label 'menial' was often used in discussing their service conditions.

---

[45] However, to the chagrin of officials, attached followers erected their own 'internal' status lines, much like Indian servants in large households. For instance, sweepers who did the 'dry' conservancy work of sweeping barracks and mule lines would refuse to do the 'wet' conservancy work of cleaning latrines.

[46] 'Caste' had to be taken account of in the follower ranks only when it affected the sepoy ranks. MacMunn observed that stretcher-bearers should always include some castes from whom Hindu sepoys would accept a drink of water. MacMunn, *The Armies of India*, p. 189.

[47] Mulk Raj Anand, *Across the Black Waters*, 1940, Delhi: Orient Paperbacks, 2000, p. 213.

[48] Fergus Read, 'Princess Mary Gift Fund 1914 Box', Imperial War Museum, https://www.iwm.org.uk/history/look-inside-the-princess-mary-gift-fund-1914-box, last accessed 10 November 2019. *Bhisti*: water-carrier.

[49] Some were hired for only part of the year—for instance, the *punkah* (fan) pullers of

In exploring this condition of 'menial' status, we have the benefit of a valuable body of writing which has shown how caste norms tended to hem powerless communities into the hardest and most stigmatised sectors of work regimes—even in those which were being refashioned under the drives of colonialism and capitalism. 'Untouchability' was thereby recast in new contexts, and low pay, degrading conditions of work, and corporal discipline were 'naturalised'.[50] The attached followers found it particularly difficult to challenge their consignment to menial status because of the presence in their ranks of 'untouchable' castes who swept, cleaned latrines, washed clothes, and crafted leather. This was work characterised both as a 'trade'—that is, as a caste-structured specialisation—and as 'polluting'.

The other dimension of 'menial' status was the reproduction, in an institutional context, of regimes of highly discretionary discipline and a requirement to be indefinitely 'on call' which resembled the dependency of domestic service.[51] Regimental followers, public and private, were, in the manner of domestic servants, expected to be constantly at hand to tend to the physical needs of their institutional superiors, who felt they had a personal right to

---

the 'hot weather establishment', or servants hired locally when sojourning at hill stations.

[50] Peter Mayer, 'Inventing Village Tradition: The Late 19th Century Origins of the North Indian "Jajmani System"', *Modern Asian Studies*, vol. 27, no. 2 (1993), pp. 357–95. See also Vijay Prashad, *Untouchable Freedom: A Social History of a Dalit Community*, Delhi: Oxford University Press, 2000; Shahana Bhattacharya, 'Rotting Hides and Runaway Labour: Labour Control and Workers' Resistance in the Indian Leather Industry, c. 1860–1960', in Ravi Ahuja (ed.), *Working Lives and Worker Militancy: The Politics of Labour in Colonial India*, Delhi: Tulika, 2013; and Ramnarayan S. Rawat, *Reconsidering Untouchability: Chamars and Dalit History in North India*, Bloomington; Indianapolis: Indiana University Press, 2011.

[51] Ravi Ahuja argues persuasively that the absence of defined working hours was a general characteristic of colonial legal regimes. Wage contracts were held to put labour 'comprehensively' at the disposal of employers, not simply to assign the wage for a fixed portion of work time. Ravi Ahuja, 'Networks of Subordination—Networks of the Subordinated: The Ordered Spaces of South Asian Maritime Labour in an Age of Imperialism (c. 1890–1947)', in Ashwini Tambe and Harald Fischer-Tiné (eds), *The Limits of British Colonial Control in South Asia: Spaces of Disorder in the Indian Ocean Region*, New York: Routledge, 2009, pp. 13–48, 16. The work of 'care' assigned to regimental followers, resembling domestic service, made it particularly difficult for them to claim a rule-governed work regime.

chastise followers for inadequate service, evasion, or questioning of demands. The fact that regiments found themselves having to supplement the income of public followers and employ 'private' followers blurred the line between public employee and domestic servant.[52] But this line was also effaced by a conviction on the part of the British Tommy, usually supported by his NCOs, that he had the white man's right to deference and care from 'menials', and that services could be appropriated by force even if they were not authorised or paid for.[53]

The Tommy's violence to some *punkah*-puller or sweeper was embarrassingly public and therefore more problematic institutionally than the beating an officer might administer to his Indian groom behind the walls of his compound.[54] Some efforts were made from the late nineteenth century onwards to curb British privates and NCOs from 'disciplining' natives with too much violence. Such initiatives were often countered by stubborn collective resistance. However, the prescribed alternative—that is, military regulations for follower discipline—were also marked by a high degree of summariness, and corporal punishment was used much more frequently than for the sepoy.

The disciplinary regime: the summary court-martial and corporal punishment

In the first half of the nineteenth century, the military authorities exercised an almost unchallenged sway over all those whose labour and services it relied

---

[52] For instance, twelve annas a month were deducted from the British private's pay to maintain regimental *dhobis* (washermen). Frank Richards, *Old Soldier Sahib*, New York: Harrison Smith and Robert Haas, 1936, p. 181.

[53] One Private Crickett punched an Indian Christian cook who had the temerity to protest against abuse, and in English too. He got off with an entirely nominal punishment because of a sympathetic Lance Corporal and Colonel. Richards account also mentions a sweeper punched for not immediately dropping his work to attend to another order, and a servant kicked for entering a bungalow with his shoes on. British privates were said to hate Curzon for his insistence that Commanding Officers punish men for violence inflicted on natives. *Old Soldier Sahib*, pp. 163–67, 181, 184.

[54] When a British cantonment magistrate asked what he should do if a European military officer assaulted his native servant, as for instance through the 'infliction of castigation by means of a Horsewhip', his superior said he 'couldn't imagine' such an incident. However, he conceded that if the military authorities at Neemuch failed to take action a report could be sent to the Governor General. Malwa Agency, no. 258 of 1870.

upon in cantonments.[55] It was only with the Indian Articles of War (Act V of 1869) that a distinction was made between enrolled followers, who came under military law at all times, and unenrolled followers and private servants, who came under military law only 'on active service, in camp, on the march or at any frontier post'.[56] However, weeks at a time could be spent in such seemingly transitional or liminal spaces, given that well into the 1890s a lot of troop movement was still through marches.[57] Ironically, the closer incorporation of the mule-drivers and stretcher-bearers into the army over the period 1902–5 improved their service conditions, but it also strengthened arguments in favour of retaining corporal punishment.[58] Summary court-martial, and with it the power to dictate corporal punishment, was held to be absolutely crucial to the reshaping of 'low-caste', unruly and unsanitary followers into efficient 'auxiliary services'.[59] The Judge Advocate General of India pointed out in 1906 that some 22,000 men had been brought under the Indian Articles of War as transport attendants in the Supply and Transport Corps, and that flogging was used more frequently to discipline them than in combatant units.[60] The Assistant Adjutant General, Richard

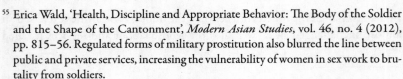

[55] Erica Wald, 'Health, Discipline and Appropriate Behavior: The Body of the Soldier and the Shape of the Cantonment', *Modern Asian Studies*, vol. 46, no. 4 (2012), pp. 815–56. Regulated forms of military prostitution also blurred the line between public and private services, increasing the vulnerability of women in sex work to brutality from soldiers.

[56] Lieutenant Colonel Andrew Cook McMaster, *A Catechism on Act No. V of 1869, the Indian Articles of War*, Madras: Higginbotham and Company, 1869, pp. 27–28. In contrast, British civilians attached to the army came under military law only in war time.

[57] Robert J. Blackham, *Scalpel, Sword and Stretcher*, London: Sampson Low, 1931, p. 93.

[58] Legislative, March 1911, 158–78. For details, see Radhika Singha, 'The "Rare Infliction": The Abolition of Flogging in the Indian Army, circa 1835–1920', *Law and History Review*, vol. 34, no. 3 (2016), pp. 1–36, 23–24.

[59] Singha, 'The "Rare Infliction"'. After the imposition of the Durand Line through Pashtun territory in 1893–95, Pashtuns were encouraged to join the army or frontier militias. This added a new argument for retaining corporal discipline, namely that this 'turbulent' and 'fanatic' transfrontier element in the Indian Army only respected summary punishment. Ibid.

[60] W. D. Thomson, JAG, 24 September 1906, Home, Judicial, A, March 1907, nos 167–83.

Wapshare, declared that desertion would become rife among transport attendants if flogging were abolished.[61]

The first consolidated Indian Army Act stated that all public followers were to be formally enrolled, thereby binding them legally to march with their units into active service.[62] Previously, only those followers who were both enrolled and attested had been bound down to general service. Knowledge about this shift was either slow to percolate down to regiments or deliberately held back. With the outbreak of World War One, as regimental followers realised that they were now compelled to march into active service, it became very difficult to procure them at the old rates of pay.[63] From April 1917, all private followers also had to be formally enrolled.[64] This was because Commanding Officers complained that if private followers refused to march into active service, or deserted at the last moment, they could be threatened with civil action but not with court-martial.[65]

Did the drawing of attached followers into the tighter ambit of military law give them some protection against summary punishment? For one category of followers this was not the case. By the terms of the 1911 Indian Army Act, the Commanding Officer of any unit could, for 'any offence, in breach of good order' on active service, in camp, in the march, or at any frontier post, still summarily sentence 'the native follower *if he was a menial servant*' to seven days' imprisonment or to 'corporal punishment not exceeding twelve strokes of a rattan'.[66] In theory, a summary caning could therefore be inflicted only on

---

[61] 17 September 1906, ibid.

[62] The *Manual of Indian Military Law* explained that enrolment was important because 'no person should be permanently subjected to an exceptional and severe code, like that contained in the Indian Army Act, without a definite act on his part, such act being susceptible of easy proof.' *Manual of Indian Military Law*, Calcutta: Government Printing, 1922, p. 7, para. 6.

[63] Army Department to SSI, 19 May 1916, AD, War, 1916–17, vol. 2, no. 38134.

[64] AD, War, 1916–17, I, no. 11207, pp. 282, 296.

[65] GOC, 6th (Poona) Division to ADG, 24 April 1915, AD, War, 1916–17, I, no. 11207, p. 295.

[66] Act VIII of 1911, section 22 (i), emphasis added. Right up to World War Two, the term 'menial servant' was never clearly defined, despite stray queries in British Parliament and in the Indian Legislative Council. The cantonment seems to be the only workspace where a summary caning was *not* permitted. The option of a fine is not even mentioned. The non-menial follower 'not otherwise subject to military

a narrow group of followers—that is, to private followers who were simply 'entertained'.[67] A court-martial would have to be held to sentence an enrolled follower to a military flogging.[68] Yet some anecdotal evidence indicates that due to the blurred line between public and private servants, all regimental followers remained vulnerable to some degree of personal violence.[69]

Nevertheless, military service had its attractions. It was precisely because the verification of caste was less rigorous among the follower ranks that 'low castes' were able to slip into less stigmatised forms of livelihood. 'Low-caste' Chamars found work as ward coolies, cooks and dressers in Indian station hospitals, and from the 1880s they were absorbed into the Army Hospital Corps on a defined institutional footing.[70] An Army Order of 30 October 1917 stated that 'musallis or sweepers or chamars who have embraced the Mohamedan faith' were specifically excluded from employment as cooks at British station hospitals.[71] Nevertheless, 'lower-caste' Muslims and Indian Christians were able to elide their origins and find work in British households

---

law' could be summarily sentenced to fifty days' imprisonment, or a fine for breach of good order.

[67] This narrowing down invited some criticism. The Chief Secretary of the United Provinces felt that summary caning should be allowed at all military stations, not only in camp or on the march, and that the term 'menial' should include 'troublesome classes of servants such as *darabis* and *syces*.' Chief Secretary, United Provinces to Secretary GOI, Legislative Dept, 7 October 1910, Leg, March 1911, nos 158–79.

[68] IOR/L/Mil/7/13738.

[69] British soldiers in World War Two were still being instructed not to give personal work to regimental followers and not to assault them, because the men might die of internal injuries, 'because it savours of bullying', and because of 'unpleasant results for the beater'. *Our Indian Empire*, General Staff India, 1940, pp. 73–78. Transport drivers also remained vulnerable. Major Thakur Hukam Singh, commanding the Jaipur Transport Corps, a princely state unit in Mesopotamia, was charged with 'illegal flogging and fining' of the mule-drivers, but a report conceded that 'he was no doubt efficient in a certain way.' F&P, Internal, B, June 1920, no. 11.

[70] Florence Nightingale, *Florence Nightingale on Social Change in India: Collected Works of Florence Nightingale*, ed. Gérard Vallée, Waterloo, ON: Wilfrid Laurier University Press, 2007, p. 177.

[71] *Compendium of the More Important Orders of the Government of India, Army Department, and Indian Army Orders, Issued from the 1st August 1914, to the 31st December 1917*, Calcutta: Government Printing, 1919, p. 225, para. 805.

and in messes.[72] In World War One a considerable number of *syces*, among them 'low castes', would be allowed to re-enrol as mule-drivers of the Supply and Transport Corps.

An 'invidious distinction': the bronze medal versus the silver medal

Just a few months before the declaration of World War One, regimental and departmental followers had notched up one victory in terms of status parity with combatants. After the Burma campaign of 1885–87, the practice began of awarding campaign medals to followers, but in bronze rather than silver.[73] By 1901, some officers were pointing out that due to the follower dislike for medals in this 'inferior' metal, many lay uncollected.[74] In the South African War (1899–1902), conducted under the command of the War Office, the boundary lines of caste and institutional status were also complicated by the race factor. Kitchener wanted non-enlisted Europeans who had served in the war, such as engine drivers and 'ward-maids', to get the silver Queen's South Africa Medal, not the bronze one kept for 'coloured' followers.[75] The response from India was that if this was the case, Indian Army followers who had served in field hospitals in South Africa, and been exposed to fire, should also get the silver medal.[76] The controversy arose at a time when the Indian Army was deeply anxious to put its transport and field medical services on a stable foot-

---

[72] At Patna, interviewing some Maghiya Doms, a community classed as a 'criminal tribe' in colonial times, a scholar listened to the following complaint: 'My father and grandfather used to work as cooks for the Englishmen. Before independence we would burn *ghee* in our earthen lamps. Independence was of course not for us! We became poor after that. Now people do not even touch the food cooked by us. For us, colonial rule was much better.' Sonali Verma, 'Criminality, Mobility and Filth: Rewriting Magahiya Doms of Bihar and United Provinces c. 1866–1947', M.Phil. thesis, Centre for Historical Studies, Jawaharlal Nehru University, 2016, p. 92.

[73] The condition was that they had to have been exposed to fire in the line of duty.

[74] TNA WO 32/4981; Military Department, Medals, A, August 1902, nos 2156–63. Of course, the other reason was that record-keeping for followers was so minimal then that they could not be traced.

[75] For a very informative post see David Grant, 'Silver or Bronze Medals to Public Followers and Others', https://www.angloboerwar.com/forum/15-important-decisions-book/641-bronze-or-silver, last accessed 22 March 2019.

[76] Secretary, War Office to Under-Secretary of State for India, Military Department, 18 December 1913 in AD, Medals, A, August 1914, nos 61–63; TNA WO 32/4981.

ing. The stance it took was therefore that nature of service, not race, ought to determine the medal. The discussion did not address the question of whether this more enlightened attitude would also apply to the 'Kaffir'—the African follower. However, in the Indian Army it led to the passing of an order on 22 May 1903 which made some categories of follower eligible for the silver medal. Nevertheless, Indian ward-sweepers, even those who were formally enrolled, were still not eligible.[77] The caste stigma attached to their occupation created a boundary to change.

In 1913 the Indian Commander-in-Chief, General Sir Garrett O'Moore Creagh, suggested that the bronze Indian General Service Medal be replaced by the silver one for all follower ranks.[78] Viceroy Lord Hardinge supported this shift, pointing out that under the Indian Army Act of 1911, all enrolled followers were liable for general service.[79] Since a war medal was 'an emblem of service in the field, only one class should be awarded'. Followers, he added, 'felt intensely the invidious distinction', and they were a class the army could not dispense with.[80] With some misgivings about the 'cheapening' of campaign medals, the Army Council in Britain issued an order on 1 May 1914 stating that enrolled followers would receive silver medals not only for operations relating to India, but also for those conducted 'under the orders of the Home Government'.[81] This time there was no clause which specifically excluded the sweeper.[82] For a clasp to this silver medal, the follower would have to be exposed to fire in the line of duty. Hence a Sikh *langri*'s jaunty assurance to General James Willcocks in France that he liked cooking close to the trenches, 'otherwise the Government may refuse to give us a clasp to

---

[77] Ward-sweepers and unattested followers, public and private, were eligible only for the bronze medal. Legislative, Unofficial, 1903, no. 807. Bronze medals received earlier could be exchanged for the silver ones, but at the cost of the follower.

[78] TNA WO 32/4981. Significantly Creagh was the first C-in-C, India, to be appointed to this post from the Indian Army, rather than from the British Army.

[79] Despatch Governor General in Council to SSI, 5 June 1913, TNA WO 32/4981.

[80] Ibid.

[81] Army Department, 29 May 1914, no. 361, in AD, Medals, A, August 1914, nos 361–63. The War Office also strenuously rejected the Government of India's contention that it could decide on the metal of the medal to be awarded. Ibid.

[82] For the saga of Ram Sarup, sweeper in the Bombay Artillery, who won an Indian Distinguished Service medal in World War Two see C. A. L. Graham, *The History of the Indian Mountain Artillery*, Aldershot: Gale and Polden, 1957.

our medals'.[83] However, the men who served in the Indian Labour and Porter Corps in France were eligible only for the bronze British War Medal. Interestingly, it was in wars conducted under the command of the Imperial Government, rather than those under the Government of India, that there was a stronger need to retain the bronze medal in order to maintain the 'colour line'.[84]

The intensification of recruitment

The central follower depots

On 13 October 1916, all recruiting for combatant, non-combatant and labour units was placed under the Adjutant General in India. As far back as March 1915 the Adjutant General had recommended the introduction of central follower depots, arguing that this would cast the net wider, ensure healthier men, check competitive bidding, and build up a reserve.[85] However, the Government of India had held off, hoping that Indian labour contractors, who regularly supplied the Public Works Department and the army commissariat, would provide followers more cheaply. Commanding Officers began to complain that contractors were not attracted by the money they received for bringing in recruits, that they passed off inferior men, and that they could not guarantee a constant supply.[86] Loosely organised follower camps, starting with the one at Meerut, were gradually reorganised as central follower depots with a Commanding Officer and subordinate staff. Public followers recruited through the central depots were uniformly enrolled for 'the period of the war', and were liable for service with any unit.[87]

---

[83] James Willcocks, *With the Indians in France*, p. 62.

[84] Men of the British Labour Battalions who had combatant status received the silver British war medal. Ironically the bronze British War Medal commands a better price on e-bay than the silver one, because of its scarcity value.

[85] ADG, 13 March 1915, AD, War, 1916–17, I, No. 11201.

[86] AD, War, 1916–17, II, No. 49806-No. 49814, pp. 1556–1564.

[87] Secy AD to ADG, 20 Sept 1916, AD, War, 1916–17, II, No. 49827, pp. 1596–1600. Central follower depots were also set up at Lucknow, Kirkee, Amritsar, and Rawalpindi. The departmental followers and the Labour Corps had separate depots AD, War, 1916–17, II, No. 49836, pp. 1605–1606.

The depots suffered from inadequate accommodation, much of it tent-age, and Commanding Officers struggled to get kit and equipment for recruits.[88] The Meerut depot, its Commanding Officer complained, resem-bled 'a large city', made up of recruits of all classes with no sense of disci-pline or sanitation.[89] Nevertheless, the imperative of separating followers from their families, and from work opportunities in the vicinity, encour-aged a militarisation of the regime. Pensioned Indian officers, appointed as 'escorting officers' and as subordinate depot staff, took the initiative in this matter. Khaki blouses, khaki *pagris* (turbans), and ammunition boots indi-cated that the men in the depot were now military property. Roll calls, drill and sanitary routines attuned them to institutional life and stricter time management.[90] Straggling and disorder had been blamed for high follower casualties in certain campaigns.

The depots allowed for more care in the compilation of follower service rolls and discharge papers, an indication of the greater value now afforded to this labour, with a correspondingly greater determination to track down deserters.[91] Commanding Officers were also asked to record caste and profes-sion so recruits could be assigned to appropriate work.[92] However, follower indents were usually framed very broadly and specified only religion or region, requesting for instance a 'Hindu cook' or a 'Gurkha bhisti'. On the supply side, there were incidents in which 'low castes' resisted their assignment to 'pollut-ing' work.[93] The emphasis on improving paperwork suggests the continuation of a trend inaugurated by the Indian Army Act—that of replacing, or at least supplementing, informal methods of disciplining the follower with contrac-tual obligation under military law. On 23 December 1916, Major P. Bramley, at the 3rd Echelon Branch in Basra, noted approvingly that the long roll sent with a batch of followers from the newly organised Meerut depot was correct

---

[88] F&P, War, B. March 1918, No. 384–386.

[89] CO, Followers Central Depot Meerut, to ADG 8/9 January 1917, AD, War, 1916–17, II, no. 49849, p. 1613.

[90] See AD, War, 1916–17, II, no. 49815, pp. 1568–71.

[91] Ibid. Mounting paperwork led to a significant rise in the employment of military clerks. The presence of educated elements in the Indian Army—for instance, the supply contractors, the clerks and medical personnel—is sometimes overlooked in accounts which focus only on the denial of King's Commissions.

[92] F&P, War, B, Secret, March 1918, nos 384–86.

[93] Officer Cdg, 6th (Poona) Division to ADG, 7 August 1916, ibid. See Chapter 3.

in all details. 'All followers were correctly labelled and in possession of identi-fication discs ... Service rolls were correctly written up in every particular.'[94]

If a centralised and militarised regime of follower recruitment offered dis-ciplinary advantages, it also provided the infrastructure for contact with fami-lies on the paternalist pattern in place for the sepoy. Followers, characterised as rootless denizens of the bazaar, were turning out to have relatives and credi-tors who would hold them back unless reassured about contact. '[L]arge sta-tions, such as Meerut,' wrote one officer, 'are full of women and children who have received no pay of any sort and in many cases have not even heard of their husbands for months and are consequently in a destitute condition and fre-quently even starving.'[95] Desperate relatives were applying for relief from the Imperial War Fund, an additional reason for insisting that followers assign a portion of their wages to dependants.[96]

Conserving follower manpower

The other reason combatant benefits were extended to the follower was that, as the war stretched on and shipping became difficult and costly, the man-power already present in theatres of war had to be conserved and deployed more flexibly. The effects of colonial backwardness in the form of a workforce too easily exhausted and prone to break down in health became very rapidly evident. The collapse of the reserve system had revealed the quick physical deterioration of the much vaunted 'martial castes' when they stayed at home on meagre prewar pensions. Scurvy among sepoys and followers in Mesopotamia reduced the effective fighting strength to an alarming extent.[97] Colonel Patrick Hehir of the Indian Medical Service pronounced that field service rations had to be reconstructed on a scientific basis.[98] On 1 January 1917 the Viceroy

---

[94] F&P, War, B, Secret, March 1918, nos 384–86.

[95] Captain A. H. R. Dodd, 22 June 1916, AD, War, 1916–17, II, no. 49815, p. 1569.

[96] GOC, 6th (Poona) Divisional Area to ADG, 24 April 1915, AD, War, 1916–17, I, no. 11207, p. 295; F&P, War, B, March 1918, nos 384–86.

[97] IOR/L/Mil/7/1828. Martin Swayne, *In Mesopotamia*, London: Hodder and Stoughton, 1917, p. 142. From East Africa, Major General T. E. Scott, comparing the ration scale of the Indian sepoy with that of the British soldier, stated flatly that it was 'ungenerous'. Major General T. E. Scott to Chief of Imperial General Staff, 31 December 1917, WW1/991/H, vol. 433, 1918, diary no. 15882.

[98] AD, Medical, A, January 1918, nos 2684–88.

announced, as a New Year boon, that all Indian combatants would get free rations on active service. Malnutrition in peacetime, he pointed out, had caused heavy invaliding in the field.[99] The measure was equivalent to a pay increase of Rs. 3–8–0, but the reason for giving it in kind was to ensure that sepoys ate better, instead of stinting themselves to send money home.[100]

However, the follower ranks, sent overseas with difficulty and expense, also had to be kept out of hospital. The prewar understanding that the follower could be sent on active service with a lesser quantity of free rations and fuel than the sepoy no longer seemed logical, and was held to compromise efficiency.[101] 'I have never been able to discover,' commented General O'Moore Creagh, 'why the appetite of a non-combatant was supposed to be smaller than that of a combatant.'[102] On 20 August 1915 regimental and departmental followers were granted free rations for active service overseas on the sepoy's scale, and on 6 December 1915 they were also permitted the same quantity of free fuel.[103] However, whereas from 1 January 1917 the sepoy got free rations both in and out of active service, for most followers at peace stations the Army held to the cheaper prewar formula of 'wages at the lowest local rates, with compensation for dearness of food grains at the follower scale'.[104]

The need to conserve all manpower is also reflected in proposals to reduce the disparity in standards of medical treatment, which existed between British and Indian troops, and between sepoys and followers.[105] The Makins

---

[99] WW1/773/H, vol. 215, 1916, diary no. 97275. In principle free rations put the Indian sepoy on the same footing as the British soldier, but the latter's rations were more varied and nutritious.

[100] Candler described the difficulty of preventing Dogra sepoys from stinting themselves to send money home. *The Sepoy*, p. 98.

[101] See GOC, 2nd (Rawalpindi) Division to QMG, 27 February 1915, AD, War, 1914–15, no. 13704, p. 455. In August 1917 the Army Department suggested free rations and better kit for stretcher-bearers in peace time as well, arguing that this would enhance their capacity to train intensively and thereby improve their efficiency. AD, Adjutant General's Branch, Medical, A, May 1919, 2238–46.

[102] Garrett O'Moore Creagh, *Indian Studies*, London: Hutchinson, 1919, p. 267.

[103] F&P, Internal, B, January 1916, no. 12.

[104] File no. 3/1917/Military, confidential list, Delhi State Archives (DSA). However, in December 1918 Labour and Porter Corps and Railway Construction companies serving within India were also granted free rations on the combatant scale. AD, B, May 1919, no. 510.

[105] *Report of the Committee Appointed by the Government of India to Examine the*

Committee, appointed on 31 October 1917 to enquire into British station hospitals in India, felt inspired to declare that:

> It is no longer reasonable, if it ever was, to rule that the Indian soldier requires less cubic air space than the British, and the Indian follower still less than the Indian soldier. A patient once admitted to a Government institution must be given the best and quickest chance of recovery possible, whatever his colour or social status.[106]

The Director of Medical Services responded repressively that the correlation of conditions between British and Indian hospitals was 'desirable where practicable'.[107] However, in December 1918 a station hospital system, modelled on the one for British troops, was introduced to cater to both sepoys and followers. Previously the regimental hospitals had only treated sepoys, and separate arrangements were made for followers.[108]

The Tommy's hold upon the British public's sympathy and attention provides an equally important explanation for the emphasis now placed on the application of training and technology to the improvement of follower services. The 'native' ward-servants, cooks, water-carriers, sweepers and washermen of the Indian Army Hospital Corps, who served British personnel in India, were criticised even before the war for not being as 'efficient or trustworthy' as the white personnel of the Royal Army Medical Corps.[109] The sharp reversals of 1915–16 in the Mesopotamia campaign would lead to a scathing denunciation of the backwardness of the medical and sanitary services of the Indian Army, reiterated by the complaints of the Territorials sent out to India. The British public had to be satisfied that measures were being taken to improve the food, sanitation and medical treatment of the British soldier-citizen. Followers were increasingly referred to as 'an integral ... part of the fighting machinery', and an 'efficient menial establishment' as 'an aid to

---

Question of the Re-Organisation of the Medical Services in India, April 1919, HMSO: Parliamentary Papers, Cmd 946, 1920. The President was Sir Verney Lovett.

[106] *Report of the Committee under the Presidency of Sir G. H. Makin*, 12 February 1918, AD, April 1919, nos 36660–66, para. 13.

[107] Ibid.

[108] *Report of the Committee Appointed by the Government of India to Examine the Question of the Re-Organisation of the Medical Services in India*, annexure I.

[109] See 1911 *Encyclopaedia Britannica*'s entry for 'Ambulance', https://en.wikisource. org/wiki/1911_Encyclopædia_Britannica/Ambulance last accessed 10 November 2019.

fighting efficiency'.[110] 'No one can doubt,' stated the Makins Committee, 'the capacity of the Indian to develop into one of the best personal attendants in the world, or an excellent house servant.' Yet nothing had been done, it complained, to develop this material in the Army Hospital Corps. Cooks and *dhobis* were using the most primitive appliances.[111]

The case for the the 'higher' followers: the mule-driver and stretcher-bearer

The pressure to improve follower conditions also came from British officers in the departmental services, who sought to improve morale and make their own war service more visible. British officers felt that an appointment to the Supply and Transport Corps was less prestigious than service with a regiment, entailed administrative drudgery, and brought fewer opportunities for promotion.[112]

A British captain in Mesopotamia buttonholed a British MP to complain that Indian cavalry officers were covered with medals but members of his mule transport unit were overlooked, despite the dangerous and onerous nature of their duties.[113] He drew up a chart to explain the disparity between sepoy and mule-driver:

Table 3: Difference in pay between sepoy and mule-driver.

	Sepoy	*Mule-driver*
Increase of pay	Rs. 2/– per month	Rs. 1/– per month
Compensation for dearness of food	Rs. 3/– to Rs. 3–8–0 per month	Rs. 1–10–0 to Rs. 2/– per month
Kit money	Rs. 60/–	Rs. 10/–
Annual allowance	Rs. 17/–	Rs. 10/–

---

[110] Army Instruction, India, no. 318 of 1919, 22 April 1919, in AD, ADG's branch, Establishment, Regimental, A, May 1919, nos 1869–73 and appendix. Commanding Officers invoked sepoy wellbeing to ask for more followers and better terms. The Commanding Officer of the Kohat Brigade demanded more cooks, pointing out that regiments had expanded in numbers and young recruits had to be fed well and punctually to accelerate their training. Brigadier General A. Eustace to ADG, 5 February 1916, AD, War, 1916–17, I, no. 15330, p. 405.

[111] *Report of the Committee under the Presidency of Sir G. H. Makin*, para. 6.

[112] IOR/L/Mil/7/6700.

[113] Aubrey Herbert, *Mons, Anzac, Kut: By an MP*, London: Edward Arnold, 1919, pp. 246–47.

He described the mule-drivers' sensitivity to the inferiority inscribed in the quality of their kit, the lack of concern for their rest and cleanliness, and their place at the back of the line for the distribution of 'comforts'. They had to work the longest hours without relief, their clothes became rags but they didn't get fresh ones, their tents were flimsy and cramped, and they didn't get milk, cigarettes, tobacco or any presents.[114] 'Concessions in kind' were a material and public signifier of institutional status, the medium through which the Indian Army conferred status on sepoys, constructed a paternalistic relationship with them, and improved the quality of its own manpower. The mule-drivers were attested, just as sepoys were, but in terms of food, kit and medical treatment they were kept at the level of the other follower ranks.[115] In 1915, explaining why it was so difficult to get mule-drivers, the GOC of the Lucknow Division wrote:

> Many of our drivers have relations in the combatant branches, and the fact of being rated as followers and laughed at as such in their villages … has greatly retarded recruiting … The expression 'followers' among Indians includes sweepers and the better class man objects to be graded in this category.[116]

The *drabis* also complained that they were treated in the cantonment general hospital 'along with the lowest class of menials' instead of in the troop hospital.[117]

The *drabis*' touchpoint for expressing their vulnerability about status was that they were put on a par with that most 'menial' of figures, the *mehtar*, or latrine cleaner. Major H. M. Alexander described the mule-drivers' ire about the coat they got for the winter in France: 'a short, shapeless garment of dirty yellow colour, lined with thin, worn-out blanket … useless for any purpose … in appearance … horrible. The men called them *mehtar ke brandi*, or sweepers' overcoats—the sweeper being the lowest type of menial in the Indian domestic system.'[118]

---

[114] Ibid., pp. 246–47. This was the picture around mid-1915 when the drabi's monthly wage had risen from Rs. 8/– to Rs. 9/–. Sepoys had followers to draw water, sweep and cook for them, but mule-drivers had only one sweeper per troop of ninety-six mules, which meant additional duties at the end of the day. GOC 3rd (Lahore) Division to QMG, 2 March 1915, AD, War, 1914–15, no. 13705.

[115] AD, ADG's branch, Supply and Transport, A, April 1919, nos 1452–58.

[116] GOC 8th (Lucknow) Division to QMG, 27 February 1915, AD, War, 1914–15, no. 13710, p. 461.

[117] Viceroy to SSI, 7 March 1917, AD, April 1919, no. 1452.

[118] Major H. M. Alexander, *On Two Fronts, Being the Adventures of an Indian Mule*

He also noted that Indian mule-drivers in France questioned their inferiority to the Indian cavalry soldiers because they had worked side by side with the British mule-drivers of the Army Service Corps, who were paid more than the British cavalry trooper.[119] British transport officers contended that their *drabis* should be placed on the same footing as sepoys, because their war work was as important, and their heroism no less so. Alexander added that 'the drabi is recruited from exactly the same classes as the sepoy, the only difference being that men of slightly inferior physique are accepted.'[120]

Interestingly, one does not find *drabis* referring to changed conditions of combat for the Indian cavalry trooper in France, although this could have constituted a possible argument for closing the status gap. In France, Indian cavalry units operated largely as dismounted troops, using bayonet and spade rather than sword and lance—a change noted with regret.[121] In his fictionalised account of 'Ram Singh', an Indian cavalry officer in France, Captain Roly Grimshaw describes him feeling very peeved about not being allowed to wander into Marseilles after disembarkation, especially because:

> he had noticed many drabies of the Supply and Transport Corps moving about with the utmost freedom ... As these good people were the very lowest caste, it annoyed Ram Singh ... Besides what could the townspeople think of the Indian Army if the only representatives they saw were these dirty untidy creatures?[122]

Later, Ram Singh complains about the way in which the cavalryman's work has come to resemble that performed by followers:

> This kind of fighting is for coolies who dig, *lohars* and such like who make all these arms and shells ... I have paid 500 rupees for the privilege of serving the Sirkar as a Cavalry soldier, not to be made to dig *morchas* like a sweeper whilst standing up to my knees in filth and water.[123]

Corps in France and Gallipoli, London: W. Heinemann, 1917, p. 40. *Brandi* could refer to brandy, as that which actually kept the sweeper warm.

[119] Ibid., p. 40.

[120] Ibid., p. 248.

[121] Major General Pratap Singh to Viceroy, 11 October 1916, describing the work of the Jodhpur Lancers. IOR Eur. Mss Chelmsford correspondence, vol. 15, no. 17.

[122] Captain Roly Grimshaw, *Indian Cavalry Officer, 1914–1915*, eds Colonel J. Wakefield and Lieutenant Colonel J. M. Weippert, Tunbridge Wells: Costello, 1986, p. 105. See image 4: 'At the horse pond, Indian muleteers, France (n.d., 1914–15)'.

[123] Ibid., p. 148. *Morchas*: trenches.

Grimshaw was weaving in an incident which occurred among the Jodhpur Lancers, but much later, in July 1920, and back in India.[124] In France itself, I could not trace any significant protest. Indian sepoys and cavalrymen had to adapt to substantial changes in routine when on active service, yet the 'martial caste' label, shored up by a war allowance, a field service allowance and free rations, acted as a status shield.[125] Practices which sepoys accepted on active service were different from those they accepted when they returned to the more visible space of the cantonment back in India. The follower ranks also aspired to this status shield, so perhaps they had no reason to highlight the changed conditions of 'martial' work.[126]

Wages and benefits: desertions and collective action

Gaps in data make it difficult to compare sepoy and follower wages over the course of World War One. The Army Department preferred to meet wartime shortfalls of departmental followers by temporary forms of supplementation, such as an enlistment bonus and additional pay for so many months of service, so it could keep their basic pay a step behind the sepoy's. The other problem

---

[124] When the Jodhpur Lancers, a princely state unit, returned to India in July 1920, they went on 'strike' demanding free rations in peacetime, like sepoys of the Indian Army. The complaint which Grimshaw puts in his fictional hero's mouth came seventh in a petition dealing with discharge, land grants, and promotions: 'Our, sepoys, work is to give head in the war and field, and not to undertake the duty of a coolie, but unfortunately for … about two years we are compelled to do that … cutting pala grass, trees, wood, carry them on our heads, and plucking Sangris, Kairs, carry earth from one place to another, ploughing, moving well, and other big and small coolie's work etc.' F&P, Internal, B, October 1920, nos 120–25.

[125] On the front line, Indian Army soldiers were now eating in platoon messes with their uniforms and leather boots on. They cleared away putrefying corpses from their trenches, work both repellant and 'polluting'. Their hours spent in fatigue dress were extending, not only because of the time spent making roads and embankments, but also because of an increased emphasis on group games such as football and hockey, which reorganised their leisure time.

[126] It was sometimes by the mode of his death that the sepoy indicated he was losing faith in the power of colonial military service to uphold his social standing. In the 1916 siege of Kut in Mesopotamia, the sepoys who chose to starve rather than eat mule flesh seem to have decided to die to preserve their family's *izzat* (honour) instead of prolonging their lives to die for the state.

was the very local frame used to determine the wages of regimental followers, public and private. This arrangement kept costs down, so it persisted, despite efforts in 1910 to fix a standard all-India rate for public followers.[127]

At the outbreak of the war the sepoy's pay was Rs. 11/– a month. The stretcher-bearer in the Army Bearer Corps received Rs. 7/–, raised in August 1914 to Rs. 9/–, and the mule-driver of the Transport Corps Rs. 8/–, raised in June 1915 to Rs. 9/–. The *Supply and Transport Manual (War)* prescribed a somewhat higher scale for public followers attached to departmental units than for those assigned to infantry or cavalry regiments, even if they did the same work. The official justification was that regimental followers were moved around less and that the regiment offered them a 'home' where they and their family got food and extra money through supplementary work for British privates.[128] So, for instance, the departmental scale for the cook, *bhisti*, *syce* and sweeper was Rs. 8/–, whereas those attached to regiments got Rs. 6/– to Rs. 7/– a month, with the sweeper getting the lowest.[129] Wages for private followers depended on the individual officer and prevailing local wages for servants. An experienced cook or bearer (valet) would get higher wages than a sepoy, but without his status, security of employment or retirement benefits.

On 20 March 1917, with the Viceroy stating that he needed 1,000 mule-teers monthly but was getting only 600, and that desertions were on the rise, the Secretary of State for India sanctioned the conversion of mule-drivers from follower to combatant service, a shift which involved formal discharge, re-enrolment and attestation.[130] The *drabi*'s basic pay remained the same at Rs. 9/– a month, as against Rs. 11/– for the sepoy, and his wound and injury pension was Rs. 1/– less than it was for the sepoy. However, he now received good service pay and free rations and fuel on the combatant's scale, in active

---

[127] AD, June 1913, nos 1302–8 and appendix.

[128] The *syces* with British cavalry regiments and batteries earned Rs. 2/– to Rs. 4/– a month extra by cleaning kit and saddlery for British troopers. *Syces* with ammunition columns were discontented because they only got their official pay. Sweepers attached to regiments could count on handouts of food, so they preferred to serve here rather than in Indian troop hospitals where this was not the case. AD, June 1913, appendix 1, Establishment, Regimental, A.

[129] Government of India (GOI), AD to SSI, 19 May 1916, AD, War, 1916–17, II, no. 38134, p. 1073.

[130] Viceroy to SSI, 7 March 1917, and SSI to Viceroy, 20 March 1917, IOR/L/Mil/7/17483.

service and in peace. The qualifying period for a pension was reduced from thirty-one years to twenty-one years, which was also the prescribed period for the sepoy, but the pension was eight annas less.[131] The Viceroy admitted that combatant status for mule-drivers might necessitate a similar change for other departmental followers in the Army Bearer Corps, the Army Hospital Corps and the Ordnance lascars.[132] He did not have to wait very long.

With the announcement on 1 January 1917 that the sepoy would get free rations on active service and in peace, and the extension in March 1917 of the same benefit to mule-drivers, the men of the Army Bearer Corps waited anxiously for a similar concession. Food prices had risen so sharply that without free rations they found it difficult to send money home.[133] In June and July 1917, the No. 7 Combined Field Ambulance at Peshawar reported incidents in which stretcher-bearers had deserted, or refused to turn up for a parade or a route march.[134] On 10 August 1917, ninety-four Gurkha stretcher-bearers, 'in a perfectly orderly manner', tied up their kit, deposited it in front of the guardhouse and marched away down the Nowshera Road.[135] Their grievance was that on a wage of Rs. 9/– they could not even eat enough.[136] They wanted

---

[131] Ibid. Interestingly, some drivers decided not to opt for combatant status. As non-combatants they had the option of leaving with a gratuity after a shorter term of service, and they could qualify for one of the higher-paid artificer ranks. ADG to Deputy ADG, Basra 10–11 January 1918, WW1/966/H, vol. 408, diary no. 3153. Pp. 43–44.

[132] Viceroy to SSI, 7 March 1917, AD, War, 1917–18, no. 1452.

[133] In the peace station of Peshawar in July 1917, a stretcher-bearer was getting Rs. 9/– a month with a grain compensation allowance which amounted to Rs. 1–12–9 at the follower's scale. In contrast, the sepoy's monthly rations were valued at Rs. 6–12 using the Peshawar *nirikh* rate, and he also received a messing allowance of ten annas a month. CO, Indian General Hospital to Assistant Director Medical Services (ADMS), 1st (Peshawar) Division, 9 July 1917, AD, ADG's Branch, Medical, A, May 1919, nos 2238–46 and Appendix.

[134] Ibid.

[135] CO, no. 1 Company, ABC to ADMS, 1st (Peshawar) Division, 10 August 1917, ibid.

[136] CO, Indian General Hospital to ADMS, 1st (Peshawar) Division, 9 July 1917, AD, May 1919, no. 2238. One Havildar Jiwand Singh was reported to have told the No. 1 ABC Company Peshawar that free rations would be sanctioned in August, and disappointment over this precipitated the desertion. Proceedings of a Court of Enquiry, 17 August 1917, ibid.

the 50 per cent war allowance and the free rations they would have received if sent on 'active service'.[137] Some Gurkhas claimed that they had been deceived into thinking they were enlisting as sepoys, adding that since all castes were recruited to the Army Bearer Corps, they would be put out of caste at home.[138] Whatever the actual 'misunderstanding', the fact that it was the most valued 'martial tribe', the Gurkhas, who had taken the decisive lead may explain why the General Officer Commanding took a lenient view of the incident.[139]

On 23 April 1918, a set of concessions were announced for the Army Bearer Corps. The stretcher-bearer remained an attested follower, and would receive the same pay as before. However, he would also receive benefits nearly equivalent to those of the sepoy, on the pattern in place for the mule-driver: a wound and injury pension at Rs. 1/ less than the sepoy, a family pension at eight annas less, free rations both in active service and in peace, at least for the duration of the war, and, in place of a meagre kit allowance, a free issue of clothing and better kit.[140]

The attached followers: 'We are at their mercy'

The Army Department was particularly reluctant to raise the permanent wage bill for attached followers, public and private, because it meant forfeiting a variety of local economies. Some officers also warned that sepoys would press for higher wages on seeing that the regimental followers, their institutional inferiors, were catching up with them.[141] However, others were quite clear that inflationary pressures had long eroded follower wages, and that the increase would have to be permanent, not just for the duration of the war.[142]

---

[137] Ibid.

[138] Ibid.

[139] '[T]he men in question did not realise the seriousness of their offence and appear to have ground for grievance in view of the promises held out to them on enlistment and after.' GOC, 1st (Peshawar) Division to ADG, 15 September 1917, ibid.

[140] GOI, AD, Army Instruction (India) no. 395, 23 April 1918, in AD, ADG's Branch, Medical, A, May 1919, nos 2238–46 and appendix.

[141] Follower committee, Delhi, 12 January 1915, AD, War, 1916–17, I, Appendix, nos 11226–36, p. 322.

[142] GOC 2nd Rawalpindi (Division), to ADG, 15 June 1915, AD, War, 1916–17, I, no. 3351, p. 109.

From 1911 onwards, infantry and cavalry regiments had been complaining of the difficulty of making up their 'menial' establishment.[143] If army stations still succeeded in getting followers at wages below the *nirikh* rate, the local market scale, it was because they could offer the follower and his family supplementary food and work. The Bannu Brigade managed to retain *bhistis* and sweepers only because every sepoy also contributed some flour from his rations.[144] But in World War One, when followers were expected to accompany their regiment for long periods overseas, such benefits were compromised and the authorised pay alone simply did not suffice. Follower reliance on family labour to put together a livelihood was also revealed by the sudden visibility during the Great War of young boys, old men and even women among followers at certain military locations.[145]

In 1916, explaining the acute difficulty of getting followers, the Government of India observed that the Indian frontier expedition was usually short in duration and low in follower casualties, but in the present war, conditions at the front had 'been abnormally hard, and losses, due both to sickness and casualties in action, extremely heavy.'[146]

---

[143] The S&T annual administrative reports for 1910–11 and 1911–12 reveal the intense dissatisfaction of 'the menial establishment' with their pay. IOR/L/Mil/17/5/259. The military contingents gathering in Delhi for the 1911 imperial assembly found it very difficult to get sweepers, *bhistis* and *beldars* (navvies). Deputy Commissioner Delhi's office, file no. 31, 1911, DSA.

[144] CO, Bannu Brigade to QMG, 20 September 1915, AD, War, 1916–17, I, no. 3383, p. 118.

[145] The CO, Bannu, reported that there were a dozen women and many children among the syces of the 31st Lancers because men simply could not be found at the authorised rate. 28 March 1917, AD, War, 1916–17, II, appendix, nos 73290–93. There were many complaints that old men or young boys were fraudulently substituted for enrolled followers. F&P, War, B, March 1918, nos 384–86. Walter Lawrence remarked upon the youth of some of the Indian followers at Marseilles and in the Indian hospital at Brockenhurst—a 10-year-old bellows-blower, two 12-year-old *syces*. Walter Lawrence to Kitchener, 15 February 1915, IOR Eur Mss F/143/65. Some of this substitution probably took place by family arrangement.

[146] GOI to SSI, 19 May 1916, AD, War, 1916–17, II, no. 38134.

Table 4: Mortality rates for sepoys and followers by theatre (italics mine).[147]

Theatre	Dead from all causes, compiled up to 31 December 1919		
	Indian officers	Indian other ranks	Followers
France	176	5,316	2,218
East Africa	67	2,405	500
Mesopotamia	364	17,567	11,624
Dunsterforce	–	158	23
Persia	25	1,779	670
Egypt	74	3,713	555
Gallipoli	33	1,591	127
Aden	7	500	79
Muscat	1	39	2
Frontier operations	17	2,245	1,621
Total	764	35,303 [according to the War Office source; the actual total was 35,313]	17,419

By the spring and summer of 1915 the follower demand from Indian Army divisions in France, Gallipoli, and Mesopotamia had outstripped supply, while units at home were struggling unsuccessfully to maintain the minimum needed.[148] The Army Bearer Corps, the Army Hospital Corps and the Supply and Transport Corps were reported to be bidding for followers at whatever rate they were obtainable.[149] The Adjutant General's Branch declared, 'We are at their mercy, which of course is absolutely wrong and must be stopped.'[150]

Follower discontent was attributed to wages being not only too low but also highly variable, even within the same category of work.[151] The concentration

---

[147] Source: Table 4, 'Total Indian casualties suffered during the war as compiled up to 31st December 1919', in War Office: Statistics of the Military Effort of the British Empire During the Great War, p. 778. The figures for wounds were 1,590 for Indian officers, 61,806 for Indian other ranks, and 954 for followers. Ibid. Followers probably suffered disproportionately from disease attributable to service, but we do not have figures for this.

[148] AD, War, 1916–17, I, nos 3351–52, pp. 109–23.

[149] Note, ADG's branch, January 1915, AD, War, 1916–17, I, appendix, p. 323.

[150] Ibid.

[151] Walter Lawrence reported that Indian followers had been recruited from different

of different units in theatres of war, as well as the circulation of personnel between them, was throwing a light on wage disparities. Public followers attached to departments got a higher wage than those attached to regiments, and those recruited at short notice for the duration of the war got higher wages still.[152] Competitive bidding for followers enhanced wage disparities and created confusion in disbursing pay.[153]

In May 1915, the Army Department sanctioned a war allowance at 50 per cent of basic pay and free rations for all public followers on active service.[154] From July 1915, follower wage discrepancies in overseas theatres were ironed out in an upward direction.[155] However, a sweeper or *syce* attached to a departmental unit still received a higher wage than one attached to a regiment.[156] In May 1916, with follower shortages continuing, the Viceroy suggested that the wages of all public followers serving overseas, whether departmental or regimental, be standardised using the scale sanctioned by the *Supply and Transport Manual (War)*.[157] This introduced the principle of same pay for same work for public followers, but only for those posted overseas.[158] The monthly pay of the regimental *bhisti*, cook and sweeper on overseas service now rose to Rs. 13/–, leading the Secretary of State for India to note anxiously that this sum was only Rs. 1–8–0 less than the sepoy's pay on active service.[159]

---

places at different rates of pay for hospitals in England, creating tension among them and discontent among sepoys. A sweeper from Peshawar was getting Rs. 10/– a month; a sweeper from Bombay or Poona, Rs. 24/–. Walter Lawrence to Lord Kitchener, 15 February 1915 and 10 March 1915, BL, Eur. F. 143/65, IOR; also Viceroy to SSI, 19 May 1916, AD, War, 1916–17, II, no. 38134, p. 1074.

[152] Ibid.

[153] GOC 6th (Poona) Division to ADG, 24 April 1915, AD, War, 1916–17, I, no. 11207, p. 295.

[154] At peace stations a money allowance would replace free rations. Secy AD to ADG, 22 May 1915, AD, War, 1916–17, I, no. 11218, p. 310.

[155] SSI to Viceroy, 6 July 1915, AD, War, 1916–17, III, appendix, p. 2214.

[156] Deputy Field Accountant General IEF (A) to India Office, 18 June 1915, AD, War, 1916–17, III, appendix, p. 2224.

[157] A 50 per cent war allowance (*batta*) would be added to this, and a field service allowance of Rs. 1/–, together with free rations. Despatch no. 44 (Army), 19 May 1916, AD, War, 1916–17, II, no. 38134.

[158] Order no. 805 of 6 November 1916, AD, War, 1916–17, II, no. 38137.

[159] SSI to Viceroy, 12 July 1916, AD, War, 1916–17, II, no. 38135, p. 1075. The autho-

Another interesting point is that the regimental sweeper's wage had levelled up to that of the cook and *bhisti*.

Back in India, however, the Supply and Transport scale was still not attractive enough to attract fresh follower recruits.[160] In September 1916, the Commanding Officer of the newly inaugurated Meerut depot was instructed to offer wages at 'a scale fixed for each class by striking a mean of the local rates quoted by civil authorities of the territorial division for which the Central Follower Depot had been set up.'[161] In other words, the follower's basic wage was to be allowed to climb up to the prevailing market rate. But it was the local market rate which was to be used as the reference point, not an all-India average. The latter would have meant a much steeper hike, because wages in western and southern India and Burma were higher than those in upper India.[162] Eventually the Meerut scale—that is, an average wage derived from the upper India region—was accepted as the universal one for all central follower depots.[163]

The problem which emerged was that this Meerut scale, which was for fresh follower recruits, exceeded the wages given to followers already overseas. Worse still, it outstripped the sepoy's wage.[164] 'It is recognised,' admitted the

---

rised pay for the regimental *bhisti*, cook, and sweeper rose from Rs. 6–8–0, Rs. 6/–, and Rs. 5–8–0 respectively to Rs. 8/–. Adding a 50 per cent war allowance, that is Rs. 4/–, and a field service allowance of Rs. 1/–, this brought their active service pay to Rs. 13/–. Enclosure to Despatch no. 44 (Army), 19 May 1916, AD, War, 1916–17, II, no. 38134, p. 1076. The *syce's* pay remained at Rs. 7/– a month, which along with allowances added up to Rs. 11–8–0 on active service. Ibid.

[160] Punjab officials said that cooks and *bhistis* would not enrol for overseas service for less than Rs. 20/– a month. AD War, 1916–17, II, no. 49821, pp. 1584–93.

[161] Secy AD to ADG, 20 September 1916, AD, War, 1916–17, II, no. 49827, p. 1598. Emphasis mine. On active service the follower would also get a 50 per cent allowance on this wage, a field service allowance of Rs. 1/– and free rations. Ibid.

[162] 'Memorandum on recruitment in India', ADG's Branch, May 1917, Military, B, 1917, file 3, DSA.

[163] On 19 January 1917 the Army Department decided that in future the terms for follower labour of a particular category were to be of 'universal application'. Secy AD to ADG, 19 January 1917, WWI/791/H, vol. 233, diary no. 4756, p. 72.

[164] Followers already overseas received the Supply and Transport scale, which was Rs. 8/– for the cook, *bhisti* and sweeper and Rs. 7/– for the *syce*. By the Meerut scale, fresh recruits to these jobs would get Rs. 10/–.[164] Adding a 50 per cent *batta* and Rs. 1/– field service allowance, I calculate that whereas the public follower sent

Viceroy, 'that these proposals will raise pay of followers above that of fighting men, but as demand exceeds supply this is unavoidable.'[165] He tried to reassure the Secretary of State that this pay rise would not affect the recruitment of fighting men, as followers were drawn from 'non-fighting classes'.[166]

Followers now preferred to join the central depots for overseas service, instead of regiments stationed in India where the pay was much lower. Regiments in India tried to draw upon the central depots, even if it meant offering higher wages, but were discouraged from doing so on the grounds that it would raise local rates and drain away followers collected for overseas service.[167] However, follower wages for regiments stationed in India could not really be sealed off from wages offered for overseas service. In January 1918 there was another attempt to rationalise wages for home and overseas service, but this meant another spike in pay.[168] A cook, *bhisti*, sweeper or *syce* enrolled on or after 1 February 1918 would get a bonus of Rs. 20/– on enlistment and a fixed wage of Rs. 12/– a month for service within India. On overseas service, he would receive an additional allowance of 50 per cent, which brought his monthly wage up to Rs. 18/–.[169] By February 1919 these rates were considered too high for peace conditions, and the Viceroy proposed to bring them down to Rs. 9/– for service in India and Rs. 14/– for service overseas.[170]

A tentative comparison around mid-1917 of sepoy and follower wages and allowances gives the following picture:

---

earlier was by this point getting Rs. 13/–, the new recruit sent overseas would get Rs. 16/– together with a bonus of one month's pay for the first six months of service and one month's pay for every subsequent three months. Viceroy to SSI, 30 August 1916, AD, War, 1916–17, II, no. 49816, p. 1582.

[165] Ibid.

[166] Ibid.

[167] F&P, War, B, March 1918, nos 384–86.

[168] Army Instruction (India), no. 64, 22 January 1918, IOR/L/Mil/7/8727.

[169] Ibid. Followers hired before this date were supposed to continue on the scale fixed by the central follower depots. WW1/999/H, vol. 441, 1918, diary no. 19703. However, *syces* stationed at the India Base Remount Depot at Marseilles, some for over three years, complained and were granted the consolidated pay of Rs. 18/–. IOR/L/Mil/7/18727.

[170] Viceroy to SSI, 15 February 1919, and Order no. 318 of 1919, AD, ADG's Branch, Establishment, Regimental, A, May 1919, nos 1869–73 and appendix.

Table 5: Follower wages and allowances in 1917.[171]

	Monthly pay in rupees	War batta (war allowance)	Field service allowance	Total monthly wage (on active service)	Bonus and other benefits
Infantry sepoy	Rs. 11/–	Rs. 5/–	Rs. 2/–	Rs. 18/–	Rs. 50/– enlistment bonus. Free rations in peacetime and active service.
Transport driver	Rs. 9/–	Rs. 5/–	Rs. 2/	Rs. 16/–	Rs. 50/– enlistment bonus. Free rations in peacetime and active service.
Army Bearer Corps	Rs. 9/–	Rs. 4–8	Rs. 2/–	Rs. 15–19	Free rations on active service.
Sweeper, langri, bhisti, syce	Rs. 10/–	Rs. 5/–	Rs. 1/–	Rs. 16/–	Free rations on active service.
Labour Corps, Mesopotamia	Rs. 15/–	Rs. 5/–	–	Rs. 20/–	Free rations on active service.
Labour Corps, France	Rs. 20	–	–	Rs. 20/–	Bonus: one month's pay for the first six months, then one month's pay every three months (Rs. 60/– for one year). Free rations.

The official justification for offering men in the Labour Corps sent to France a monthly wage of Rs. 20/– in comparison to the sepoy's Rs. 18/– was that labourers were drawn from a different social stratum and were not part of

---

[171] The figures are based on data from Secy Recruiting Board to Chief Commissioner Delhi, 29 June 1917, file no. 3/1917, Military, DSA; and Secy AD to ADG, 9 July 1917, in F&P, War, B, Secret, March 1918, nos 384–86.

the permanent military establishment, so the gap would not affect combatant recruitment. However, from April 1918 the total pay of the sepoy on active service was also raised to Rs. 20/–.[172] On field service, sepoys and followers were now getting free rations at the same scale. However, in peacetime, whereas combatants continued to get free rations, followers received either free rations at a lower scale, or a money allowance or compensation for dearness of grain at a lower follower's scale.[173] Overall, the Indian Army seems to have managed, though with difficulty, to keep the sepoy's basic pay and total active service pay somewhat ahead of that of the departmental follower and the lower ranks of public followers.[174]

The new pension rules sanctioned in January 1915 also favoured the sepoy in evaluation of life and limb.[175] Followers earning Rs. 8/– to Rs. 12/– monthly received a family pension of Rs. 4/– at the higher rate and Rs. 3/– at the lower rate, as compared to Rs. 5/– and Rs. 4/– respectively for the sepoy, and a wound and injury pension at three-fourths of the sepoy rate.[176] This was the scale which applied to mule-drivers and stretcher-bearers.[177] Followers with a wage below Rs. 8/–, a category which included a substantial number of attached followers, public and private, received a wound and injury pension at half the sepoy rate, with a minimum of Rs. 3/–.[178] The heirs of 'temporary public followers … engaged on high rates of pay for a particular service' and of 'private followers of the servant class' would get the lowest pension of Rs. 3/–

---

[172] Rs. 11/– a month with Rs. 5/– war *batta* and Rs. 4/– war allowance, totalling Rs. 20/–.

[173] 'Combatant' now included the mule-driver.

[174] Within the parameters of 'unskilled labour', sepoy service retained its status and wage superiority.

[175] Departmental followers and public followers earning a wage of Rs. 13/– and above received the same wound and injury pension as the sepoy, and the same family pension. Army Regulations (AR), no. 1062, in AD, War, 1914–15, no. 2250, pp. 74, 77.

[176] AR no. 1073, and AR no. 1062, in AD, War, 1914–15, no. 2250, pp. 74, 77.

[177] In April 1918, the stretcher-bearer's family pension was increased from Rs. 4/– to Rs. 4–8 at the higher rate and Rs. 3/– to Rs. 3–8 at the lower rate. GOI, AD, Army Instruction (India), no. 395, 23 April 1918, in AD, ADG's Branch, Medical, A, May 1919, nos 2238–46 and appendix.

[178] AR no. 1062, ibid., p. 74. 'Private followers of the servant class' received a wound and injury pension on the same scale. AR no. 1063, ibid., p. 75.

a month if the follower died in action or from wounds sustained in war.[179] This 'temporary' category came to include 'organised labour and unorganised labour'—that is, the Labour and Porter Corps and other discrete labour categories such as boatmen, watchmen, guides and so on, 'classes not ordinarily represented in the army in peace time'. However, from January 1918 the worth of a 'life' in this temporary category was reduced further. The family pension was withdrawn and, instead, if the man died on his way to active service his heirs would get a one-off gratuity of Rs. 150/–, and if he died on field service one of Rs. 300/–.[180]

The Great War and the 'servant problem'

The higher risk of wounds and fatalities in this war and the reluctance of servants to travel into overseas theatres created a problem for the officer ranks as well.[181] In November 1914, the Adjutant General in India observed that to expect the British officer to assist his servant's family if he died or was disabled on active service was an 'unfair liability ... seeing that civilian servants are taken to relieve the State of providing soldier servants, as in European armies, and leave the latter available to strengthen the effective firing line.'[182] He proposed that the government extend the benefit of the lowest class of pension to private followers, and to 'the recognised servants engaged and paid for by the troops, and taken into the field under authority'.[183] The new pension rules of 1915 sanctioned this.[184]

---

[179] AR, no. 1074, AR no. 1075, ibid., p. 84. The heirs of 'temporary public followers' could receive the capitalised value of the pension instead if they requested this, or if it was difficult to arrange for pension payment. Ibid.

[180] If the man died before embarkation, the heirs would receive a gratuity of Rs. 150/–. AD to ADG, 2 January 1918, IOR/L/Mil/7/18302, pt I.

[181] Officers proceeding to Persia were told they would have to take private servants with them, as they were 'unobtainable in that country'. Indian Army Orders 1918, no. 332, p. 257.

[182] ADG's report, 26 November 1914, AD Progs, War, 1914–15, no. 2230, p. 46.

[183] Ibid.

[184] AR, no. 1063, no. 1075 prescribed a wound and injury pension of 'half the combatant scale with a minimum of Rs.3/–' for 'private followers of the servant class authorised to be taken on active service', and, in case of death on service, a family pension of Rs. 3/–. AD, War 1914–15, nos 2250–51, pp. 75, 84.

Further problems arose when private followers were taken as prisoners of war in Mesopotamia. Officers, regardless of whether they were prisoners themselves, chafed at the idea that they were morally obliged to go on paying wages to their servant, or an allowance to his family.[185] Regiments did not want to dip into mess funds to support mess-bearers taken prisoner and their dependants. More generally, officers complained about the difficulty of getting servants to accompany them into active service and the high wages they demanded. The Adjutant General said that the Army was not officially obliged to provide private followers, but suggested that officers fix servants' wages using the *nirikh* rate and stick to it.[186] Nevertheless, when British officers of the Indian service were given the benefit of free rations overseas on 30 June 1916, the concession was also extended to their horses and their authorised private servants.[187]

Eventually, on 29 March 1917, the central follower depots were instructed to take on the task of recruiting private followers for both officers and regiments. Private followers would be enrolled and given an identity disc marked E.P.F. (enrolled private follower) and clothing on the follower's scale. The government would pay them a lower fixed wage while they waited at the depot, and their employer would pay a higher fixed wage once they joined him overseas.[188] The government also undertook to pay servants taken as prisoners of war at half the depot scale, with a quarter remitted to the family if asked for.[189] The Commander-in-Chief in India justified this expansion in the army's responsibilities by arguing that 'the lack of servants was liable to react on the health and efficiency of officers on field service'.[190] The 'servant problem' in World War One probably consolidated officers' expectations of domestic work at public expense within the Indian Army.

---

[185] IOR/L/Mil/7/18061.

[186] Note, ADG's branch, January 1915, AD, War, 1916–17, I, appendix, p. 324.

[187] AD, War, 1916–17, I, no. 8898.

[188] Deputy Secy, AD to ADG, 29 March 1917, IOR/L/Mil/7/18061. Officers were instructed to pay enrolled private followers exactly those wages which were written into their service book. Ibid. See also IA Order no. 114, 14 February 1919, IOR/L/Mil/17/5/261.

[189] IOR/L/Mil/7/18061; also F&P, War, B, Secret, January 1918, nos 192–96.

[190] C. C. Monroe to SSI, 26 July 1918, AD Despatch no. 57 of 1918, IOR/L/Mil/7/18061. Nevertheless, it was the pleasantly sepia-tinted vision of a life made comfortable by personal and regimental servants on which the postwar Indian Army counted to attract British officers.

Such was the popularity of servants from India that even British officers at Basra who were entitled to a British soldier-servant preferred to take a 'coloured batman'.[191] The Deputy Adjutant General there actually ran a Servants Bureau, which allocated Indian servants and trained more from the Indian Labour and Porter Corps.[192] Another such pool of enrolled *khidmatgars*—bearers or valets—was maintained at Bombay.[193] However, the 'officialisation' of the private follower system increased the Indian Army's administrative burden, perhaps one of the reasons for a discussion at the close of the war about introducing the British Army practice of assigning combatants as servants and grooms on active service to the Indian Army.[194]

Public employment and personal subordination: 'Remember an orderly is not a servant.'[195]

Even on the eve of the Great War, the epithet 'menial' for someone employed entirely by one household for domestic services was not quite archaic in Britain.[196] The *Encyclopaedia Britannica* of 1911 had this to say:

> Menial, that which belongs to household or domestic services, hence, particularly, a domestic servant. The idea of such service being derogatory has made the term one of contempt.[197]

---

[191] GOC 'D' to Chief of General Staff, 23 January 1917, WW1/791/H, vol. 233, diary no. 4942.

[192] Memorandum, 8 December 1917, WW1/959/H, vol. 401.

[193] An officer going to Mesopotamia or Persia was warned that he would not be supplied with a servant there. He was instructed to enrol his own servant or to take an enrolled private follower from this pool. 'Recruiting in India Before and During the War of 1914–18', appendix N, p. 195, IOR/L/IL/17/5/2152.

[194] Assistant ADG, 3rd Echelon Basra to Chief of General Staff, 5 January 1917, WW1/783/H, vol. 225, pp. 152–53; Chief of General Staff to GOC, 'D', 7 January 1917, WW1/789/H, vol. 231, diary no. 3623, p. 41.

[195] A general to his bride, who had just handed their tiffin basket to his orderly, a Dogra Brahmin. John Travers, *Sahib-Log*, London: Duckworth and Co., 1910, p. 56. 'John Travers' was the pseudonym of writer Eva Mary Bell.

[196] Certain amendments to the British National Insurance Act in 1914 stated that 'the expression "domestic servant" shall be deemed to include a menial servant employed in whole time service in and about a private residence.' *The London Gazette*, 30 June 1914.

[197] 'Menial', *Encyclopaedia Britannica*, 1911, https://theodora.com/encyclopedia/m/menial.html, last accessed 10 November 2019.

This hierarchical attitude affected the standing of the batman—the white soldier-servant—as well. The Australian soldier was said to be reluctant to take up this post, giving it the rude label of 'bumbrusher' and leaving it to British migrants in the Australian Imperial Force.[198] On the other hand, for Harvey Cushing, the famous Harvard surgeon, the British batman came as a joyous discovery: 'these Britishers of the lower classes make extraordinarily good servants'.[199]

In India, there was a pervasive expectation that Europeans in official employment should have access to 'menials' for sweeping, cooking, and laundry, and that if they could not pay for them personally these servants should be provided institutionally or from the public exchequer. Related to this was an understanding that the performance of these services could expand fluidly from the circumference of official duty into the domestic sphere. Indians in official positions had the same expectations of their subordinate staff.[200]

What attracted comment was that in India even the rank and file British soldier had access to native servants. Writing on the 1882 Egypt expedition, an American naval commander noted that giving the British soldier the luxury of Indian servants maintained European prestige, and also served to 'render him a mere fighting machine'.[201] The British soldier cost about three or four times more than his Indian counterpart, so he had to be reserved for combat-

---

[198] W. H. Downing, *Digger Dialects*, Melbourne; Sydney: Lothian Book Publishing Co., 1919, p. 14; and personal communication, Peter Stanley, 15 November 2019.

[199] However, his next batman was disappointing. Harvey Cushing, *From a Surgeon's Journal: 1915–1918*, Boston: Little, Brown and Company, 1936, p. 143.

[200] A Madras Police Order of 1863 stated that under no circumstances were the police to be employed in domestic or personal service. E. S. B. Stevenson, *The Station House Officers' Vade-Mecum*, Madras, 1879, p. 708. Controversies about the use of *sahayaks* (soldier-orderlies) in household work continue to surface in contemporary India. See Sushant Singh, 'Simply put: Why Sahayak is "Buddy" for Army, Servant for Critics', *Indian Express*, 16 March 2017, https://indianexpress.com/article/explained/lance-naik-roy-mathew-sindhav-jogidas-simply-put-why-sahayak-is-buddy-for-army-servant-for-critics-4560889/, last accessed 13 November 2019; and 'Sahayaks in Army not to be Employed for Menial Tasks: Govt', *Economic Times*, 12 July 2018, https://m.economictimes.com/news/defence/sahayaks-in-army-not-to-be-employed-for-menial-tasks-govt/articleshow/57756206.cms, last accessed 10 November 2019.

[201] Caspar Frederick Goodrice, *Report of the British Naval and Military Operations in Egypt 1882*, Washington: Bureau of Navigation, 1885, p. 302.

ant work.[202] However, the reason the Tommy wanted access to servants was to resist being reduced to a cog in the military machine. In an environment which treated him like a juvenile and made very little room for marriage and a family life, he could assume the role of employer and carve out a space for domesticity.[203] Memoirist Frank Richards recalled that at Indian cantonments the British private only had to clean his own rifle and bayonet.[204] He was absolved of all the barrack duties he had to perform in England, such as peeling potatoes and washing dishes—the stuff of jokes about the 'feminine' roles men assume in army life.[205] British soldiers drew upon public followers and those paid out of regimental funds, such as the cook-boy, the *dhobi*, the barrack sweeper and the 'latrine-wallah', but they also pooled their money to get 'boys' to polish, clean, fetch and carry, and cook special meals. If they did not get the 'care' they felt was their due they often enforced it by boot and fist, but their relationship with the follower ranks was also marked by an acute dependence upon them when on the march or in the field.[206] This is one reason for the shift in colonial representa-

---

[202] The prewar entry-level pay was Rs. 11/– for the Indian soldier and Rs. 30/– for the British soldier; postwar it was Rs. 16/–, compared to Rs. 55/–.

[203] Douglas M. Peers points out that in India servants satisfied a number of roles played by the British soldiers' wives in England, so the latter were valued less in the colony. Douglas M. Peers, 'The Raj's Other Great Game: Policing the Sexual Frontiers of the Indian Army in the First Half of the Nineteenth Century', in Steven Pierce and Anupama Rao (eds), *Discipline and the Other Body*, Durham; London: Duke University Press, 2006, pp. 115–150, 132. However, wives of British soldiers and of Indian followers did assist, for paltry sums, in station hospitals before the Indian Army Nursing Service was set up in 1893. Colonel A. Ghosh, *History of the Armed Forces Medical Services, India*, Orient Longman: New Delhi, 1988, p. 99.

[204] Richards, *Old Soldier Sahib*, pp. 182–84. Richards recalled that in Britain recruits had to wash up and remove the urinal tub, but their laundry was done by wives of corporals and old soldiers.

[205] Ibid. Forced to darn his own socks, the Harvard professor of surgery Harvey Cushing argued furiously that the British War Office should penalise suffragettes. 'Damn the Votes, Darn the Socks'. Cushing, *From a Surgeon's Journal*, p. 159.

[206] In July 1857, pulling up the discipline of the British forces besieging Delhi, General Wilson wrote of 'ignorant soldier' who 'too often repaid the camp-followers, without whose services, given at the risk of their lives, they could not have existed for a day, with brutal words and savage blows; and few of their officers cared or ventured to restrain them....' T. R. E. Holmes, *A History of the Indian Mutiny*, London: Allen and Co., 1888, pp. 339–342.

tions of the follower ranks, from descriptions of 'scum of the bazaar' to praise for the 'gentleness' with which the *kahar* and *bhisti* tended to the Tommy.[207] Rudyard Kipling captured this dependence, not only in his well-known poem 'Gunga Din' but also in 'Epitaphs of the War':

NATIVE WATER-CARRIER (M.E.F.)
Prometheus brought down fire to men,
This brought up water.
The Gods are jealous—now, as then,
Giving no quarter.[208]

Previously, one of the arguments used by the Army Department to request better terms for Indian stretcher-bearers had been that 'in Asiatic warfare, every wounded man must at once be carried off the field to the rear. Humanity to the wounded cannot be expected from semi-civilised races'.[209] In World War One, it was once again the *kahar* who had to allay the Tommy's fear of mutilation at the hands of 'ghoulish' Arabs in Mesopotamia or 'vengeful Pathan women' during the Third Afghan War and the Waziristan campaign (1919–20).[210] The supply of British nurses from Queen Alexandra's Military Nursing Service for India was limited, so it was still the follower ranks on which the Indian Army counted to reassure families that the British officer and the Tommy were being tended to.[211] The

---

[207] *Kahar*: a specific caste, but also the term for stretcher-bearers, whatever their caste; M.E.F.: Mesopotamian Expeditionary Force.

[208] From 'Epitaphs of the War', a sequence of epigrams published in Rudyard Kipling's verse collection *The Years Between*, 1919.

[209] 'Changes in Indian Army System', *Parliamentary Papers*, House of Commons, 1884–85, p. 152, para. 421.

[210] Reminiscing about his 1917 service in Waziristan, one officer of the Royal Engineers declared that capture could result in 'death by torture, in which, so I was told, the womenfolk used to luxuriate.' Francis Stockdale, *Walk Warily in Waziristan*, Devon: Arthur H. Stockwell Ltd, 1982, p. 24. About a British Officer who had gone missing in a frontier operation, A. N. Peckham wrote that something must have gone wrong, 'for it is a point of honour always to bring in even a sepoy's body'. 3 April 1917, IOR, Arthur Nyton Peckham, Mss Eur D078.

[211] By late 1918 there were approximately 520 trained army nurses in India, consisting of eighty from the Indian Nursing Service, 120 from Queen Alexandra's Indian Military Nursing Service and 320 from the Australian Army Nursing Service. Ashleigh Wadman, 'Nursing for the British Raj', Australian War Memorial,

assignment of this feminine role to the follower ranks is captured in Willcocks's description of *Bhutia* stretcher-bearers in France rendering first aid with 'touching tenderness'.[212]

British officers in prewar India, whether in the British Army or the Indian Army, were not allowed a British batman (soldier-servant). The official reason was that white combatant strength had to be kept up, but British privates also resisted the performance of 'menial' tasks in the sight of 'natives'. British officers in India expected their domestic comforts to stretch quite significantly into 'active service', but, conversely, official accoutrements underpinned many domestic amenities. Army officers received an allowance for a *syce*, and took him into active service as a 'private follower'. However, they also took along their household bearer, or valet, whose ingenuity in rustling up food and hot tea in the most extraordinary circumstances was a staple of war anecdotes. The reader of a tribute to a fallen friend in Mesopotamia learns more about the hero's private servant, Antoni, a 'Madrasi Christian', than they do about the hero himself. It is the devotion that his friend inspires in Antoni which does him credit. Antoni can ride, sew, string a racquet, cook a priceless dinner, and is ready to resort to deeds of felony to ensure that if his master 'gave voice to a want ... the want did not exist any longer'.[213]

There was one context in which the work of the Indian sepoy could take on a dangerous resemblance to that of the attached follower—the rendering of bodily care to an institutional superior. British officers in Indian regiments were assigned a sepoy as an orderly, who on active service took messages, cleaned his kit, and found him food and a billet. European officers were reminded repeatedly that the batman or orderly was not a 'servant'—his status as a combatant had to be preserved.[214] Yet memoirs and novels about army life reveal that the

---

28 October 2014, https://www.awm.gov.au/articles/blog/nursing-british-raj, last accessed 13 November 2019.

[212] Interview with Lieutenant General James Willcocks, former Commander of the Indian Corps in France: 'India's Military Potentialities', *The Indian Review*, June 1917, p. 374. *Bhutia*: sometimes linked to Bhutan or Tibet, the term describes communities widely distributed across the central Himalayas in the region from Garhwal to Sikkim.

[213] Joatamon, *A Mug in Mesopotamia*, Poona, 1918, pp. 33–35.

[214] 'Batmen are not permitted to work in regimental clothing and they must never be employed in menial or domestic duties'. Captain F. M. Wardle, *Barrow's Sepoy Officer's Manual*, Calcutta: Thacker, Spink and Co., 1922, p. 48; Charles Chenevix Trench,

orderly was inducted into the officer's household, and sometimes accompanied him like a personal retainer from one posting to another.[215] Gordon Corrigan's attempt to clarify the position actually underlines the ambiguity of the orderly's status: 'The British officer's orderly was emphatically not a servant—although he did carry out some menial tasks'.[216] The orderly gained some patronage from this connection, but the relationship could also cast the shade of 'menial' work over a combatant. This, one surmises, is the reason accounts of the Indian Army dwell on the devotion of the sepoy orderly not only to his officer's person, but also to his officer's personal effects—to stress that this 'extra' measure of care derived from attachment, not obligation.

Sepoys attached as nursing orderlies to the Army Hospital Corps could also suffer a drop in status because of the resemblance between their duties and those assigned to the follower ranks of the medical services. They might also find themselves under the supervision of a British or Australian 'sister-sahib', the title given to trained army nurses in India.[217]

By the close of World War One, the Indian service was said to be unpopular with British officers, so it was felt that they had to offer more concessions 'in kind'. The Esher Committee appointed in 1919–20 to suggest army reforms proposed that officers of the British service be allowed a British soldier-servant from the ranks when in India, as in the United Kingdom. Correspondingly, British officers of the Indian service could be given a soldier-servant from the Indian ranks, deploying special enlistments if necessary.[218] To paraphrase, if

---

The Indian Army and the King's Enemies, 1900–1947, London: Thames and Hudson, 1988, p. 26. See image 1 for an idealised portrait of 'the devoted orderly'.

[215] 'Tulsi, my soldier orderly, regarded himself as being superior to the servants ... In a peace station orderlies could not be used as domestic servants but a point was stretched in letting them look after a car'. R. C. B. Bristow, *Memories of the British Raj*, London: Johnson, 1974, p. 78.

[216] Gordon Corrigan, *Sepoys in the Trenches: The Indian Corps on the Western Front, 1914–1915*, Staplehurst: Spellmount, 1999, p. 19.

[217] Writing of her encounters with Indian Army nursing orderlies, an Australian nurse wrote of a Garhwali so immune to admonition that, although they weren't supposed to beat orderlies, she caned him 'weekly—sometimes daily'. 'In an Indian Army Hospital, Devoted Orderlies', *The Singapore Free Post and Mercantile Advertiser*, 11 November 1925, p. 24.

[218] *Report of the Committee Appointed by the Secretary of State for India to Enquire into the Administration and Organisation of the Army in India*, Cmd 943, 1920, II, p. 41

high-caste sepoys objected to 'menial' work, lower castes could be specially recruited as soldier-servants. The committee also recommended a free charger for the British cavalry officer and an Indian groom who would again be 'an enlisted soldier, paid, rationed and clothed by Government'.[219]

To understand why such suggestions could be made at all, one has to keep in mind the severe manpower shortage of spring 1918, which forced the Indian Army, particularly units stationed overseas, to discuss ways of using sepoy labour more flexibly.

Visions of manpower rationalisation

'[T]he follower is an anachronism and his continued existence as a class is irrational.'[220]

In April 1918, the Commander-in-Chief in India was urging the War Office, and the General Officers Commanding overseas, to use non-combatant labour from India with stringent economy, to substitute it with local labour, and finally to take more 'fatigue duties' from soldiers.[221] He pointed out that the demand for sweepers simply could not be met 'despite every inducement', and suggested that those already at hand could be confined to latrine work and heavy-duty cleaning and that soldiers and other labourers could clean camps: 'There should be no difficulty in making some such arrangements provided long handle brooms, rakes and spikes for picking up waste paper were provided, thereby eliminating all question of assimilating the work to that ordinarily performed by the sweeper in India.'[222]

In February 1919, H. Cooke, the Director of Organisation, suggested that by enlisting the follower and changing his designation—for instance, by

---

(*Esher Report*). It also suggested replacing unofficial with official allocation of soldier-orderlies for the Indian Officers, the Viceroy's Commissioned Officers: 'The Indian Officer is not allowed a soldier servant by regulation. We think this should be permitted and regularised.' *Esher Report*, II, p. 59, para. 57.

[219] *Esher Report*, II, p. 41.

[220] H. Cooke, Director of Organisation to SSI, 15 February 1919, AD, ADG's Branch, Establishment, Regimental, A, May 1919, nos 1869–73 and appendix.

[221] C-in-C, India to War Office, London, 23 April 1918, WWI/1023/H, vol. 465, diary no. 31812, p. 86.

[222] C-in-C, India, to GOCs, 23 April 1918, WWI/1023/H, vol. 465, diary no. 31810, p. 85.

replacing the word 'syce' with the term 'horse orderly'—follower work could be made more honourable, thereby persuading the sepoy to diversify his tasks.[223] The sole exception he made was that sepoys should not be put to 'sweeper's work'.[224] The suggestion was therefore that a change of tools and of institutional labels could destigmatise certain kinds of work, thereby allowing for more flexible use of the Indian sepoy.[225] The Tommy was held up as the model for a self-sufficient modern masculinity—someone who attended to his own toilet, for example, instead of requiring a regimental barber. In fact, British soldiers in India routinely pooled their money for an Indian barber to shave them in bed while they caught some extra sleep in the morning.

If one way to rationalise the use of manpower was to diversify the sepoy's work, then the other way was to equip the non-combatant for combat duties. 'How often in this war,' wrote Cooke, 'has the stupidity of the follower class caused casualties from hostile fire which might otherwise have been avoided?'[226] A 1919 follower committee suggested that all public followers be enlisted— that is, given combatant rank—and trained in defence.[227] Soldiers would not have to be deputed to guard baggage trains, and it would reduce the number of follower casualties.[228] In World War One, the steadiness of stretcher-bearers, water-carriers and mule-drivers under fire had been praised anew.[229] But the

---

[223] H. F. Cooke to SSI, 15 February 1919, in AD, ADG's Branch, Establishment, Regimental, A, May 1919, nos 1869–73 and appendix. Ibid.

[224] Ibid.

[225] For the poet-idealist in *Untouchable*, it was the flush system, 'the machine which cleans dung without anyone having to handle it', which would free sweepers from untouchability by enabling them to change their profession. Anand, *Untouchable*, p. 155. Viceroy Lord Curzon's technological solution for ending the violence inflicted on sleeping punkah-pullers—those who pulled ceiling fans—was electricity in barracks. Jordanna Bailkin, 'The Boot and the Spleen: When Was Murder Possible in British India?', *Comparative Studies in Society and History*, vol. 48, no. 2 (2006), pp. 462–93, 486.

[226] H. F. Cooke to SSI, 15 February 1919, AD, ADG's Branch, Establishment, Regimental, A, May 1919, nos 1869–73 and appendix.

[227] Ibid.

[228] Ibid.

[229] Colonel Hehir of the Indian Medical Service in Mesopotamia said that Indian stretcher-bearers ought to be liberally treated, for they had been 'invariably kind'. IOR/L/Mil/7/18281.

Indian Army also began to take credit for having drilled a workable kind of bravery into classes said to lack the 'hereditary' spirit of the martial castes and tribes.[230] Signs of a more impulsive bravery were observed among the 'menial followers', but as a touching aberration.[231] Candler wrote that at Givenchy, sweepers carried ramrods over the open ground to the men in the firing line. 'In Mesopotamia,' he added, 'a sweeper of the —th Rifles took an unauthorised part in an assault on the Turkish lines, picked up the rifle of a dead sepoy, and went on firing till he was shot in the head.' But Candler hastened to add that this was an exceptional man.[232] In the 'normal drudge', signs of bravery were attributed to lack of imagination, fatalism, and most of all to 'order, continuity, routine'.[233]

The short two-page section on the follower ranks in the Esher Committee's recommendations for the postwar administrative organisation of the Army in India exhibits the same kind of rationalising drive, a theme touched upon again in the Afterword to this book.[234] This rationalisation, while extending somewhat to the British soldier, focused primarily on Indian sepoys and followers. I can offer only a sketchy picture of the changes which were actually implemented. The improved status of departmental followers was confirmed and extended in the 1920s, because the Indian Army had to compete with

---

[230] An officer who had laughed at the 'antics' of 'ill-conditioned' Indian stretcher-bearers drilling on a troopship in August 1914 said it was hard to realise they were the 'smart, well-set-up' units he later saw in France. Alexander, *On Two Fronts*, p. 19.

[231] In the fighting around Cambrai, an officer of the 19th King George's Own Lancers recorded this note: 'In the afternoon, the Squadron Sweeper asked to see me ... His father, he said had served the regiment for thirty-five years, and he had been born and brought up in it. If the squadron was going into battle, he should go with it ... if it ... was going to suffer he wanted to be with it. Might he have a bandolier and rifle and march with the squadron? ... I searched his face for signs of his being an actor but found none ... He was a nice, clean-made fellow with a good face and chin—the chin was what I looked for. My eyes smarted'. General Sir Havelock Hudson, *History of the 19th King George's Own Lancers, 1858–1921*, Aldershot: Gale and Polden Ltd, 1937, p. 202.

[232] 'The Indian Follower', in Candler, *The Sepoy*, p. 233.

[233] Ibid., p. 234.

[234] *Report of the Committee Appointed by the Secretary of State for India to Enquire into the Administration and Organisation of the Army in India*, Cmd 943, 1920, II, pp. 97–98 (Esher Committee).

wages in an expanding industrial and commercial sector.[235] However, demobilisation and cost-cutting pushed out low-caste combatant units and recruitment for the departmental services was also curtailed, so lower castes were
probably hemmed into the ranks of the attached followers again.

A comparison between the position of the stretcher-bearers and that of the
public followers in the new Indian Hospital Corps, constituted in June 1920,
indicates that the association between 'polluting' castes and 'polluting' trades
continued to impose an institutional ceiling. The stretcher-bearers were placed in
the 'Non-combatant Branch' of the Indian Hospital Corps. This was a category
which also included the nursing, clerical and store-keeping staff. Here, all personnel were attested in addition to being enrolled, and they received rations, allowances, furlough, leave, clothing and equipment on the combatant's scale.[236]
However, other public followers of the medical services were relegated to the
'General Section' of the Indian Hospital Corps, where personnel were enrolled
but not attested, and clothing and equipment were issued on an inferior scale. The
Viceroy's explanation for this distinction was that 'owing to the caste and status
of some of the personnel necessary for Hospital work, e.g. *dhobis* and sweepers, it
is considered undesirable to include them in the Non-Combatant Branch.'[237] In
this 'General Section', the epithet 'menial' was replaced by the phrase 'trade
denominations', but in the frame of colonial understanding, this phrase implied
forms of work which could only be carried out by the lower castes.[238]

In regiments, the tradition of maintaining private followers—those paid by
individual officers, groups of British soldiers, or the regiment collectively—
persisted; so too, therefore, did the condition of 'menial status', a situation in
which employment was insecure and conditions of work and discipline continued to take very personal and summary forms. British officers did not get
the enlisted *syces* envisaged by the Esher Committee, but continued to receive
a monthly allowance for a civilian groom, who was expected to accompany
them into active service.[239] The private follower system was cheap because men

---

[235] The lascars of the Indian Ordnance Department were given combatant status in the
1920s.

[236] Viceroy to SSI, no. 67, 28 August 1919, IOR/L/Mil/7/324.

[237] Ibid.

[238] Ibid.

[239] Officers complained that the *syce* allowance of Rs. 15/– was too low, and that there
was no guarantee that a civilian groom would accompany them into active service.
AD, 1922, note no. 377 of 1922.

could be employed and laid off without any long-term financial and institutional commitment. In the light of complaints that military service in postwar India had become very unpopular with British officers and soldiers, followers and 'barrack boys' constituted one of the luxuries of a colonial posting. Their presence absolved British privates and NCOs of 'dirty', tedious or exhausting duties, and elevated their status as white men.[240]

The persistence of the menial trope in institutional culture is also evident in the fact that although corporal punishment was abolished for the Indian soldier and enrolled follower in 1920, a provision permitting summary punishment with a rattan for 'the native follower if he was a menial servant' was retained.[241] There are anecdotes which hint that on active service summary punishment may have continued to constitute the norm for all followers 'of the servant type'. Major L. W. A. Lyons, from the 4th Indian Division at Genifa, Egypt in World War Two, recalled that Indian camp followers such as the sweepers and the cooks were 'subject to a special code of discipline and could be flogged or summarily imprisoned, though I never heard of this ever happening.'[242]

Nevertheless, a growing recognition of the importance of the ancillary services, along with pressure on follower supply from 1916 and a postwar drive to curtail army expenditure, encouraged the positing of a new, more integrated model of military organisation, one in which differences between sepoys and followers would be narrowed down.[243] Followers, circulating with

---

[240] Major Leslie Hore-Belisha voiced this expectation when he complained in Parliament about some personnel of the Royal Army Medical Corps having to subscribe towards the employment of native labour. By 'the custom in the British army in India', he pointed out, it was this native labour which did 'the menial work of various regiments, such as lavatory cleansing, water carrying, etc.', and the Government of India paid for it in depots with British regiments. House of Commons, Hansard Archives, 15 July 1924, http://hansard.millbanksystems.com, last accessed 10 November 2019. One Indian critic pointed out that British troops were not only more expensive, but they also accounted for an inflated follower establishment. Captain G. V. Modak, *Indian Defence Problem*, Poona: G. V. Modak, 1938.

[241] Section 22, Indian Army Act (Act VIII of 1911). See Singha, 'The "Rare Infliction"'.

[242] Rupert Lyons, 'Audio memoirs of Major L. W. A. Lyons', https://www.bbc.co.uk/history/ww2peopleswar/user/91/u2169891.shtml, last accessed 10 November 2019.

[243] See Afterword.

greater velocity between stations and theatres of war and comparing wages, service conditions and labour markets, also contributed to this shift. However, followers associated with 'polluting' trades, and those whose work positioned them somewhere between the status of 'public employee' and 'domestic servant', found it difficult to climb up from the menial rung. In addition, as the Indian Army demobilised, caste and ethnic criteria for combatant service tightened again.

Nevertheless, the figure of the follower gives us a much wider social and spatial vista on recruitment into military work. It shows how migration networks intersecting at bazaars, construction sites, and cantonments along the frontier, and labour regimes emerging at these sites, could generate both 'martial races' and their non-combatant 'others'. Sukha Kalloo's resting place is one of the sites from which a history of the different forms of work which make up the practice of war can be excavated, one in which actual combat is only the most spectacular:

Sukha's epitaph

This stone was erected by
Parishioners of Brockenhurst
To mark the spot where is laid
The earthly body of
Sukha
A resident of Mohulla Gungapur
City Barielly United Provinces of India
He left country, home and friends to save our
King and Empire in the Great European War
As a humble servant in the Lady Hardinge
Hospital for Wounded Indian Soldiers
In this parish
He departed this life on January 12th 1915
Aged 30 years
By creed he was not Christian
But this earthly life was sacrificed in the interests of others
There is one God and Father of all who is
For all and through all and in all
Ephesians IV.[244]

---

[244] 'WW1 memorial to India—an Indian soldier is remembered at Brockenhurst', https://www.newforest-life.com/WW1-memorial-India.html, last accessed 10 November 2019.

3

MAKING THE DESERT BLOOM?

THE INDIAN LABOUR AND PORTER CORPS IN IRAQ, 1916–21

In the bleak spring of 1916, a note from Mesopotamia complained bitterly about the tardiness with which India was responding to desperate calls for military labour:

> Could there possibly have been a greater opportunity for India with millions of men not usable as soldiers, to take a larger share in the war, or even a larger share in helping its own Indian Army? From all accounts India was burning to get such a chance, yet what happened? The honour of India was upheld first by aborigines and then by convicts.[1]

Delays in sending manpower and 'parsimony' in sanctioning funds—these were the recriminations heaped upon the Government of India after the dis-

---

[1] Lieutenant Colonel W. B. Lane, 'A Summary of the History with Suggestions and Recommendations of the Seven Jail Labour and Porter Corps employed in Mesopotamia from October 1916 to July 1919', Home, Jails, B, January 1921, nos 9–11, and appendices, p. 2, para. 2. Henceforth 'Summary' for Lane's overview and 'History' for reports on the individual Jail Corps. Lane was echoing the complaint of Arnold Wilson, acting Civil Commissioner, Mesopotamia. Arnold Wilson, *Mesopotamia 1917–1920: A Clash of Loyalties*, London: Oxford University Press, 1931, p. 48. The 'aborigines' referred to the 'tribal' or 'Santhali' labourers from Bihar and Orissa.

asters which overtook the British invasion of Ottoman Iraq at the close of 1915.[2] One response was that in India only specific communities, the so-called martial castes and races, could be recruited as soldiers. The question that hung in the air regarded the supply of labourers and followers. After all, India, with her population of 320 million, seemed to have a vast reservoir of coolies.

The conduct of industrialised warfare in a theatre where the population was low and the transport infrastructure rudimentary meant that Britain drew upon Egypt and India for the human and animal resources needed for that abstract subject, military logistics.[3] This chapter focuses on the men enrolled in the Indian Labour and Porter Corps, although the Inland Water Transport, the Mesopotamian railways and a variety of other units also made very substantial use of Indian labour.[4] Two Punjab Labour Corps and one Madras Porter Corps, raised for Gallipoli, were diverted to Mesopotamia. Thereafter, the Army placed itself in the path of *Santhali* labour migration from Bihar and Orissa towards Bengal and Assam. 'Santhal' was both the designation for a specific community and a generic label for 'tribals' from Chota Nagpur and the Santhal Parganas in Bihar and Orissa—those referred to as 'aborigines' in the opening complaint.[5] This process began so casually that the Secretary of State for India only learnt of it from a newspaper snippet announcing that the arrival of two military recruiters at Purulia had given 'rise to a rumour that Government was offering high wages in order to get people to bury the dead'.[6]

---

[2] Secretary, Army Department (AD), India, 18 September 1916, Home, Political, February 1917, nos 353–96; *Report of the Commission Appointed by Act of Parliament to Enquire into the Operations of War in Mesopotamia*, House of Commons, 1917, cd 8610, 41, 129; Sir Charles Lucas (ed.), *The Empire at War*, vol. 5, London, 1926, p. 342; Arnold Wilson, *Loyalties; Mesopotamia, 1914–1917: A Personal and Historical Record*, London: Oxford University Press, 1930, pp. 169, 203.

[3] Kristian Coates Ulrichsen, *The Logistics and Politics of the British Campaigns in the Middle East, 1914–22*, Palgrave Macmillan: London, 2011.

[4] Nineteen Indian Labour Corps and twelve Indian Porter Corps were sent to Mesopotamia. *India's Contribution to the Great War* (*ICGW*), Calcutta: Superintendent Government Printing Press, 1923, p. 92 (henceforth ILC, IPC, and for the Jail Labour and Porter Corps, JPC and JLC).

[5] One Santhali detachment reinforced the 2nd Punjab ILC, and there was a strong Santhali component in the 3rd and 7th ILCs. TNA WO 95/4991, The National Archives, London, UK (TNA).

[6] IOR/L/PS/11/107.

With such stories about high casualty rates swirling through India, labourers showed a tendency to bolt. From May–June 1916, Lieutenant Wishart reported that on two occasions when he had collected a large number of men from the Central Provinces for embankment work in Basra, 'they suddenly had an attack of nerves and refused to embark.'[7] To deal with the bottleneck in supply, the government explored the penal and policed end of the labour spectrum. Over the period October 1916 to July 1919, some 15,234 prisoners were sent to Mesopotamia. The majority were in the Jail Porter and Labour Corps, but this figure also included 1,602 recruited for miscellaneous services such as sweeping, laundry work and gardening.[8] In August 1917, as the Persian theatre rose to prominence, the demand from Mesopotamia surged.[9] An official report stated that:

> The maintenance of our troops on the Caspian necessitated road construction and the provision of mechanical transport on a large scale in North West Persia involving large demands on India for MT [Motor Transport] drivers and road making personnel and equipment. The extension of the railway system towards Khanikin was also a serious drain on India's resources in railway material.[10]

Labour demand remained high even after the Armistice.[11] In March 1919, four new Labour Corps were raised in India to replace the four being repatriated from Mesopotamia.[12] By December 1919, the total number of Indian combatants and non-combatants who had circulated through Mesopotamia amounted to 675,391, of whom 348,735 were non-combatants.[13]

World War One had in fact witnessed the first major influx of Indian labour into the Persian Gulf. Yet, all too often, supply had lagged behind demand. The

---

[7] F&P, Secret, War, February 1917, nos 235–66; Home, Political, Deposit, June 1916, no. 25.

[8] 'Recruiting in India Before and During the War of 1914–18', appendix XVI, IOR/L/MIL/17/5/2152; and Lane, 'Summary', p. 8, para. 11.

[9] F. D. Frost, *Report of the Labour Directorate, Mesopotamian Expeditionary Force from October, 1916 to October, 1918*, Baghdad, 1919, p. 14 (henceforth *RLD*); war diary, WW1/271/H, Force D, vol. 49, pt II, nos 16–31, August 1918. From September 1918 the 14th, 17th, 18th, 20th and 109th ILCs arrived for the Persian road and the Kermanshah railway extensions. *RLD*, p. 15.

[10] *Supplement to the London Gazette*, 28 July 1919, p. 2544.

[11] *RLD*.

[12] WW1/278/H, IEF, 'D', vol. 56, nos 1–15, March 1919.

[13] *ICGW*, p. 98.

Army Department proposed some form of labour impressment on two occasions, but the Government of India rejected this solution, choosing to deal with shortfalls by piecemeal measures such as drawing upon jail labour and deploying 'customary' and statutory forms of corvée. However, it also responded by offering short-term contracts and better terms of employment.[14] There is a huge body of literature on conscription debates across the empire, but not very much on this secretive discussion in 1916–17, and the more open discussion of spring and summer 1918, about introducing some form of conscription.[15] Among the factors complicating the issue was the ongoing campaign in India to end the system of indentured migration, replete with allegations about the use of force and fraud in overseas recruitment.[16] This explains the prolonged and anxious discussions of 1916–17 about the most prudent legal form in which to send labour for 'military work overseas', and the equally detailed discussions about the form in which to retain it after the Armistice.

In contrast to this voluminous correspondence, there is very little in the archives about the actual working and living conditions of Indian non-combatants in wartime Mesopotamia and Persia. The entries made by Commanding Officers in the war diaries for the Indian Labour and Porter Corps expand from one line to two or three only when sickness, or a sudden flurry of desertions, jeopardised the viability of the unit. After the surrender of the British and Indian troops garrisoning Kut al-Amara on 29 April 1916, the Government of India was eager to showcase the reconstruction of medical and transport arrangements in Mesopotamia. The infrastructure being put in place for military occupation was cast as an exercise which would also pull Ottoman Arabia out of the state of backwardness imposed on it by Turkish

---

[14] To speed up recruitment for the 6th and 8th ILC for Mesopotamia, men were enrolled on six-month agreements. 'Recruiting in India', p. 38, IOR/L/MIL/17/5/2152.

[15] As a Punjab paper, *The Tribune*, pointed out, the condition for conscription in India was the transformation of the State 'on a modern democratic basis'. Every individual had to feel that the state he was defending was 'his own higher self.' *The Tribune*, 8 May 1918, p. 1.

[16] On 20 March 1916, Madan Mohan Malaviya had passed a resolution in the Imperial Legislative Council demanding the abolition of indentured migration. For a comprehensive account of the widely supported campaign to abolish indentured migration see Hugh Tinker, *A New System of Slavery: The Export of Indian Labour Overseas, 1830–1920*, Oxford: Oxford University Press, 1974. In March 1917 the Government of India passed a war ordinance suspending the system.

'mis-rule'.[17] Priya Satia puts it very well: 'If technology's dark side was exposed in France, a new aspect of it was unveiled in Iraq: in the hands of "experts", it could resurrect a military campaign and, at once, a devastated civilization.'[18] But one catches only the occasional glimpse of the various labour units, Indian, Persian, Arab, and Kurd, who were bringing about this transformation.[19] The political motivation for downplaying the influx of Indian labour was nervousness on the part of the British Foreign Office that Arab notables would read in it a portent of the permanent absorption of Ottoman Iraq into the Empire of India, and an open door policy for Indian settlers.[20]

Ironically, the source material is richer for the Indian Jail Porter and Labour Corps sent to Mesopotamia than for the 'free' Indian Labour and Porter Corps. This is because Lieutenant Colonel W. B. Lane, the Inspector General

---

[17] Minute, J. E. Shuckburgh, Under-Secretary, Colonial Office, 11 October 1917, IOR/P/1417/1917. In 1915, when General Nixon demanded 'an irrigation engineer with staff' from India, he stressed the importance of river navigation for military mobility. However, he also mused on the transformation which intensive agriculture would bring about in 'degenerate marsh Arabs' and 'thieving Buddoos'. F&P, Secret, War, February 1917, nos 235–66. However, even Gertrude Bell had to admit that military works drained agricultural labour and were often not of public benefit, some 'even directly contrary to local interests.' Gertrude Bell, *Review of the Civil Administration of Mesopotamia*, 1920, pp. 19–20, 126.

[18] Priya Satia, 'Developing Iraq: Britain, India and the Redemption of Empire and Technology in the First World War', *Past and Present*, vol. 197, no. 1 (2007), p. 225.

[19] The American journalist Eleanor Egan decided that the 'peculiarities of the coolie labour corps' were too complex to be written about. Eleanor Franklin Egan, *The War in the Cradle of the World: Mesopotamia*, New York; London: Harper and Brothers, 1918, pp. 4, 216.

[20] Political Resident, Persian Gulf to Secy, F&P, GOI, 6 April 1917, in IOR/P/1417/1917; F&P, Secret, War, February 1917, 235–66; F&P, Secret, War, December 1917, 345–64; Brigadier General F. J. Moberly, *History of the Great War Based on Official Documents: The Campaign in Mesopotamia, 1914–1918*, vol. 2, London: HMSO, 1925, p. 280; William Willcocks, *Sixty Years in the East*, London: W. Blackwood, 1935, pp. 233, 266. And yet, in spring 1918 we find Basra elites demanding the import of Indian or Persian labour for military purposes, to release Arab labour for agricultural operations. *Eastern Committee, Mesopotamia: Civil Administration*, 12 April 1918, IOR/L/PS/18/B/283, in Qatar Digital Library (QDL), https://www.qdl.qa/en, last accessed 10 November 2019.

for Prisons in India and advisor for this Corps, wanted to cast the recruitment of jail labour as a hugely successful experiment in penal reform, one he hoped would conclude in a permanent Convict Legion scheme for Iraq on the lines of the French Foreign Legion Scheme in Algeria.[21]

The proportion of 'jail' to 'free' labour was not insignificant. In October 1918 the tally was 8,212 for the Jail Porter and Labour Corps as against 22,946 men for the free Indian Labour and Porter Corps.[22] But how far can we draw upon the war experiences of the Jail Corps to generalise about the rest? Jail and free labour worked side by side at many sites, and ground-level conditions of deployment were much the same. Measures to increase output and to punish desertion began to creep out from the Jail Corps to the 'free' Corps. Yet jail labour was always more vulnerable to over-exploitation, a vulnerability reflected in the relentless regime of flogging and fines which emerges from the official war diaries.[23] This was the grim reality lurking behind Lane's proud boast that no task was too hard for jail recruits. However, we also see jail labourers trying to efface the stigma which distinguished them from the 'free' Corps. And on 4 December 1918, when a section of the 11th Bombay Jail Labour Corps staged a brief protest against the arbitrary extension of their term of service, military authorities interpreted it as a signal that with the end of the war a 'labour problem' was emerging, even in a militarised construction complex.[24]

The surrender at Kut al-Amara and the reconstruction of the Mesopotamian campaign

The declaration of war with the Ottoman Sultan on 5 November 1914 brought into prominence the longstanding rivalry regarding legitimacy of rule over Muslim populations which ran along the tangled boundaries between the Empire of India and the Arab territories of the Ottoman Empire.[25] From the

---

[21] 'Summary', p. 9, para. 13. Lane drew upon his quarterly inspection reports and information from the Cos of the seven Jail Corps for his 'History'. See 'Summary', pp. 1–2.

[22] F. D. Frost, *RLD*, p.12.

[23] See below.

[24] Lane blamed the strike on jail labourers being allowed to feel that they were 'free'. 'History', 11th Bombay JLC, p. 7.

[25] This rivalry found expression in disputes about the management of the pilgrim routes

perspective of Delhi, the Gulf chiefs, Kuwait, Bahrain and the Trucial States were already under British protection. The absorption of the Basra *vilayat* would confirm Britain's commercial and strategic dominance in the Gulf and block Germany's entry into this body of water. The protection of the Anglo-Persian Oil Company's works in Abadan, southern Persia, was a further motivation for the dispatch of Indian Expeditionary Force D into the Gulf. In 1912–13, recognising the vital importance of oil for the Royal Navy, Winston Churchill had acquired a controlling interest in the Anglo-Persian Oil Company for the British government.

Easy victories for Indian Expeditionary Force D at the outset of conflict made Mesopotamia 'the only bright spot' for empire at a time when casualty rates in France and Flanders were appalling and the Turkish army was putting up a stiff resistance in the Dardanelles.[26] After failures at Gallipoli, the Home government longed for a quick rush up to Baghdad.[27]

However, men and supply lines were dangerously overstretched. On 22 November 1915, Turkish forces massed at Ctesiphon inflicted a savage blow on the Sixth Division of the Indian Army advancing under General Townshend. Retreating down the Tigris to Kut al-Amara, some 13,500 British and Indian troops and followers waited out a siege for five months before a humiliating surrender to Turkish forces on 29 April 1916.[28] Such was the

---

to the Hijaz. See Radhika Singha, 'Passport, Ticket, and India-Rubber Stamp: "The Problem of the Pauper Pilgrim" in Colonial India c. 1882–1925', in Harald Fischer-Tiné and Ashwini Tambe (eds), *The Limits of British Colonial Control in South Asia: Spaces of Disorder in the Indian Ocean Region*, New York: Routledge, 2009, pp. 49–83.

[26] Hardinge, Mss vol. 3, 1915–16, Cambridge University Library, Cambridge.

[27] '[I]t seems that German attempt to break through to Constantinople will succeed, and our ... prospects in Gallipoli are most uncertain. Persia seems to be drifting into war on German side, whilst Arabs are wavering ... We are therefore in great need of striking success in the East.' Private telegram, Secretary of State for India (SSI), Chamberlain, to Viceroy, Lord Hardinge, 21 October 1915, Hardinge Mss, vol. 94, Cambridge University Library. See also Hardinge to Governor General, Sudan, 15 October 1915, vol. 3, no. 116, 159. Ibid.

[28] To correct the humiliating impression, put about by Turkish propaganda, that the surrendering force was entirely British, one military engineer underlined that of the 13,300 who surrendered, only 2,950 were British, and of the Indians, a large number were non-combatants such as *bhistis*, *dhobis*, and sweepers. E. W. C. Sandes, *In Kut and Captivity: With the Sixth Indian Division*, London: John Murray, 1919, pp. 261–62.

importance placed on averting this event that three attempts were made to lift the siege, with casualty figures for the relieving force rising to the heartrending figure of 33 per cent.[29] The 'flower of the Indian Army was buried on the banks of the Tigris from Shu'aiba to Ctesiphon'.[30] In July 1917, Kipling wrote in 'Mesopotamia' that:

> They shall not return to us, the resolute, the young,
> The eager and whole-hearted whom we gave:
> But the men who left them thriftily to die in their own dung,
> Shall they come with years and honour to the grave?[31]

Kipling, like many others, blamed the Government of India for trying to conduct the occupation of Mesopotamia too 'thriftily'.[32] But in fact the Mesopotamian campaign was already putting a strain on India's fragile economy.

This was a 'sea borne, sea supported, sea victualled' war.[33] However, Basra had to be reconstructed, and docks, wharfs, quays, storage units and barracks built, to handle this huge volume of traffic.[34] Nine-tenths of Basra was covered by water in the flood season, so a twelve-mile-long protective embankment also had to be built from the Tigris at Magil to higher ground at Shaiba, and a second embankment up to the Zubair Gate.[35] The advance of the army depended on river navigation, yet rivercraft were in short supply and the water fell to levels which would not sustain heavy traffic. Canals had to be deepened and extended, and road and railway lines set out. However, Arab labourers were characterised as 'unsteady', coercive methods of obtaining them raised civilian discontent, and they were suspected of spying for the Ottoman army.[36]

---

[29] *Report of the Commission*, p. 35.

[30] Wilson, *Loyalties; Mesopotamia, 1914–1917*, p. 111.

[31] Kipling's poem 'Mesopotamia' was published on 11 July 1917 in the *Morning Post* (London) and the *New York Times*.

[32] For accusations about the Government of India's parsimony, see *Report of the Commission*, pp. 37–38, 74, 104–5.

[33] Ibid., p. 9.

[34] Ibid. 'Shipping and Congestion of Stores at Basra', Simla: Government Press, 1916, IOR/L/Mil/17/15/132, QDL.

[35] Lieutenant General Sir Percy Lake, C-in-C, IEF, 'D', Army Despatch, 27 August 1916.

[36] Philip Graves, *The Life of Sir Percy Cox*, London: Hutchinson, 1941, p. 193. An Indian journalist who visited Basra and Amara in spring 1917 wrote, 'Bitter oppo-

[It is the environment, above all, that dominates contemporary accounts of this campaign. Blistering heat in summer and freezing rains in winter; rivers which flooded the country, liquefying mud into swamps; flyblown hovels and disease-ridden settlements: these were the hellish images used to represent a landscape that had to be invested in and transformed not only to win the war, but to lay down the infrastructure for colonisation.[37] This was where the image of the Indian coolie, artisan and domestic servant began to flash before the official eye.

Jail-recruited labour

Convict sweepers and the mission of sanitary reform

In March 1916, among the letters and telegrams flowing in from Mesopotamia which called for labour of every possible description, we find a letter marked 'confidential' and pressing for 450 latrine sweepers.[38] One of the reasons for this secrecy was that news had spread about military setbacks and harsh living conditions in this theatre, and military and civil authorities were discussing the option of impressment. In addition, cholera had broken out in Basra—something which had to be concealed from those being sent into the thick of this epidemic.[39] In this context, the Quartermaster General in India suggested the assistance of the Salvation Army, 'already largely connected with Doms and [the] class from which latrine sweepers are drawn'.[40] Frederick Booth-Tucker, Special Commissioner for the Salvation Army in India and Ceylon, proposed that sweepers be recruited from jails using Section 401 of the Criminal Procedure Code, which allowed conditional release. He also sug-

---

sition radiated from their [Arabs'] eyes ... They earned only a couple of *paise* [pennies] and behaved like defeated and dependent enemies.' Indulal Kanaiyalal Yagnik, *The Autobiography of Indulal Yagnik*, trans. from Gujarati by Devavrat N. Pathak, Howard Spodek, and John R. Wood, vol. 1, Manohar: Gujarat Vidyapith, 2011, p. 264.

[37] Evans, Roger, *A Brief Outline of the Campaign in Mesopotamia*, London: Sifton, Praed, and Co., 1926, pp. 6–9.

[38] Home, Jails, A, November 1916, nos 42–48 (confidential).

[39] Sir Reginald Craddock, 26 May 1916, in Home, Jails, A, November 1916, nos 42–48 (confidential).

[40] Quartermaster General, 23 May 1916, in Home, Jails, A, November 1916, nos 42–48 (confidential).

gested that some 'Dom' communities, targeted as 'criminal tribes' in India, could be tapped:

> in Gorakhpur and other districts members of the Dom tribe not yet ordered into settlements but who it is desired to bring under control, should be given the option of enlisting as sweepers, but failing this they should be required to find security in the usual manner, and if they fail, should then have the same offer repeated to them in lieu of going to jail.[41]

Some background will explain why a Quartermaster General turned to a Salvation Army Commissioner when sweepers were required. As pointed out in the previous chapter, work regarded as 'traditional' for certain 'untouchable' communities often turns out to be an occupation forged under modern institutional and economic imperatives. Vijay Prashad has shown how much the equation between latrine sweepers and the community known as 'Chuhras' owes to colonial municipal and public health drives.[42] Under one such drive, some of the communities being registered as 'criminal tribes' were forcefully made over into sweepers for municipalities and military cantonments.[43] This was also the conjuncture at which the Government of India was drawing upon missionary organisations, in particular the Salvation Army, for assistance in turning 'stigmatised' and 'vagrant' populations into useful labour. Such exercises were cast as measures through which the 'welfare' of such strata could be secured and their potential criminality contained.[44] Missionary organisations found a position at the policed end of the labour and services market in India, one made up of industrial and agricultural settlements for 'criminal tribes' and juvenile reformatories.

---

[41] Ibid.

[42] Vijay Prashad, *Untouchable Freedom: A Social History of a Dalit Community*, Delhi: Oxford University Press, 2000.

[43] In Gorakhpur in the United Provinces, there was a concerted effort to compel the Maghiya Doms, one such stigmatised group, to live within a walled enclosure, and to use them as municipal sweepers. The vagrancy and bad livelihood sections of the Criminal Procedure Code were used to deter them from running away. Home, Police, A, June 1913, nos 6–7.

[44] Home, Police, A, June 1913, nos 6–7; Home, Police, Deposit, May 1916, no. 5; Manjiri N. Kamat, 'The War Years and the Sholapur Cotton Textile Industry', *Social Scientist*, vol. 26, nos 11–12 (1998), pp. 67–82; Meena Radhakrishna, *Dishonoured by History: 'Criminal Tribes' and British Colonial Policy*, Delhi: Oxford University Press, 2001.

However, at this conjuncture the government was single-mindedly concerned about getting sweepers, whereas the Salvation Army clung to its broader agenda of social and moral transformation. Booth-Tucker wanted 'the wives and families of prisoners and tribesmen ... to be ordered into a Salvation Army settlement, to be supported by a family allotment of Rs. 8/– deducted from the wages of each sweeper.'[45] The Home Department concluded that high-handed intrusion into domestic life would compromise recruitment, and decided not to involve the Salvation Army for fear of associating recruitment with proselytising.[46] Instead, provincial governments were directed as a matter of 'utmost importance' to get prisoners to volunteer as sweepers.[47] In addition, district magistrates of the United Provinces and Bihar and Orissa were urged to recruit sweepers

> from among the criminal tribes of Doms, noticeably in Gorakhpur, Saran, and Champaran, *who, although not in jail at the moment, are always more or less on the verge of it.* If the opportunity of earning an honest and lucrative living were explained to them, in preference to the precarious mode of living which they now follow ... it is to be hoped that further recruits might be obtained.[48]

At the level of such a deeply 'polluting' occupation, the line between criminal and low-caste mattered little. Jail recruitment could be used without embarrassing questions about the degree of pressure used, and no particular offence was regarded as a bar to service; the Home Secretary noted that '[n]o one is likely to worry much where we get sweepers from'.[49] The blurring of this line had one advantage for jail-recruited sweepers. They were initially given the same wage, Rs. 15/–, as free sweepers, a decision attributed to the higher risk of disease they faced.[50] There may have also been fewer restrictions on

---

[45] Home, Jails, A, November 1916, nos 42–48 (confidential).

[46] H. Wheeler, 24 May 1916, Home, Jails, A, November 1916, nos 42–48 (confidential). However, the Salvation Army did raise one free IPC from some 'criminal tribes'. Home, Political, B, February 1917, nos 353–96. There was intensive use of 'criminal tribe' labour for war purposes within India, in Bombay Presidency, the United Provinces and Punjab.

[47] The prisoner who 'volunteered' as sweeper was offered a monthly wage of Rs. 15/–, with a two-month advance, free rations, and clothing. His sentence was suspended under Section 401 of the Criminal Procedure Code, and remitted on his return. Home, Jails, A, November 1916, nos 42–48 (confidential).

[48] Ibid. (emphasis added).

[49] 22 May 1916, in Home, Jails, A, November 1916, nos 42–48 (confidential).

[50] Home, Jails, B, June 1916, no. 1. However, their pay was later brought down to

them because they were not organised into a distinct Labour Corps.[51] Lane commented disapprovingly that '[t]hey were in every sense "free" in the Force, so much so, that two jail-recruited sweepers, who had been in the country under a year, were given leave in the spring of 1917 from some unit.'[52] This fact became known because a Jail detachment at Qurna found out and asked for the same privilege.[53]

With suspicious swiftness, no less than 1,017 prisoners were found ready to 'volunteer' to go to Mesopotamia as sweepers in 1916.[54] Securing sweepers in sufficient number was crucial to the improvement of military hospitals in Mesopotamia, an issue on which the British public demanded reassurance. By autumn 1916, the accumulation at Basra of one Egyptian and ten Indian Labour Corps, together with dock labourers and craftsmen for the Inland Water Transport, had built up fears of a sanitary catastrophe.[55] As one Health Officer observed: 'in the first years of the British occupation, I suppose on an average there was no square yard of open space in Basrah free from a faecal deposit.'[56] Where homes did not have cesspits, any open space was used. The solution, he wrote, was to build latrine blocks with receptacles fashioned from disused kerosene tins, and to dispose of the solid waste in incinerators: 'For this work the Indian sweeper caste were imported, and they trained a number of Arab sweepers—although it must be admitted that the Arab never took kindly to these duties.'[57] Modern sanitation and modern medicine were also expected to encourage the demographic growth of the Arab population, without which commercial and agricultural expansion could not be contemplated.[58] Health

Rs. 10/–. Home, Jails, B, August 1917, nos 26–32. Jail-recruited *dhobis*, some trained before being sent, were kept at the higher wage of Rs. 15/ on the grounds that 'men of this caste were scarce and their work involved some risk, as they were required mainly for the Disinfecting Sections.' 'Recruiting in India', p. 41.

[51] The miscellaneous units were less supervised. Home, Jails, B, July 1917, nos 5–6.

[52] 'Summary', p. 9, para. 11.

[53] Ibid.

[54] Summary', p. 8, para. 11. Another official report put the number of jail-recruited sweepers sent in 1916 at 1,199. 'Recruiting in India', appendix XVI.

[55] F. T. H. Wood, 'Civil Sanitary Work in Mesopotamia', *Public Health*, vol. 33, no. 10 (1920), pp. 159–64.

[56] Ibid.

[57] Ibid. See image 9 for the 'closed incinerator'.

[58] Major General Sir W. G. Macpherson and Major T. J. Mitchell, *Medical Services,*

reports from Mesopotamia give us a glimpse here and there of the Indian sweeper engaged in this mission of sanitary reform.[59]

However, municipalities and jails in India could not be entirely denuded of sweepers, so 'untouchables' in the Indian Labour and Porter Corps and among the hospital followers were also hustled into latrine work.[60] Some of the men in the Jail Corps resisted this work, arguing 'that they were only sent out to sweep mule lines, and remove litter ... but they would not deal with human excreta.'[61] Others, wrote Lane, claimed that they did not know they had been brought out for this task.[62] Some of those who refused were sent back to India to serve their original sentence; others were given no choice at all. Colonel Patrick Hehir, Assistant Director of the Medical Service, admitted that '[a] certain proportion of those sent out were of the wrong class: many of them would not at first do conservancy work in latrines, although the conditions of field service necessitated our compelling them to carry out whatever duties were assigned to them.'[63] There is a tragic entry in the war diary of the 14th ILC recording the summary court-martial of one Medid Ramaswamy, for attempt-

---

General History, vol. 1, London: HMSO, 1924, pp. 260–61. 'The Arabs bear many but raise few, and a generation of dispensaries and kindly medical aid will populate the banks of the canals to be.' George F. MacMunn, 'Mesopotamia: The Land Between the Rivers', *The Cornhill Magazine*, 7 December 1918, in http://jfredmacdonald.com/worldwarone1914–1918/ottoman-18mesopotamia.html, last accessed 10 November 2019.

[59] *Report of the Health Officer, Ashar*, p. 2, in *Report of the Departments of the Civil Administration*, 1917.

[60] Describing his stay at a military hospital in Amara in 1917, the Indian journalist Indulal Yagnik said some 'mochis [cobblers], bhois [watermen], dhobis—gave vent to their anger when the work of bhangis [latrine-sweepers] was imposed on them.' Yagnik, *The Autobiography of Indulal Yagnik*, vol. 1, p. 269. A letter listing this grievance as well as others was published by Gandhi in *Young India*, 27 January 1921. See Home, Political, B, June 1921, nos 285–86.

[61] 'Summary', p. 9, para. 11.

[62] Ibid.

[63] Colonel Hehir, 'Recommendations for Improving Medical and Sanitary Efficiency on Field Service', 4 February 1917, IOR/L/Mil/7/18281. The *Bombay Chronicle* of 30 June 1920 reported that with the dismantling of Indian military hospitals in Mesopotamia, Indian sweepers were transferred to civil hospitals despite their pleas for repatriation. 'They have no place for Indian administrators, barristers, engineers and doctors, but are willing to welcome any number of sweepers and menials.' *Report on Native Newspapers, Bombay Presidency* (RNPB), no. 27, 3 July 1920, p. 13, para. 11.

ing to commit suicide by tying his legs and neck with his turban and throwing himself in the river. He was sentenced to six lashes, the officer noting that '[t]he case was very unfortunate as the fault lay with the Enlister. The man being of a caste which could not do sweeping work.'[64]

The Jail Labour and Porter Corps: an 'interesting experiment'

The first consignment of sweepers was blamed for an outbreak of crime in Basra, prejudicing some military authorities against jail recruitment.[65] However, by August 1916 the labour situation became critical again, with the shortage of dock labour crippling the delivery of supplies to the front.[66] The Quartermaster General requested 4,000 coolies, 1,300 camel-drivers, 500 washermen and 200 tailors for Force D, but admitted, 'men of the follower class are reluctant to serve in Mesopotamia and ... even high pay and a bonus will not overcome their somewhat natural reluctance.'[67] This reluctance was heightened by an excellent harvest in India, which had generated a bustling local demand for labour. In August 1916, the Army Department asked the Government of India to consider impressment, but for reasons discussed below that solution was rejected.[68] And once again we find the indefatigable Booth-Tucker at the elbow of the Army establishment.

Booth-Tucker suggested that a remission of sentence scheme for juvenile offenders at Lahore Jail could provide the framework for intensifying jail recruitment. Under this scheme, juvenile prisoners were transferred from the jail to a Salvation Army settlement in Danapur and given work at a minimum wage to ready them for release.[69] The Army Department outlined the advan-

---

[64] 3 September 1918, TNA, WO 95/5058.

[65] Lane, citing the Provost Marshall at Basra, 'Summary', p. 2, para. 2. '[S]cattered through every kind of unit at the base are convict sweepers, convict dhobis, convict bullock drivers, convict syces &c,' complained the Deputy Commissioner of Police for Basra. The Jail Labour Corps was kept under supervision, but these men, he said, were free to engage in crime. *Reports of Administration for 1918 of Divisions and Districts of the Occupied Territories in Mesopotamia*, vol. 1, IOR/L/PS/20/250, p. 275, QDL.

[66] Home, Political, B, February 1917, nos 353–96.

[67] Note, 28 August 1916, in Home, Political, B, February 1917, nos 353–96.

[68] Home, Political, B, February 1917, nos 353–96.

[69] 18 September 1916, Home, Political, B, February 1917, nos 353–96; for the Borstal scheme, see Home, Jails, A, June 1913, nos 37–50.

tages: 'The utilisation of prisoners ... may be regarded as a development of the Borstal system, with the additional merit that it is cheap, and does not disturb wages or interfere with economic needs.'[70] The prisoner who 'volunteered' to go to Mesopotamia in a Porter or Labour Corps would be enrolled as a follower under the Indian Army Act, to serve 'for two years or the duration of the war, whichever is less'. The unexpired period of his sentence would be suspended under Section 401 Cr. P. C., and remitted when he returned. He would receive Rs. 10/– per month, food, clothing, and a bonus of one month's pay every six months.[71] In comparison, the monthly wage for men in the 'free' Porter Corps, including allowances, was Rs. 15/–, and for those in the 'free' Labour Corps it was Rs. 20/–.[72] The men in the 'free' Corps were also entitled to a wound and injury pension at three-fourths of the combatant rate, and a family pension if they died on service—benefits not extended to jail-recruited corps.[73]

Why were the prisoners asked to 'volunteer' for this Corps, and why were wages given at all? In Indian jails, prisoners were not consulted when they were assigned to outdoor labour on public works.[74] Nor was it the practice to pay prisoners anything for their labour, although those elevated to the position of overseer or warder received a small monthly allowance.[75] Reginald Craddock, member of the Viceroy's executive council, had in fact suggested that there was no need to cast the scheme as a voluntary one, or to give wages. Prisoners could simply work out their sentences in Mesopotamia.[76] However, the Home Department pronounced that this 'would have wrecked the whole

---

[70] Note, 17 October 1916, Home, Political, February 1917, nos 353–96.

[71] Ibid. Cr. P. C. Indian Code of Criminal Procedure.

[72] As if to make up for this difference, a three-month pay advance was given to the men of the Jail Porter and Labour Corps. 'Summary', p. 4.

[73] F&P, Internal, B, August 1917, nos 110–15. An earlier file mentions a wound and injury pension for the Jail Corps, but a later one indicates that this was not given. See Home, Political, February 1917, nos 353–96; and F&P, Internal, B, August 1918, nos 11–18. Army Department Order, no. 50, of 2 January 1918 withdrew the family pension for all categories of 'temporary followers' substituting it with a one-time gratuity. *Compendium of the More Important Orders of the Government of India, Army Department, and Indian Army Orders, Issued from the 1st August 1914, to the 31st December 1917*, Calcutta: Government Printing, 1919, p. 53.

[74] Home, Jails, Deposit, September 1918, No. 3.

[75] *Indian Jails Committee*, vol. 1, report and appendices, 1919–20, 1920.

[76] Home, Political, February 1917, nos 353–96.

scheme ... The Indian prisoner has a pretty good idea of Mesopotamia's reputation.'[77] This time entire corps were being recruited, so publicity was inevitable, and these were not prisoners of the 'sweeper class'.

With the recruitment of some 3,200 prisoners, an official press communiqué was issued in October 1916 referring carefully to an 'interesting experiment' in 'giving well behaved and short term prisoners a "locus poenitentiae" by granting them conditional remission and employing them as labourers in Mesopotamia.' The communiqué glided over the fact that the first call had just been for sweepers, with little distinction as to class of offence.[78] The *Times of India* gave a rousing description of prisoners at Lahore Jail stepping forward smartly to be enrolled. The scene 'resembled nothing so much as recruits coming forward to take the King's shilling'.[79] Readers were reassured that the prisoners' transformation had already begun.

At first, the Army Department suggested the exclusion of certain categories of prisoner from this scheme: adolescents and prisoners sentenced for military or political offences, or for murder.[80] Perhaps there was a concern not to expose young boys to the danger of potential inappropriate sexual contact with adult prisoners in the unregulated environment of a labour camp. But juvenile reformatories were a source of trade-trained labour, and the argument that war service offered them a chance to 'make good' smoothed the way. The Punjab government, presumably 'in loco parentis', sent 405 juveniles from the Lahore Borstal to the Jail Corps, and the Bombay government sent thirty-seven adolescents from the Dharwar Juvenile Jail.[81] Recruitment helped to

---

[77] S. R. Hignell, 21 September 1916, Home, Political, February 1917, nos 353–96. In 1917 and in 1918, when fresh drafts of jail recruits were needed, the use of compulsion was discussed but rejected again. Home, Jails, March 1918, no. 6 (file not traceable, index notation used). Interestingly, prisoners working at the Kirkee (Khadki) arsenal were paid 6 annas a day, until the return of the JLC from Mesopotamia. *Indian Jails Committee*, 1919–20, 1920, p. 1174, para. 1937, p. 1180, para. 19502.

[78] *The Pioneer* (Allahabad), 23 October 1916, p. 13. The newspaper report did refer to the despatch of sweepers.

[79] *TOI*, 25 October 1916, p. 7.

[80] Home, Jails, B, December 1917, no. 1. The Bombay Government decided to exclude 'sodomites', 'lightly sentenced murderers', and political prisoners. Home, Political, B, February 1917, nos 353–96.

[81] 'Summary', p. 3, para. 5. *Administrative Report, Bombay Jail Department*, 1916, para. 16. In 1918, those confined in jail not because they had been found guilty of an

decongest jails, which were bursting at the seams with people swept in by the hardship caused by wartime inflation.[82] The number of military men among offenders had also gone up, and their absorption into these non-combatant units sent them back into the 'zone of the armies'.[83]

The framework of 'volunteering', the wage, and the promise of a remission of sentence allowed the Jail Corps to be cast as an experiment which placed the Government of India in the flow of international discussions about 'scientific penology'.[84] It hoped to contend thereby with reports in the Indian press, and sometimes in the British Parliament, about the backwardness and brutality of the Indian police and jail regime.[85] Some officials in India had begun to take an interest in the theme of 'indeterminate sentencing'—namely the idea that instead of a fixed term of imprisonment, a term could be reduced or extended depending on the individual prisoner's ability to demonstrate, by steady work and good conduct, his fitness for reintegration into society.[86] The decision to offer prisoners in Indian jails a chance to 'earn' a remission of sentence could be cast as an enlightened experiment in reform. In reality, some unreconstructed and regularly critiqued features of the Indian jail regime turned out to be eminently suitable to the deployment of prison labour in Mesopotamia: a heavy reliance on convict-recruited warders, the deployment of convict work gangs for outdoor labour, and the extensive reliance on flogging to enforce work and discipline.[87]

---

offence, but because they had failed to provide 'security for keeping the peace' or 'security for good behavior', were declared eligible for the Jail Corps. Home, Jails, A, May 1918, nos 3–4.

[82] To add to the problem, some central jails had been taken over for military needs. 'Summary', p. 10, para. 13.

[83] Judicial Department, 1917, no. 1412, Maharashtra State Archives, Mumbai (henceforth MSA). Soldiers sentenced for purely military offences could volunteer for the free Labour and Syce Corps.

[84] The international discussion on 'indeterminate sentencing' resonated at two sites in India—namely borstals for juveniles and settlements for 'criminal tribes'. See *Report of the Indian Jails Committee, 1919–1920*, Simla: Government Press, 1920.

[85] F. C. Mackarness, a Liberal MP, had published a very critical pamphlet: *The Methods of the Indian Police in the Twentieth Century*, San Francisco: The Hindustan Gadar Office, 1915.

[86] See *Report of the Indian Jails Committee, 1919–1920*.

[87] Jail-recruited warders and mates were given a monthly wage of Rs. 30/– and Rs. 20/–

One can only speculate about the combination of persuasion and coercion used to raise the Jail Corps. Some refusals were effective; the sweepers of Delhi Jail, for example, refused to go. On the other hand, it is difficult to understand why one Samandarkhan Samankhan, with barely a month and a half left to serve, would voluntarily leave with the Bombay JLC to replace a prisoner who had died.[88] Likewise, why would four prisoners from Bihar and Orissa who had completed their terms go with the Corps?[89] Perhaps they had not understood that they would have to carry on serving for the duration of the war, under special restrictions, and that any misconduct would result in recommitment to jail.[90]

Prisoners themselves attributed a lot of significance to the fact of being asked to 'volunteer', interpreting it to mean that they had regained some rights over their person. A prisoner at Thane Jail, waiting to be shipped, 'adopted the attitude that having volunteered he would only do such work as he liked. There had been a good deal of this kind of thing ... and he was given fifteen stripes not only for his own offence, but as a warning to others.'[91]

Recruiting 'free' labour: the case against impressment

The only form of compulsory military service employed in India during the war, was that applied to European British subjects.[92]

Jail recruitment alone could not meet the demand for non-combatant labour, hence the Army Department's suggested use of <u>impressment</u> in August 1916.[93] However, the Home Department turned down the suggestion, point-

---

a month respectively, instead of the Rs. 10/– given to the convict labourer. The Deccan work gang digging a tank reservoir at Visapur was tapped for Mesopotamia, and the Sind work gang was tapped for dock work at Karachi and for stacking and loading salt at Khewra mines in Jhelum district. *Report of the Indian Jails Committee, 1919–20*, p. 131, para. 222.

88 Home, Jails, B, August 1917, no. 16.

89 Home, Jails, B, December 1917, no. 2.

90 'Summary', p. 7

91 *Administrative Report, Bombay Jail Department*, 1917, para. 14.

92 *ICGW*, p. 203. Under the Registration Ordinance of 2 February 1917 all European British citizens in India between the ages of 18 and 41 were liable to general service, and those between 41 and 50 to local service in the Indian Defence Force. F&P, General, A, July 1917, nos 1–21.

93 Note, 28 August 1916, Home, Political, B, February 1917, nos 353–96.

ing out that it would be too difficult to work out an all-India scheme for labour impressment and too onerous to apply the scheme only to a particular locality. The biggest objection, it stated, was that conscription for labour service 'particularly outside India went enormously beyond anything on the statute book.'[94] It also pointed out that although there were officially sanctioned forms of labour corvée in some hill tracts, these were distinct to the locality and objections to them were picking up.[95] Under some irrigation and forest acts, officials could impress labour for emergencies. However, impressment for war service, the Home Department noted, was different, and there would be a strong political reaction to any such law or ordinance.[96] As pointed out earlier, the government was apprehensive about giving the impression that it was opening up a new form of indentured migration. Interestingly, the rioting and strikes with which the urban poor had resisted seizure and segregation in the Bombay plague epidemic of 1896–98 had also left a legacy of caution.[97] 'We know,' noted Deputy Home Secretary S. R. Hignell, 'what dangerous consequences attend any form of compulsion towards the person in this country, even if it be undertaken in the interests of the person himself.'[98]

Another point of concern was that impressment for the army might send labour into flight at crucial worksites and along transport nodes. This would jeopardise the production of war supplies, the generation of export surpluses, and the maintenance of communication networks, which were by this point all tightly oriented to military needs. In addition, landlords and tenants, the class from which the Punjabi soldier was drawn, would resent the depletion of

---

[94] Note, 3 September 1916, Home, Political, B, February 1917, nos 353–96. See below.

[95] Note, 1 September 1916, Home, Political, B, February 1917, nos 353–96. In the Kumaon hills a campaign against *coolie utar*, forced porterage for officials and forced provision of supplies to travellers, stepped up during the war. *Selected Works of Govind Ballabh Pant*, ed. B. R. Nanda, vol. 1, Delhi: Oxford University Press, 1993, p. 188. The authority structures of corvée were used to push up recruitment numbers in certain tracts, but emancipation was offered as a reward. See Chapter 4.

[96] Home, Political, B, February 1917, nos 353–96.

[97] See Aditya Sarkar, 'The Tie That Snapped: Bubonic Plague and Mill Labour in Bombay, 1896–1898', *International Review of Social History*, vol. 59, no. 2 (2014), pp. 181–214.

[98] Note, 3 September 1916, Home, Political, B, February 1917, nos 353–96. Major General A. H. Bingley, Secretary to the Army Department (1916–21), had done plague duty in Bombay in 1897–98.

labour, particularly when agricultural operations were in full swing.[99] '[T]hough we may not care to introduce impressment by law,' noted Craddock, 'we refrain, not because we regard it as absolutely immoral, but because it would cause a panic.'[100] British businessmen in India were particularly quick to underline this danger.[101]

The suspension of indentured migration

The army's other suggestion was to be allowed 'first choice' of the coolies collected by emigration agents for plantation work in the West Indies and Fiji.[102] In January 1917 it went on to propose the suspension of all labour migration, 'free' and indentured, until the demand from Mesopotamia and France for non-combatant labour had been satisfied.[103] The local governments of Bihar and the United Provinces pointed out that the flow of indentured migration had significantly diminished, and would not meet the military demand for labour.[104] Nor was there any certainty that labourers would agree

---

[99] Ibid. In south-east Punjab, 'menial castes' had responded well to recruitment but it was stopped because it was affecting the supply of agricultural labour. *Record of War Work in the Gurgaon District*, Government of the Punjab: Lahore, 1923.

[100] Note, R. H. Craddock, 10 September 1916, Commerce and Industry (C&I), Emigration, October 1916, no. 2. In Belgaum in Bombay Presidency a rumour about forced recruitment led to the flight of labour, cutting timber for railway fuel. Home, Political, May 1917, no. 70. There were many such instances.

[101] See *Report of the Bombay Chamber of Commerce for the Year 1917*, Bombay, 1918, Appendix A3, p. 107. As the army began to pick up Gurkhas around tea gardens and markets in upper Bengal and Assam, planters complained vociferously that recruiting parties were panicking their labour.

[102] Major General Sir Arthur Phayre to Chief Secretary Madras Presidency, 26 February 1916, C&I, Emigration, A, January 1918, nos 1–34. The Commerce and Industry Department pointed out that military recruitment would get linked with the dubious figure of the emigration agent, but did not reject the idea outright. Ibid.

[103] General Richardson, 25 January 1917, and 13 February 1917, in C&I, Emigration, January 1918, nos 1–34.

[104] Bihar and Orissa Government, 26 January 1917, United Provinces Government, 9 February 1917, C&I, Emigration, January 1918, nos 1–3. Nevertheless, the Colonial Office still pressed for the continuation, in some form, of indentured migration. The world price of cane sugar had gone up due to the curtailment of continental beet sugar, and with Afro-Caribbeans in the West Indies being recruited to the army it was important to sustain the supply of plantation labour.

to be rerouted from emigration depots towards the army.[105] What eventually precipitated the suspension of indentured migration was the fallout from an embarrassing statement made by the Secretary of State for India in Parliament. On 22 February 1917, Austen Chamberlain blithely declared that indentured labour would be maintained for five years 'at the outer limit' while an alternative form of labour migration was worked out.[106] Viceroy Chelmsford was less than thrilled, pointing out that public opinion had been stirred up by 'further revelations with regard to the moral issue'—that is, by accounts of the sexual exploitation of the female coolie—and that the demand in India was for immediate abolition.[107]

It is worth dwelling on this issue because some scholars ascribe the suspension of indentured migration in March 1917 to the shortage of shipping and the need to divert labour into military channels.[108] The military demand for labour was important, but although it provided an excuse for suspending indentured migration it was not the reason for doing so. The citation of war needs gave the Government of India the leverage it needed with the Colonial Office to take this step instead of working out a 'reformed' system. The Commerce and Industry Department in India had hinted at this manoeuvre:

> The army authorities emphasise the importance of restricting all emigration of Indian Labour overseas at the present time. We must necessarily accept this view. I incidentally mentioned this case to His Excellency this morning, and he was of the view that *we should seize the opportunity to discontinue, at any rate temporarily, recruitment of indentured labour*.[109]

---

[105] A. H. Bingley, 14 February 1917, C&I, E, January 1918, nos 1–34. It would be 'absurd to upset the economics of the East for the sake of a few questionable Tamil recruits', noted D. N. Strathie, a Madras civil servant, 9 January 1916, in GO, no. 1046, 30 May 1916, Public, Press Series, TNSA.

[106] Viceroy to SSI, 28 February 1917 (private telegram), and 9 March 1917, C&I, E, January 1918, nos 1–34.

[107] Viceroy to Secretary of State for India (SSI), 28 February 1917, C&I, E, January 1918, nos 1–34. For the 'moral issue' see John D. Kelly, *A Politics of Virtue: Hinduism, Sexuality, and Countercolonial Discourse in Fiji*, Chicago; London: University of Chicago Press, 1992.

[108] See Goolam Vahed, 'End of a dehumanising system', *The Mercury*, 20 April 2017, www.pressreader.com/south-africa/the-mercury/20170420/281724089428371, last accessed 10 November 2019.

[109] Note, H. F. Howard, 10 February 1917 and 14 February 1917, in C&I, E, January 1918, nos 1–34. My emphasis.

On 12 March 1917, therefore, the Government of India passed a Defence of India Ordinance declaring that:

> in order to conserve the man-power of India for the purposes of labour in connection with the war the Government of India have decided to prohibit all labour emigration except to the extent necessary to supply the minimum requirements of Ceylon and the Federated Malay states.[110]

What this meant in effect was that indentured migration, by this time largely restricted to Fiji and Trinidad, was stopped, but that Indian labourers were still permitted to leave in reduced numbers for Ceylon and the Federated Malay States, where their presence was vital to the production of plantation crops, rubber, petroleum and tin, and to the maintenance of dock and transport infrastructures.[111]

The military use of labour: problems and possibilities

The label of 'war service' helped to distance the sending of labour to Mesopotamia from the now stigmatised system of indentured migration. The entirely masculine nature of recruitment also removed the problematic figure of the female coolie. Viceroys had often lamented that 'the moral degradation' of the female labourer had made it difficult for them to defend the indenture system.[112] Very importantly, the military framework also allowed for the blanket of censorship to be imposed over conditions of work and treatment.[113]

Schematically put, there were three forms in which Indian manpower was sent into the Persian Gulf. Under the terms of the Indian Emigration Act (Act XVII of 1908), labour migration under contract for hire was permitted only from certain specified ports and destinations. One approach was to simply bypass this Act and contract civilian overseers to take labour to Mesopotamia for short-term periods. This was probably the method used in early 1916 when labourers had to be rushed to Basra to construct a flood embankment around the military base. The Department of Commerce and Industry commented that:

> It seems undesirable for political reasons to draw attention to the fact that we are recruiting a large number of coolies from the very unwarlike tracts of

---

[110] C&I, E, January 1918, nos 1–34.

[111] The ports of Colombo and Rangoon were heavily dependent on Indian stevedore labour.

[112] Hardinge to SSI, 28 February 1917, C&I, E, August 1916, file 104, no. 5.

[113] General Department, 1916–17, no. 90, part II, MSA.

Gorakhpur and the East U.P. for work in however safe a portion of the war area, and ... it seems undesirable to treat these coolies as emigrants *thereby putting them in a position to make afterwards complaints* of a nature which may be troublesome.[114]

And again, sending railway contractor Rai Bahadur Chotay Lal to recruit labour for railway-laying in Mesopotamia on 10 June 1916, the government informed the United Provinces and Bihar and Orissa that:

> though the recruitment and embarkation of such coolies comes technically within the scope of the Indian Emigration Act (XVII of 1908), *the Government of India find it desirable to treat this form of labour recruitment otherwise than under the Act*, and to allow the labourer to proceed to Basra *without the formal issue of a notification under Section 107 relaxing the provisions of the Act*.[115]

If there were objections, observed the Commerce and Industry Department, it could be said that the coolies were 'only technically emigrants', that they were actually being sent 'as a war measure', and that the 'desirability of maintaining secrecy' could be pleaded.[116] The Railway Board merely had to certify that 'the coolies will be properly paid and fed and otherwise looked after ... food will be supplied free. The actual rates of pay given will be such as to satisfy the responsible officer in charge of the work.'[117]

Section 107 of the Indian Emigration Act allowed rules to be waived if labour was being sent overseas 'under an agreement made with, or on behalf of, His Majesty's Government to labour for hire'.[118] This provision had been used to send Indian labour overseas to build the Ugandan railway.[119] Why was

---

[114] Note, C. E. Low, Secretary, Department of Commerce and Industry, 11 January 1916 in C&I, E, B, March 1916, no. 43, serial no. 1, my emphasis. Also C&I, E, B, March 1917, no. 17. Some labourers and artisans were rushed to Mesopotamia from Surat district in the early phase of the war without being enrolled. *India's Services in the War*, Bombay, vol. IV, Lucknow: Newul Kishore Press, 1922, p. 80.

[115] General Department, 1916–17, no. 90, part II, MSA, my emphasis.

[116] Ibid.

[117] Note, M. R. Anderson, Railway Board, 10 June 1916, in C&I, E, June 1916, file 95, B, Sl., nos 1–3.

[118] Indian Emigration Act (Act XVII of 1908), chapter XIV, section 107.

[119] The 1909–10 Parliamentary Committee (the Sanderson Committee), which recommended some modifications to the system of indentured migration, carefully factored in an exception for labourers required for official purposes in a British colony overseas. Such labourers, it said, were 'throughout their indenture, practically

this eminently suitable procedure not deployed for Mesopotamia? The fact was that a gazette notification under Section 107 could be issued only after the Governor General in Council was 'first satisfied that the fair treatment of Natives of India ... has, by rules or otherwise, duly been secured.'[120] In this instance, labourers were being sent not to a British colony, but to territory under military occupation, and there was no agency there to monitor their treatment. A gazette notification would bring unwanted publicity, and the very invocation of the Indian Emigration Act instituted a legal and procedural framework which labourers, or public figures critical of indenture, had sometimes used to lodge complaints with the Protector of Emigrants.

The second method of sending Indian labour overseas during the war was that used by the powerful Anglo-Persian Oil Company. Emigration rules were more relaxed in relation to skilled labour than to unskilled labour, and in theory Persia was neutral territory. The Government of India therefore allowed the company to continue recruiting Indian artisans.[121] The APOC used this concession to surreptitiously import unskilled labour as well—at one estimate, some 1,000 men annually throughout the war.[122] The government turned a blind eye to this illegality until the close of 1920.[123] And yet the APOC continuously complained about the very minimal formality it was required to observe, namely that the artisans were to register themselves with

---

servants of the State and under the constant care of officers of the Government.' *Report of the Committee on Emigration from India to Crown Colonies and Protectorates, June 1910*, London: Eyre and Spottiswode, 1910.

[120] Indian Emigration Act (Act XVII of 1908), section 107.

[121] Under section 2 (v) of the Indian Emigration Act, 'labour' meant 'unskilled labour'. Artisans were dealt with under chapter XI, section 75.

[122] F&P, General, A, February 1916, nos 1–6; F&P, War, B (Secret), May 1916, nos 259–63. The covert recruitment of Indian labour by private firms in the Persian Gulf, in violation of the ordinance of 12 March 1917, was quite extensive during the war. General Dept, 1920, no. 989, MSA. Tetzlaff points out that in passing off unskilled Indian labour as skilled labour, the APOC also evaded its undertaking to use Persian labour as much as possible. Stefan Tetzlaff, 'Entangled Boundaries: British India and the Persian Gulf Region During the Transition from Empires to Nation States, c. 1880–1935', MA Thesis, Magisterarbeit, Humboldt University, 2009, p. 211.

[123] In December 1920 India's Foreign and Political Department finally stated to the APOC that this illegal migration had been condoned due to the war, but was going to be stopped from 1 January 1921. Home, Political, B, January 1921, no. 2.

the Protector of Emigrants at Bombay. It insisted, in contradictory fashion, both that the men found this procedure 'irksome', and that it fostered a 'litigious spirit' in them.[124] And, indeed, some artisans did complain to the Protector of Emigrants about miserably cramped accommodation, gruelling work hours, forcible transfer from Persia into the war zone of Turkish Arabia, and the threat of punishment under military law if they refused to work beyond the expiry of their contract.[125] The military authorities also assisted the APOC by lending it a detachment of 300 men for the period February–July 1918 from the Burma Jail Labour Corps, a unit with a large number of skilled artisans.[126]

And, finally, there was the third method—the enrolment of non-combatant labourers as 'temporary followers' under the Indian Army Act. Instead of the architecture of indentured contract, where penal provisions were used to enforce work and discipline, another form of extra-civil law, the Indian Army Act, was put in place.[127] One difference was that the planter was not legally permitted to flog his coolie, whereas the Commanding Officer of a Labour or Porter Corps presiding over his own one-man tribunal, the summary court-martial, could order a sentence of thirty lashes.[128] However, some of the formalities of the Indian Army Act would also pose a conceptual problem for officers commanding labour units, both in Mesopotamia and in France.

The terms of service: the imprint of off-farm work

Officials who hoped that channels of migration for waged work could simply be diverted for wartime needs were often disappointed. Jobbers who supplied

---

[124] F&P, General, B, June 1918, no. 79. After some initial resistance, the Government of India agreed in February 1918, as a 'war measure', to waive all formalities. Home, Political, B, January 1921, no. 21; General Department, 1920, no. 989, MSA. See also Tetzlaff, 'Entangled Boundaries', p. 70.

[125] F&P, General, B, June 1918, no. 79.

[126] 'History', 12th Burma JPC, p. 5, p. 7; TNA WO/95/5038.

[127] Once enrolled as a follower, the recruit faced police arrest and court-martial for being absent without leave or for desertion. Indian Army Act (Act VIII of 1911), section 123(2).

[128] See Radhika Singha, 'The "Rare Infliction": The Abolition of Flogging in the Indian Army, circa 1835–1920', *Law and History Review*, vol. 34, no. 3 (2016), pp. 783–818.

labour for plantations could not have been enthused by the Rs. 1/– offered as 'bringing in' money for a non-combatant, given that they stood to make Rs. 8/– to Rs. 10/– for each 'Santhali' labourer presented at a tea plantation in northern Bengal, and even more in Assam.[129] Some recruiting officers from the Madras Presidency complained about the apathy of brokers who shipped labour to Ceylon, Malaya, the Straits and Burma.[130] However, railway and military contractors in North India who had links to the army's Supply and Transport Department and were heavily dependent on state patronage rallied around. Rai Bahadur Chotay Lal, 'landholder, banker, merchant and general contractor of state railways', raised some 4,900 men from the United Provinces for railway work and for the ILC, and his son Ram Sarup raised 400 men for the Porter Corps depot at Faizabad.[131] Boota Singh, a wealthy Punjabi military contractor, opened his own recruiting agencies at Rawalpindi, Peshawar, Lahore and Delhi and claimed he had supplied 11,842 combatants and non-combatants.[132] However, contractors were also criticised for passing off men who were too old or too young, and physically not up to par.[133]

The larger princely states were not very responsive to the call for labour.[134] Supplying soldiers was more prestigious, and combatant formations retained the title of the princely state, whereas labourers were absorbed into provincial Labour or Porter Corps. The most reliable way to ensure that quotas were met was to fall back on subordinate officials who collected the land tax or handled

---

[129] See Tirthankar Roy and Anand V. Swamy, *Law and the Economy in Colonial India*, Chicago; London: University of Chicago, 2016, pp. 113–14. The jobber received Rs. 45/– for an indentured labourer sent to Fiji, or the West Indies. The army later raised the 'bringing in' money for a non-combatant to Rs. 3/–.

[130] For complaints about the apathy of Muslim businessmen said to control coaling labour at Nagapatam, Mandapam and Tuticorin in the Madras Presidency, see Public, GO, no. 669, 23 May 1917, TNSA.

[131] Chotay Lal and his family merited a five-page entry in the provincial war record: *India's Services in the War*, United Provinces, vol. II, Lucknow: Newul Kishore Press, 1922, pp. 181–86. He was awarded the OBE on 2 May 1918, ibid.

[132] J. Wilston Johnston, *The History of the Great War, Rawalpindi District*, Lahore, 1920, pp. 22–23. Mian Nadar Din, contractor of Sarai Kale Khan, supplied recruits for the Labour Corps and the Railway Labour Corps. Ibid., p. 30.

[133] 'Recruiting in India'.

[134] There were exceptions—the Banaras Raj supplying labour for Mesopotamia, the Manipur Raj for France.

the roster for the labour tax, and to call on large landholders, headmen and chiefs to induce tenants to enlist. Associations for the uplift of lower castes were sometimes approached.[135] Missionary bodies responded fulsomely, both to secure work for their impoverished laity and to demonstrate how they had shaped 'backward' populations into useful, sober labour.[136] The Salvation Army offered to raise two Porter Corps for service in the Persian Gulf, and the Wesleyan Methodist mission at Hyderabad raised a Labour Corps composed of 'low-caste' Malas and Madigas, with two of their chaplains going along to Mesopotamia as Commanding Officers.[137]

Military recruitment also had to accommodate itself to some of the norms which shaped migration for off-farm work, notably the preference of Indian labourers for fixed terms of six months, a year or two years, rather than indefinite 'duration of war' agreements. A December 1918 report put the number of Indian non-combatants in Mesopotamia at 138,648, of whom 71,735 were on 'duration of war' agreements and 66,913 on fixed-term engagements. Skilled labour was usually on fixed terms.[138] The situation in October 1917 was that practically all Indian railway personnel were on one-year engagements.[139]

Writing in glowing terms of the Santhal Labour Corps, the war journalist Edmund Candler explained that they had entered into one-year service agreements because they had to 'get back to their harvest', but could be trusted to sign on again.[140] One wonders which harvest cycle follows the annual calendar. In fact, labourers understood the value of a fixed exit point in dealing with

---

[135] Among the new classes being enlisted were the Jadubans Ahirs from the United Provinces and the Nandbans Ahirs from Bihar. The Ahir Sabha helped in recruitment. *India's Services in the War*, United Provinces, vol. III, p. 13; 'Recruiting in India', appendix XVIII, p. 75.

[136] *127th Annual Report of the Baptist Missionary Society, 1918–19*, London: Carey Press, 1919, pp. 8, 11.

[137] 'Porters Coolie Corps for the Persian Gulf', *The War Cry*, XXII, 10 October 1916, p. 11; *The Wesleyan Methodist Church: The Twenty-Sixth Report of the South India Provincial Synod*, Madras, 1919, p. 69.

[138] C&I, E, August 1919, nos 8–9. In February 1917, when Labour Corps were being raised for France, a proposal to enrol men for 'the duration of the war' had to be dropped for one-year agreements. F&P, Internal, B, August 1917, nos 110–15.

[139] General Officer Commanding (GOC), Mesopotamia to C-in-C, India, 13 October 1917, IOR/L/MIL/7/18490.

[140] Candler, *The Sepoy*, p. 222. Candler was probably referring to the 'Santhalis' recruited in 1916, attached to the 2nd Punjab Labour Corps and repatriated in 1917.

this formidable employer, the army in wartime. Madras officials complained that when the term of service for railway labour companies was changed from one year to 'period of war' many potential recruits backed away. The very reference to war, they said, 'leads to an apprehension that the men are to be sent into the firing line.'[141] The promised point of termination was often an object of struggle. Nevertheless, it allowed non-combatants to bargain for some paid leave, to change their unit, or to seek a recategorisation as skilled labour. Eager to stress that labour recruitment for the Inland Water Transport in Mesopotamia was 'nothing in the nature of conscription', Lieutenant Colonel L. J. Hall wrote of hundreds who returned to India at the expiry of their contract then came back to enrol for second and third terms.[142]

Labour recruits had to be constantly reassured that they 'would not be called upon to fight', and their caution was not misplaced, for they were not warned that front lines could move or that worksites could lie within range of the guns.[143] In recruiting men for the Indian Labour Corps for France, the Chief Commissioner of the North-West Frontier Province had wanted a military or semi-military designation.[144] However, he was told this would have adverse consequences elsewhere, as 'the one stipulation we have always found labourers insist upon is that they shall not be either employed, or treated as soldiers.'[145] One of the benefits on offer for men in the Labour Corps was a wound and injury pension. In civil life, most labourers in India could expect no compensation at all for workplace injury. Yet district officers were warned that in explaining this novel feature of the contract, they should guard against giving the 'erroneous impression that they [the ILC recruits] would be at the firing line.'[146]

---

[141] *Fortnightly Report*, Madras Presidency, 17 January 1918, TNSA.

[142] Lieutenant Colonel L. J. Hall, *The Inland Water Transport in Mesopotamia*, London: Constable and Co., 1921, p. 126.

[143] Non-combatants at the central follower depot at Kirkee (Khadki), near Pune, were regularly asked if anyone wanted to join for combatant service. In Mesopotamia, some men from the 2nd Punjab Labour Corps were transferred to combatant service. During the Arab uprising in 1920, many men of the ILC were trained in the use of arms for the defence of Basra.

[144] The men of British labour battalions had combatant status.

[145] To expedite recruitment for Mesopotamia, the men of the 6th and 8th ILC had to be offered terms of just six months. 'Recruiting in India', p. 38.

[146] See Assam Secretariat, Political, Political Branch, B, April 1918, nos 316–499, Assam State Archives, Guwahati.

The quest for follower labour also turned up some exceedingly uxorious husbands. No sweepers were available at Trichinopoly 'owing to their refusal to accept military service unless accompanied by their wives'.[147] Lieutenant Sargisson, formerly of the South Indian Railway Company, observed that there were 'many good working castes' who would go for railway work in Mesopotamia only if they could take their families with them.[148] Some men were clearly testing the ground. If work behind the lines was safe enough for them, it ought to be safe enough for their wives. For 'coolies and menials' spousal presence was certainly a better guarantee of care than reliance upon institutional arrangements. But such encounters also reveal the clash between family-based livelihood strategies and the all-male work gangs required for theatres of war. Ian J. Kerr gives us an excellent account of the imprint of family labour units upon work processes and the wage structure in railway construction.[149] The prime minister of Baroda State pointed out that women were an integral component of construction work gangs from Kathiawar, where the men did the digging and the women carried away head-loads of earth and stones. If women were excluded, he said, it would create the impression that the risk was greater than it actually was.[150] In World War One, the pattern of family-based livelihood which prevailed in the follower lines of cantonments was disrupted by the expectations placed on regimental followers to leave for active service. This then increased the pressure to raise their wages.[151]

Another method used to assemble work gangs was deploying the police to draw them out from communities labelled 'criminal tribes'. In World War One the reform agenda of pressing these groups to adopt a fixed location and a stable family life was often bypassed because of the need to secure predominantly male work gangs who could be moved around from site to site—for

---

[147] Fortnightly Report, Madras, 17 July 1916, para. 6, TNSA.

[148] Lieutenant Sargissson, Recruiting Officer, Mesopotamia Railway Training Camp, Tirupatthur to Chief Secretary, Madras, 19 May 1917, Public, GO, no. 66, 23 May 1917, TNSA.

[149] Ian J. Kerr, *Building the Railways of the Raj, 1850–1900*, Delhi: Oxford University Press, 1995, pp. 87–88, 175.

[150] Acting Dewan, to British Resident, 11 December 1916, Baroda Residency, War, W-65. Candler noted the unmasculine readiness of Santhal labourers to acknowledge that their women could carry larger head-loads of firewood than them. Candler, *The Sepoy*, p. 223.

[151] See also 'Recruiting in India', p. 35.

instance, from a public works project to an irrigation works, or from a military grass farm to a lumber extraction camp.[152]

However, the service package shows that in recruiting non-combatants some effort had to be made to placate the family and the creditor. From the army's point of view, forms of deferred payment—such as, for instance, one month's extra pay for set periods of service—allowed better control. Too much money 'up front', as in the form of an enlistment bonus, was said to encourage 'the professional deserter and the professional malingerer'.[153] Viewed from the recruit's position, however, a lump sum at enrolment allowed him to pay off debts and leave something for his family.[154]

Men recruited to the free Labour and Porter Corps for Mesopotamia were offered a one-month advance, but what is interesting is that jail-recruited sweepers were offered a two-month advance and jail-recruited labourers a three-month advance to tempt them. Officers of the Labour Corps were instructed to systematise the deduction of a family allowance, which gave non-combatant recruitment in the Madras Presidency an edge over combatant recruitment.[155] However, in 1918 the army took advantage of agricultural drought in India and a stable situation in Mesopotamia to rationalise the wage package for all categories of temporary labour. From February 1918, the consolidated wage for temporary labour was fixed at Rs. 12/– within India and Rs. 18/– overseas, with a bonus of Rs. 20/– at the point of enlistment. Enrolment was for general service and for the duration of the war.[156]

---

[152] For the most marked illustration of this tendency, see *Report on the Administration of Criminal Tribes in the Punjab for the Year Ending December 1918*, Lahore: Government Printing, 1919, appendix A, p. iv.

[153] 'Recruiting in India', p. 28, IOR/L/MIL/17/5/2152.

[154] Men from the Chittagong-Sylhet belt, an area regularly tapped for lascars (seamen), were the first to respond to the labour demand from Mesopotamia because they were 'accustomed for generations to leave their homes'. 'Recruiting in India'. Submarine warfare had also made this the safer option. However, as lascars they were used to getting a one-month wage advance. They also put other time-tested strategies for securing the survival of their family into play. Father Douglass, commanding a Bengal labour company, was scandalised by 'rough sea-men from Chittagong' who divorced their wives before leaving for France. Anonymous, *Father Douglass of Behala, By Some of His Friends*, London: Oxford University Press, 1952, p. 92. This was a practice which left the woman free to make alternative arrangements to sustain herself and her children.

[155] Fortnightly Report, Madras, 18 October 1918, TNSA.

[156] *Army Instruction (India)*, no. 48 of 1918; *RLD*.

The camp under military guard and the play of ethnic comparison

At first there was no discernible drive to give the Indian Labour and Porter Corps in Mesopotamia a specific territorial or ethnic label, although a prefix such as Punjab, Madras, or Santhal was sometimes used. In theory, enlistment in the Labour and Porter Corps was for general service—that is, the recruit could be assigned to any unit. In fact, language and therefore region had to be given some consideration, for too much of a variety compromised recruitment and created administrative problems. The Madras Government reported that it was easier to induce men to join a railway training camp in their own area than in a distant depot.[157] It also complained that the people being placed in command over 'Madrasis' did not know their language, and assumed that they were stupid.[158] Commanding Officers objected to the difficulties caused by linguistic heterogeneity, and by the mixing of wheat-eaters with rice-eaters and of vegetarians with non-vegetarians.[159] Labourers were also very resistant to any move to detach them from their original unit, because it disrupted the support systems on which they relied so substantially.

In contrast to language and region, caste and religion were not given any great attention in institutional provisions for the Labour and Porter Corps. The cautiousness about cooking and messing arrangements for combatants was an index of their higher standing. In 'coolie units' the expectation was that collective cooking, which saved on fuel and work time, could be adopted.[160] They were assumed to be made up of 'low castes' or 'caste-less' tribals, yet when names are listed for those drawn from the Gangetic tracts of the United Provinces and Bihar and Orissa they reveal a broad caste spectrum.[161]

In January 1918 the General Officer Commanding in Mesopotamia suggested that each ILC be given a territorial designation and renamed as 'Labour Battalions' to distinguish them from local labour corps, 'as there appears to be some confusion in the public mind as regards these Corps.'[162] The aim was

---

[157] Fortnightly Report, Madras, 5 March 1918, TNSA.

[158] Ibid.

[159] See, for instance, WO 95/5277 about the transfer of ten 'non-flesh eaters' into the 5th Madras Labour Company.

[160] The selection of cooks probably took place by internal arrangement.

[161] Some but not all Labour Corps had this profile. The Labour Corps raised from around Hyderabad with the help of the Wesleyan mission (probably the 14th ILC) had a large number of Malas and Madigas, treated as 'low caste'. TNA WO 95/5038.

[162] GOC, Force 'D', 11 January 1918, WW1/976/H, vol. 418, diary no. 8177.

both to reassure Arabs that there was no intention to settle Indian labour in Mesopotamia and to create a sense of *esprit de corps* to stimulate recruitment.[163] When they compared the quality of the different 'ethnicities' in the Labour and Porter Corps, British officers drew upon stereotypes shaped by the distinction between 'martial' and non-martial races and emerging from worksites such as plantations and docks. Manpower from the wheat-eating colder regions of India was held to be healthier and stronger than that from the rice-eating regions of eastern and southern India.[164] However, such comparisons were also bound up with political agendas. The commanding officer of the 2nd Punjab Labour Corps, a 'free' unit, clearly felt he had to preserve the prestige of all military employment in Punjab. He objected to the sending of a jail detachment to work with his men, and to an order stating that labourers punished for serious offences would continue to work but in shackles.[165] This 'most degrading punishment', he noted, was 'unfit for a free volunteer Punjabi Corps'.[166]

The notion that 'aboriginal' communities provided 'a particularly valuable kind of coolie' shaped Candler's decision to select a 'Santhali' unit when he wrote about the Labour Corps in Mesopotamia.[167] By the early twentieth century, Candler, in common with paternalist administrators in internal and external 'borderlands' of India, was discovering a happier affinity with 'primitive man' than with the politically assertive, educated Indian. His article in *The Times* carried the following subtitles: 'The Model Coolie in Mesopotamia', 'Recruits from an Indian Utopia', and 'The Simple Santal'.[168] Quoting an Indian veteran, Candler cast the Santhal Corps as the absolute opposite of the Jail Corps: 'There is no fighting, quarrelling, thieving, lying among them, Sahib ... No trouble with women folk, no gambling, no tricks of deceit.'[169]

When Lane wanted to highlight the capacities of jail-recruited labour he had to cut the 'Santhali' down to size: 'Now the Santhali is not without his

---

[163] Ibid.

[164] *RLD*, p. 14. For an insightful assessment of dietary stereotypes, see David Arnold, 'The "Discovery" of Malnutrition and Diet in Colonial India', *The Indian Economic & Social History Review*, vol. 31, no. 1 (1994), pp. 1–26.

[165] 27 October 1917, TNA WO 95/5036.

[166] Ibid.

[167] See Chapter 4.

[168] *The Times*, 20 June 1917, p. 5.

[169] Candler, *The Sepoy*, p. 218.

merits, but he is quite useless for work requiring intelligence. What we wanted were Corps with a fair proportion of artisans ... and intelligent labourers of the type found ... amongst the daily labourers of the P.W.D. and the M.W.S.'[170] The Labour Directorate in Mesopotamia similarly described Santhali labour as 'slow but steady, of low intelligence and poor physique, extremely easy to control'.[171] Looked at from a different perspective, the 'Santhalis' were protecting themselves from overuse by sticking to earth-work and keeping to their own measured pace.[172] Jail labour was far more vulnerable to exploitation.

The main axis of comparison in Mesopotamia, and the most politically significant one, was between Indian and locally recruited labour units. Arab labour was described as 'most uncertain', with workers declining to work in the wet weather and deserting when fields had to be prepared for cultivation, or date trees pollinated or harvested.[173] Regarding Kurds, the complaint was that in summer they had abandoned worksites on the Persian road to leave for the hills.[174] This 'unsteadiness' is hardly surprising given the disruption caused to agricultural and pastoral life by the military demand for labour. Keeping the price of Arab labour down was another problem, as local labour contractors drove hard bargains. The solution was forcible recruitment through local sheikhs and *mukhtars* (headmen), a strategy used in the area between Basra and Kut al-Amara, and again in Baghdad.[175]

The necessity of importing labour to ensure continuity at crucial worksites is illustrated by the problems which emerged in the construction of the Shaiba Bund, a crucial flood embankment around Basra. Once date-picking started and the ground had to be prepared for cultivation, Arab labour could not be

---

[170] Lane was citing two notes. See 'Summary', p. 2. The Jail Corps certainly had the advantage of social diversity, and some units, such as the 12th Burma JPC, had a remarkable number of artisans. TNA WO/95/5038. PWD: Public Works Department; MWS: Military Works Service.

[171] *RLD*, p. 27.

[172] 'Summary', p. 2.

[173] Moberly, *The Campaign in Mesopotamia*, vol. 2, p. 359. The 'unreliability' of Arab labour was given as the reason for bringing in, successively, Indian lascars, the Egyptian Labour Corps, one JLC, and finally 'Madras coolies and Kurdish labourers' to man the Inland Water Transport. Hall, *The Inland Water Transport*, p. 47.

[174] *RLD*, p. 9.

[175] *RLD*, p. 7. The Labour Directorate complained that Arabs released for agricultural work actually left for better-paid sites elsewhere, or worked for local contractors.

found. This was harsh toil in the desert when work at high wages was freely available in Basra. The Chief Political Officer was ordered to impress Arab labourers. With heavy rains in February 1916, they had to be placed in camps under military guard to prevent desertions.[176] The 11th Bombay JLC was eventually put to work on the Shaiba Bund.

Imported labour ensured continuity: it was more mobile than local labour; it reduced the leverage of local contractors and local labourers; and it enabled the periodic release of Arab labour for agricultural work.[177] However, if Iraq was to be ruled with an Arab rather than an Indian façade it was important to maintain that Arab labour could be steadied—that is, bound down to continuous work and trained to new kinds of tasks.[178] An article penned by Major General George F. MacMunn, Inspector General of Communications in Mesopotamia, gives us a sense of this imperative:

> The Arab ... is eager for progress ... Civilisation and government are eagerly looked for ... Oil pumps and machinery are eagerly used, while the military organization of labour and native craft have proved the Arab to be a first-class worker ... The farmers, and even the marsh Arabs, have hurried to work on roads and railways.[179]

The camp under military guard was described as the site where Arab, Persian and Kurdish labour was being moulded to habits of steady work and sanitary living, although at one camp in Kut men from the Arab Labour Corps had decamped 'at the rate of a 100 a day ... scared of de-lousing and inoculation.'[180]

---

[176] F&P, Secret, War, February 1917, nos 235–66.

[177] A detachment of the 11th Bombay JLC was deployed to break a strike of Arab labourers employed in brick-making. 'History', 11th Bombay JLC, p. 3. In August 1918, the Deputy Assistance Director of Labour on the Persian road demanded that one ILC break strikes held by local labourers. TNA WO 95/4991. In September 1919, the Arab Labour Corps was released to bring in the date harvest, their work being taken up by the Indian and Persian Labour Corps. 'Labour in "Mespot"', *TOI*, 30 September 1919, p. 12.

[178] Despite drastic differences of opinion about the advisability of settling Indians in Mesopotamia, it was accepted that these were careful agriculturalists in contrast to the nomadic 'Buddoo'. Martin Swayne, author and doctor, declared that Arabs had long feared the incursions of Indians, 'for they knew that the India farmer under the British engineers would make Mesopotamia blossom like a rose.' Martin Swayne (Maurice Nicoll), *In Mesopotamia*, London: Hodder and Stoughton, 1917, p. 161.

[179] MacMunn, 'The Land Between the Rivers'.

[180] 20 October 1919, TNA WO 95/5026. A newspaper commented on the remark-

British 'Arabists', resistant to the Government of India's policy interventions in Iraq, held that there was an affinity of humour and masculine independence which created common ground between Briton and Arab—the 'real' outsider was the Indian.[181] Thus, when the San Remo Conference confirmed on 25 April 1920 that Iraq had been handed over to Britain as a 'Class A mandate' and an uprising broke out, some British MPs blamed all the unrest on Arab hostility towards Indians. The Earl Winterton said that Arabs harboured a 'colour prejudice' against Indians, leading to friction with the Indian garrison.[182] Similarly, William Ormsby-Gore said that British officers and troops were 'perhaps less alien' to the Arab than the Indian, so the solution to unrest was to build an Arab army.[183] Such declarations proved such an embarrassment in India that the Civil Commissioner Arnold Wilson had to send a telegram stating he had 'seen little or nothing to justify the statement made at home regarding the prejudice of Arabs against Indians'. He acknowledged that Indian railway, telegraph and postal employees had rendered 'notable service' during the uprising—they had remained and died at their posts.[184]

Work and Wastage

The command structure

At first, the Indian Porter Corps was placed under the Director of Supplies and Transport, the Indian Labour Corps under the Director of Military Works, and

---

able transformation in the sanitary habits of Persian labourers within the well-kept lines of their military camp. 'Labour in "Mespot"', *TOI*, 30 September 1919, p. 12. Egan claimed that Arabs who had never worked before were working now with 'rapidity and cheerfulness'. Egan, *The War in the Cradle of the World*, p. 105. Gertrude Bell declared that Arab labour, handled properly, compared favourably with the Indian Labour Corps. Bell, *Review of the Civil Administration of Mesopotamia*, p. 20.

[181] 'The Indian as a rule is easier to handle', wrote General Haldane, but he lacked the sense of humour of the Kurd and the Arab, and 'suffered from a want of stamina'. Aylmer Haldane, *The Insurrection in Mesopotamia, 1920*, London: Blackwood, 1922, p. 109. For General MacMunn, on the other hand, it was the Turk and the Chinese, both 'almond-eyed' outsiders, who had to be excluded from Iraq. MacMunn, 'The Land Between Two Rivers'.

[182] *HC, Deb, 23 June 1920, vol. 130, nos 2223–85.*

[183] Ibid.

[184] Wilson, *Mesopotamia 1917–1920*, p. 317.

local labour units under the Department of Labour.[185] On 24 October 1917 the Department of Labour, now renamed the Directorate of Labour, was authorised to advise on the allocation of all labour, Indian and local, and in June 1918 it took control of all labour units. European officers selected for the Indian Labour and Porter Corps were expected to have some 'experience in handling native labour'.[186] Many were drawn from pools of Europeans employed in India in the police, the railways, the Public Works Department, and tea estates.[187] However, the combination of illness and frequent transfers meant that in some labour units a lot rested on the Indian regimental clerk and the Indian *subedar*, a Viceroy's Commissioned Officer. The establishment list of an ILC in Mesopotamia also included two civilian overseers.[188]

Diary entries for the ILC and IPC in Mesopotamia are very brief. However, from Commanding Officers concerned about the high rate of 'wastage' we get glimpses of relentless work in a harsh environment, with pitifully inadequate winter clothing and frequent ration shortages telling on the health of the men. At Basra in 1916 the 1st Madras Porter Corps unloaded supplies in day and night shifts through blistering heat, exposed sometimes to shelling along the riverfront. 'The attitude regarding the men of my unit as "niggers"', complained their CO, 'without a sense of feeling, who should be beaten and worked to a "stand-still" is wrong in every way.'[189] In September 1917 the CO noted that this unit had been on active service for two years without a single free day.[190] By this time, due to sickness and death only 200 men remained of the original 1,000 recruited from the Madras Presidency.[191] Lieutenant M. M. Knight, a tea-planter from southern India commanding a detachment of the 1st Madras Labour Corps, reported in October 1918 that a great number of his men, cutting with bruised hands through shingle and gypsum to extend the Khanikin railway, had 'no boots at all, and only one blanket apiece', though the temperature was below fifty degrees.[192]

---

[185] Home, Political, B, February 1917, nos 353–96.

[186] *RLD*, pp. 10, 12.

[187] In 1918, the Department of Labour began to give Indian Army Reserve Officer commissions to British NCOs.

[188] There were no civilian overseers sent with the ILC to France.

[189] TNA WO/95/5039.

[190] Ibid.

[191] Ibid.

[192] TNA WO 95/5277.

In 1916, and again during the Arab uprising of spring and summer 1920, the men of the ILC and IPC were exposed to combat situations. But bodies without any protective gear or proper training were also vulnerable to work accidents. In the 12th Burma Jail Porter Corps five men died when a Stokes mortar shell was put unwittingly into a forge in a bid to turn it into a dumbbell. Left in ignorance about these 'pieces of cyclindrical iron' lying around their camp, they had also been using mortar shells as mallets to drive in tent pegs.[193] In the 7th IPC, one man had his hand amputated in an accident, another lost his left hand in an explosion, and seventeen were injured in a separate ammunition explosion.[194] Outdoor work in the cold and the wet and a continuous insufficiency of warm clothing meant that large numbers were felled by respiratory disease.[195] Disruptions in the supply chain affected everyone. British personnel subtly communicated news of shortages through fervent thank you notes for gift packages.[196] However, race and institutional hierarchy mediated access to whatever there was in the way of food, warm clothing, and medical care. The heavy incidence of scurvy among Indian soldiers and followers was attributed to the deficiency in field rations compared to the British other ranks, particularly in the allocation of potatoes and meat.[197] Commanding Officers of the ILC and IPC complained regularly about ragged uniforms, inadequate footwear, delays in the provision of warm clothing and blankets and the total absence of any medical care at scattered worksites.

Skilling labour

The working experience of the men of the Indian Labour and Porter Corps in Mesopotamia was riven by the paradoxes of setting up the infrastructure for

---

[193] 'History', 12th Burma JPC, appendix 1, p. 10.

[194] Entries, 30 August 1917, 19 March 1918, 16 July 1918, TNA WO/95/5026.

[195] TNA WO/95/5278, TNA WO/95/5026.

[196] '[M]any a half-naked soldier', wrote the CO of the 1/6th Devons at Dujailan on 30 August 1916, had the ladies of England and India to thank for 'the shirt he wears today and washes tomorrow.' Thanking the Madras War Fund for towels, cheroots, tea, and Horlicks, the first gift package they had received, the CO of the 1st Madras Porter Corps added, 'Any further gifts will be gratefully received.' 2 November 1916, *Madras War Fund, Report of Transactions to 31 March 1917*, TNSA.

[197] W. H. Willcox, 'The Treatment and Management of Disease Due to Deficiency of Diet: Scurvy and Beri-beri', *The British Journal of Medicine*, vol. 1, no. 3081 (1920), pp. 73–77. There was a high incidence of scurvy among the men of the 10th Punjab Corps. In a Corps of 1,180 men, 250 casualties were reported for the first five months due to sickness, death and desertion. 'History', 10th Punjab JLC, p. 2.

occupation in conditions of extreme infrastructural backwardness. Yet the context for this was one in which oil, the new global fuel, was transforming both warfare and everyday life.[198] Given the scarcity of wood in Mesopotamia and the fact that coal haulage took up too much labour and valuable shipping space, oil in one form or another penetrated the work life of Indian followers. Crude oil fired the cooking-stoves in Arab, Indian and Persian labour camps, and left its reek in their food. The military sweeper 'toiled with his kerosene tins and brushes', and the *bhisti*, the water-carrier, put his *massakh* (leather bag) aside and filled up kerosene tins with water.[199] In India, fuel costs lessened the use of incinerators to dispose of waste. In Mesopotamia, the journalist Eleanor Egan marked the round mud domes of incinerators among the serried ranks of military huts at Basra.[200]

It was not just engineers from the railways, irrigation projects and Public Works Department in India who brought their technological expertise to occupied Iraq.[201] Clusters of men in the Indian Labour and Porter Corps revealed skills acquired on docks and construction sites in India.[202] The 18th ILC arrived in Mesopotamia in August 1918 and was put to work on the Khalisi canal, and by 25 October 1918 it had '50 trained drillers, a party of light railway men, over 100 of some skill in rock work and the bulk hardening up as diggers and carvers of earth.'[203]

Sometimes skill in Indian labour was viewed as an ethnic attribute rather than something acquired by application, prompting declarations such as the following: 'The Pathan ... is the best digger in the Punjabi Corps'.[204] If skill was a hereditary characteristic, then by implication higher wages were not called for. However, quarrymen enrolled in the 101st Indian Labour Corps, raised

---

[198] Dan Tamir, 'Something New under the Fog of War', in Richard P. Tucker, Tait Keller, J. R. McNeill and Martin Schmid (eds), *Environmental Histories of the First World War*, Cambridge: Cambridge University Press, 2018, pp. 117–35.

[199] 'Labour in "Mespot"', *TOI*, 30 September 1919, p. 12; *RLD*, p. 8; Swayne, *In Mesopotamia*.

[200] Egan, *The War in the Cradle of the World*, pp. 113–14. See illustration No. 9.

[201] Even as late as 1920, the Public Works Department was being drawn on for skilled workmen and draftsmen for Mesopotamia.

[202] The 12th Burma JPC, later the 148th Burma JLC, had 300 carpenters in addition to masons and other artisans. TNA WO/95/5038.

[203] War diary entry, 25 October 1918, TNA WO/95/5038.

[204] *RLD*, p. 27.

for rock-cutting, blasting and road construction in southern Persia, had to be offered a higher monthly wage of Rs. 25/– at the very outset.[205] Some IPC units were speedily shifted to a more diverse range of tasks, in part because Arab labourers around Basra refused to go out into the desert so had to be reserved for haulage. This relieved the monotony of porterage, but their wages did not rise from Rs. 15/– to Rs. 20/– until they were formally recategorised as an ILC unit.[206] Brigadier Frost, the Director of Labour, ruled that the formal conversion of a Porter Corps into a Labour Corps was a reward which had to be earned.[207]

Nevertheless, the Mesopotamian theatre offered some men entry into new fields such as electrical work, motor mechanics and the maintenance of oil-driven pumps and engines.[208] 150 men from the 5th United Provinces Jail Porter Corps sent to the Electricity and Mechanical Section learnt to fix wiring and electric lights and fans, and some became blacksmiths and fitters.[209] The Government of India also arranged for training camps and trade certification to raise skill levels. Month-long courses were offered at railway camps set up at Puri, Tirupattur and Monghyr to train labourers in track-laying, first in Mesopotamia and then, in 1919, along the North-West Frontier. Recruits were promised that after a year's service they would receive a trade certificate.[210] Men of the ILC who had acquired certain skills used this point of re-engagement to seek higher paid positions as artisans.[211]

---

[205] IOR/L/MIL/7/18558.

[206] When the 8th Indian JPC was converted into the 145th JLC, some men were reclassified as carpenters, masons, and blacksmiths and began to get higher wages. TNA WO/95/5038.

[207] Director of Labour, 2 November 1918, 6th JPC, TNA WO/95/5026.

[208] 'History', 5th United Provinces JPC, p. 3.

[209] Ibid.

[210] Terms of service for road and railway work in Mesopotamia were published in English and in the vernacular in the village sheets of district gazetteers. Public Dept, GO, no. 669, 23 May 1917, TNSA. After the war, the denial of trade certification became one of the means of disciplining Indian labour in the Persian Gulf—so, too, did the threat of deportation, even if no criminal offence had been committed.

[211] For Indian sub-overseers in the Works Department, see *History of the Corps of Royal Engineers*, vol. VII, Chatham: The Institute of Royal Engineers, 1952, pp. 76–78. For a reference to Persian-speaking Indian overseers on the Persian road, see GOC 'D' to Secy, WO, 30 September 1918, WW1/273/H, vol. 1, pt II, 16–31 October 1918, diary no. 86805.

The social diversity of men in the Jail Labour and Porter Corps permitted the replacement in Mesopotamia of free clerks, warders, and artisans with jail recruits.[212] Social standing allowed some prisoners to take greater advantage of this situation than others. Ex-soldiers and the occasional ex-policeman were selected as convict officers almost as a matter of course, and European prisoners were selected as convict clerks with a monthly salary of Rs. 30/–.[213] The added advantage of jail recruitment was that men were already attuned to the discipline of a daily timetable, and to a structure of command through the figure of the jail-recruited warder. Many also had previous experience in extramural penal labour in India.[214]

Time-work, task-work, piecework

Fleeting entries in war diaries reveal that the issues on which the men of the Labour and Porter Corps spoke out were the scale of their daily task, the length of the working day, and the duration of their contract. A fixed monthly wage, unrelated to a measurable output, was unusual for Indian labour.[215] When conditions were stable, the men in the ILC and IPC worked for eight and a half to nine hours daily, and ten during a night shift.[216] The actual working day was much longer due to long treks from camp to worksite and a four-hour midday break to shelter from the blazing sun.[217] On construction sites, where the men were strung out in small parties, it was difficult to intensify the pace of work. One Captain Mathews of the 8th United Provinces Jail Porter

---

[212] The free warders often came reluctantly, were termed 'useless', and were sent back. Home, Jails, B, November 1917, no. 13. By 1918, with the exception of the 11th Bombay JLC, all the jail units were reliant entirely on jail-recruited warders. 'Summary', p. 4.

[213] Home, Jails, B, November 1917, no. 13; 'History', 6th Punjab JLC, p. 4, para. 11.

[214] General, 1916–17, no. 90, pt II, MSA.

[215] However, when the demand for labour was high then employers in India did prefer to pay by the week or the month, but held the payment in arrears.

[216] In October 1917, when work hours were raised from forty-eight hours a week to fifty-four, the CO of the 2nd Punjab ILC noted disapprovingly that this did away with the much-needed weekly rest day. 12 October 1917, TNA WO/95/5036.

[217] The work hours for the 7th IPC were 5.30am to 10am and 4pm to 10pm, which is eight and a half hours with a six-hour interval. TNA WO 95/5026. At one point, men of the 145 United Provinces JLC (formerly 5th United Provinces JPC) had to walk seven miles to their worksite and seven miles back. TNA WO 95/5038.

Corps tried to foster *esprit de corps* by urging work gangs to lay small bets and compete for a higher output.[218] In other contexts, gambling was punished as an offence on the grounds that it broke down hierarchy, dissipated savings, and encouraged theft.[219] Another method, also explored in labour units in France, was to induce the men to work harder by the promise of 'earning' leisure.[220] The length of the day was increased for the 6th Jail Porter Corps, to allow them to 'earn' one day off in seven. But the new daily task was so demanding that the men either could not or would not complete it, and they asked for a return to the seven-day week.[221]

The more successful strategy was to allow the men to top up their monthly wage by paying them for piecework, at the same rate as for local labour, after they had completed a fixed daily task. This experiment began with the Jail Corps, but in June 1918 it was extended to all Indian Labour and Porter Corps.[222] The Labour Directorate argued that the difficulty of securing labour had made it necessary to offer fixed monthly wages, but this was an arrangement 'most unsuitable for men of the coolie class' because of 'the Indian's natural tendency to consider himself a pensioner'.[223] Given that prices were spiralling in both India and Mesopotamia, the bonus system operated as a useful drag on the wage bill while increasing output.[224]

The uses of 'rest' time

Rest days were few and far between.[225] Time opened up if the weather was too harsh, or if the next assignment was stalled, but then there was the necessity

---

[218] 'History', 8th United Provinces JPC, p. 4. A case of robbing Peter to pay Paul?

[219] 'History', 12th Burma JPC, appendix IV, p. 11; 'History', 11th Bombay JLC.

[220] The CO of the 2nd Punjab ILC pointed out that when work was fixed by task rather than by the length of the work day, his men would work in the middle of the day to save an hour for themselves in the evening. 12 October 1917, TNA WO 95/5036. Lights out was at 8pm. 4 May 1917, TNA WO 95/5277.

[221] 22 March 1918, 6 March 1918, no. 1, Military Prisoner Labour Company, TNA WO 95/5008.

[222] 'History', 11th Bombay JLC, p. 2; *RLD*, p. 25.

[223] *RLD*, p. 12.

[224] Ibid. It is interesting, nevertheless, that labourers tested contractual honesty by hanging back to check whether the extra payment would be withdrawn once their work speeded up.

[225] Of the 1st Madras Porter Corps, which had left Madras in September 1915, their

of delousing, bathing and cleaning the camp. A major religious festival secured a reprieve from work, but only for labourers of the relevant denomination. The 10th Madras Jail Porter Corps set aside Muslim and Sikh places of worship.[226] Christian carpenters from Chota Nagpur described a 'very large and beautiful' wooden church they were building.[227] Men offered each other the consolation of their gods. A Tamil Christian in the Artisan Corps read the story of Christ healing palsy to a sick Hindu carpenter, who then sent Rs. 5/- to the Wesleyan church in Hyderabad.[228] A prominent feature of the war publicity emanating from the European theatre was respectful attention to the disposal of the dead, each according to their religious creed, but there is little of that sort of literature from Mesopotamia.[229] One account of the Inland Water Transport in Mesopotamia declared that scrupulous care was taken to bury or cremate those who died.[230] But letters from APOC employees complained of the denial of spiritual needs: 'Muhammadans are burnt by Hindus and Hindus have been buried by Mahomendans etc. When protest has been made the usual reply "It is Field Service" "what does [it matter?] when man is dead".[231]

CO noted in September 1917 that '[t]his Corps has been on active service for two years without a single free day.' TNA WO 95/5039.

[226] 'History', 10th Madras JPC, p. 5.

[227] *Chota Nagpur Diocesan Paper*, October 1917, Bishop's Lodge, Ranchi. Ten Indian chaplains were sanctioned for Mesopotamia.

[228] *Seventy-Eighth Annual Report of the Wesleyan Mission in the Mysore Province*, Mysore: Wesleyan Mission Press, 1918, pp. 12–13.

[229] See S. Hyson and A. Lester, 'British India on Trial: Brighton Military Hospitals and the Politics of Empire in World War I', *Journal of Historical Geography*, vol. 38, no. 1 (2001), pp. 18–34.

[230] Hall, *The Inland Water Transport*, p. 125. A photograph titled 'Hindus of an Indian Army Labour or Supply and Transport Unit prepare to cremate the body of a dead comrade in Baghdad' shows men standing around a corpse laid out on a few palm tree logs. The tone is sombre, and attentive, but there is no suggestion of an institutional framework. IWM photograph, HU 104981, S. K. Fletcher (private) collection.

[231] Letter to Shaukat Ali, with 'copy to Lala Lajpat Rai, Dr Ansari, Mr Mazharal Haq, Babu Bepin Chandra Pal, C. R. Das, Esq., Maulana Shaukat Ali' published by Mahatma Gandhi in *Young India*, 27 April 1921. Home, Political, B, June 1921, nos 285–86. The *Arya Gazette* complained that the APOC made no arrangement for Hindu cremation, whereas a priest came for Christian funerals. Indian employees of the APOC complained to the *Bande Mataram* about ill treatment and a disregard for their religious beliefs. *Punjab Press Abstracts*, 19 February 1921, no. 8.

Some Commanders tried to organise group games such as football. The YMCA provided the occasional lantern slide lecture and played gramophone records.[232] However, when the 10th Punjab Jail Labour Corps got 25 and 26 December off, they asked for a 'real "loaf" and rest' in preference to sports or a *tamasha* (an entertainment programme).[233] The kind of unsupervised, unstructured time the men yearned for is often to be discovered in lists of offences—gambling, smoking hemp, and absence without leave.

Taking advantage of a more stationary post, the 10th Madras Jail Porter Corps set up a 'Madras Dramatic Society' and performed Tamil and Kanarese plays.[234] Theatricals and skits were the medium through which sepoys and labourers could assume a variety of other roles, low-caste followers could display their creativity, officers could be parodied, race could be changed, and 'women' could materialise in highly masculine spaces. In one publicity photograph the men of an Indian Porter Corps at Kut squat in a circle, one taps a drum, and three twirl around in sheets impersonating women. It is a bare bones spectacle, not a very successful advertisement for service in Mesopotamia, but revealing of the consolations of the imagination.[235] Describing a burlesque by Indian soldiers in Mesopotamia, one officer noted that just as a white man blackened his face, so the brown man whitened his to play a British officer or a memsahib.[236] Performance provided the opportunity for soldiers and labourers to engage in subtle dialogues with their audience, and even with officers in that audience, hinting at opinions which might otherwise get them into trouble. Shortly after severe sentences were handed out for a short half-day strike by some men of the 11th Bombay Jail Labour Corps, the 8th Jail Porter Corps put on a play which Lane watched. When the villain of the narrative pleaded for mercy, he received the following response from the King: '*Rahim Kamzuri ki nishan hai*' ('mercy is a sign of weakness').[237] Had the performer dared to mime, even to critique, the harsh stance taken by Lane? Open mimicry was of course

---

[232] Harald Fischer-Tiné, '"Unparalleled Opportunities": The Indian Y.M.C.A.'s Army Work Schemes for Imperial Troops During the Great War (1914–1920)', *The Journal of Imperial and Commonwealth History*, vol. 47, no. 1 (2019), pp. 100–37.

[233] 'History', 10th Punjab JLC, p. 4. *Tamasha:* a performance, a spectacle.

[234] Ibid., p. 5.

[235] 'Outdoor theatre of Indian Porter Corps at Kut', Imperial War Museum (IW), photograph Q24574.

[236] Arthur Nyton Peckham, 14 March 1917, IOR, Mss Eur. D078.

[237] 'Summary', p. 12, para. 15.

one of the deadliest insults a prisoner could offer, but Lane chose to interpret this dialogue as proof of a lesson well learnt.[238]

For resourceful individuals, everyday performance was a means by which the stigmatising disciplines of the Jail Corps could be converted into the more honourable disciplines of a military formation. Some of the men took pleasure in acquiring a soldierly bearing, and styling their headgear and clothes in a way which suggested military service. Of a stretcher-bearer from the Bombay Jail Corps, Lane noted disapprovingly:

> No. 5 was wearing a red and blue band with a fringe to his *pagri* and would have easily been taken as belonging to a regiment. There have already been instances of habituals impersonating Indian officers in this Force, and so, any attempt at being anything more than what the corps is, viz. a Labour formation, must be stopped.[239]

Lane was always on the lookout for such signs of presumption.[240] Performance was also a crucial element in plans for escape, as in the case of four men who disguised themselves as telephone-fitters and covered quite some distance pretending to repair the line before their detection.[241]

Labour units under military discipline

> The Germans made us take to gas and it seems as if the bombing of towns will have to be done ... in the same way the convict is doing all he can to make us ... have more of the prison out here than was intended.[242]

Tabular statistics of offences and punishments are available only for the Jail Corps, and these paint a dark picture. In September 1917, wanting to issue an inspiring press communiqué, the Madras government asked for information on the 10th Madras Jail Porter Corps, but backed away hurriedly because of a

---

[238] Of the strike of 4 December 1918, Lane had noted that when the men saw themselves surrounded by British soldiers with bayonets, 'they became insulting, offensive and mimicked orders ... It was now my time to have no mercy'. 'History', 11th Bombay JLC, p. 6, para. 6.

[239] 'History', 11th Bombay JLC, p. 4. *Pagri*: turban.

[240] Yet he had hailed the repatriation of 'useless' civilian officials and warders, and the shift to a reliance on largely jail-recruited warders and overseers.

[241] 'History', 11th Bombay JLC, p. 10, appendix 10.

[242] W. B. Lane, report on 10th Madras JPC, 8 October 1917, in Home, Judicial, GO, no. 2466, 27 November 1917, TNSA.

dismaying account of sickness and frequent flogging.[243] We do not have similar statistics for the 'free' ILC and IPC, but going by the qualitative evidence of their war diaries, fines and flogging were not used so relentlessly. Nor did they present any serious disciplinary issues until the Armistice, when they became restive due to long delays in repatriation and the rearrangement of units which disrupted their support systems.[244] Officers of the Jail Corps complained that, due to the innate nature of jail-recruited men, they were much more burdened than those who commanded a 'free' Corps.[245] The fact was that a regime based on labour servitude required a high degree of routine violence to keep it in place.[246]

Commanding officers of Indian labour units, both in Mesopotamia and in France, were able to draw upon two distinctive features of the Indian Army Act. One was the summary court-martial, in which the Commanding Officer was the sole judge; the other was the retention of flogging as one of the penalties which could be dealt out to rank-and-file soldiers and followers, even though it was abolished for the British soldier in 1881. The standard explanation for these two 'peculiarities' of Indian as opposed to British military law was that with an 'oriental soldiery' the commanding officer had to wield a large measure of summary authority to sustain his personal charisma.[247] At the same time, to maintain the standing of military service, it was used sparingly.[248] With the follower ranks and labour units, particularly with jail labour, there was no such status inhibition. However, in World War One the need to keep manpower 'in the field' meant that even the 'rarely flogged' Indian sepoy and cavalryman became more vulnerable to corporal punishment.[249] In

---

[243] Home, Judicial, GO, no. 2466, 27 November 1917, TNSA. Fines were also frequent, but only up to a quarter of a man's monthly pay.

[244] See war diary for the 1st Madras ILC (earlier the 1st Madras IPC). TNA WO 95/5277/9. However, there was some variation between jail units. The discipline in the 10th Madras JPC was described as very good, even though the percentage of invaliding back to India was as high as 21.9 per cent. 'History', 10th Madras JPC, p. 6.

[245] 'Summary', appendix 5, 'Offences'. Lane commented: 'The number of offences will appear appalling to those unaccustomed to jails'.

[246] There are no consolidated statistics for offences in the 'free' ILC and IPC. I have made a qualitative comparison based on war diaries.

[247] Singha, 'The "Rare Infliction"'.

[248] Ibid. See also General, 1917–18, no. 1284, MSA.

[249] Singha, 'The "Rare Infliction"'. Sentences of over three months' imprisonment had to be carried out in India. 'Summary', p. 3.

France, the flogging of Indian soldiers or followers had sometimes posed an embarrassment.[250] East of the Mediterranean, in Egypt, Palestine and Mesopotamia, the sight of 'native' labourers being flogged was passed off more easily as a 'traditional' method of managing labour gangs.[251] However, it was the sound rather than the sight of 'natives' being flogged which the irrigation engineer George Buchanan recalled of his service in Mesopotamia. Hearing some 'extraordinary noises' at lunch in the officers' mess in Basra, he was told that the room where corporal punishment was administered was next door. His informant added:

> that they had grown so knowledgeable ... that they could tell from the nature of the cries whether the sufferer was an Arab, Persian, or Indian. The man who flogged was an extraordinarily robust sergeant, and at the end ... marched off whistling a hymn tune, 'The voice that breathed o'er Eden' being a favourite.[252]

At first, Commanding Officers of both 'free' and Jail Labour Corps in Mesopotamia simply handed down a flogging for various 'misdemeanours'. On frontier expeditions porters were summarily caned, and superintendents of Indian jails had considerable discretion to order the corporal punishment of prisoners.[253] But the military authorities objected, pointing out that as the men were enrolled under the Indian Army Act a summary court-martial had to be convened to pass sentence.[254] Lane felt that flogging alone was not suf-

---

250 See Singha, 'The "Rare Infliction"'.

251 'A desert canteen', in *Wanganui Chronicle*, LX, 16852, 4 January 1917, p. 6, paper-spast.natlib.govt.nz, last accessed 15 November 2019; Cecil Sommers, *Temporary Crusaders*, London: John Lane, 1919. The Levantine presence in the Zion Mule Corps at Alexandria made it acceptable to use flogging in this unit too. Jewish Virtual Library, http://www.jewishvirtuallibrary.org, last accessed 15 November 2019.

252 George Buchanan, *The Tragedy of Mesopotamia*, Edinburgh: William Blackwood and Sons, 1938, p. 108. Under the 'Iraq Occupied Territories Code' of 1915, the military administration had applied the Indian Whipping Act of 1864 then shifted to its modified 1908 version. In 1920, there was a discussion about whether this provision for flogging could be retained in the transition to a civil administration. Some held that flogging was the only way to deal with thefts by Persian coolies and 'professional thieves' around military areas and the railways. One Inspector General of Jails with long experience in India (probably W. B. Lane, in fact) was stated to be in favour of its retention. IOR/L/S/11/160, file 7510.

253 See 'Summary', p. 3, para. 4.

254 'Summary', p. 12, para. 15; also 'History', 10th Punjab JLC, p. 8.

ficient: 'Flogging to a prisoner, especially a habitual, has very little effect, because it is a code of honour with them to take it without a murmur. One also runs a risk of the man being openly impertinent after it or being "dumbly insolent" by saluting and walking off.'[255] In search of a longer, slower punishment, he proposed that labourers sentenced to terms of imprisonment be made to go on working but in fetters. However, under military law prisoners could be fettered only if their offence was one punishable by death.[256] In May 1917, the Army Commander agreed that men of the Labour and Porter Corps found guilty of desertion could be made to work in shackles for six months. However, fetters hampered work, so Lane set up a 'Disciplinary Camp' in Kut—a barbed wire enclosure within which a harsh regimen of brick-making was instituted.[257] All Indians sentenced to imprisonment were sent to this camp, where they wore prison clothes and worked without pay.[258]

Desertion figured prominently among the offences tried by summary court-martial and summary general court-martial in the Jail Corps.[259] Some commanding officers of the Jail Corps protested when the long sentences of imprisonment they handed out to 'habitual' deserters were reduced substantially by the higher military authorities.[260] The latter's understanding was that labourers did not fully understand the seriousness of this offence.[261] Yet the death penalty was awarded for some 'flagrant' cases of desertion in the Jail Corps.[262]

---

[255] Ibid.

[256] Summary', p. 3; 'History', 10th Punjab JLC, p. 8.

[257] 'A short history of the Disciplinary Camp, Kut', in 'Summary'. There are images here which parallel the descriptions later circulated of Indian and British prisoners of war making bricks and breaking rocks in the Taurus Mountains.

[258] 'Summary', p. 3.

[259] In the 5th United Provinces, JPC desertion accounted for 180 out of 223 major offences. 'History', 5th UP JPC. Appendix 4, p. 8.

[260] War diary, 145th JLC, WO 95/5083, file 3.

[261] 'Summary', p. 3; TNA WO 95/5038. For this complaint, see 'History', 10th Punjab JLC, appendix III, p. 9 and diary entry, 8 November 1917, TNA WO 95/5278.

[262] 'Summary', p. 3, para. 4. Cases in which men were hung for desertion: one in the 6th Punjab JLC; one in the 10th Punjab JLC, 29 September 1917; one in the 12th Burma JPC, of a man who had deserted twice before. One man who had deserted from the 10th Punjab JLC on two previous occasions was deemed a 'habitual' and shot. Collated from 'Summary'.

Desertion

'all of them made queer and incoherent statements'[263]

Some jail-recruited men tried to escape at the very outset. Travelling down to Bombay, the men of the 5th United Provinces Jail Porter Corps pulled the train communication cord 'no less than seven times', and by the end of the journey seven of them were missing.[264] Overland pilgrim routes to India and *dhow* traffic along the Persian Gulf which swelled during the date season facilitated flight.[265] Niches for shelter also opened up within the burgeoning military construction complex in Iraq and southern Persia. An Indian Christian from the 6th Punjab Jail Labour Corps was discovered as one Abdur Rahman at Muhammera, where a large Indian colony had come up for the oil works.[266] Mickie, a jail-recruited European clerk with the 12th Burma Jail Labour Corps, deserted and joined the civil police at Amara. He was detected only because he embezzled money there.[267] The pressure under which labourers and followers had been dispatched to Mesopotamia resulted in a general looseness of documentation that was useful to the deserter.[268] Many convicts had been sent off without a verification of their residential address.[269] However, many escapes also ended in death or recapture. 'An Indian deserter, presumably from the Mesopotamian Labour Corps,' reported a consular officer in Persia, 'was brought in yesterday in the last stage of exhaustion, and died from exposure and hunger without being able to state his identity.'[270]

---

[263] CO's note, December 1918, describing the response of the deserters from the 145th JLC whom he questioned. However, the diary had noted the daily march of seven miles to the worksite, along with inadequate rations and hard work. TNA WO 95/5038, file 3.

[264] 'History', 5th United Provinces JPC, p. 1.

[265] F&P May 1916, nos 463–78; F&P (Secret) War, B, December 1918, nos 51–52; Albert Charles Wratislaw, *A Consul in the East*, London: Blackwood, 1924, pp. 162–63.

[266] 'History', 6th Punjab JLC, p. 7.

[267] 'History', 12th Burma JPC, p. 1.

[268] Army, War, 1916–17, B, nos 35936–38, nos 49801–54, and appendix.

[269] F&P, Secret, War, B, December 1918, nos 51–52.

[270] File 52/1912, pt 3, 'Persia Diaries' [372v] (755/1128), IOR/L/PS/10/211, in QDL.

[271] January 1919, 6th JPC TNA WO/95/5026. On 10 January 1919, men of the 10th Punjab JLC suspended work on an embankment at Ruz, complaining in an 'orderly way' of a poor measurement of tasks and of being overworked. TNA WO/95/5037.

An impressionistic comparison of war diaries suggests that the incidence of desertion was much higher for the jail as compared to the 'free' labour and porter units. Is this difference self-explanatory? Officers of the Jail Corps attributed desertion not to any innate desire to escape, but to harsh conditions of work. Between the emergency duty often imposed on jail recruits and the piecework they undertook to pull up their wages, there was an inbuilt tendency to overtask them. A detachment of the 6th Jail Porter Corps expressed its 'dissatisfaction' when in addition to a ten-hour working day on jetty construction at Abadan they were also expected to load and unload steamers at night.[271] The only way to get some relief was to absent oneself and face a flogging, or to desert. In the 5th United Provinces Jail Porter Corps, out of 223 major offences 180 were for 'desertion' and for being 'absent without leave'. Captain W. S. Dickens attributed a rush of seventy-five desertions from this Corps simply 'to the men getting tired and wanting a rest'.[272] Captain McGrath blamed desertions from the 12th Burma Jail Labour Corps on the want of opium—that is, to the want of a substance which would take the edge off the men's exhaustion.[273] The Mashad intelligence summary for 25 August 1917 reported that deserters from the ILC had 'one and all assigned the same cause for their action—(a) the withholding of their pay by native officers and NCOs; (b) harsh treatment involving frequent beatings by the latter.'[274] The 'NCOs' in the Jail Corps were the jail-recruited warders whose position depended on their ability to ensure that work was completed. Another reason for desertion was a complaint common to all Indian units, combatant and non-combatant, who were serving on 'duration of war' engagements—years of service away from home without any leave.[275]

---

[272] 'Summary', appendix 4, p. 16. Overwork left its mark on this Corps. It had the second highest death rate, at 6.95 per cent for thirty-four months, the highest invaliding rate, at 35.46 per cent, and the highest figures for offences punished by court-martial. Ibid. The largest percentage of 'Major offences' were for 'Desertion and Absent without Leave', 'Summary', passim.

[273] 'History', 12th Burma JPC, appendix III, p. 11. The men had been confined to the lines and put on very heavy road work, and 'opium subjects, who were without it … could not stand the strain and became desperate.' Ibid.

[274] File 52/1912, pt 3, 'Persia Diaries' [372v] (755/1128), IOR/L/PS/10/211, and file 52/1912, pt 3, 'Persia Diaries' [331v] (673/1128), IOR/L/PS/10/211, in QDL.

[275] When some labourers of the free 2nd Punjab ILC did not return home from a short leave, the CO blamed this on their having served for two and a half years without any leave. TNA WO 95/5036.

The alternative form of escape was, to use Mark Harrison's suggestive phrase, through the 'retreat into one's body'.[276] Convict labourers could not pass off self-inflicted injuries as war wounds but disabled themselves by other means—for instance, by injecting their legs with an infusion of jequirity seeds.[277] In the case of Indian soldiers, there were anxious and secretive investigations into rumours of self-injury.[278] For convicts, suspicion was open and routine. Lane held that the point of medical inspection was to root out 'malingerers'. He offers no comment on the high figures for illness and mortality in some of the Jail Corps.

The closer supervision and tighter restrictions considered appropriate for a jail-recruited corps also generated an extraordinary number of 'orderly room punishments'.[279] Referring to the high figure for 'minor offences'—'irregular conduct', leaving camp without permission, gambling, being 'found with prohibited articles'—one Commanding Officer concluded: 'At first they were unable to understand their semi-free position, and in some cases very severe punishment had to be exercised.'[280]

Under the Indian Army Act 'unnatural offences' were categorised as 'disgraceful conduct', the punishment for which was imprisonment or a lesser penalty.[281] 'Sex problems are always acute in convict life,' commented Lieutenant General Sir George F. MacMunn, 'and they are even more so in their Eastern aspects and altercations, and these naturally took a somewhat different angle in the semi-free atmosphere of the war-time labour encampments.'[282] However, even though

---

[276] Mark Harrison, 'Disease, Discipline and Dissent: The Indian Army in France and England, 1914–1915,' in Roger Cooter, Mark Harrison and Steve Sturdy et al. (eds), *Medicine and Modern Warfare*, Amsterdam: Atlanta, 1999, pp. 185–203. In military law, rendering oneself unfit was an illegal attempt to repossess one's body. To attempt suicide was to die for something other than the state.

[277] 'History', 6th Punjab JLC, p. 6. Porter Dhuke, 7th Indian Porter Corps, thirty lashes for 'producing a disease in himself', 30 August 1917, TNA WO/95/5026.

[278] Jeffrey Greenhut, 'The Imperial Reserve: The Indian Corps on the Western Front, 1914–15,' *The Journal of Imperial and Commonwealth History*, vol. 12, no. 1 (1983), pp. 54–73, 57–8.

[279] 'Summary', p. 16, appendix 5, 'Offences'.

[280] 'History', 10th Madras JPC, p. 8.

[281] Indian Army Act (Act VIII of 1911), section 31 (i), 'commits [or attempts to commit] any offence of a cruel, indecent or unnatural kind'.

[282] George F. MacMunn, *The Underworld of India*, London: Jarrolds, 1933, p. 192.

officers expected this 'perversity' to be especially prevalent in a Jail Corps, there was no great effort to detect or prevent such relationships. The cases listed are few and, except for four cases in the Bombay Jail Labour Corps defined as 'major' offences, are categorised as 'minor'.[283] What was risky was to lodge a charge of 'unnatural sexuality' against a superior officer, because the party who complained could be punished for a 'false accusation' if the charge collapsed.[284]

'Were we not promised to be free?'

The prisoner's path to 'rehabilitation'

What about rehabilitation, the other component of the 'experiment'? Prisoners had been told that by volunteering they would erase the stigma of jail and rise in public estimation. In fact, 'common usage' prevailed and the more euphemistic term 'Disciplinary Labour Corps' never caught on.[285] Men whose sentences would have expired had they stayed in India were retained in the Jail Corps, although on higher wages, instead of being transferred to a 'free' Labour Corps.[286] This circumvented the tasks of transferring papers, altering service books, and issuing new identity discs. But it also allowed the police in India to keep returning men under surveillance.[287] This penal tag also sustained Lane's claims to expertise in 'handling convicts'.

Convict labourers made their own efforts to efface the stigma of jail. The 10th Madras JPC complained about the label 'J', which was displayed on their khaki blouses.[288] A tally clerk was handled roughly by the 10th Punjab Jail

---

[283] 6th Punjab JLC: two cases; 8th United Provinces JPC: seven including attempts; 11th Bombay JLC: four cases. Were some of these incidents buried under the 'miscellaneous offences' charge—that is, as acts 'prejudicial to good order and military discipline'? Indian Army Act (Act VIII of 1911), section 39 (i).

[284] When an Indian NCO was acquitted of the charge of committing an 'unnatural offence', the men who made the complaint were given ten and twenty lashes for a false accusation. 14 May 1917. TNA WO 95/5277.

[285] 'Summary', p. 3.

[286] Lane supported this policy, arguing that if the men misbehaved, section 401 could be used to send them back to jail to serve their original sentences. 'Summary', p. 7, para. 10.

[287] Home, Jails, Deposit, October 1917, no. 1.

[288] 'Summary', p. 3, para. 3.

Porter Corps for calling them *kaidis*, or 'jailbirds'.[289] One 'minor offence' arising more frequently in a Jail Corps was refusing to wear identity discs—those for prisoners carried the stigmatising inscription 'JLC'.[290]

Some prisoners embraced the military framework to cast themselves in a different kind of relationship to the state—that of soldiers, rather than convict labourers. This aspiration to military status was probably most marked among prisoners who had been able to remove themselves from rough labour—stretcher-bearers such as the man that Lane complained about, and those selected as jail-recruited NCOs. For Lane, the figure of the jail-recruited warder or overseer and the 'habitual offender' overlapped. His own expertise, as he saw it, lay in knowing how to tap the initiative and agency of the 'habitual offender' without allowing him to get the upper hand.[291] Yet such was the reliance on jail-recruited overseers that despite Lane's misgivings about their mimicking of military command, they managed to secure a promotion for themselves—from *naik* to *havildar*.[292] Lane said he had originally chosen the term *daffadar*, from cavalry usage, because he wanted a distinct term for jail-recruited officers. 'Usage ... proved too strong' and the designation *havildar*, used in regular infantry units, became common.[293] In fact, *daffadar* was also the title used in Indian jails for the convict-recruited warder. Lane probably wanted to gloss over this fact because the excessive reliance on 'convict officers' was criticised as a very retrograde feature of the Indian jail regime.[294]

Prisoners tried to turn their forced encounter with the law and institutional life to their advantage in other ways. Lane complained about 'the legal mindedness of convicts' because of their efforts to use his inspection visits as an occasion to present petitions.[295] Ironically, these petitions often deployed the

---

[289] 'History', 6th Punjab JLC, p. 5.

[290] After some discussion, it was decided to put 'JLC' on identity discs instead of reserving this tag for service books. F&P, Internal, B, August 1918, nos 11–18. On one occasion, ninety-one men were fined for not wearing these discs. 'History', 8th United Provinces JLC, p. 11.

[291] 'Summary', p. 6, para. 8, and 'History', 11th Bombay JLC, pp. 4, 6. The legal criteria for categorising someone as a 'habitual offender' was the subject of continuous debate, but jail classification gave this figure a satisfying concreteness.

[292] 'History', 10th Punjab JLC, p. 3.

[293] 'History', 10th Punjab JLC, p. 4.

[294] *Report of the Indian Jails Committee, 1919–1920*, chapter VI.

[295] 'History', 10th Punjab JLC, p. 10. In India, convicts presented petitions to sessions judges during prison inspections.

language of contract. The prisoners repeatedly went back to that moment when they had been asked to 'volunteer' for Mesopotamia, insisting that it marked their emancipation to the status of 'free' labour. Lane had to keep reminding them that their sentences had been suspended, not remitted. And they would counter: 'Were we not promised to be free?'[296]

The more paternalist discourse that prisoners mobilised was the special bond which military service had established between the *sarkar* (the government) and those who had rallied to its call.[297] Lane noted indignantly that one Jail Corps 'seemed to think that they were conferring a favour on Government by coming out.'[298] He also complained that the habituals wanted an 'entire washout'—that is, to have their names removed from the police register in India.[299] Nevertheless, the Jail Corps had created a place for itself, and when fresh drafts were needed in 1917 some additional inducements, such as the remission of fines, were added.[300]

The most important way in which the jail-recruited labourer could erase his institutional past was through recourse to that all-encompassing category, 'Asiatic labour' or 'Eastern labour'. These were the labels commonly used to describe the jumble of followers, labour gangs, and *mistris* (artisans) in British-

---

[296] 'Summary', p. 7, para. 9.

[297] From the days of the East India Company, prisoners labouring on public works would claim that that they were *sarkar ke naukar*—that is, that they had entered the service of the ruling power, turning that entity into a patron who could be supplicated for concessions. Radhika Singha, *A Despotism of Law: Crime and Justice in Early Colonial India*, Delhi: Oxford University Press, 1998, pp. 274–75. Of course, such declarations also had their ironic inflections.

[298] 'History', 10th Punjab JLC, p. 10.

[299] 'Summary', p. 7. Nevertheless, when some men who had returned to India protested about rough handling by the police, an order was issued that they were not to be hauled up for failing to register their residence. '[I]t would be hard on a man who has done satisfactory military service and who would naturally think that he was a free man on return to India, to find that he had to undergo further police supervision.' Home, Department note, 11 May 1917, Home Jails, A, September 1917, nos 10–13.

[300] Home, Jails, B, September 1917, no. 6. As with recruitment of soldiers, the need to force the pace of manpower recruitment brought the family into view. In January 1918, the Bombay Government included the Jail Labour Corps in its scheme to give free primary education to children of soldiers and followers. General Department, 1917–18, no. 1284, pt I, MSA.

occupied Iraq.[301] Civil Commissioner Arnold Wilson's description shows that on the ground a blurring of the line between jail-recruited and 'free' labour was taking place:

> Thirty to forty languages could be heard in the bazaar. Among the latter under the strict but kindly supervision of Col. W. B. Lane were several Indian Jail Labour Corps. Many were professional thieves, and taught the local Arab a few lessons in an art in which he had hitherto regarded himself as *hors concours.* They gave little serious trouble.[302]

Spreading out helped to efface stigma, and prisoners working in detached units made themselves so useful that it was difficult to gather them in again.[303] The engineer at Aziziyah complained about returning a detachment from the 5th United Provinces Jail Porter Corps which had become proficient in brick-moulding and masonry.[304]

The strike

On 4 December 1918, a batch of 229 men from the 11th Bombay Jail Labour Corps refused to work, contending that that their 'agreement' with government had ended and they should be sent home. They were not violent, and their strike lasted barely half a day before they were marched away by British troops.[305] But the incident set off alarm bells for the army command about a potential labour crisis if men began to demand repatriation after the Armistice.[306] In Bombay, the major port of embarkation for Mesopotamia, there were signs that strike actions were picking up, and officials feared that the postwar assertiveness of labourers in India would be a source of contagion for the Persian Gulf.[307] But why was it this particular Jail Labour Corps detachment which precipitated a confrontation? I offer some lines of enquiry rather than a definite conclusion.

---

[301] See Hall, *The Inland Water Transport*, p. 26.

[302] Wilson, *Loyalties; Mesopotamia, 1914–1917*, p. 280.

[303] 'Summary', p. 6, para. 8; also 'History', 5th United Provinces JPC, pp. 2–3, 8.

[304] 'History', 5th United Provinces JPC, p. 3.

[305] Home, Jails, B, December 1918, no. 12; 'History', 11th Bombay JLC, pp. 5–7.

[306] Home, Jails, B, April 1919, no. 1; C&I, E, August 1919, nos 8–9.

[307] Judicial Department, 1918, no. 253, MSA. *The Persian Gulf Administration Reports, 1873–1947* (Archive Edition 1986), vol. VII (1912–20), p. 44; vol. VIII (1921–30), pp. 24, 38–40.

On 1 December 1916, 935 men were enrolled at Yeravada Jail in Pune for the 11th Bombay Jail Corps on a two-year agreement, and they began to receive their wages from this date.[308] Among them were 515 men from a Deccan convict work gang, which had been building a canal at Visapur in Ahmednagar district, and eighty-two from a Sindhi convict work gang.[309] There is an affecting bundle of forms in the Maharashtra State Archives in Mumbai, attested by thumbprints or by laboured signatures, which marks the transfer of the men from the Deccan work gang to the Jail Corps.[310]

Networks forged earlier probably came into play when negotiating new situations in Mesopotamia, hence Lane's dark references to the clannishness of 'Sindhi habituals'.[311] To encourage volunteering, the earlier batches of men recruited from jails were offered this fixed two-year term; subsequently, recruits were enrolled on 'duration of war' agreements.[312] The Commandant of the 11th Bombay Jail Labour Corps, Captain F. F. Mackay, worked for a business firm, and of the four Lieutenants under him, E. G. Nielson and W. S. Dickens were from the police service, C. M. Galvin was from railway accounts, and N. N. Farrell was from the Public Works Department. All five were said to have a working knowledge of many vernacular languages.[313]

With the end of effective fighting and the signing of the Armistice, jail-recruited men began to argue that since the war was over they should be sent home.[314] 'I had to repeat over and over again,' wrote Lane, 'that "Peace" was not signed, and that it was the "Cease fire" and not the "Dismiss..."'[315] If 'the end of the war' was a phrase open to interpretation, the two-year limit seemed to provide firmer ground.

On 30 November 1918, the Commanding Officer of the 11th Bombay Jail Labour Corps noted in his diary: 'On the conclusion of work today, the men

---

[308] General Department, 1917–18, no. 1284, pt 1, MSA; 'History', 11th Bombay JLC, p. 5.

[309] General Department, 1916–17, no. 90, pt II, MSA. Military Works in India co-opted the rest of the Sindhi convict work gang to build barracks and haul stores in Karachi—a port rising in importance as the second gateway for dispatching war supplies from India. *Indian Jails Committee*.

[310] Judicial Department, 1917, no. 689, pt VI, Convicts. MSA. See below.

[311] 11th Bombay JLC, p. 4.

[312] F&P, Internal, B, August 1918, nos 11–18.

[313] Ibid.

[314] The Armistice with Turkey was signed earlier, on 30 October 1918.

[315] 'Summary', p. 9, para. 12.

Enrolment form, Jail Corps, Judicial Dept. 1917 No. 689 Pt. IV, Maharashtra State Archives Mumbai.

G.C.P.—H 425—1,100-11-16—K2

In exercise of the power conferred by Section 401 of the Code of Criminal Procedure, 1898, the Governor of Bombay in Council hereby remits, with effect from the date of embarkation for Mesopotamia, subject to the conditions hereinafter set forth, the remainder of the punishment awarded to *Kaloo Lala Jail R. No. 3510* , a convict at present undergoing sentence of imprisonment in the ~~POONA EXTRA-MURAL~~ Prison.

The conditions are these:—

(1) That he will be enrolled and attested as a follower under the Indian Army Act on arrival in Mesopotamia.

(2) That he will, for the period of two years or the duration of the war, whichever is less, be employed there under the Military works service on embankment work, on loading and unloading stores from and into steamers and river craft, or on such other work as the Military authorities may direct.

(3) That he will behave well and perform satisfactory service during the period of his employment.

(4) That he will not commit any offence punishable by any law in force in British India.

(5) That he will not associate with notoriously bad characters, or lead a dissolute life.

By order of the Governor of Bombay in Council.

Dated the 1st Dec 1916.　　　　　Acting Secretary to Government.

I hereby accept and agree to abide by the above conditions; and I acknowledge that, should I fail to fulfil those conditions, or any portion of them, the Governor of Bombay in Council may cancel the remission of my punishment, whereupon I may be arrested by any Police officer without warrant and remanded to undergo the unexpired portion of my original sentence.

　　　　　　Prisoner.　　　　　Dated the 8 December 1916.

Left hand Thumb impression of Kaloo Lala No. 3510.

CERTIFIED that the foregoing conditions were read over to the Prisoner *Kaloo Lala no. 3510* and accepted by him under Section 401 of the Code of Criminal Procedure in my presence.

Witness.

　　　　　　　　　　　Superintendent.

Poona Extra-mural Prison

Dated the 　　　 1916.

cheered a good deal.'[316] However, on 3 December Lane told them that it had been a mistake to give them their salary when they were enrolled on 1 December 1916, and that in fact their contract began when they boarded ship on 15 December 1916. The next day 229 men refused to work, surrounding Lieutenant Nielson, their former Commanding Officer, and appealing to him to intervene as their *maa-baap* (protector). Lane chose to interpret this as the men taking Nielson hostage. The threat could not have been very imminent, because Nielson was told to collect them for a palaver in which tact was not the keynote. Lane now put the starting date of their contract even later, at 23 December 1916 when the Corps originally arrived at Basra. When the men asked for a definite date of departure, he refused to give it.[317] He acknowledged that the tone taken by those refusing to work was not insubordinate until British troops arrived with fixed bayonets: 'When the men saw themselves surrounded ... they became insulting, offensive and mimicked orders ... It was now my time to have no mercy.'[318]

Twenty-four were singled out as ringleaders, and tried for mutiny by a special general court-martial which handed down terms of rigorous imprisonment ranging from one to eight years.[319] The others were returned to India to serve their original sentence. Lane contended that if the ringleaders had got off, 'the whole of the Indian Porter and Labour element, and especially the Jail Corps ... would have downed tools.'[320]

For Lane, the explanation was almost self-evident. He hinted that the Commanding Officers had allowed the 'habituals' to get out of hand, locating two alleged strikers in the *havildars* of the A company, though they had not actually been in the crowd.[321] The degree to which the 11th Bombay Jail

---

[316] 'History', 11th Bombay JLC, p. 5.

[317] Ibid. There was some administrative bungling, because the men were enrolled twice over: on 1 December 1916 in Bombay, and once again in Basra on 23 December 1916. Home, Jails, B, December 1918, no. 12.

[318] 'History', 11th Bombay JLC, p. 6.

[319] Ibid.

[320] The strike did not spread to the other units, though a company of the 10th Punjab JLC did 'down tools' on 10 December 1918 when 204 men were taken across the Diala for return to India and recommitment to jail. 'History', 11th Bombay JLC, p. 7. The 18th ILC, a 'free' unit, also working on the Khalis canal, was said to be 'rather disturbed' in mid-December due to 'an infection caught from a prison corps' in which there was 'trouble'. 29 December 1918, TNA WO 95/5038.

[321] Of the strikers, 131 belonged to the A company. 'History', 11th Bombay JLC, p. 6.

Labour Corps was dispersed would certainly have created a marked dependence on jail-recruited NCOs.[322] This unit, noted their Commanding Officer in June 1917, was 'strung out from Qurnah to Samarra in 14 or more different stations, in detachments of all sizes from 500 to 1.'[323]

On arrival, the men had been put onto a crucial embankment, the Shaiba Bund, but Captain Mackay felt the pace was very slack. Rejecting harsher punishment as impractical, he formulated a bonus money scheme based on piecework after the completion of a fixed daily task.[324] Mackay had been a partner in a commercial firm, and Lane felt he tried to manage his corps as 'labour' rather than as convicts:

> He steadily worked to get all reference to the word 'Jail' or 'convict' removed and interpreted the freedom given them *in the fullest sense that the men did*. He did not want to know anything of their antecedents, and so in this he differed from myself … His pre-war training gave him an intimate knowledge of labour contracts.[325]

Detached work, whatever its intensity, probably led to a reduced sense of duress, as compared with the Jail Corps working together at Headquarters.[326] However, with wages rising for other labour units in Iraq, jail-recruited labourers must have become increasingly restive about their lower wage scale. Hauling coal side by side with Inland Water Transport coolies who got Rs. 30/– a month, men of the 10th Madras Jail Porter Corps, who received Rs. 10/–, had asked for increased pay.[327] Another reason men of the Bombay Jail Corps were waiting anxiously for the end of their two-year term was that they had been denied any home leave, on the grounds that priority had to be given to those on 'duration of war' contracts.[328] Finally, from October 1918 the Bombay Jail Corps had been cutting stone and earth in the Khalisi Canal. This was brutally taxing work in water and slush, often exposed to sharp win-

---

[322] However, the 11th Bombay JLC still had some non-convict NCOs.

[323] 'Summary', p. 6.

[324] 'History', 11th Bombay JLC, p. 2.

[325] Ibid., p. 7, my emphasis.

[326] Desertions were sometimes more frequent from Headquarters, where discipline was stricter, than from dispersed detachments. Ibid., p. 10.

[327] Their commanding officer commented: 'The economy of working the convict coolies stands out in this instance very plainly.' 'Summary', 10th Madras JPC, p. 3.

[328] 'Summary', p. 8, para. 10.

ter rain, and the uncertainty about when their ordeal would end must have bitten cruelly.[329]

Shortage of shipping could make dates of embarkation uncertain. British personnel were pushing for demobilisation and convict labour could not have had high priority, especially when the need for labour was still acute. In addition, the Bombay police favoured a phased repatriation of Jail Corps.[330] The Bombay Jail Corps thought they would have to press to get a date for embarkation. The harshness of the response brought home once again the particular vulnerability of men working under the constant threat of being sent back to jail to serve their original sentence.

Nevertheless, the episode convinced the General Officer Commanding for Force D of the wisdom of maintaining contractual honesty with labour units, including those recruited through 'duration of war' agreements.[331] He pronounced that '[o]n various occasions when Asiatics viz Egyptians, Chinamen and Indians have been kept under the stress of circumstances beyond their agreements trouble has resulted.'[332] Therefore, he argued, those who wanted to go home should be allowed to do so, and fresh one-year agreements should be drawn up for those who agreed to stay.[333]

The strike ensured that all jail-recruited men on two-year agreements were repatriated towards the end of December 1918.[334] The 10th Punjab Jail Labour Corps, engaged for the duration of the war, built up its own pressure for repatriation—this time not by a strike, but by creating a 'crime wave'.[335] As the withdrawal of military units began, forced labour units demonstrated their unviability and desertions increased.[336] The strike also dashed Lane's hopes of presiding over a future Convict Legion scheme for Iraq.[337] In October 1919 the

---

[329] 'History', 11th Bombay JLC, p. 3.

[330] Ibid., p. 6; General Department, 1916–17, no. 90, pt II, MSA.

[331] GOC, Force D, to Chief of General Staff, 29 December 1918, C&I, E, August 1919, nos 8–9.

[332] Ibid.

[333] Ibid.

[334] 'History', 11th Bombay JLC, p. 8.

[335] 'History', 10th Punjab JLC, p. 3.

[336] Adjutant General, India to Chief Secretary, Bombay, 19 May 1919; Judicial Department, 1919, no. 817, MSA.

[337] Summary', p. 9, para. 13. However, he did secure the post of Inspector General of Jails in Iraq. Bell, *Review of the Civil Administration of Mesopotamia*, p. 124.

Government of India sent a telegram saying it did not approve of the employment of convict labourers in postwar Iraq, and the last batch left for India in January 1920.[338] In fact the official summary, 'Recruiting in India Before and During the War of 1914–18', swept the October 1916 communiqué about giving prisoners a *locus poenitentiae* under the carpet. It declared that '[t]he formation of the Jail Labour and Porter Corps was admittedly a measure of emergency. It was not intended as an experiment in criminology'.[339]

1918: a 'labour problem' in Mesopotamia and in India

In April 1917, shortly after the entry of British forces into Baghdad on 11 March 1917, the Indian Army brought in a party of Indian and British journalists to demonstrate the extent to which operational conditions had improved since the breakdown of 1915–16.[340] As journalists began to ask about prospects for Indian trade and migration and the nature of the future administration envisaged for Mesopotamia, Percy Cox, Political Resident in the Persian Gulf, sent a frantic telegram to the India Office. Local notables, he complained, might suspect that Basra and Baghdad *vilayats* were destined for absorption into the Empire of India.[341] Held back in Amara for a fortnight, the party was finally allowed to proceed to Baghdad, but only on the condition that their articles would not touch upon the political future of Mesopotamia.[342] This *contretemps* exemplified the paradoxes of a campaign which drew heavily upon the manpower and material resources of India but

---

[338] 'Summary', p. 11, para. 13; p. 13. A proposal to use convict-recruited labour for the North-West Frontier in 1919 was also rejected.

[339] 'Recruiting in India', chapter 3, p. 42. It concluded that the results regarding the men's reform were 'promising', but that a definite pronouncement could be made only after their return to normal occupations. Ibid.

[340] F&P, Secret, War, December 1917, nos 345–64. A GOI circular of 8 May 1917 stated it was 'desirable to avoid as far as possible any discussion in the Indian press of the future of Mesopotamia.' IOR/P/1417/1917.

[341] Political Resident, Persian Gulf to Secy, F&P, 6 April 1917, IOR/P/1417/1917. In March 1917 the SSI had informed the Viceroy that the occupied territories would be administered by the British government rather than the Government of India, and that Basra would remain permanently under British occupation but Baghdad would have the façade of an Arab state. IOR/P/1417/1917.

[342] F&P, Secret, War, December 1917, nos 345–64.

left the Government of India at a loss when it came to explaining what Indians stood to gain from this outlay.[343]

At the close of the Mesopotamian campaign there were 113,000 Indian combatants in Mesopotamia and 183,000 followers, the latter including twenty-six Indian Labour and Porter Corps and a large number in the Inland Water Transport and Railways.[344] As late as April 1920, 80 per cent of the 24,928 railway personnel of all grades in Iraq were Indian.[345] The problem was that once peace was declared, the sending of Indian labour to Mesopotamia became illegal because it was not one of the destinations sanctioned under the Indian Emigration Act. 'Once we do away with the shield of a military organisation,' wrote the British Political Resident in the Persian Gulf, 'we are confronted with the problem of indenture labour and the emigration laws'.[346] Yet even as British authorities in Iraq kept demanding labour and personnel from India, they started deporting 'unauthorised' Indians, particularly peddlers and merchants, to prevent a settler population emerging.[347] With South Africa pushing for the 'voluntary' repatriation of Indians and the East African highlands being claimed exclusively for European settlers, Mesopotamia seemed to add another chapter to a story in which territory was acquired for empire by the deployment of Indian soldiers and labourers, but where Indian merchants and settlers were unwelcome.[348] The other problem was that with the relaxa-

---

[343] Hardinge and Chelmsford demanded a substantial role for the Government of India in the future administration of Mesopotamia, referring repeatedly to the dependence upon India for soldiers, personnel, and labour to hold this territory. Robert J. Blyth, *Empire of the Raj: India, Eastern Africa and the Middle East, 1858–1947*, Basingstoke; New York: Palgrave Macmillan, 2003, pp. 146, 161.

[344] *Supplement to the London Gazette*, 28 July 1919, p. 2544. In August 1920, there were 1,092 Indian Post and Telegraph employees in Mesopotamia. IOR/L/PS/11/145, file P143. On 1 April 1920, when the personnel of the railway department were transferred from the military to the civilian administration, there were 24,928 personnel, of whom 80 per cent were Indians and 3 per cent Europeans.

[345] Bell, *Review of the Civil Administration of Mesopotamia*, 3 December 1920, p. 18.

[346] Telegram from Political Resident in the Persian Gulf, 31 January 1919 in F&P, Secret, External, March 1921, nos 46–51.

[347] Home, Political, File 51/2/1922; C&I, E, August 1919, nos 8–9.

[348] White settler lobbies in Africa denounced Indian business ethics, standards of morality and hygiene, saying they had a demoralising effect on the 'indigene'. Indian settlers contended with colonial taxonomies about the civilisational ranking of different races, and got enmeshed in them. For an insightful exploration, see Renisa Mawani,

tion of centralised recruitment for the army, competitive bidding for labour and services resumed and wages began to rise.[349]

The strategy adopted in Mesopotamia was to keep all labour from India under military command even if it was deployed by the civil administration, as in the case of the railways, and to continue to cast it as part of the army of occupation.[350] In May 1920, to sustain this fiction, the term 'Military Labour Corps' was interpreted to apply to all Indian subordinate personnel and labour, skilled and unskilled, in Iraq.[351] The condition was that they were to remain government servants, not employed by private contractors.[352]

The Arab uprising of May–November 1920 highlighted the continued dependence on Indian manpower. Of the 102,000 troops deployed to crush the rebellion, 17,000 were British and 85,000 were Indian.[353] Incidentally, 2,500 men from the Indian Labour Corps were also deputed for guard duty. Aylmer Haldane, the General Officer Commanding, recalled that blockhouses constructed around Baghdad and Basra were placed under the 'charge of Indian labour coolies, who, by the expenditure of vast quantities of ammunition, maintained their morale and discouraged attempts to rush their posts'.[354]

Conclusion: 'A wail from Mesopotamia'

In 1917–18, Indian newspapers pointed out that revelations about the failures of the Mesopotamian campaign had exploded the myth that that an authoritarian executive guaranteed efficiency of rule in the colony.[355] Indian leaders seized with delight upon Edwin Montagu's scathing description of the Government of India as 'too wooden, too iron, too inelastic, too antediluvian to be of any

'Law As Temporality: Colonial Politics and Indian Settlers', *UC Irvine Law Review*, vol. 4, no. 1 (2014), pp. 65–95.

[349] IOR/L/PS/11/145, file P143.

[350] Viceroy, Foreign Department, to India Office, 21 March 1919, IOR/L/P/11/145, file P143; C&I, E, August 1919, nos 8–9.

[351] Commerce Department, Note, 11 October 1920, F&P, External, B, December 1921, no. 242.

[352] Viceroy, Foreign Department to India Office, 5 May 1920, IOR/L/P/11/145, file P143.

[353] Haldane, *The Insurrection in Mesopotamia*, pp. 64, 108.

[354] Ibid.

[355] 'Bureaucratic inefficiency', *The Tribune*, 8 January 1918, p. 2.

use for modern purposes'.[356] What was needed, they argued, was a rapid advance towards representative government. However, it was the extended presence of Indian military and civilian personnel in Iraq after the Armistice which impinged strongly upon Indian politics. Earlier, there had been some calls in the press for Indians to be given opportunities to trade and settle in Mesopotamia. Now, from a variety of political positions, a demand gathered for the recall of Indian troops and labourers, fuelled by the growing conviction that India had nothing to gain by underwriting the occupation of Iraq.[357]

Even as the Khilafat and non-cooperation movements in India gathered strength, the grievances of subordinate Indian personnel in Iraq began to surface in newspapers. One anonymous petition complained of the harshness with which military authorities bent Indian civil and military personnel to their needs, riding roughshod over caste and respectability. Indian clerks carried out 'menial' work such as constructing roads while they waited for their passage home. Brahmins and high-caste Hindus of the Jail Corps were made to do sweepers' work (that is, to clean latrines), as were those recruited as hospital orderlies: 'There are hundreds of high-class people doing this work.'[358] The religious needs of Hindus and Muslims were disregarded, and bodies were disposed of without proper burial or cremation. Indians were mistreated by the Arab police and there was no redress.[359] Gandhi published a similar letter in *Young India* on 27 January 1921, which asked Indian leaders to take up the cause of their 'fellow citizens' in Mesopotamia, just as they had in Africa and British Guiana.[360] The signatories went on to state confidently that if non-cooperation could be started in Mesopotamia, 'Government may be coerced in a day what they would not have given India in a decade.'[361] Here was the echo again of complaints which had resonated during the campaign against indentured migration: namely that the trajectories of empire had positioned

---

[356] Edwin Montagu, Speech, 12 July 1917, para. 2205. HC, Deb, 12 July 1917, vol. 95, nos 2153–268, 2205.

[357] See Chapter 6 for further discussion.

[358] 'The Poor Sufferers of Mesopotamia, A Suffered and Suffering', anonymous petition, n.d., Home Political, 1922, file 51/2.

[359] Ibid.

[360] The letter was published as an attachment to Gandhi's own piece titled 'A Wail from Mesopotamia', *Young India*, 27 January 1921, in Home, Political B, June 1921, nos 285–86.

[361] Ibid.

Indians across a variety of geographical sites, but they were denied the means of cultural reproduction.

However, this chapter deals with the war experience of those in Mesopotamia who did not fit this portrayal of the high-class Indian. Here were men who had navigated arduous work regimes, wasteful of life and health, and went on doing so. By speech, petition and everyday actions, they held onto that fragile element of contract which was acknowledged in their labour regime, trying to deepen its significance in order to put some boundaries on the use of their person. Another theme taken up here is carried further in the following chapter—that of the government's efforts to reorient circuits of labour mobility towards the military worksites opening up along India's frontier and overseas. One manifestation of this drive was the deep interest in seeking out bodies of 'caste-less coolies' who might be harnessed to the manpower needs of war. 'Backward tracts' and 'primitive' populations came to be reframed as resources not just for India but for empire, regarding both the immediate needs of the war and the reconstitution of imperial legitimacy in postwar India.

4

THE RECRUITER'S EYE ON THE 'PRIMITIVE'

THOSE WHO WENT TO THE GREAT WAR
AND THOSE WHO WOULDN'T

'At present by far the most interesting map in the world is the map of France', wrote the Reverend Frederick William Savidge in 1917, describing the intense interest taken in the war by mission schoolboys at Lungleh in the Lushai hills, some of whose companions had gone to Europe in the Indian Labour Corps (ILC).[1] In January 1918, Reverend James Herbert Lorrain, of the same outpost in Assam, would visit the Lushai labourers in France and show the men '[l]antern entertainments which have transported them in imagination to their beloved hills and have made them ... forget their present surroundings ... and revel in the joy of being HOME once more.'[2]

Visual technologies allowed for landscapes to be transported across space and viewed in different frames: a map to conceptualise 'France' sitting in a schoolroom in the Lushai hills, or a flickering vision of the Lushai hills as a 'home' for men working at the battle lines in Europe. This chapter examines

---

[1] *South Lushai Hills Report, 1917*, in *Reports by Missionaries of Baptist Missionary Society (B.M.S.) 1901–1938*, Baptist Church of Mizoram, 1993, p. 140 (henceforth *SLRBMS*). Lushai, or Mizo: an umbrella ethnic term for the inhabitants of the contemporary state of Mizoram in North-East India.

[2] Reverend J. H. Lorrain to Mrs Lewin, 5 January 1918, MS 811/IV/65(10) (i), Lewin papers, Senate House Library, University of London archives (henceforth SHL).

the way in which remote hill districts running north to south along the Assam-Burma frontier were reframed in France, the most prominent theatre of the Great War. Along an intersecting axis, it also explores the deepening of colonial interest during World War One in the military, labour and political potential of those it categorised as 'primitive' populations. To do so, it focuses on two examples of 'tribal' populations targeted as labour for France: men from the Assam-Burma ranges, described in colonial ethnographies as 'hillmen of Tibeto-Burman or Mongolian stock', and men labelled 'aboriginals' of 'autochthonous Kolarian races', prominent in the plateau and forest topography of Chota Nagpur and the Santhal Parganas in the province of Bihar and Orissa.[3] The identity discs issued by the Indian Army to combatant and noncombatant ranks were stamped not only with 'H' for Hindu, 'M' for Muslim, and 'C' for Christian, but also 'A' for Animist.[4]

Sub-imperial ambitions along India's long land frontier left their imprint upon manpower recruitment for World War One. Labour regimes which had served militarist border-making in India were tapped more intensively. This set out pathways for the movement of men, information and military hardware between longstanding conflict zones and the new theatres which had opened up in France and the Persian Gulf. India's frontiers were not carrying on, 'business as usual', in some parallel timeframe. There was an escalation of ambitions and anxieties, and the implosions taking place along India's frontiers over 1917–20 led to the redrawing of spheres of influence. The instance explored here is the incorporation of a stretch of virtually autonomous territory between the formal borders of Assam and Burma.[5]

India was said to have escaped the horrors of war, but this transborder frame exposes the intensity with which World War One was experienced in

---

[3] I have used the word 'tribal' despite its connotations of evolutionary backwardness because most of the communities so labelled accept it as a term of political self-identification and as a basis for claiming constitutional rights.

[4] The 1911 census stated that '[a]nimism is used as the name of the category to which are relegated all the pre-Hindu religions of India.' Sir E. Gait, *Census of India, 1911*, vol. 1, part 1, Calcutta: Government Printing, 1912, p. 126, para. 174.

[5] IOR/L/MIL/7/6899. The other instance, not taken up in this book, is the Marri-Khetran uprising of March 1918, sparked off by a demand for recruits, but more generally by war-generated intrusion along the Baluchistan-Persia border. For images, see 'Fighting the Marris and the Khetrans', The Soldier's Burden, http://www.kaiserscross.com/304501/478822.html, last accessed 15 November 2019

certain pockets along its frontiers. In late November 1918, even as the armistice was being celebrated along the Western Front, Lieutenant General Sir Henry D'Urban Keary, of the Burma command, was sending military police columns equipped with Stokes mortars, Lewis guns and rifle grenades to occupy some 6,000 miles of rugged hill terrain surrounding the Manipur valley and extending to the Somra tract and the Thaungdut State in Burma.[6] This was the second attempt to bring rebel chiefs to submission—one which this time involved 6,234 combatants, 696 non-combatants and 7,650 porters, with some of the final group often deployed as scouts and auxiliaries.[7] After pressure from British officials who had participated in this campaign, it would be categorised as one of the 'minor military operations' of the Great War.[8] It is along this frontier, too, that men's rendering of war service in Europe, or refusal to go, have left a permanent mark upon narratives of ethnic nationalism and the competing territorial claims that are based on them.[9]

The war also escalated the labour demand in seemingly wild and remote areas through colonial and corporate drives to access mineral and forest resources, and it legitimised the use of greater force to do so.[10] In the process, the distinction between corvée work and contract work began to blur. The longstanding justification for labour tax in certain areas was that it had a 'customary' sanction; that it was not burdensome, because it was limited to a few days in the year; and that it was necessary to maintain communications and

---

[6] IOR/L/MIL7/6899; file 5115/1917 in IOR L/PS/10/724. D'Urban Keary had participated in the conquest and pacification of upper Burma, 1885–93. After service in France and Mesopotamia, he took command of the Burma division in August 1918.

[7] IOR/L/MIL7/6899.

[8] F&P, Secret, External, July 1921, nos 1–7. Shakespear, commandant of the Assam Rifles, was outraged that the largest military operations this side of the frontier since the 1911 Abor campaign were covered by two Calcutta papers as 'outings of Political Officers and their escorts'. Colonel L. W. Shakespear, *History of the Assam Rifles*, 1929, Aizawl: Tribal Research Institute, 1977, pp. 235–37. For the list of awards, see *Supplement to the London Gazette*, 23 July 1920, pp. 7757–61.

[9] In Manipur and Nagaland, such tensions resurfaced in commemorations of the centenary of World War One. See Kham Khan Suan Hausing, 'Unmindful of History: On Biren Singh and Manipur', *The Hindu*, 29 December 2017, https://www.the-hindu.com/opinion/op-ed/unmindful-of-history/article22320391.ece, last accessed 10 November 2019.

[10] See below.

'public works'.[11] Resistance to forcible recruitment and the intensified appropriation of natural resources was not limited to 'tribal' communities.[12] But their grievances could more easily be dismissed as that millenarian longing for autonomy which periodically stirred up 'primitive' populations. The Chief Secretary of Bihar and Orissa accepted that labour recruitment in Mayurbhanj, following hard on the heels of a war loan collection drive, had been harsh and hasty. Nevertheless, his conclusion was that defiance of these impositions arose from that 'yearning for a return to the golden age when they had no overlords, one that periodically returns to the Santhals and other aboriginal tribes.'[13]

On the other hand, when recruitment quotas were met in remote tracts then officials said that this demonstrated the benevolent face of imperial rule at the margins of society, where caste-conscious Indian leaders did not venture.[14] More generally, from the late nineteenth century onwards, a disillusionment with the consequences of industrialisation had fostered a romantic attitude to primitivity as a condition which sustained physical vitality and a closeness to nature.[15] J. H. Hutton, the administrator-ethnographer who recruited Nagas for both the ILC in France and punitive operations against the Kukis, declared that the Naga 'has mental outlooks and mental processes far more consonant with those of the European than has the ordinary native of India, whose thought has for generations been stunted by the cumbrous wrappings of caste and Hinduism'.[16] Such representations fed into debates about the postwar con-

---

[11] In fact, the 'opening up' of such areas led to an intensification of corvée.

[12] Rosters for *bent* and *begar*, the compulsory supply of labour and provisions at low fixed prices, also shaped the tax regime of Kumaon and Garhwal in the central Himalayas. World War One would witness the intensified exploitation of the forest resources of this region, to the detriment of local needs for fodder and fuel.

[13] 8 July 1918, in F&P, Internal, A, September 1918, nos 84–100.

[14] Lord Northbrook, a former Viceroy, declared that 'outlying districts' such as Chota Nagpur and Kumaon gave a stronger impression of the benefits of British rule than the well-known Provinces. Francis B. *Bradley-Birt, Chota Nagpore: A Little-Known Province of the Empire*, London: Smith, Elder, & Co., 1903, Introduction, p. xiii.

[15] Administrator-ethnographer R. V. Russell warned against the tendency to cast 'savage life' as Arcadia, saying that this obscured 'the gulf between savagery and civilisation' and hence 'the measure of human progress'. R. V. Russell, 'Review of Sarat Chandra Roy's *The Oraons of Chota Nagpur*', in *Folklore*, vol. 27, no. 1 (1916), pp. 107–9.

[16] J. H. Hutton, *The Angami Nagas*, London: Macmillan, 1921, p. 38. James Henry

stitutional dispensation for 'backward areas where the people are primitive and there is no material on which to found political institutions'.[17]

Missionaries contributed to this paternalist discourse, but in the Assam-Burma hills there were areas of disagreement with officials about the pace of movement away from the 'savage' past.[18] The story of military recruitment in 'backward areas' is not, however, only constituted by the actions of a handful of European officials and missionaries; it is also about the emergence into public life of a small, newly literate tribal element, Christian and non-Christian, which began to press for education, employment, and a political space in the face of the colonial preference for 'indirect rule' through chiefs and headmen.

Profiling the Indian Labour Corps: 'from the remotest confines of India'?

The literature on India's contribution to the war has focused overwhelmingly on the rushing of the Indian Corps to France and Belgium in autumn 1914. As it became clear that there were not going to be any swift and easy victories, the accolades dimmed. In December 1915, amid rumours that they had been 'broken' by shellfire, the Indian infantry divisions were shifted to Mesopotamia, although the cavalry was retained until March 1918. What did not register in public perception was the second flow of South Asian personnel to France in 1917–18, to deal with the manpower crisis that had overtaken that theatre.

In January 1917, the Secretary of State for India informed the Viceroy that 50,000 'South African kaffirs' were being sent to France and asked if he could supply an equal number of labourers.[19] Battered by the ongoing and very public enquiry into the disasters of the Mesopotamian campaign, the Government of India hoped to restore its reputation by a renewed presence in the most prestigious theatre of the war. Presented with this fresh demand, some local

---

Hutton, Indian Civil Service (1909–36), served for extensive periods in the Naga hills, acquiring a formidable reputation as Naga ethnographer.

[17] This was the formulation used in the Montagu-Chelmsford report on constitutional change to categorise areas excluded from the general scheme for representative government. 'Summary of constitutional reform for India, 22 April 1918', *Report on Indian Constitutional Reform*, London: HMSO, 1918, cd 9109.

[18] See below.

[19] SSI to Viceroy, 22 January 1917, IOR/L/MIL7/18398. The number actually supplied was probably around 30,000. See Chapter 1.

governments remained non-committal, but Archdale Earle, Chief Commissioner of Assam, responded fulsomely with the offer of some 'eight to ten thousand able-bodied hill-men'.[20] Quite remarkably, the labour companies sent from this province would be raised from its most sparsely populated tracts: the Garo, Khasi and Jaintia hills, and, down along the Assam-Burma frontier, the Naga hills, the mountainous tracts of the princely state of Manipur, and the Lushai hills.[21] The Assam administration would also be congratulated for the speed with which it met Labour Corps quotas.[22] Earle's response to an anonymous petition from the Khasi and Jaintia hills, accusing him of being 'the most violent Chief Commissioner of Assam', was that it might have emanated from the 'social upheaval' produced by sending '2000 voluntary workers within a month' from a small district.[23] The Manipur Raja offered two 'hill-men' Labour Corps, and the Viceroy signalled his 'grateful acceptance'.[24] Across the border, in the Chin hills of Burma, Deputy

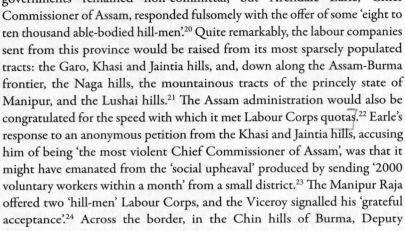

[20] Chief Commissioner (CC), Assam to Chelmsford, 8 February 1917, IOR, Papers of Viscount Chelmsford as Viceroy of India, 1916–21, vol. 18, no. 81, pp. 76–78. The Assam government also responded positively to a Central Recruiting Board circular of 29 June 1917 asking about the feasibility of introducing some form of conscription. It pointed out that '[i]n the Naga Hills and the Lushai Hills the people are still accustomed to impressment'. For the Manipur hills, Kanrei Shaiza put the situation bluntly: 'During World War 1, we were sent to France in 1917 under the system of *thoukai*.' Kanrei Shaiza, *Āpuk Āpaga Rairei Khare, France Khavā, 1917–18, Khala Republic Day, 1974, Delhi Kakā*, Imphal: City Press, 1974. *Thoukai*: tributary labour for the Manipur raja. Families who could not provide a recruit put together thirty to forty rupees to get a substitute. Ibid.

[21] The Assam government's description of the hills stated that 'there was practically no labouring class' among the plain's Assamese and that their physique was poor. Chief Secretary, B. C. Allen, 29 January 1917, Assam Secretariat, Political Dept, Political, B, April 1918, nos 316–499, Assam State Archives, Guwahati (ASA). 'Caste-less' hill-men also made it easier to adopt collective cooking arrangements, thereby saving fuel and labour time. H. C. Barnes, Deputy Commissioner, Naga Hills, 28 March 1917, Assam Secretariat, Political, Political B, April 1918, nos 316–499, ASA.

[22] F&P, External, B, August 1917, no. 21.

[23] CC, Assam to Home Dept, 19 May 1917, IOR Chelmsford Mss Eur. E. 264, vol. 18, no. 246, p. 290.

[24] F&P, Internal, B, March 1917, nos 85–86. Asked to supply 'hill-man' labour for Mesopotamia, the British Political Agent at Manipur had demurred, arguing that 'such very primitive and unsophisticated persons ... were unfit for service beyond

Commissioner E. O. Fowler raised 1,000 men from Tiddim, remarking: 'This response by the Northern Chins is more remarkable when it is considered that there are only about 5000 males between the ages of 20 and 40 in this Sub-division.'[25]

The Viceroy stated that he would also be able 'to raise some thousands of Santhali coolies' for the first ILC contingent for France.[26] As pointed out earlier, 'Santhali' had emerged as a generic label for labour drawn from Oraons (or Kurukhs), Mundas, Kharias, Hos and other 'tribal' communities from a forest and plateau terrain stretching from central India into Chota Nagpur and the Santhal Parganas. At two very separate locations, therefore, certain populations, categorised by colonial ethnography as belonging to a 'rudimentary' state of civilisation, had been targeted as labour for the European theatre of war.

It has to be stressed that the ILC that was sent to France was not raised only from 'tribal' areas. Recruitment stretched over a broad swathe of upper India: the North-West Frontier Province (NWFP), the United Provinces (UP), Bihar and Orissa (B&O), Bengal, Assam and Burma.[27] However, in war propaganda the ILC which went to France was cast as a force drawn largely from 'primitive people who had never been beyond their villages'.[28] Their

---

the seas and were likely to suffer very severely from the climate'. F&P, Internal, B, October 1917, nos 126–45. The climate of France seemed better for 'hill-men', but it was the cachet of registering a presence in this theatre which was irresistible.

[25] *Administrative Reports of the Chin Hills and the North Eastern Frontier of Burma for the Year Ended 30 June 1917*, Government of India, 1917.

[26] Viceroy to India Office, 20 February 1917, IOR/L/MIL7/18302.

[27] See table. A detachment of 100 men from the Central Provinces was incorporated into the United Provinces Corps. A draft from Bombay was sent to the NWFP companies. The Madras Presidency supplied labour for Mesopotamia, but not for France.

[28] Stanley Reed, 'Introduction' to Captain Pandit Kashi Nath, *Indian Labourers in France*, Bombay: Oxford University Press, 1919. Ironically, Kashi Nath's description of his United Provinces company is of a heterogenous assortment: peasants, ex-soldiers, seasoned followers, and even men of some means and education. There are hints that he also wanted to distance his men from any association with the 'primitivism' of other companies. He joked that at Marseilles they had to let people know they were not cannibals but 'only harmless *Indiens*, mostly vegetarians'. Elsewhere he remarks that there were Khasis and Nagas some miles away, 'but beyond the realisation that they were from our own soil the strangeness of language and demeanour prevented a closer intimacy'. Kashi Nath, *Indian Labourers in France*.

journey to Europe was presented as proof of the trust which colonial officials and missionaries had won at the 'civilisational fringes' of empire.[29] The Nagas and Chins came in for special attention because at the point of their repatriation they were returning to a frontier which was in the throes of insurgency.[30] This propaganda slant has been reproduced in some contemporary historical accounts which describe the ILC in France as made up largely of 'tribal' elements.[31] The politics of commemoration, feeding into ethnonationalist agendas, have also encouraged a monoethnic framing of the labour companies raised from the hill districts of Assam. Several elements within the companies drawn from the Assam hill districts, such as 'Santhals', Bengali Muslims, and Gurkhalis (or Nepalis), have been written out of the story.[32] For instance, there was a Gurkhali cluster in the 69th Garo company, and of the 145 men sent by one headman, Helik Pasah, for the Khasi Labour Corps, over half were non-Khasis.[33]

---

[29] The Commander-in-Chief, India, acknowledged the diversity of elements in the ILC but underlined the presence of 'men from the remotest corners of India'—those from the Assam-Burma hills and 'Santals and aborigines from Chota Nagpur.' Despatch from the C-in-C, India, *The London Gazette*, 25 July 1919, p. 9541. See also George F. MacMunn, *The Martial Races of India*, London: Sampson Low, 1933, p. 339.

[30] *The Times* declared that the Nagas had made themselves so popular with the French 'that "Naga" is the generic name in certain districts for all Indian labour.' 'An Army of Labour', *The Times*, London, 26 December 1917. The British MP Edward Pearson described the ILC as made up of 'no less than 15 tribal units', and singled out the Nagas and the Chins as having done well. E. Pearson, 'Report on Labour Organisation in France', January/February 1918, TNA CAB 24/58.

[31] Claude Markovits, 'Indian Soldiers' Experiences in France during World War I: Seeing Europe from the Rear of the Front', in Heike Liebau, Katrin Bromber, Katharina Lange, Dyala Hamzah and Ravi Ahuja (eds), *The World in World Wars*, Leiden: Brill, 2010, pp. 29–54, 13.

[32] Kyle Jackson notes the presence of Limbus (Nepalis) and 'Santhalis' in graveyard registration for the Lushai Labour Corps, and comments that histories of the Assam hill districts which view all of their non-British inhabitants as part of a unified 'Mizo' ethnicity reinforce an impression of remoteness and unchanging tradition. Kyle Jackson, 'Globalizing an Indian Borderland Environment: Aijal, Mizoram, 1890–1919', *Studies in History*, vol. 32, no. 1 (2016), pp. 39–71.

[33] See correspondence of A. W. Dentith, October 1917, Assam Secretariat, Political Department, Political, B, nos 315–26, ASA. Sylvanus Lamare separates out thirty-

Table 6: The Indian labour companies in France.[34]

Province	Territorial or ethnic label	Reconstituted Companies	Descriptive remarks from the time
North-West Frontier Province (NWFP)	NWFP	48, 49, 50, 83	1,607 transfrontier men and a draft from 'Jews, Parsis and low-caste Hindus from Bombay'[35]
United Provinces (UP)	UP	21, 23, 24, 25, 44, 45, 46, 47, 71, 72, 74, 75, 79, 82	
	Kumaon	70, 73, 76, 77, (85)	
Bihar and Orissa (B&O)	Bihar	22, 30, 31, 32, 33, 56	
	Ranchi	41, 42, 43, 51	
	Santhal	52, 53, 54, 80, 81	
	Oraon	57, 58	

six 'non-Khasis' in his list of men in the Khasi Labour Corps. Sylvanus Lamare, *The Role of the Khasi Labour Corps in World War I*, Shillong: Eses Plus Publications, 2017, pp. 78–91. Their details indicate family connections with Cachar, East Bengal, Nepal, and the 'Santhali' diaspora. Dentith's correspondence suggests that the actual number of non-Khasis was larger.

[34] Raised as corps of 2,000 men, the ILC was reorganised in June 1917 in France into companies of 500 and renumbered. Some companies acquired an ethnic designation; others retained the original territorial label. The 67th and 68th companies are missing, perhaps because the Garo hills only sent the 69th company. The table draws upon various sources, among them 'Confidential reports on officers employed with Indian companies of the Labour Corps in France during First World War', IOR/L/MIL/7/17120. There was some reconstitution of companies in February 1918, with one and a half companies agreeing to stay on for the duration of the war.

[35] Ampthill to Cox, 4 January 1918, IOR/L/MIL5/738.

Assam	Naga	35, 36, 37, 38	1,000 Semas, 400 Lhotas, 200 Rengmas, 200 Aos, 200 Changs 'and other trans-frontier tribes'[36]
	Manipur (princely state)	39, 40, 65, 66	1,200 Tangkhul Nagas, 500 Kukis, and some Meiteis and Koms[37]
	Lushai (Mizo)	South Lushai: 26, 27	
		North Lushai: 28, 29	
	Khasi	22, 34, 55, 56	
	Garo	69, reconstituted as 84	
Burma	Burma	59, 6, (78)	From the 'agricultural classes of upper Burma'[38]
	Chin	Tiddim: 61, 62	250 Sukhte, 105 Sizang and 700 Kamhau
		Falam: part of the 78th	300
Bengal		63, 64	East Bengal Muslims and 300 Bengali and Santhali Christians

[36] Robert Reid, *History of the Frontier Areas Bordering on Assam from 1883–1941*, Delhi: Eastern Publishing House, 1942, p. 162; F&P, External, B, August 1917, no. 21.

[37] This ethnic distribution is being reassessed. The Mao Nagas now claim the 39th company. '"France li Kata Ko": Mao Naga Labour Corps in First World War', *The Morung Express*, 30 December 2018, http://www.manipur.org/news/2018/12/30/france-li-kata-ko-mao-naga-labour-corps-in-first-world-war-morung-express/, last accessed 10 November 2019. Kanrei Shaiza puts the Tangkhuls and Kukis at 750 each, and adds 500 from the Mao-Senapati area. Kanrei Shaiza, *Āpuk Āpaga Rairei Khare, France Khavā, 1917–18*.

[38] F&P, General, B, January 1919, nos 460–63.

The imprint of border-making

One pattern which emerges from this table is the repurposing of infrastructures and practices which had evolved to navigate and consolidate boundaries at the edges of administered territory.[39] The cantonments, military police posts, roads, railheads, and sawmills along India's frontiers, pressing as it were into 'wild territory', generated a range of labour regimes which tactically balanced local and migrant populations. The military construction complex along the North-West Frontier was linked to the port of Bombay, the third largest city of the empire, creating a Punjabi and Pashtun labour diaspora there which was also tapped for Mesopotamia.[40]

Some ethnicities otherwise visible in frontier labour gangs were put out of bounds for ILC recruitment in order to preserve the combatant pool. In March 1917, follower recruitment was prohibited from 'Punjabis of all classes, Garhwalis, Rajputs, Nepalese, cis-Frontier Pathans'.[41] The recruitment of transfrontier Pashtuns had been stopped for combatant units in November 1915 and was stopped for non-combatant units for Mesopotamia in 1917, because they were suspected of sympathy for the Ottoman side. However, George Roos-Keppel, the autocratic Chief Commissioner of the North-West Frontier Province, allowed their enlistment in labour companies for France. In the tone of someone taking care of a problem, he said that he wished the entire Mahsud tribe could be sent off: 'they are splendid navvies and might eventually marry and settle in France.'[42] Of the four NWFP companies, three were drawn from

---

[39] For an excellent exploration of the portering economy in Baltistan, which 'made possible the delineation of empire and allowed imperialists to travel to its margins', see Kenneth Iain MacDonald, 'Push and Shove: Spatial History and the Construction of a Portering Economy in Northern Pakistan', *Comparative Studies in Society and History*, vol. 40, no. 2 (1998), pp. 287–317, 302.

[40] Chief of General Staff to GOC, Force 'D', 4 December 1916, WW1/771/H, vol. 2134, war diary no. 96088; F&P, Frontier, B, September 1918, nos 21–27.

[41] F&P, Internal, B, August 1917, nos 110–15. However, Nepalis continued to find their way into non-combatant units, and Garhwalis enlisted at Bhimtal for the Kumaon labour companies. Report on services rendered by the Tehri Durbar, 31 August 1920, Political Agent for Tehri Garhwal State, File T-C/108/D, no. 702.

[42] Roos-Keppel to Viceroy, Lord Chelmsford, 16 April 1917, F134, George Roos-Keppel Papers, IOR Mss Eur. D 613. To keep the peace in Waziristan, government looked for some alternative employment. In February 1917, a proposal to offer Mahsud chiefs contracts for the repair of the road between Madh Hassan and Spinkai

Mahsuds, Swatis and Punjabi Muslims.[43] The fourth was put together from what Lord Ampthill, the labour advisor, referred to contemptuously as 'Jews, Parsis, Christians and low-caste Hindus from Bombay'.[44]

Moving down to the United Provinces, we find four companies recruited from the central Himalayan belt of Kumaon and its adjoining submontane tract, a terrain dotted with labour gangs working in road construction, forest-work and porterage.[45] The other fourteen companies were drawn from 'mixed castes' of the Gangetic plains, with a substantial number taken from zones of high labour migration in eastern UP.[46]

The Assam government sent seventeen companies: one from the Garo hills, and four each from the Khasi, Naga, Lushai and Manipur hill districts. From Burma, two companies from the adjoining Chin hills acquired the ethnic label 'Chin', whereas two, drawn from the 'agricultural classes of Upper Burma', retained the Burma label.[47] The official need to ensure a steady labour pool for portering and road-building marked the tax and tributary structure of these sparsely populated hill tracts. The crucial instruments were an annual house tax of Rs 2/–to Rs 3/–, and ten to fifteen days of corvée labour annually from each household, a demand which stepped up with frontier expeditions.[48] In

---

stalled due to the opposition of religious leader Mullah Fazl Din, who pointed out that better roads made for easier invasion. *Operations in Waziristan, 1919–1920*, Calcutta: Government Printing, 1921, p. 32.

[43] J. W. Keen, *The N.W.F. Province and the War*, n.d., p. 20; IOR/L/MIL5/738.

[44] Ampthill to Cox, 4 January 1918, IOR/L/MIL5/738. This draft included some Mahars.

[45] The Kumaon labour depot was located at Bhimtal, an area dotted with tea planta-tions. Robert Bellairs, from a planter family, helped in recruitment, and went to France as CO of a Kumaon labour company. His friend James 'Jim' Corbett, who was from a local Irish family and would rise to fame as a writer and conservationist, was CO of the 70th Kumaon company.

[46] *India's Services in the War*, United Provinces, vol. III, Lucknow: Newal Kishore Press, 1922.

[47] The Chin companies were made up of 1,000 men from Tiddim and 300 in drafts from Falam. F&P, General, B, January 1919, nos 460–63.

[48] For important work see Lipokmar Dzuvichu, 'Roads and the Raj: The Politics of Road Building in Colonial Naga Hills, 1860s–1910s', *Indian Economic Social History Review*, vol. 50, no. 4 (2013), pp. 473–94; and 'Empire on their Backs: Coolies in the Eastern Borderlands of the British Raj', *International Review of Social History*, vol. 59, no. 22 (2014), pp. 89–112.

1. Mohammedans of the empire.

2. Maintenance train on the Bolan Pass line, 1890.

3. Indian mule cart train embarks from Alexandria for Gallipoli, April 1915.

1914... A l'abreuvoir - Muletiers Indiens | At the horse-poud - Indian muleteers

11ᵐᵉ Série

Cliché marchand (BLD)

4. At the horse pond, Indian muleteers, France (n.d., 1914–15).

5. Stretcher bearers, Gallipoli.

6. Washerman *dhobis*, Swat campaign, 1915.

7. Pumping up water for the *bhistis*, watermen, Swat campaign, 1915.

GUERRE 1914. — Au Camp de "l'Indian Army" — Marseille.

8. Indian camp followers, Marseille, 1914.

9. The Tigris Front, Iraq (formerly Mesopotamia): First Corps British Army camp sanitary area at Sandy Ridge: view of closed incinerator, sweeper's tent, drying shed for litter and latrine huts.

10. Pyarelal, a Dom catechist, and his wife, Varanasi, n.d. Pyarelal accompanied Dom Christian troops fighting in Mesopotamia.

11. Headmen, Naga Coolie Corps, Kobo, Assam, Abor expedition, 1911.

MANIPUR STATE

This is to Certify that *Kuinga* .... of
Samdal ....Village, Lam No........ Manipur State
is exempted for life from payment of house tax, Pothang and
begar as he served with the Manipur Labour Corps in France.

মনিপুর কেটকী লম নং............তুবা..................
দস্তিদা লৈবা শ্রী.................................হাইবা অসি তংসদা
মনি ন্র লেবার কোর চৎলুবগী দমক সার্টিফিকেট অসি পিদুনা য়ুমগী
খাজনা, পোৎপাং পুরা অমসুং বেগার ওইবা অসি মাগী মপুন্লি চুরা
কোকপিরবনি। ইতি তাং...................১৯১৮ইং

Dated Imphal,   President Manipur State
The 12th .... 1918.   Durbar.

12. Kuinga Muivah's certificate of exemption from house-tax and corvée.

13. Labourers from Manipur dressed for a war dance near Arras, 20 October 1917.

14. The 26th Lushai labour company, France.

15. Kuinga Muivah of Somdal and his friend Pashi Ruivah with the Manipur Labour Corps in France.

16. Burmese troops receive their mail at Contalmaison, Autumn 1917.

17. Members of an Indian Labour Battalion reading papers during a work break, 1917.

18. At a wayside station, the Indian Labour Corps in France.

19. Manipur 'hill-men' positioned around a motor-car, 20 October 1917.

20. Elderly Gurkha husband and wife coming down to a recruiting depot to take their son's estate, who has been killed in action. They may well have marched as many as 150 miles on foot.

The Sikh kitchen. Turning chappaties on the gas stoves.

21. The Sikh kitchen, Brighton.

unadministered areas along the borders of these districts, the obligation to provide porters and supply rice for expeditions was worked into treaty arrangements with chiefs. Those who met official demands for porters and armed auxiliaries were hailed as fine patriarchal figures.[49] However, a market for contract labour had also emerged in portering, mining, and forest-work, pushed along by the need to pay the house tax. Portering work runs like a thread through colonial ethnographies of the Assam hill districts, leaving its mark on consumption patterns and religious rituals.[50]

Caste-less labour: 'a particularly valuable sort of coolie'

The premise that some 'primitive' populations provided a particularly valuable sort of coolie emerged from the stream of 'Santhali' migration flowing from Chota Nagpur and the Santhal Parganas in Bihar and Orissa towards docks, coal mines, construction works and tea plantations in Bengal and Assam.[51] For tea-planters, writes Kaushik Ghosh, caste 'in so far as it was embodied in any sense of boundary, pollution or refusal to do any work' was presumed to lie outside the consciousness of the 'aborigine', making him or her the ideal labour import.[52] Santhali porter gangs had also been raised for militarist forays along the borderlands of Assam, as in the Chin-Lushai wars of 1889–90 and the

---

[49] J. P. Mills described the Sema Nagas, a prominent component of the Naga Labour Corps, as ideal porters for any expedition, cheerful, warlike and with 'very autocratic chiefs'. J. P. Mills, 'The Assam-Burma Frontier', *The Geographical Journal*, vol. 67, no. 4 (1926), pp. 289–99. James Philip Mills, Indian Civil Service (1913–47), a contemporary of J. H. Hutton, also emerged as a significant Naga ethnographer with the publication of *The Lhota Nagas*, London: Macmillan, 1922, and *The Ao Nagas*, London: Macmillan, 1926.

[50] The coats or clothes of Khasi porters who died away from home were brought back and incorporated into funerary rites. P. R. T. Gurdon, *The Khasis*, 1907, London: Macmillan, 1914, p. 185. The consumption of opium increased along the line of Angami Naga road-working gangs. J. H. Hutton, tour diary, Kohima, Zubza, 13 August 1920, Naga Exploratour, http://himalaya.socanth.cam.ac.uk/collections/naga/record/r72100.html, last accessed 15 November 2019.

[51] Kaushik Ghosh, 'A Market for Aboriginality: Primitivism and Race Classification in the Indentured Labour Market of Colonial India', in Gautam Bhadra, Gyan Prakash and Susie Tharu (eds), *Subaltern Studies No. 10: Writings on South Asian History and Society*, Delhi: Oxford University Press, 1999, pp. 8–48.

[52] Ibid.

1913 Mishmi expedition, and Santhalis were visible in road construction gangs and mines in the Assam hill districts.[53] So intense was the wartime demand for 'Santhali' labour that the Government of India had to broker a division between commercial concerns, the Indian Army and civilian departments.[54] Chota Nagpur and the Santhal Parganas would send labour to Mesopotamia, France and the North-West Frontier.

Santhali labour had a presence in the two Bengal labour companies as well. A description of one of the Bengal companies refers to some 300 Santhali and Bengali Christians as well as Muslims from East Bengal, 'of the class from which lascars of the P&O [a British shipping company] ships are drawn'.[55] Some of these Christians were recruited from Behala, a settlement for Christian artisans and apprentices run by the Oxford mission at Calcutta.[56]

The 'small war' in the Great War

> After the British came to our land, we were away from home most of the time. We went off to war in their service eleven times. In our own Naga areas, I went nine times … I got *dogmas* [medals of honour] only for the Abor and France wars.[57]

In contrast to the North-West Frontier, garrisoned by regular Indian Army units as well as militias, border-making along the North-East Frontier was characterised by decentralised expeditions conducted 'on the cheap'.[58] Food supply limited the depth and duration of a frontier promenade, as 'a coolie

---

[53] A. S. Reid, *Chin-Lushai Land*, Calcutta: Thacker, Spink and Co., 1893, pp. 184–99. F&P, External, January 1915, nos 53–54.

[54] ILC recruitment was prohibited in Manbhum and Hazaribagh districts to reserve labour for coal and mica mines in Bihar and Orissa and for wolfram mines in Burma. Commerce and Industry, March 1918, nos 29–31.

[55] Anonymous, *Father Douglass of Behala, By Some of His Friends*, London: Oxford University Press, 1952, p. 92.

[56] F&P, Internal, B, August 1917, nos 110–15.

[57] From a conversation between Watingangshi Ao and his son, as reported in W. Chubanungba Ao, *Havildar Watingangshi Ao Longkhum: Off the Coast of Tunis 1917*, Shillong: Galaxy Book Centre, 2017, p. 12. There were Lushais who received medals both for the Abor campaign and for service in France. Vanlalchhuanawma, *Christianity and Subaltern Culture: Revival Movement as a Cultural Response to Westernisation in Mizoram*, Mizoram: ISPCK, 2007, p. 432.

[58] L. W. Shakespear, *History of Upper Assam, Upper Burmah, and North-Eastern Frontier*, London: Macmillan, 1914, p. 254.

would normally eat the whole of his own load [60lbs] in a fortnight'.[59] The labour of local hill-men and hill-women was cheaper because they were expected to bring along their own food or forage for it.[60] By working along the line of feud, district officers in the Assam and Burma hill tracts gave local chiefs a political stake in their frontier 'promenades'. The porters whom chiefs supplied were in fact also being used as guides, scouts, and spear- and *dao*-wielding auxiliaries.[61] However, local hill-men porter gangs could desert more easily, as they did during the season for *jhum* (swidden cultivation in forest tracts), so they had to be interchanged with Gurkhali, Punjabi and Santhali gangs.[62]

While 'head-hunting' (taking the head of a slain enemy home) was usually viewed as the epitome of savagery, officers organising a frontier expedition found it useful to hint that porters would be able to take home the heads, or other body parts, of those killed, thereby qualifying them to wear the warrior's ornaments.[63] The duality of the coolie warrior is never fully acknowledged in accounts of frontier expeditions, but it is there if one looks for it. Protesting against the threats used in 1917 to force them into providing men for the Labour Corps, Kuki chiefs reminded the British Political Agent that 'Kukis helped Government in fighting with Cachar, Khonoma, Manipur, Suktim Poi, Lushai and Abor'.[64]

Kukis, along with Lushais and Angami and Sema Nagas, did indeed have a presence among the scouts and porters taken for the 1911–12 Abor expedition, which was launched from upper Assam along the Dihong river. The venture was publicised as an act of imperial vengeance for the killing of an Assistant Political Officer, Noel Williamson, so steps had to be taken to guard

---

[59] E. T. D. Lambert, 'From the Brahmaputra to the Chindwin', *The Geographical Journal*, vol. 89, no. 4 (1937), pp. 309–23, 310.

[60] Burmese coolies, noted one Political Officer, were more expensive than local Chins, because 'we have to sell them rice.' June 1892, J. Shakespear, IOR, Mss Eur. E361/14.

[61] *Dao*: machete. The possession of firearms was strictly licensed.

[62] During the Chin-Lushai expedition of 1889–90, 700 Chakma coolies returned home 'to *jhoom*', so they were replaced by 300 Santhali coolies from Chittagong. Reid, *Chin-Lushai Land*, p. 199. Gurkhali coolies replaced Naga coolies at the conclusion of the Abor expedition, 1911–12, Foreign, Secret, E, May 1912, nos 201–337.

[63] '[T]he Naga coolies on any trans-frontier expedition manage to return with a finger, ear, or other trophy'. A. G. E. Newland, *The Image of War, or Service on the Chin Hills*, Calcutta: Thacker, Spink and Co., 1894, p. 79.

[64] Petition, 18 May 1919, F&P, Secret-1, January 1920, nos 4–12.

against any embarrassing setbacks.[65] Arthur Bentinck, the Political Officer attached to the Abor expedition, commented on 'the necessity of appearing always in sufficient force to ensure against accidents.'[66] Precautions included the import of Airedales to counter Abor (Adi) hunting dogs. It was the first time in British military history, proclaimed the *New York Times* in excitement, that dogs were being used.[67] On hearing a rumour that the Abors had stopped an advance guard, a forest officer noted with relief the sound and spectacle of the Naga porters marching along at their side: 'every Naga had his blanket round his belly, and they twisted their spears and chanted right through the village, which put the fear of god into the Abor.'[68] The Naga scouts and porters, contracted for three months to accompany the Abor expedition, were actually kept away from their homes for four and a half months.[69] The catapulting of hill tribes from the Assam-Burma frontier to France in World War One was an extension, if a breath-taking one, of strategies to generate manpower for 'small' wars.

'Primitives' who went to war: the Assam-Burma 'hill-men' companies

In the Assam-Burma hill districts officials turned to headmen and chiefs to send in recruits for the Labour Corps, an affirmation of strategies of 'indirect rule'.[70] In the Khasi hills, assemblies of the Siems (chiefs) were held, and

---

[65] The long-term imperative was to stake a claim, in competition with China, over the trade route leading from Sadiya along the Dihong river to Tibet. Reid, *History of the Frontier Areas*, pp. 222–23.

[66] A. H. W. Bentinck, 'The Abor Expedition: Geographical Results', *The Geographical Journal*, vol. 41, no. 2 (1913), pp. 97–109, 97.

[67] 'Real Dogs of War: England Will Send a Force to Act in Expedition Against the Abors', *New York Times*, 20 August 1911, https://www.nytimes.com/1911/08/20/archives/real-dogs-of-war-england-will-send-a-force-to-act-in-expedition.html, last accessed 10 November 2019.

[68] A. J. W. Milroy, diary, Abor expedition, p. 73. IOR, Mss Eur. D1054. See image 11.

[69] Foreign, Secret, E, May 1912, nos 201–337.

[70] The deployment of recruiting to reinforce the ideology of indirect rule is also visible in the South African Native Labour Contingent. In France, 'for purpose of discipline and for political reasons', ruling chiefs, their relatives, and natives of standing in the SANLC were given the title InDuna—meaning headman or councillor—Class One or Two, and a distinctive badge. TNA WO 107/37, p. 27.

recruitment was left to them.[71] The Chief Commissioner in Assam said the Siem of Rambrai had not only 'mobilised practically the manhood of his State' for the ILC, but had supplied labour to a British syndicate working the local corundum mines as well.[72] J. P. Mills, then Sub-Divisional Officer at Mokokchung, recalled proudly that it was not necessary to issue notices calling for recruits. Naga chiefs were called for a discussion, and afterwards they not only sent in their men but went along themselves or sent a relative.[73] In France, no less a personage than the Commander-in-Chief sent a spear to the son of a Naga chief to mark his accession to chiefly status when his father died. All the headmen and assistant headmen of the Lushai Labour Corps, except one, were appointed from young Sailo chiefs.[74] In the Chin hills, Hau Chin Khup, chief of the Sukhte clan, sent men for the the Chin Labour Corps and provided auxiliaries for the Kuki-Chin campaign; his standing with the government rose by leaps and bounds.[75]

However, it was not pressure alone but also economic need which channelled men towards France. In the Lushai hills and south-west Manipur, the burden of government-sponsored rice loans, taken during the terrible famine of 1911–12, encouraged men to enlist.[76] This motivation was captured perfectly in a Lushai periodical, *Mizo leh Vai*: 'Everybody knows it's mostly the

[71] Assam Secretariat, Political Dept, Political, B, April 1918, nos 313–499, ASA.

[72] CC Assam to Viceroy, 3 March 1918, Chelmsford IOR Mss Eur. E264, vol. 20, letter no. 110, p. 179; Demi-official, 19 March 1917, Assam Secretariat, Political Department, Political, B, April 1918, nos 316–499, ASA. The ILC memorial erected at Jowai in the Jaintia Hills has the inscription *Ka Ri Khadar Doloi*—the land of the twelve chiefs.

[73] 'J. P. Mills and the Chittagong Hill Tracts, 1926/27: Tour Diary, Reports, Photographs', ed. Wolfgang Mey, http://crossasia-repository.ub.uni-heidelberg.de/548/1/J.P._Mills_and_the_Chittagong_Hill_Tracts.pdf, last accessed 15 November 2019. At the time, Mills was Sub-Divisional Officer at Mokokchung.

[74] Vanlalchhuanawma, *Christianity and Subaltern Culture*, p. 232, n. 5.

[75] *Acts and Achievements of Hau Cin Khup, Chief of Kamhau Clan, Chin Hills, Tedim*, 1927, in Khup Za Go, *Zo Chronicles: A Documentary Study of History and Culture of the Kuki Chin Lushai Tribe*, New Delhi: Mittal, 2008.

[76] *SLRBMS, 1916*, p. 134. See 'Regarding giving an award to Mr Needham, Sap', *Mizo leh Vai*, September 1919. Also Ningmuanching, '"As Men of One Country": Rethinking the History of the Anglo-Kuki War', in Jangkhomang Guite and Thongkholal Haokip (eds), *The Anglo-Kuki War*, London; New York: Routledge, 2019, pp. 168–97, p. 191.

poor who have gone; and that more had gone voluntarily than had been forced to go'.[77]

The monthly wage offered was Rs 20/–, higher than the Rs 18/–paid to the soldier on active service, and there was the additional attraction of a three-month advance up front. One month's extra pay was added for the first six months of service, and thereafter for every three months.[78] One of the most attractive inducements was the promise of a lifelong remission from the annual house tax and the labour tax, the latter exemption a mark of status usually reserved for headmen, government employees, and those who enlisted in the military police battalions.[79] Now men joining as labourers were being offered the same inducement—many of them from the sections of the community which were most vulnerable to this periodical seizure of their person.[80] 'No greater reward,' observed an Assam missionary, 'could possibly be given to any Lushai than perpetual exemption from this part of his taxes.'[81]

Missionary 'frontier work'

Missionary networks provided the other crucial element in recruitment from the hill districts of Assam and Burma, as well as the 'aboriginal' tracts of Bihar and Orissa. By one estimate there were some 5,000 Christians in the first batches of men sent in the ILC to France, 'accompanied by 11 chaplains in addition to several lay readers'.[82] In the Assam-Burma hills the administration

---

[77] 'Lekhathawn', *Mizo leh Vai*, April 1918, p. 51

[78] F&P, Internal, B, August 1917, nos 110–15.

[79] See image 12: 'Kuinga Muivah's certificate'. ILC recruits from the Kumaon hills in UP and from the Garhwal Raj were promised a similar exemption from the compulsory requisitioning of labour and supplies.

[80] C. I. Khama, 'Regarding going to France', *Mizo leh Vai*, February 1919.

[81] J. H. Lorrain to Mrs Lewin, 21 July 1917, MS 811/IV/65/7(i), Lewin collection, University of London.

[82] The first Labour Corps sent from Ranchi district, Chota Nagpur, Bihar had 1,200 Catholics. In addition, the Anglican mission helped to recruit 415 Anglicans and 391 Lutherans from Chota Nagpur and the Santhal Parganas. IOR/L/MIL5/738. T. H. Cashmore, SPG (Anglican Society for the Propagation of the Gospel) missionary in Ranchi, recalled that members of the Anglican laity were present in four Bihar and Orissa companies. Thomas Herbert Cashmore, 'The Raj', recording, 16 October 1973, IWM, no. 4912. Reverends F. W. Douglass and G. W. Shaw of the Oxford

drew upon the linguistic, medical and personnel resources of the missions to extend its very limited infrastructure of rule.[83] These resources were also, usefully, at hand when expeditions into unadministered territory were organised. Sadiya, the launching point for the 1911–12 Abor expedition, was the site of a small Baptist station.[84] The perpetual shortage of personnel made it a highly unstable base, yet annual reports of the Assam Baptist mission cast it as a gateway to evangelical paths leading to Tibet on the one side and Yunan on the other.[85] From the missionary perspective, colonial conquest was the necessary prelude to a lasting peace; in mission histories, 'punitive' exercises were therefore stripped of their violence, and the destruction of villages was often described as an incidental event.[86] Bloodshed was only retained in the world of tribal raids, their savagery epitomised by the custom of taking home the heads of enemies killed in these encounters. At the same time, church members back home had to be reassured that hearts and minds were being won over. The Assam frontier was cast as the 'pliable' if 'savage' one, in contrast to the North-West Frontier.[87] 'The head-hunters who lost their hearts': so went one of the chapter titles in *Lorrain of the Lushais* (1944), a biography of the Scottish Baptist missionary James Herbert Lorrain.[88]

Mission helped to raise the 64th Bengali company, which included 300 Bengali and Santhali Christians. IOR/L/MIL5/738, p. 188. There was a substantial Christian presence in the Khasi Labour Corps, and of the 2,100 men in the Lushai Labour Corps 600 were Christians, of whom 420 were affiliated to the Baptist mission and 180 to the Welsh Presbyterian mission. IOR/L/MIL5/738; IOR/L/MIL5/738, p. 188; *SLRBMS, 1917*, p. 142. The Naga and Manipur companies had Christians among the clerks, interpreters and mates, but very few among rank and file labourers.

[83] In Manipur, Baptist missionary William Pettigrew conducted the 1910–11 census of the hill areas with the assistance of students from the Ukhrul school. Lal Dena, *History of Modern Manipur, 1826–1949*, Manipur: Orbit Publishers, 1991, p. 107.

[84] The Baptist station at Sadiya gave medical assistance during the Abor expedition. *Assam Baptist Missionary Conference Report*, Calcutta: American Baptist Mission Press, 1913, pp. 2–6, 20, 71.

[85] Ibid.

[86] See Mary Clark's account of the 1889 annexation of Ao Naga territory. Mary Mead Clark, *A Corner in India*, Philadelphia: American Baptist Publishing Society, 1907, pp. 126–27.

[87] Reverend David Kyles, *Lorrain of the Lushais: Romance and Realism on the North-East Frontier of India*, Stirling: Stirling Tract Enterprise, 1944.

[88] Ibid.

However, there were areas of disagreement between missionaries and officials about the terms on which the 'savage' past was to be made usable. Whereas Welsh and Baptist missionaries recalled the 'head-hunting' past to emphasise, with a delicious shiver, the depth and rapidity of the transformation they had effected, administrator-ethnographers such as J. H. Hutton and and J. P. Mills wanted to refurbish it for militarist border-making.[89] Missionary efforts to reconstruct social relationships could clash with the customary entitlements of chiefs and headmen to the labour and services of their dependants. The local administration, on the other hand, wanted to uphold the power of chiefs and headmen to enforce 'community obligations', because this term had been usefully stretched to include the supply of labour and porterage for official purposes.[90] For instance, to illustrate his complaint that Christianisation eroded a sense of community responsibility, J. P. Mills pointed out that very few Christian Aos had joined the Naga Labour Corps.[91]

World War One meant a shortage of funds and personnel for missions in India, but it also opened up some new and unexpected contexts for evangelical work. Missionaries agreed to assist in recruitment to prove to sometimes sceptical officials that Christianity did not 'spoil' converts and create an aversion to manual labour, but shaped 'primitive' or stigmatised populations into productive and loyal subjects.[92] The military framework also offered an orderly environment in which first-generation Christians might be instructed in the principles and practices of belief. If a mission managed to raise a significant proportion of a labour company, then a priest or a chaplain could accompany it, and some were given commissioned rank and appointments. This was a convenient arrangement given the immense strain on the Indian Army Officer Reserve and the difficulty of finding British officers who knew

---

[89] See below.

[90] J. P. Mills, *The Ao Nagas*, London: Macmillan, 1926, pp. 419–20.

[91] Ibid., p. 420.

[92] Missionaries often felt compelled to offer reassurance on this point. Father Douglass declared that the Christians of his Bengal company 'worked better and kept their billets cleaner than the other Indian Labour Corps'. Speech in London, reprinted as 'Oxford Calcutta Mission', *The Times*, 11 January 1918. A. W. McMillan, missionary and YMCA worker, said Indian Christians in military service had displayed an 'active loyalty, keen intelligence, and literacy, and a preparedness to engage in manual labour'. A. W. McMillan, 'Indian Echoes from France', *The East and the West*, vol. XVIII (1920), pp. 1–20.

the local language. The YMCA was strictly prohibited from any religious activity when working with Indian troops and followers, but it was permitted to address religious themes in those labour companies which had a large number of Christians.

In the Naga and Manipur hills the pace of Christian conversion was still painfully slow. A 1918 American Baptist Mission report stated that J. Riley Bailey of the Impur mission in the Naga Hills would spend his furlough with the Nagas in France. 'Twenty-five hundred Naga Gospels furnished by the Publication Society will be distributed to the members of the Coolie Corps, and the promising evangelist work begun in their own villages will be continued in France.'[93] It also noted the 'unexpected opening of work among Burmans with BEF [British Expeditionary Force] in France.'[94]

The American Baptist Mission hoped that the presence of Nagas, Garos and Chins working behind the lines in Europe would stimulate public support for the missions, a hope raised further by the entry of America into the war in April 1917.[95] The 1918 report notes that:

> During the last four years, strange things have happened ... Perhaps one of the most startling to the Christian world, which has been ... sending its missionaries to the uttermost parts of the earth, has been to find that the 'uttermost parts' are coming nearer and are actually taking a share in the great war for democracy 'overseas'.[96]

However, when Baptists set out from Asia for Europe, it was not only to safeguard those 'ignorant of temptations of so-called Christian nations' but also to save American troops from the many girls in France waiting to cause them 'an untold injury'.[97] Taken aback by the religious ignorance of British

---

[93] *Baptists in World Service*, Boston: American Baptist Foreign Mission Society, 1918, p. 110 (henceforth *BWS*).

[94] E. Griggs, 26 January 1918, *BWS*, p. 106. Whether this effort succeeded is not clear. In 1919–20, the missionary F. J. Sandy noted, gratefully if obliquely, that young men 'whose religious life had been adversely affected by their stay in France' had 'been brought back to the Church in penitence.' Vanlalchhuanawma, *Christianity and Subaltern Culture*, pp. 232–33, 263.

[95] *BWS*, p. 110. To interest an American readership in the Garos, Ewing referred to their 'valiant work as soldiers in Europe', digging trenches for British and American troops. Ruth Grimes Ewing, *Our Life with the Garos of Assam, India*, Philadelphia: Dorrance and Company, 1971, pp. 72, 80.

[96] *BWS*, pp. 107, 110.

[97] J. Riley Bailey to Reverend Aitchison (n.d.), *BWS*, p. 111.

troops in Palestine, an Anglican chaplain wrote that it was 'just as much missionary work here as in Chota Nagpur'.[98]

By assisting in recruitment, missionaries could offer work with a regular wage to their economically hard-pressed laity. The appointment of local catechists and mission schoolteachers and schoolboys as headmen, mates or interpreters vindicated the value of mission schooling.[99] Service in France was also supposed to make visible that wider Christian ecumene to which the laity were told they now belonged. The Baptist missionary William Pettigrew would use an extraordinarily cataclysmic image to claim that this objective had been fulfilled. One Tangkhul Naga declared that they had previously had:

> little faith in your stories of lands across the seas and oceans, peopled with beings who believed in the Christ you preached to us, but we have seen with our own eyes the emblem of the cross over thousands of graves on the battlefields, and the beautiful grave stones in the cemeteries of France.[100]

It would be a mistake, however, to overestimate the persuasive influence of the European missionary, thereby overlooking the far wider reach of the 'native' catechist.[101] In 1912 Pettigrew had in fact been forbidden to move around in the Kuki areas of Manipur, and he had been away in Gauhati since 1916. He himself acknowledged the crucial role played by the Meitei headmaster of the Ukhrul school, Angom Porom Singh, and other local catechists in the raising of the Manipur Labour Corps.[102] For this educated stratum, enrolment in the

---

[98] *Chota Nagpur Diocesan Paper*, vol. 43, March 1918, p. 3.

[99] The staff and schoolboys of the American Baptist School at Ukhrul went as mates, headmen and interpreters in the Manipur Labour Corps. William Pettigrew, 'My Twenty-Five Years 1897–1922 at Ukhrul Mission School', in *Reverend William Pettigrew: A Pioneer Missionary of Manipur*, Imphal: Fraternal Green Cross, 1996. Appendix, p. viii. Educated boys from Shillong were appointed as interpreters and mates for the Khasi Labour Corps.

[100] Pettigrew, 'My Twenty-Five Years', appendix, p. viii.

[101] Lorrain acknowledged that it was the 'travelling evangelists' of the American Baptist and Welsh Calvinist missions, 'trusted everywhere', who had been crucial to Lushai recruitment. J. H. Lorrain to Mrs Lewin, 21 July 1917, MS 811/iv/65/7(i), SHL. Some seventy to eighty Christian Thadou Kukis in the Manipur Labour Corps had been converted by Dala, a Lushai missionary. *SLRBMS, 1919*, p. 152.

[102] Some of the educated recruits who went with the Manipur Labour Corps as interpreters emerged as prominent figures in the Baptist church: R. S. Ruichumhao, a famous Tangkhul Naga evangelist; Ngulhao Thomsong, a teacher at Tujang

lower command ranks of the Labour Corps, like participation in evangelical activity or the acquisition of literacy, offered opportunities for self-transformation which would emplace them in the new political order.[103]

The 'aboriginals' of Bihar and Orissa

This recruiting will prove a blessing for the country. More than 2,000 Catholic families are saved from poverty; some 200 pagans have joined the Catholic corps, cut their *'chungis'* and bought rosaries. I expect the bank deposits to reach the sum of 2 lakhs, a third of which will go to the families, and two-thirds will constitute a clean profit for the country and our men.[104]

Many stupid rumours have been running wild ... The Padris are now doing *arkatia* work and sending their Christians to be slaughtered in Europe.[105]

In Bihar and Orissa the local government drew upon prominent landlords to raise men for the ILC for France, praising in particular the assistance of Raja Krityanand Singh of the Banaili estate and Raja Rajendra Narayan Bhanja Deo of Kanika in Orissa.[106] In the 3,546-acre Damin-i-Koh estate in the Santhal Parganas, the government, which was itself the landlord, sanctioned an annual rent remission of up to Rs 10/–for ten years to every tenant who enlisted in the ILC. Tea-planters were apprehensive that military recruitment would disrupt the supply of 'Santhali' labour, but the Assam Labour Board did give some help in recruitment and recommended two planters as 'supervisors'.[107] The local government also drew upon the assistance of the Belgian Jesuit Mission and the Anglican Society for the Propagation of the

---

Vaoichong in Kuki territory; and Teba Kilong, a Kom evangelist. *BWS, 1918*; Pettigrew, 'My Twenty-Five Years', p. viii.

[103] See Chapter 5; also Vanlalchhuanawma, *Christianity and Subaltern Culture*; and Joy L. K. Pachuau and William Schendel, *The Camera as Witness: A Social History of Mizoram, Northeast India*, Delhi: Cambridge University Press, 2015, pp. 36–212.

[104] 'Ranchi, From Rev. Fr. Molhant s.j.', *The Catholic Herald of India*, 27 June 1917, p. 410 (henceforth *TCHI*). The Jesuits insisted that converts cut their *chungis* (topknots) so that they could not pass themselves off as 'pagans'.

[105] Father Bodson, diary entry, 11 June 1917, in M. Vermeire, *History of Barway Mission*, Katkahi, n.d., p. 157.

[106] 13 March 1918, *Proceedings of the Legislative Council of the Lieutenant-Governor of Bihar and Orissa Legislative Council, 1918*.

[107] Secretary Army Dept to CC Assam, 8 December 1917, IOR/L/MIL7/18302.

Gospel (SPG) Mission.[108] The missions were facing a situation in which poverty-driven migration to tea plantations was making it difficult to stabilise the promising Christian communities emerging in Chota Nagpur.[109] The Jesuit mission was exploring the idea of setting up a kind of 'labour exchange' through which members of the laity could be sent to those tea gardens or mines where the management might give time off for Sunday mass and allow a priest or catechist to keep in touch.[110] The other challenge was the Tana Bhagat movement, whose messianic call for religious and social transformation was receiving a response from poorer and more marginal sections of tribal society.[111] In Jesuit histories of Chota Nagpur, the 'pagan revival', or the 'great apostasy', competes with the Great War as one of the significant events of the time.[112] To guard against its allure, the rudiments of Catholic or Protestant belief and practice had to be inculcated more rigorously, but financial constraints imposed by the war made it difficult to organise religious instruction

---

[108] The SPG mission had also taken charge of the Gossner Evangelical Lutheran Mission after the internment of its German pastors.

[109] The exodus to tea plantations was family-based, so it disrupted primary schools where the next generation might be brought up properly Catholic, or Protestant. Nor was it always possible to provide a pastor at the other end. The Jesuit mission tried to build up a buffer against bad seasons through the organisation of grain banks, the *gola dhan*, and the founding in 1909 of the Catholic Co-Operative Credit Bank at Ranchi. Peter Tete, *A Missionary Social Worker in India; The Chota Nagpur Tenancy Act and the Catholic Cooperatives (1893–1928)*, Ranchi: Satya Bharatchi Press, 1986. The SPG mission ran a much smaller co-operative bank.

[110] Father T. Van Der Schueren, *Moral and Intellectual Uplift of the Aboriginal Races of Chota Nagpur, India*, London: East and West, 1928, p. 10; Edward A. Violett, 'Faith Based Development: The Social Development Perspective in Catholic Social Teaching, With an Illustrative Case Study of the Ranchi Archdiocese', Ph.D. thesis, University of London, 2003, p. 258–60. Members of the Catholic laity did not always move obediently to the favoured employer. Vermeire, *History of Barway Mission*, pp. 192–94.

[111] See Sangeeta Dasgupta's nuanced exploration, 'Reordering a World: The Tana Bhagat Movement, 1914–1919', *Studies in History*, vol. 15, no. 1 (1999), pp. 1–41.

[112] 'Like the World war for Europeans so the great subject of interest here ... is the Oraon pagan revival.' 'Mandar', in *TCHI*, 19 January 1916, p. 41. In February 1917, 'Bhagatism' was reported to be wreaking havoc among Catholics in Chechari, Palamau, with 'some 4500 having "apostatised"'. Vermeire, *History of Barway Mission*, p. 193.

camps.[113] Military service offered the opportunity to address the laity in an orderly, routinised environment, and Fathers Henri Floor and Frans Ory, who accompanied the labour companies recruited from this area, would grasp it with both hands.[114]

The Jesuit mission agreed to assist in recruitment on condition that priests would accompany lay people, and that wages would be paid through the Catholic Co-operative Credit Bank at Ranchi. Recruitment to the ILC allowed families to stay where they were. The wives of some of the men recruited from Ranchi went on working at piece rates at the lace school run there by the Ursuline nuns.[115] The Jesuit and Anglican missions constituted the link between the men overseas and their families, so community interactions deepened. Reverend Cashmore of the SPG mission recalled that he used to cycle out to the rural surrounds of Ranchi to hand over remittances while his clerk read out letters to an excited audience and composed letters for France.[116] The savings deposited by the laity in the Catholic bank pushed its capital assets up by Rs 450,000/–(four and a half lakhs) in 1918.[117]

Lest the *padres* loom too large in this story, it is necessary to note another more powerful, if less visible, layer of authority which shaped the decision to enlist or not to enlist. This was the *panchayat*, an assembly either of a village or a group of villages, usually dominated by the Bhuinhars—those tribal families who claimed they were the original settlers of a tract, and held larger farms on privileged tenures. Such *panchayats* had played a key role in the decision to approach a particular mission (Lutheran, Anglican or Jesuit), to shift from the one to the other, or to 'apostasise'—that is, to join the Tana Bhagat cult. The Jesuit mission encouraged the setting up of *panchayats* under its own aegis, in a bid to exercise disciplinary control over the laity and to participate in the running of the grain reserve and the co-operative bank.[118] Father Dejardin

---

[113] *TCHI*, 30 May 1917, p. 346. Conference of 17–18 October 1917 at Ranchi on schools in Chota Nagpur. Typescript, Vidya Jyoti Library, New Delhi.

[114] See Chapter 5.

[115] 'Over There!', *TCHI*, 28 November 1917, p. 802.

[116] Cashmore, 'The Raj'.

[117] These savings were said to have enabled returning men to redeem or buy lands, or purchase cattle. Van Der Schueren, *Moral and Intellectual Uplift of the Aboriginal Races of Chota Nagpur*, pp. 13–14. The SPG mission also tried to direct the use of savings to 'productive' ends. *Chota Nagpur Diocesan Paper*, October–November 1918, Bishop's Lodge, Ranchi.

[118] Vermeire, *History of Barway Mission*, pp. 194–98.

said his efforts to recruit around Noadih were uncertain until a 'panchayat was made' which allowed him to enlist 150 men in eight days, although forty-nine cancelled their undertaking.[119] From Katkahi, Father Bodson reported that recruiting began on 27 May 1917, when a *panchayat* of 1,400 men was held.[120] On the other hand, in September 1917 a *panchayat* was held 'on the sly' at Dumberpatha which declared that 'they had resolved to become *bhagat* if they were forced in any way.'[121]

And 'primitives' who wouldn't go: the 1917 Mayurbhanj uprising

> *Bhanjabhuiye meli hailo*
> *Kanka Majhir phansi hailo*
> *Oh tusu haar agdali*
> *Kalia Mahator phanshi hailo*
> *Baripada jhar jhanai*
> *Retu Kol-Kumar aur*
> *Nayan Singh Munda marod bhathe bhai.*[122]

'Success' in recruiting for the Labour Corps was actually a very textured phenomenon, with many smaller disturbances excised from subsequent accounts. However, within roughly contiguous tracts some communities went more willingly than others. To cope with the escalating demand for 'aboriginal labour', the government of Bihar and Orissa decided to extend recruitment to the 'feudatory' states under Indian chiefs and princes. In May 1917 the British Political Agent J. E. Scott launched a recruiting drive in the princely state of Mayurbhanj, pressing headmen to meet their quotas in a fortnight.[123] However,

---

[119] 'Noadih', *TCHI*, 4 July 1917, p. 426.

[120] Vermeire, *History of Barway Mission*, p. 157.

[121] Ibid., p. 157.

[122] Song collected from Sukhi Mahato, of Chitroda village, in Pashupati Prasad Mahato, 'Assertion and Reassertion as Jharkhandi: A History of Indigenous People of 1763–2007', in Asha Mishra and Chittaranjan Kumar Paty (eds), *Tribal Movements in Jharkhand, 1857–2007*, New Delhi: Concept Publishing, 2010, pp. 43–57. The song refers to the *meli* (rebellious gathering) which took place in the land of the Bhanja ruler—that is, Mayurbhanj. Kanka Majhi, Kalia Mahato, Retu Kol Kumar and Nayan Sing Munda Mahato threw Baripada into turmoil and were sent to the gallows. 'These were real men indeed!' Ibid.

[123] F&P, Internal, A, September 1918, nos 84–100. Father Op de Beeck at Krishnachandrapur wrote that going by the description of his catechist, Joseph

the 'Santhalis' refused to turn up and began to deploy a pointedly traditional form of assembly to resist the demand:

> The aboriginal population had withdrawn their confidence entirely from all persons ... connected with the administration of the State ... *Ganthias* were generally circulated, forbidding coolies to carry the luggage of State officers, to pay *chaukidari* [watchmen] tax and to pay for *handia* [rice beer] at *hats* [markets].[124]

The railway line at Betanoti was ripped up, the cart road was cut off, and telegraph wires were pulled down.[125] Some subordinate officials and village headmen engaged in recruitment were assaulted, some Marwari traders were looted, and, significantly, the forest pass office was destroyed.[126] However, there was no loss of life, and troops and military police met with no resistance. The government called off recruitment in Mayurbhanj, and on 26 May 1917 the Commissioner of Orissa declared that the trouble was over.[127]

However, the 'Santhals' continued to hold assemblies in which grievances were aired about forest and excise regulations. On 15 June 1917 one such gathering clashed with the police at Rairangpur, resulting in the death of one constable and two tribals, and the sensational plundering and burning of the marketplace and the police station. Armed police made extensive arrests and 1,118 prisoners were tried, 712 for major offences and 406 for minor. Of the 977 who were convicted, four were sentenced to death and many others to long terms of imprisonment.[128]

Massia, recruiting methods were 'very un-English and rather Prussian!' His own account features a 'jungly race' stirred up by 'false rumours'. However, he had to accept that they knew about submarines, drifting mines and aerial bombing. 'The Santal Rising in Mayurbhanj, A Diary', *TCHI*, 6 June 1917, pp. 359–60.

[124] Political Agent, Orissa Feudatory States to Commissioner Orissa Division, 15 July 1917, F&P, Internal, A, September 1918, nos 84–100. *Ganthias* were knots on a rope indicating a day of assembly. The circulation of *ganthias* was officially prohibited except as summons to a hunt.

[125] *TCHI*, 6 June 1917, pp. 359–60.

[126] Home, Political, Deposit, October 1917, no. 47.

[127] Ibid. To address alarmist press reports about the danger of stirring up a 'backward' people, the Government of Bihar and Orissa issued a press communiqué on 27 May 1917 reassuring the public that labour units for France would be 'staffed by civilian officers acquainted with the languages and customs of the aboriginals.' Ibid. No such reassurance was found necessary in 'Santhali' recruitment for Mesopotamia, or later for the North-West Frontier.

[128] Of the 'disturbance cases', four were sentenced to death; thirty-three to transporta-

Trying to understand why 'aborigines' in Mayurbhanj had risen against labour recruitment when similar communities in the Santhal Parganas and Chota Nagpur had provided 4,000 men for France, the Bihar administration concluded that the former were more 'backward', whereas the latter had 'for many generations been in close contact with European officials and missionaries'.[129] Interestingly, a petition presented by one Baiju Manjhi to the Commissioner on 25 May 1917 invokes these same ideas of ignorance and isolation to make its case.[130] The British Political Agent claimed that it had been drafted by Oriya elites, reluctant to lose Santhali labour.[131] However, the assertiveness with which the 'Santhals' fashioned a collective self at this point, recalling their chiefs to community norms and attacking 'outsider' trading groups such as the Marwaris, is a clear indication of broader agency:

> Respected Sir:
>
> We are practically living with wild animals and as it were have not been in the society of human beings ... We do not know what service is and we have never seen any place outside the Mayurbhanj State. We only wear coarse cloth and do not know what a coat or shirt is.[132]

However, further into the petition certain cracks emerge in this picture of panicked 'primitives'. The terms of service are carefully outlined, to clarify that they have been understood in generous detail but not accepted:

> The *Hakims* [persons in authority] of this place came to us and said that we shall have to go to England, have to wear coats, shirts, pants and hats, get Rs. 20/–pay per month, besides half a seer of meal, one seer rice, two chittacks dal with salt, spices, oil, earthen pots and fuel daily and that we shall get an advance of

---

tion for life; one to rigorous imprisonment (RI) for life; thirteen to fourteen years' transportation; nineteen to ten years' transportation; thirty to seven years' transportation; eight to ten years' RI; sixty-eight to seven years' RI; three to six years' RI; 193 to five years' RI; sixty-six to between five and three years' RI; 368 to between three years' and one year's RI; 163 to RI for one year or less; seven to payment of a fine; and one to whipping. Twenty-seven men under trial died in jail. *Report on the Administration of Mayurbhanj for 1917–1918*, Baripada: State Press, Mayurbhanj, 1918. The death sentences were commuted to transportation for life. F&P, Internal, A, September 1918, nos 84–100.

[129] F&P, Internal, A, September 1918, nos 84–100.
[130] Ibid.
[131] Ibid.
[132] Ibid.

Rs. 60/–per man. We did not agree to this. We were then threatened saying that we shall have to go in handcuffs, bound in pair[s] and marched under strong guard armed with guns. The Officers ... forcibly took our thumb impressions under threats.[133]

As one judge pointed out, the Santhals of Mayurbhanj were familiar with long-distance migration, some travelling regularly to Assam, or to the Sunderbans for railway work and forest clearance.[134] The petition itself indicates that waged work was a familiar and important means of livelihood.[135] But recruitment to the Labour Corps was experienced not as contract work but as a capture of the person, an extension of state corvée.[136] The petition also requested an investigation into the rising number of forest and excise cases, an index of the conflict over natural resources.[137]

The construction of the Mayurbhanj State Light Railway, inaugurated in 1905, had advanced far enough by 1912 to boost the extraction of forest products, a trend stimulated further by the wartime demand for railway sleepers and tanning bark.[138] The other factor at play was the discovery of rich iron ore reserves in Mayurbhanj, and the awarding of a licence to the Tata Iron and Steel Company in April 1917 which permitted it to prospect for ore over a forested tract of 1,588.16 square miles.[139] On 4 June 1917 a Santhal gathering had taken place at Gurumahisani, close to Tata's iron ore mine. The administration insisted that the choice of site had no significance, and yet it posted 100 riflemen there.[140] To defend their person, and their access to forest resources and a competitive wage structure, Santhals in Mayurbhanj flaunted a cohesive ethnic identity and humbled headmen who had grown too powerful.[141] As the British

---

[133] Ibid.

[134] Ibid.

[135] The petition noted that when there were many contractors for public works wages were competitive, but now monopoly prevailed. Ibid.

[136] The petition complained that *padhans* (headmen) had been forced to put their signature or thumb-impression to an undertaking to produce recruits, and that the *sardar* (chief) of Chitrada had measured the chests of the men sent up. Ibid.

[137] Ibid.

[138] Sailendra Nath Sarkar, *Biography of the Maharaja Sri Ram Chandra Bhanj Deo, Feudatory Chief of Mayurbhanj*, Calcutta: Mayurbhanj Estate, 1918, pp. 60, 90; *Report on the Administration of Mayurbhanj for 1917–1918*.

[139] F&P, Internal, B, April 1917, no. 460. The total area of the state was 4,243 miles.

[140] Home, Political, Deposit, October 1917, no. 47.

[141] F&P, Internal, A, September 1918, nos 84–100. The Santhal chief of Murda was

Political Agent pointed out, even after ILC recruitment was brought to an end the Santhals had 'got used to holding meetings' and discussing their grievances.[142] Once they were reassured about forced recruitment, wrote *The Catholic Herald of India*, 'out came ... the usual threnody on excise, forest and monopoly.'[143] However, the trial of 1,118 men and the severity of the sentences handed out underlined the government's determination that there would be no disruption to the wartime supply of iron ore and timber.

The Kuki-Chin 'punitive operations', 1917–19

Hundreds of miles eastwards, ILC recruitment set off even more violent convulsions in the hills encircling the Manipur valley and stretching in the east to the unadministered tract of Somra and in the north up to the Naga Hills district. When they proposed to extend the area of control across the border of upper Assam, the local government could emphasise the importance of inhibiting Chinese influence along trade routes to Tibet and protecting British investments in tea, coal, lumber and rubber against 'tribal forays'.[144] The Government of India had also begun to express its unease about Japan's communication networks with Tibet.[145] However, it was more difficult to build up an imperial case for absorbing the tribal 'Alsatia' between the borders of Assam and Burma, although many Assam officials viewed its existence as an anomaly.[146] In a dispatch dated 13 November 1908, Lord Morley, the Secretary of State for India, had rejected the Eastern Bengal and Assam government's proposal to extend the boundary of the Naga Hills district eastwards into unadministered territory, warning that unauthorised extensions could have 'wider and more serious

---

not admitted to one Santhal meeting until he had humbled himself and conformed to the prescription that shoes, umbrella and a coat were not to be worn. Ibid.

[142] Political Agent, Orissa Feudatory States to Commissioner Orissa Division, 15 July 1917; ibid.

[143] *TCHI*, 30 May 1917, p. 341. It also hinted at the hand of a 'seditionist' Bengali professor. Ibid.

[144] Reid, *History of the Frontier Areas*, pp. 212–13; p. 139.

[145] WW1/1161/H, vol. 603, no. 100797, p. 95. A temporary North-East Frontier Intelligence Corps, based on tribal informants, was set up during the war. In 1919 the C-in-C, India wanted it to be made permanent in order to monitor Japan. Army Despatch, 1918–19, nos 81–109, no. 95.

[146] Ibid.

results' than anticipated.[147] This directive slowed, but did not stop, the incremental movement to close the gap, which continued even after Britain declared itself at war with Germany in August 1914.[148]

The most formidable resistance to the slow merger of the Assam-Burma border was expected to come from the Kuki chiefs. In 1910, the Assam administration had begun to restrict the migration of Kuki clans into unadministered territory by trying to prevent the hiving off of new villages, amalgamating existing villages into larger settlements, controlling access to firearms, and exacting house tax and corvée more rigorously.[149] Another strategy was to sponsor the building up of Naga ethnic borders in an attempt to hem the Kukis into a smaller zone of influence, a tactic which sharpened ethnic distinctions and escalated feuding.[150]

Against this backdrop, the Assam government's willingness to supply labour for France sprang from its eagerness to display the hold its officers had over the hill tribes, especially those in the lightly ruled or transfrontier tracts where it aimed to redraw the border.[151] A large number of the men in the Naga Labour Corps were drawn from the transfrontier Semas and Changs.[152]

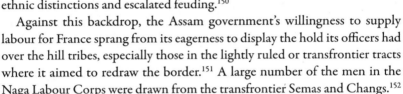

[147] Despatch no. 128, Political, 13 November 1908, in Reid, *History of the Frontier Areas*, pp. 141–42.

[148] Ibid., pp. 142–44.

[149] Ibid., pp. 143–46.

[150] In 1906, and again in 1913–14, the Assam government pressed the Government of India for permission to extend the area of political control eastwards from the Naga Hills, incorporating Sema and Chang territory and pushing out Kuki settlements. Ibid., pp. 137–41.

[151] Of the Naga Hills, the Chief Secretary, Assam reported that '[t]he Angamis, Kacha Nagas and Kukis refused to volunteer'. F&P, External, B, August 1917, no. 21. However, unlike the Kukis of Manipur they were not threatened with retribution.

[152] Ibid. In January 1917, J. H. Hutton had raised a Sema Naga Coolie Corps for an expedition to upper Assam. A couple of months later he began to recruit them for the Naga Labour Corps for France, and in April 1918 he was using Sema scouts and porters to launch attacks on the Kukis at Lapvomi and Akhan. F&P, Secret, External, August 1919, nos 54–156. Reid described the Naga Labour Corps as drawn from '1000 Semas, 400 Lhotas, 200 Regmas, 200 Aos, 200 Changs and other trans-frontier tribes.' Reid, *History of the Frontier Areas*, p. 162. In September 1921, arguing that recruitment had forged a close relationship with them, the Assam government secured the incorporation of Sema and Chang territories into the Naga Hills district. Ibid., pp. 151–54.

The refusal of the Thado, Haokip and Mangum Kuki chiefs in Manipur and its borderlands to send men for the Labour Corps was, therefore, a blow to this ambition.[153] These Kuki chiefs probably balked at supplying recruits because it would have stripped them of fighting men when they were already feeling encircled.[154] For some chiefs of southern Manipur and the Chin hills, the sense of threat became more imminent; for others, opportunities to change the local balance of power opened up.[155]

Military police columns began burning villages and destroying or capturing food and livestock to starve rebels into submission. Kukis started to trek from the Manipur hills into unadministered territory to the north-east.[156] On the Burma side, as Labour Corps recruitment extended beyond Tiddim it triggered an uprising among the southern Chins, who besieged the military post at Haka on 12 December 1917.[157] Laura Carson, of the American Baptist Chin Mission, painted a shocking picture of the military reprisals which followed:

> The Relief Column ... went to Hniar Lawn ... the leading village in the rebellion, and shot the cattle and hogs, confiscated the grain and fowls and burned the village—a thoroughly German performance ... I do not see what is to prevent many of them [women and children] starving to death.[158]

Yet by February 1918 the GOI had to inform the India Office that the 'the Kuki-Chin disturbances have been found more difficult to tackle than was anticipated.'[159] The onset of the rains in mid-1918 compounded the difficulty

---

[153] F&P, External, B, August 1917, no. 21.

[154] According to Bhadra, chiefs feared that if they forced their clansmen to join the ILC, the latter could easily desert them for rival chiefs along a mobile ethnic frontier. Gautam Bhadra, 'The Kuki (?) Uprising (1917–1919): Its Causes and Nature', *Man in India*, vol. 55, no. 1 (1975), pp. 10–56.

[155] For a close analysis of local stakes see David Vumlallian Zou, 'Patriots and Utilitarians in the Anglo-Kuki War: The Case of Southern Manipur, 1917–1919', in Guite and Haokip, *The Anglo-Kuki War*, pp. 157–67.

[156] F&P, Secret, External, July 1918, nos 7–131.

[157] J. Shakespear papers, IOR Mss Eur. 361/14, IOR; Reid, *History of the Frontier Areas*, pp. 79–81.

[158] Laura Carson to Dr and Mrs Tilbe, 13 December 1917, in Robert G. Johnson, *History of the American Baptist Chin Mission*, vol. 1, Valley Forge, PA: R. G. Johnson, 1988, p. 419.

[159] F&P, Secret, External, July 1918, nos 7–131.

of the terrain, and the Burma Military Police requested airfields and 'punishment from the air'.[160] Punitive operations began to blur the line between hostiles and 'friendlies'. The Tangkhul Nagas of Manipur, counted among the 'friendlies', were very reluctant to enter the concentration camps set up for them at Ukhrul in July 1918, which were intended both to protect them from Kuki reprisals and to remove supplies from rebel reach.[161] Impressing porters for the 'operations' caused friction and put immense pressure on agricultural production—still more so as the influenza pandemic took its ghastly toll in winter 1918.[162]

The scope of the operations was also under debate. Blaming the local governments for 'injudicious' recruiting, the India Office and the Foreign and Political Department of the Government of India argued that where rebel chiefs surrendered, or the inhabitants were well-disposed, it was not desirable to occupy their territory.[163] However, the Assam and Burma governments favoured a thoroughgoing pacification and tighter cross-border control over the Manipur hills and the adjacent tracts of Somra and Thaungdut State.[164] D'Urban Keary shared this sentiment, defining, in October 1918, the goal of the winter operations as the complete occupation of all territory, friendly or

---

[160] Ibid.; F&P, External, B, August 1918, no. 13.

[161] Chief Secy Assam to Secy F&P, 6 July 1918 and 7 August 1918, F&P, Secret, External, August 1919, nos 54–156.

[162] *Report on the Administration of Assam for 1918–19*, Government of India, 1919, p. 4; F&P, General, B, January 1919, nos 460–63; F&P, Secret, External, August 1919, nos 54–156. The C-in-C, Assam attributed a drop in revenue collection to 'the removal of thousands of the [Manipur] State's subjects to act as transport columns.' 22 May 1919, Home, Political, A, 1919. The informality of recruitment for porters during this campaign meant that whereas the heirs of those who died in France received a gratuity of Rs 300/–, the heirs of those who died in the Kuki-Chin operations received only Rs 100/–. Home Police, B, September 1918, nos 238–39; Home Police, A, September 1918, nos 82–83.

[163] Note by K.F., in F&P Dept, 22 October 1918, in F&P, Secret, External, August 1919, nos 54–156. Writing in confidence to the Viceroy on 8 March 1918, the SSI had noted disapprovingly that the Assam government's position amounted to saying that 'local arrangements governing the supply of labour for local services are applicable to service in Europe under military conditions.' F&P, Secret, External, July 1918, nos 7–131.

[164] F&P, External, A, December 1917, nos 1–6.

otherwise, until a complete settlement was reached.[165] Three columns of the Burma Military Police advanced into Somra in December 1918 even though the Kukis there had surrendered, blockading villages to extract arms and enforcing punitive labour to construct mule-paths.[166] 'I decided', D'Urban Keary reported, 'to break up (when not already done in the course of operations) small outlying hamlets, and make larger settlements under responsible men—these ... to be linked up with mule roads.'[167]

The operations were concluded by April 1919, and the territorial changes crystallised by 1923. Somra was integrated into the Chin Hills division in Burma and the Manipur hills were broken up into three sub-divisions under British officers to reduce Thadou-Kuki influence.[168] Jurisdictional boundaries were plotted out on more strongly ethnicised lines, as between the hill and valley people of Manipur and between Nagas and Kukis along the Manipur-Naga Hills border.[169] The Kuki-Chin operations were heavily censored, but they drew attention to the hill-men companies in France, who were thereafter cast as exemplars of loyalty to the Raj.

The problems and possibilities of 'primitivity'

In France, Lord Ampthill, advisor to the Department of Labour for the ILC, wondered how men 'from the hills and jungles, who have barely emerged from barbarism' would shape up as labour.[170] '[A] distinct limit', he wrote, 'is

---

[165] Chief Secy, Burma to A. H. Grant, F&P, 18 October 1918, F&P, Secret, External, August 1919, nos 54–156. Lieutenant General Henry D'Urban Keary to Chief of General Staff, June 1919, IOR/L/MIL7/16899.

[166] D'Urban Keary, June 1919, IOR/L/MIL7/16899.

[167] Ibid. This strategy would become a chillingly familiar one in 'counter-insurgency operations' along this frontier in independent India. See Nandini Sundar, 'Interning Insurgent Populations: The Buried Histories of Indian Democracy', *Economic and Political Weekly*, vol. 46, no. 6 (2011), pp. 47–57.

[168] F&P, Secret, External, August 1919, nos 54–156.

[169] Ibid. The Assam government allowed the Baptist mission to expand its activity in the Manipur hills, and its students supplied the 'clerks, peons, road *muharrirs*, supervisors, vaccinators, compounders' needed when the hill districts were reorganised. Pettigrew, 'My Twenty-Five Years'; William Pettigrew, 'Manipur State 1891–1932', *The Baptist Missionary Review*, vol. XXXVIII, no. II (1932). *Muharrirs*: accountants overseeing road construction.

[170] Ampthill to DOL, 18 July 1917, IOR/L/MIL5/738.

imposed to their utility by their inferior physique and intelligence and by their exotic nature.'[171] Inspecting the Naga companies at Beaumetz, he cautioned the Department of Labour about the tendency of the British soldier 'to treat the Indians as Gollywogs'.[172] However, Ampthill was not invulnerable himself to the charms of exoticism, confessing in a rush that 'these Nagas, Khasis, Manipuris and Lushais' were after all 'very engaging savages':

> Their friendly smiles, their childish adornment, their weird chants and the stark nudity which they affect at every possible opportunity all combine to disarm professional military criticism and in its stead to excite ethnological interest.[173]

Ampthill, former Governor of Madras and briefly *pro tem* Viceroy in 1904, was a paradoxical figure. Educated Indians, struggling against civic discrimination in South Africa, counted him as a sympathiser, and at Gandhi's request he wrote the foreword to the Mahatama's first biography.[174] Yet his position in 1917 was at the far right of the British political spectrum.[175] On Indian affairs, he was one of a set of luminaries bitterly critical of Edwin Montagu's promise in August 1917 of an advance to self-government, holding that trusteeship remained the most viable model for India.[176] No wonder, then, that the confident paternalism of Assam officers who had been appointed to command positions in the ILC struck a chord with Ampthill.[177] He suggested that the Assam-Burma hill-men had come all the way to France not to earn a wage but

---

[171] Ampthill to H. V. Cox, 31 July 1917, IOR/L/MIL5/738.

[172] Ampthill to DOL, 15 August 1917, IOR/L/MIL5/738. The war journalist Candler used the same phrase—'happy black golliwogs'—for Santhal labour in Mesopotamia. Edmund Candler, *The Sepoy*, London: John Murray, 1919, p. 218.

[173] Ampthill to DOL, 15 August 1917, IOR/L/MIL5/738, p. 228.

[174] Reverend Joseph J. Doke, *M. K. Gandhi: An Indian Patriot in South Africa*, London: London Indian Chronicle, 1909.

[175] See W. D. Rubinstein, 'Henry Page Croft and the National Party, 1917–1922', *Journal of Contemporary History*, vol. 9, no. 1 (1974), pp. 129–48.

[176] See 'Indo-British Association: Inaugural meeting', *TOI*, 10 December 1917, p. 12. For Ampthill's bitter opposition to the Government of India Bill of 1919, see *HL*, Deb, 16 December 1919, vol. 38, nos 111–202. Lord Sydenham, former governor of Bombay, was another prominent figure in this lobby.

[177] Among the Commanding Officers of the Assam labour companies were senior civil servants such as Lieutenant Colonel H. W. G. Cole, Political Agent at Manipur, H. C. Barnes, an ICS officer of twenty-two years' service, and Lieutenant Colonel Alan Playfair, who was also the author of an official ethnography: *The Garos*, London: Nutt, 1909.

out of friendship for the Raj, so their loyalty had to be nurtured to secure the legitimacy of empire in postwar India.[178]

For the Department of Labour in France, the 'primitivity' of some components of the ILC was a vexatious illustration of the difficulty of replacing white manpower with 'coloured' labour.[179] The Chins at Abancourt, asserted one report, were so filthy that they ought to be fumigated before being allowed to handle food supplies, and the Nagas would have to be trained 'in the rudiments of discipline and sanitation'.[180] But the presence of Nagas and Chins in France allowed the Assam-Burma officers to highlight the importance to empire of seemingly obscure reaches of India's frontier, and to make a case for the preservation of a paternalist order of rule in these geopolitical spaces. This agenda was given a further push in spring 1918, when local governments were asked to step up combatant recruiting.[181] The Assam administration responded by drawing upon an administrative-ethnographic tradition which essentialised the 'war-like' proclivities of forest and hill tribes, and their supposed distance from the politically contentious Hindus and Muslims of the Assam valley and the Bengal plains.[182] The Garos and the Northern Chins already had some presence in provincial military police battalions, from which drafts were being taken for the regular army.[183] When Lieutenant General

---

[178] Ampthill reassured the Department of Labour that the Nagas would not get spoilt by the attention they were getting, as they were used to 'friendly chats' with Europeans. The British Deputy Commissioner of their district, no less, would sit down by the wayside to converse informally with them. Ampthill to DOL, 15 August 1917, IOR/L/MIL5/738, p. 228. On the other hand, he cast the 'Santhalis' as 'difficult to manage' and 'not even good carriers', a prejudice also probably filtering in from the Assam officers. Ampthill to DOL, 1 September 1917, and Ampthill to Cox, 10 December 1917, IOR/L/MIL/5/738.

[179] The Department of Labour (DOL) was set up in December 1916 to administer and allocate all unskilled labour, white and 'coloured', in the British sector in France.

[180] TNA WO 95/83.

[181] In May 1918 the Central Recruiting Board assigned a monthly combatant quota of 400 to Assam, with a warning that recruitment in frontier areas had to proceed with 'utmost caution'. F&P, External, B, July 1918, no. 8.

[182] See Foreign, Secret, E, May 1912, nos 201–337. From 1916, *Jheruas* or 'forest tribes', a term which included the Garos, Koches, Meches, Kacharis, and Rajbansis, were recruited more extensively to the Assam military police and the army. Home, Police, A, May 1916, no. 142; F&P, External, B, July 1918, no. 8.

[183] Ibid; and 'History of the Chin Hills Battalion', IOR, Mss Eur. E 250. From June

H. V. Cox came on a tour of the ILC in March 1918, he noted that the Garos 'stood on parade like well drilled soldiers. The Chins ... have a very martial bearing.'[184] Burma wanted to reduce its dependence on 'martial races' from India, and the performance of the Northern Chins in the ILC would be cited as proof of their pluck and their amenability to discipline.[185]

'Sudden contact with higher civilisations at war'

What had to be reconciled in such narratives of loyalty were the ethics of taking 'primitives' across the sea to expose them to modernity in its most horrific avatar. After all, colonial ethnography was marked by a 'salvage mentality': the conviction that primitive cultures were so fragile when brought into contact with advanced civilisations that the ethnographer had to ensure he could record 'original' beliefs and structures before they were eroded.[186] One of the few instances of introspection is to be found in the foreword written by Henry Balfour, first curator of the Pitt Rivers Museum in Oxford, to J. H. Hutton's 1912 monograph *The Sema Nagas*:

> One wonders what impressions remain with them from their sudden contact with higher civilisations at war. Possibly, they are reflecting that ... the White Man's condemnation of the relatively innocuous head-hunting of the Nagas savours of hypocrisy. Or does their sang-froid save them from ... endeavouring to analyse the seemingly inconsequent habits of the leading peoples of culturedom? Now that they are back in their own hills, will they settle down to the indigenous simple life and revert to the primitive conditions which were temporarily disturbed?[187]

Clearly what appealed to Balfour was the notion that 'primitivity' had acted as a shield against any disturbing effect of exposure to modern war. The ethno-

---

1920, the Assam Rifles experimented with the enlistment of 'our late rebels the Kukis'. L. W. Shakespear, *History of the Assam Rifles*, p. 204.

[184] 'Notes on a tour', 9 March 1918, IOR/L/MIL5/738.

[185] F&P, External, A, August 1919, nos 1–2; *TOI*, 27 February 1919. In 1922 a Karen-Chin battalion would be taken across the length and breadth of India to crush a major peasant uprising in coastal Malabar.

[186] James Clifford and George Marcus (eds), *Writing Culture: The Poetics and Politics of Ethnography*, Berkeley: University of California Press, 1986.

[187] Henry Balfour, 'Foreword', in J. H. Hutton, *The Sema Nagas*, London: Macmillan, 1921.

grapher could keep focusing therefore on the more important objective—that of investigating 'the indigenous culture of the Nagas ... before the inevitable changes have wrought havoc with the material for research.'[188] Balfour's other suggestion was that, given the slaughter of the Great War, the interrogator of Naga culture might also reassess the 'barbarity' of head-hunting.[189]

David Zou has argued persuasively that discourses around head-hunting became a site for contestation around codes of masculinity.[190] I suggest that with World War One and the Kuki-Chin operations, the balance shifted from contestation to co-option. Administrators like Hutton and J. P. Mills were beginning to feel that the only way to slow down the debilitating effect upon the Nagas of their exposure to Hinduising or Christianising forces was to give them scope to achieve warrior status in the train of colonial military expeditions.[191]

In 1911–12 we find Bentinck, the Assistant Political Officer, describing with revulsion foraging and plundering by Naga porters during the Abor expedition, even though this was clearly an extension of colonial retribution.[192] The shift in attitude emerges clearly from Hutton's ethnography, *The Sema Nagas*, in which he embraces the idea that it was 'the desire to wear the warrior's pigs tushes and cowrie gauntlets' which kept young men going on expeditions as carriers.[193] 'It is partly this desire, as well as loyalty,' he conti-

---

[188] Ibid.

[189] Ibid.

[190] As Zou explains, colonial administrators and ethnographers derided the idea that head-taking was a mark of bravery, pointing out that heads were taken by treachery and that any head counted, including those of women and children. Colonised communities, for their part, began to invoke an already vanishing practice as 'heritage' for the construction of modern nationalism. David Vumlallian Zou, 'Raiding the Dreaded Past: Representations of Headhunting and Human Sacrifice in North-East India', *Contributions to Indian Sociology*, vol. 39, no. 1 (2005), pp. 75–105.

[191] See below. A drop in the number of taxable households in some Naga villages in 1920–21, possibly a fallout from the influenza epidemic, seemed to confirm Hutton's forebodings that the suppression of headhunting had led to apathy and population decline. See J. H. Hutton, 'Tour diaries in the Naga Hills', 166/952, March 1921, Naga Exploratour, http://himalaya.socanth.cam.ac.uk/collections/naga/record/r72165.html, last accessed 17 November 2019.

[192] Arthur Harold Walter Bentinck papers, Mss Eur. D 1024/3, personal diary.

[193] Hutton, *The Sema Nagas*, p. 173. Hutton was writing in 1917–18.

nued, 'which at the time of writing has just taken 1000 Semas to France.'[194] In his 1923 presidential address to the Folklore Society, Balfour, who was in regular correspondence with Hutton and Mills, suggested delicately that head-hunting was 'not such a bad thing' if it was reciprocal. Any mortality arising from it might well be 'counter-balanced by a higher birth-rate due to the vigour, alertness and the greater physical and mental fitness.'[195] Mills enthused that addresses of this sort were of valuable help in countering missionary perspectives on primitive society.[196]

Warrior dances were incorporated into colonial public spectacle to show that empire made room for the celebration, not the denigration, of this past. The Government of India was seeking at this point to exclude certain areas, including the Assam hill districts, from the model of representative government being worked out for postwar India. In October 1918, outlining its position on constitutional change, the Assam government stressed that two-thirds of the province was made up of tracts populated by 'simple hill tribes governed in patriarchal fashion', which should be excluded from the new electoral dispensation or included with safeguards.[197] The Government of

---

[194] Ibid. Hutton had photographs taken of himself with Sema, Lhota, Ao, Chang and Rengma recruits to the Naga Labour Corps. J. H. Hutton, 'Black and White Photographs', Naga Exploratour, http://himalaya.socanth.cam.ac.uk/collections/naga/record/r57389.html, last accessed 17 November 2019. The Assam government sent spears and shawls along with the Naga and Kuki companies going to France. These are visible as ethnic props in propaganda photographs of the 39th Manipur company taken on 20 October 1917 at Arras, France. IWM, Q6117, Q7243, Q6125. See image 19.

[195] Henry Balfour, presidential address, 'The Welfare of Primitive Peoples', Folklore, vol. 34, no. 1 (1923), pp. 12–24. If the Nagas were to emerge as 'an efficient ethnic unit', he added, the pace and nature of change should be left to the paternalist and ethnographically informed administrator. Ibid. The Pitt Rivers Museum would receive a stream of Naga artefacts via Hutton and Mills, a good many of them acquired in the course of their punitive transborder forays.

[196] J. P. Mills to Balfour, 1 June 1923, Naga Exploratour, http://himalaya.socanth.cam.ac.uk/collections/naga/record/r73841.html, last accessed 17 November 2019. After a 1936 attack on Pangsha in transfrontier territory, Mills exulted that the Nagas in his column, even the Christians, could now don warrior ornaments: 'after all, they are no more heathen than medals gained in war!' J. P. Mills to Pamela Mills, 12 December 1936, Naga Exploratour, http://himalaya.socanth.cam.ac.uk/collections/naga/record/r73909.html, last accessed 17 November 2019.

[197] Chief Secy, Assam to Secy, GOI, Home, 28 October 1918, from 'First Despatch

India Act of 1919 broadened the electorate and gave greater powers to the provincial legislative councils, but section 52A (2) authorised the Governor General-in-Council to declare any territory in British India a 'backward tract', and to withhold the application of any Act of the Indian Legislature to it. Large areas of the Assam province were classified as 'backward tracts'. When the Government of India Act was extended to Burma in 1923, the Chin hills, the Kachin hills and the Shan states were also excluded from the new system of representation.

For these reasons, even as village after village was being burnt to crush the Kuki-Chin uprising, the Chief Commissioner in Assam was commenting: 'We must recover the confidence and affection of those misguided savages.'[198] By the summer and autumn of 1919, it was abundantly clear that political reconciliation with imprisoned Kuki chiefs would be the order of the day.[199] At the other end, in France, it was crucial to send the Assam-Burma companies back feeling well-disposed to government. Observing some 'home-sickness' in the 35th and 36th Naga companies in March 1918, Lieutenant General Cox noted: 'It is no doubt of great importance to send these Nagas back as soon as possible and they should be given priority.'[200] In May 1918 the 62nd Chin company had agreed to be reconstituted into a pioneer company and to stay for the duration of the war, but 'owing to receipt of uncensored letters regarding disturbances near their homes' they became reluctant.[201] In the meantime, on 1 June 1918, the Burma government sent a telegram asking for the Chins to be repatriated on a priority basis because their families were becoming anxious and unrest could not be allowed to spread to the northern Chin hills.[202]

The Indian Labour Corps and the construction of public memory

It was therefore not only the sending of the 'hill-men' to France, but also their return in mid-1918 to a situation of local insurgency and a changed political

---

on Indian Constitutional Reforms', Calcutta, Government of India, 1928, https://archive.org/details/firstdespatchoni029261mbp, last accessed 10 November 2019.

[198] N. D. Beatson-Bell, C-in-C Assam, to Viceroy, 13 May 1918, F&P, Secret, External, July 1918, nos 7–131.

[199] F&P, Secret, 1 January 1920, nos 4–12; Reid, *History of the Frontier Areas*, p. 81.

[200] Tour diary, 2 March 1918, IOR/L/MIL/5/738.

[201] F&P, External, B, August 1918, no. 4.

[202] Ibid.

landscape, which gave the Assam government an interest in encouraging the celebration and commemoration of war service.[203] In contrast, the Chief Commissioner of the North-West Frontier Province complained that whereas other companies were feted, the transborder Pathan companies were received back 'with fear and suspicion'.[204] The United Provinces companies were praised for their steadiness in France, but after a modest reception they melted out of official sight.[205] Of the thousands who served in the Bihar and Orissa Corps, only the Catholics found a small niche in community events organised by the Belgian mission. Father Van der Scheuren describes them making up the guard of honour at the annual Sacred Heart Procession in 1922: 'They looked magnificent and impressive in their grand uniform and with their battle-axes glittering in the brilliant sunshine.'[206] The high-caste educated classes of Bihar and Orissa were either indifferent to the war services of 'aboriginals' or ambivalent about the potential effect of 'stirring them up'.[207] Of the men who served in the Bengal companies we hear nothing at all.

At Aizawl, the Lushai Labour Corps was pipped to the parade ground by the military police band.[208] At Tura, in the Garo Hills district, a cenotaph was erected in memory of the fifty-five men who had died away from home.[209] The date of return, 16 July 1918, became an annual event on the official calendar.[210] The American Baptist missionary at Tura, a Great War veteran himself, organised a parade of scouts in red scarves.[211] Ruth Grimes Ewing, his wife, recalled that '[m]any of the old Garo dances' were revived, 'and sports contests were held.'[212] In Shillong, now the capital of Meghalaya, a memorial named Mot Phran (Stone of France) was erected in 1924 to honour the Khasi Labour

---

[203] See also Chapter 6.

[204] F&P, Frontier, B, September 1918, nos 21–27.

[205] IOR/L/MIL7/18510; IOR/L/MIL7/18759.

[206] Vermeire, *History of Barway Mission*.

[207] See *The Behar Herald*, 13 February 1918, pp. 2–3.

[208] Sainghinga Sailo, *Indopui 1914–1918: Mizote France Ram Kal Thu*, trans. Joy L. K. Pachuau, Aizawl, n.d.

[209] Ewing, *Our Life with the Garos of Assam*, pp. 72–73.

[210] 'Garo Labour Corps Recruits Remembered on 100th Anniversary', *The Shillong Times*, 16 July 2018, www.theshillongtimes.com/2018/07/16/garo-labour-corps-recruits-remembered-on-100th-anniversary/, last accessed 17 November 2019.

[211] Ewing, *Our Life with the Garos of Assam*, pp. 72–73.

[212] Ibid.

Corps, but it became an urban orientation point and a tourist site rather than a locus of public memory. The Manipur Raja was rewarded with the title of Maharaja, but colonial officials also laid the blame for the Kuki uprising at his door. The somewhat contradictory allegation was that the insurgency had arisen both from his neglect of the hill tracts and from the oppression of his *lambus* (interpreters and tax-collectors), who were also accused of deliberately exaggerating the dangers of going to France.

Posted to the Naga hills in November 1919, shortly after the conclusion of the Kuki-Chin campaign, Keith Cantlie recalled that one of his first public duties

> was to hold a great ritual dance in honour of the return of the Naga Labour Corps from France. All the tribes were represented. The dancing dress is gorgeous with feathers in the Angami tribe with a huge erection on the head in which many wear long feathers of the hornbill, each feather in the old days a sign of a head taken in war. Every man carried a spear. The Angamis marched onto the parade ground with deep sounding rhythmic cries of 'How. How.' The smaller statured Semas danced in a quick and lively way. I gave out quantities of rupees provided by Government and a number of buffaloes were presented to them and killed and eaten that night.[213]

Cantlie gives us a vivid and pleasurable account of the reframing of porters and labourers as warriors.[214] However, Hutton's tour diaries reveal that the

---

[213] Keith Cantlie, 'Memoir of time in the Naga Hills as a Deputy Commissioner, 1919–1920', Naga Exploratour, http://himalaya.socanth.cam.ac.uk/collections/naga/record/r74103.html, last accessed 17 November 2019. The occasion was in fact the 'peace celebrations' of December 1919 at Kohima. The Naga Labour Corps had returned the previous year in July 1918. Very few Angamis had joined the Labour Corps, but many had been recruited as porters for the Kuki operations, so what was being acknowledged was war service both in France and locally. See also J. P. Mills, photographs of warrior dances at the 1919 'Mokokchung peace celebration', J. P. Mills photographic collection, H.009, H.011, H.016, School of Oriental and African Studies.

[214] The botanist Frank Kingdon-Ward, on a trip to northern Burma in 1919, recalled the same event: 'I happened to be in Kohima when the Naga *coolies* came home from France ... a great festival was held in Kohima, to which all the tribes sent their warriors to dance ... We saw Angamis, Aos, Semas, Lhotas, and others doing their dances dressed in full war paint ... I remember that several of the *warriors* who had come home from France joined in the dance wearing German helmets, which they had picked up on the field of battle.' F. Kingdon-Ward, discussing J. P. Mills's paper,

acknowledgement of loyalty could also be a taxing business. Right up to 1925 we find him trudging around the Naga Hills, signing medal rolls and distributing medals to everyone who had gone to France in the Labour Corps or participated in the Kuki operations. '[G]ot rid of some more', he notes in exhaustion on 7 August 1925, remarking that some Angamis who had deserted from a column in Manipur were annoyed at not getting any medals.[215] The lines of 'loyalty' and 'rebellion' on the ground were never as clear as commemorative exercises suggested.

Of course, warrior codes were celebrated only in the context of colonial militarism, and not if they were resurrected in struggles to maintain territorial autonomy.[216] That Kukis and Chins could have even entertained the idea of autonomy was attributed to their deep geographical ignorance. William Shaw, Subdivisional Officer in the Manipur hills, wrote that the 'ill-conceived' action of the Thadou Kukis in 1917–18 sprang from their belief 'that they were destined to be rulers of their earth ... many of those who went to France in the Manipur Labour Corps are now convinced that the earth is not quite as small as they held it previously.'[217]

In Kuki ethnonationalist accounts, the refusal to go to France as 'coolies' is treated as a 'Zo', or Kuki-Chin-Lushai, national uprising against colonial conquest. Its crushing is therefore seen as the fatal point at which Zo territory was divided up between India and Burma and the border between Manipur and the Naga hills was restructured to Naga advantage. However, centenary commemorations of World War One generated considerable pride in the heroism of those Kukis who did cross the seas and gave their community a presence in the European theatre of war. Naga ethnohistories treat enrolment in the Labour Corps going to France, and the establishment in 1918 of a Naga club at Kohima and Mokokchung by some *dubashis* (interpreters, clerks, schoolmasters and other government employees), as key

---

titled 'The Assam-Burma Frontier: Discussion', *The Geographical Journal*, vol. 67, no. 4 (1926), pp. 299–301, 300 (emphasis added).

[215] J. H. Hutton, tour diary, 6–7 August 1925, Naga Exploratour, http://himalaya. socanth.cam.ac.uk/collections/naga/record/r72543.html, last accessed 17 November 2019.

[216] For a serious assessment of the war strategies of the Kukis, see Jangkhomang Guite, '"Fighting the White Men till the Last Bullet": The General Course of the Anglo-Kuki War', in Guite and Haokip, *The Anglo-Kuki War*, pp. 37–77.

[217] William Shaw, *Notes on the Thadou Kukis*, Calcutta: Asiatic Society of Bengal, 1929.

events in the emergence of a modern sense of Naga nationhood, one which transcended the different clan identities.[218]

El Dorado? Back in the tides of migration, 1918–19

> The crops have failed badly and my poor people will soon be in terrible distress ... and alas! To make things worse, the influenza has invaded my district ... the villages are empty and dead, and in the fields the work is at a standstill.[219]

In counterpoint to the narrative of valorous war service, or resistance to it, there were many who returned only to place themselves once again within the flow of migration.[220] Interpreters or clerks returned with healthy savings.[221] However, given the soaring price of cloth and food in 1918–19, rank and file labourers probably enjoyed only a brief spell of prosperity.[222] In Hutton's estimation, the sums accumulated from wages received during the Abor expedition and service in France set up a 'wild but short-lived inflation', but the distribu-

---

[218] One contemporary controversy is whether the Naga Club was set up in January 1918 by Naga employees at Kohima or by returning members of the Labour Corps.

[219] 'Trials', Rev A. Bossaers, Gholeng, 6 November 1918, in *TCHI*, 20 November 1918; also *Chota Nagpur Diocesan Paper*, November and December 1918.

[220] The kingdom of Nepal pressed for the return home of its military personnel, but many Nepalis chose instead to stay on in India working in coalmines, on rubber plantations and in the service sector. F&P, External, B, April 1915, nos 171–203; C. G. Bruce and W. Brook Northey, 'Nepal', *The Geographical Journal*, vol. 65, no. 4 (1925), pp. 281–98. Nepali court historian Bhim Bahadur Pande gave a lively description of the emulative migration set off by demobilisation: 'All the way from Nautanawa, these youngsters spent so much money that porters charged more, taverns opened up along the foot trails, minstrels got enough to eat, innkeepers got fatter, and land-prices soared ... everyone started hoarding Indian currency at home and people migrated to India and Burma because Kathmandu couldn't provide the lifestyle that they were dreaming of.' Cited in Sunir Pandey, '100 Years of Platitudes', *Nepali Times*, 3–9 January 2014, http://archive.nepalitimes.com/article/nation/100-years-of-platitudes,1025, last accessed 10 November 2019.

[221] As against the labourer's wage of Rs 20/–, interpreters received Rs 75–100/–, headmen initially Rs 100/–but later Rs 50/–, clerks Rs 50–60/–, and mates Rs 30/–.

[222] Hutton's tour diary for August 1918 describes a situation of food scarcity and high cloth prices. J. H. Hutton, tour diary, 2 August 1918, Naga Exploratour, http://himalaya.socanth.cam.ac.uk/collections/naga/coll/8/records/detail/all/index.html, last accessed 17 November 2019.

tion of wealth and influence, he noted approvingly, remained as before.[223] Some men deferred their return home to seek work in a large town. Many from the Garo labour company, for instance, stayed on at Gauhati or Gaolpara after their discharge, leaving only 120 to return to Tura on 16 July 1918.[224]

In Chota Nagpur, drought left a trail of devastation in 1918. 'After all,' commented one missionary, 'the expedition [to France] had not proved an "El Dorado"; the crops that year were bad, and money was wanted at home.'[225] Another rivulet of military movement emerged as men from Chota Nagpur and the Santhal Parganas enrolled in Labour Corps and railway construction companies raised for military work along the North-West Frontier.[226] In November 1918 the *Behar Herald* reported that some of the Oraons and Mundas who had returned from France were also enlisting as soldiers, saying that they had experienced danger as labourers and now wished to do so as combatants and have others serve them.[227] Some returning men enlisted in the Mechanical Transport Corps and joined the motor training school at

---

[223] J. H. Hutton, *Problems of Reconstruction in the Assam Hills: Presidential Address for 1945*, Royal Anthropological Institute of Great Britain and Ireland, 1945, pp. 1–2. However, pleasing accounts of men returning flush with money from service in the Labour Corps were circulated again in World War Two to inspire hill communities along the Assam-Burma frontier to resist the Japanese invasion. Some paternalist officials also wished to interest the British public in schemes to constitute this area as a crown colony. Reid, *History of the Frontier Areas*, p. 163. See also Anthony Gilchrist McCall, *Lushai Chrysalis*, London: Luzac and Co., 1949, chapter 10.

[224] 'Tura Remembers Garo Recruits to France during WWI', *The Shillong Times*, 17 July 2012, http://theshillongtimes.com/2012/07/17/tura-remembers-garo-recruits-to-france-during-ww-i/, last accessed 10 November 2019. Some soldiers and followers stayed on in Bombay and Calcutta as stokers and lascars.

[225] *Voices from India*, Calcutta, November 1922, pp. 39–40.

[226] In July 1918 the SPG missionary A. T. Williams, who had commanded the 51st Ranchi labour company in France, left for the North-West Frontier with the 115th Labour Corps, one section of which was recruited from the local laity. Men from around Ranchi were also present in the 143rd Labour Corps, raised for this theatre. *Chota Nagpur Diocesan Paper*, October 1918. Father Ory went with a 'Catholic Labour Company' to this front. For 'Santhali' recruitment to the railway training camp at Puri, see 'Supply of Labour for the Andamans, Puri, Tea Garden Area Sirdars, 1922', Gossner Evangelical Lutheran Mission Records, Ranchi, Jharkhand.

[227] *The Behar Herald*, 2 November 1918, p. 7.

Rawalpindi.[228] The SPG mission referred to twelve who joined the new Engineering Works set up at Kumardhubi.[229] Skilled and secure work of this kind, however, was not usually open to 'Santhali' labour, and for many the only option was to step into the river of 'Santhali' migration flowing towards northern Bengal, Bhutan and Assam, or to join the new stream leading to the Andaman islands. Here the Forest Department negotiated with missions to find labour for forest clearance and road-building, and another Santhali diaspora emerged.[230] War service therefore folded almost seamlessly into the story of further migration.[231]

---

[228] *Chota Nagpur Diocesan Paper*, October 1918.

[229] Ibid.

[230] Van Der Schueren, *Moral and Intellectual Uplift of the Aboriginal Races of Chota Nagpur*, p. 11; Violett, 'Faith Based Development', pp. 258–60.

[231] Revenue and Agriculture, Forests, B, August 1920, no. 36.

5

THE SHORT CAREER OF THE INDIAN LABOUR CORPS IN FRANCE

EXPERIENCES AND REPRESENTATIONS

Scattered over miles of desolate country, where the villages have been literally pulverised and the shell-pocked land is like the surface of a rough sea, there are many colonies, containing thousands of India's working classes.[1]

This chapter adds the story of the Indian Labour Corps (ILC) to the now multiplying accounts of the various 'coloured' units brought in to deal with the manpower crisis which had overtaken the European theatre in 1916.[2] Even in the face of the devastating losses of the Somme, there was intense public criticism in Britain about this decision. Stories circulated that Indian troops sent in 1914 had been unable to cope with the cold and the trauma of modern warfare. A correspondent for the *Evening Standard* claimed to have heard

---

[1] YMCA worker's account, IOR/L/MIL/7/18577, India Office Library and Records, British Library, London (IOR).

[2] Michael Summerskill, *China on the Western Front: Britain's Chinese Work Force in the First World War*, London: Michael Summerskill, 1982; Robin Wallace Kilson, 'Calling up the Empire: The British Military Use of Non-White Labor in France, 1916–1920', Ph.D. dissertation, Harvard University, 1990; Glenford Deroy Howe, *Race, War and Nationalism: A Social History of West Indians in the First World War*, Oxford: James Currey, 2002; Xu Guoqi, *Strangers on the Western Front: Chinese Workers in the Great War*, Cambridge, MA: Harvard University Press, 2011.

British officers speak 'of the feeling of shame that came over them when in France we turned to black races for help'.[3] It was therefore 'impossible to imagine', he claimed, that Sikhs, Gurkhas, Zulus and the like should be sent into the battlefields of France, but for war work behind the lines 'a stronger case can be made.'[4] Arguments about climatic and cultural incompatibility were easier to override, therefore, when Indian labourers, rather than combatants, were contemplated for France.

Following the Secretary of State for India's request in January 1917 for 50,000 labourers for France came another request on 24 March 1917 for 18,286 horse- and mule-drivers to replace British personnel in supply and divisional artillery columns.[5] Batches of the Indian Labour Corps began to arrive in June–July 1917, and the drivers followed later that year. Yet this second influx of South Asian manpower was barely noticed in either Britain or India.

The Department of Labour (DOL), established in December 1916 to administer and allocate all unskilled labour, white and coloured, in the British sector in France, would deliver a very unenthusiastic verdict on the Indian Labour Corps. It judged that the ILC had not justified the expense of bringing it over, because its contract had been too short, its organisation had been confused, and its men had not been able to withstand the winter.[6] This chapter proposes not so much to revise these representations as to assess them for what they reveal about the experiences of the ILC.

There are very few sources in which the labourers communicate their own understanding of this historical moment. However, their experience becomes more visible at the points where it had to be probed by those raising and supervising the ILC, and reordered to provide propaganda material. Discussions about the capacities and limitations of recruits to the ILC give us a sense of their embodied experience of this conjuncture, and of their activity as sentient beings in the orders of time, object-worlds, and environments in which they were positioned.

---

[3] 'In Winter's Grip, Lessons of the Somme', *Evening Post*, 5 January 1917, p. 10, paperspast.natlib.govt.nz, last accessed 15 November 2019.

[4] Ibid.

[5] Secretary of State for India (SSI) to Viceroy, 22 January 1917 and 26 January 1917. IOR/L/MIL/7/18354.

[6] 'Report on the Work of Labour during the War', TNA WO/107/37, p. 45.

The labour advisor to the ILC, Lord Ampthill, wanted the corps to be treated as an extension of the Indian Army, not placed in the general frame of 'coloured labour'.[7] There were some organisational features, notably the presence of Indian NCOs in the lower ranks of command, that supported this distinction, but Ampthill never managed to get the men recategorised as combatants on the lines of those serving in British Labour Battalions. The range of encounters that the ILC were permitted in France was very limited, and their worksites were often stark and isolated. Nevertheless, the rank and file tried to generate resources from the social and material environments in which they were positioned, not only to soften harsh conditions but also to create suggestive equivalences between themselves and other military personnel. They thereby sought to lift themselves from the position of mere wage-workers to the status of participants in a common project of war service. At the same time, they indicated that they had not put their persons at the disposal of the state in exactly the same way as the sepoy. The Government of India wanted, for fiscal and ideological reasons, to keep the line between labourer and sepoy manipulable without allowing it to collapse. For different reasons, the men in the ILC also had an investment in maintaining this separation.

Probing, constraining, and reordering experience

A corpus of letters preserved by the operations of censorship in Europe provides one of the most evocative sources for exploring the war experience of Indian sepoys and labourers, but it yields just a handful of letters from the ILC. 'The bulk of the Labour Corps letters received are in languages which we cannot read,' wrote Captain Tweedy, chief censor of Indian mail, 'and the few in Hindi and Urdu contain nothing of the slightest interest.'[8]

Commanding officers of the ILC have left virtually no account of their experiences. Some had very short tenures, and others probably felt their service with

---

[7] To boost the morale of ILC officers, Ampthill stressed that their men did the same work as base or line of communication troops and were therefore 'honourably distinguished from Coolies working under indenture.' 18 June 1917, IOR/L/MIL/5/738.

[8] Censor's notes, 7 April 1917 and 14 November 1917, IOR/L/MIL/5/828. However, the censor kept an eye out for anyone in the ILC taking an interest in British labour politics. Note, 13 February 1918, ibid., pp. 395, 399.

a 'coolie' formation was not worth writing about.[9] In his novel *The Dripping Tamarinds* (1933), C. C. Lewis, a retired civil servant who served with the ILC, hints at the condescension its officers could encounter. When the character Fendle, who is commanding a Burma company, meets Miss Underwick in France, she has never heard of the ILC, is incredulous that he is serving with it, and finally concedes, 'That's because you're wounded, I suppose.'[10]

There are scraps of information on regimental followers and the Indian Labour Corps in missionary periodicals that hailed the transformation of the 'primitive' and 'untouchable' into useful, loyal, intelligent subjects of empire, and staked a political claim for them in the postwar dispensation for India.[11] This chapter draws upon a hitherto unexplored source in the form of newsletters sent to *The Catholic Herald of India* by two Belgian Jesuits, Fathers Henri Floor and Frans Ory, who went as supervisors to France with labour recruited from Chota Nagpur.

Recruiters promised experiences normally inaccessible to the labouring classes—a monthly wage, some savings, and a plentitude of food and clothing.[12] Experience itself was one of the attractions on offer: 'Young men will get a chance to see the world in a safe job on good pay.'[13] A propaganda paper remarked that labourers returned as prosperous and *samajhdar* (intelligent

---

[9] There are just a few glancing references to the war in the entire corpus of the writings of hunter and conservationist James (Jim) Corbett, such as the following: 'Shortly after the Kaiser's war, Robert Bellairs and I were on a shooting trip'. Jim Corbett, *The Temple Tiger and More Man-Eaters of Kumaon*, New York: Oxford University Press, 1955, p. 1. In 1917, Corbett was working as a Transshipment Inspector at Mokameh Ghat, Bihar, supervising the shifting of goods between two different railway gauge lines, when he was picked up to serve as officer to a Kumaon labour company in France. His contacts in the Kumaon hills and his experience handling labour gangs on piecework payment worked in his favour, even though he was forty-two years old. See the chapter 'Loyalty' in Jim Corbett, *My India*, Delhi: Oxford University Press, 1952. An Indian revenue official who commanded the 23rd United Provinces company composed a highly enthusiastic propaganda pamphlet: Pandit Kashi Nath, *Indian Labourers in France*, Bombay: Oxford University Press, 1919.

[10] Cecil Champain Lowis, *The Dripping Tamarinds*, London: Laurie, 1933, p. 163.

[11] A. W. McMillan, 'Indian Echoes from France', *The East and the West*, vol. XVIII (1920), pp. 1–20.

[12] ILC recruitment poster, *Jangi Akhbar*, no. 18, 1918.

[13] Circular, 14 May 1917, IOR/L/MIL/2/5132.

and capable) beings.[14] Joy Pachuau points out that Lushai interpreter Sainghinga Sailo's memoir of his trip to France is informed by the educated Mizo's drive for *changkanna*, or self-improvement through knowledge of the modern world, a characteristic of travel accounts published in the periodical *Mizo leh Vai*.[15] War travel as a non-combatant offered literate Indians of modest means a chance to experience that metropolitan world which had come to their doorstep through print media and commodity retailing. However, Sainghinga joked that the young men of his village also wanted to return as figures of interest to women.[16] For sepoys and labourers, the hope of returning with the wherewithal to marry was an important inducement. On the other hand, there was the disturbing prospect that death away from home might write them out of the generational cycle.

If encounters with novelty in intriguing, pleasurable, or horrifying forms constituted one aspect of war service, another was an ever-present sense of the constraints put upon sights, encounters, new tastes, and the communication of experience.[17] Crammed into the lower deck of very rundown ships, the men were marched away immediately on disembarkation at the outskirts of Marseilles. Soon after, they were moving northwards in trains bound for remote worksites in the Third Army area, often in landscapes devastated by war.[18] One account describes how disappointed the Lushais were that only those sent to a hospital got to see Marseilles.[19] The labourer stayed in Europe for a much shorter period than the Indian cavalryman, who remained there for over three years. The cavalryman was billeted at times in village barns,

---

[14] *Ladai ka Akhbar*, 21 August, 1918.

[15] Joy L. K. Pachuau, 'Sainghinga and his Times: Codifying Mizo Attire', in *MZU Journal of Literature and Cultural Studies*, vol. 2, no. 2 (2015), pp. 272–93.

[16] Sainghinga Sailo, *Indopui 1914–1918, Mizote France Ran Kal Thu*, Aizawl, n.d.

[17] An additional censorship rule for 'coloured labourers' prohibited them from sending home pictures, postcards, photographs, printed matter, and newspaper clippings. TNA WO 107/37, p. 63.

[18] IOR/L/MIL/7/18410. Lowis describes Contalmaison, the worksite for a Burma labour company, as 'a ghastly hole' in which 'everything was battered flat into the mud.' Lowis, *The Dripping Tamarinds*, p. 159. For a passing reference to 'Indian troops' (the ILC) building an RFC aerodrome at Rambervillers in a 'stretch of bleak sopping countryside', see Maurice Baring, *R.F.C.H.Q., 1914–1918*, London: G. Bell and Sons, 1920, p. 255.

[19] Lianbuka, 'Lekhathawn', *Mizo leh Vai*, 23 February 1918.

whereas the ILC was more usually housed in camps or barracks. In addition, the sheer length and intensity of the ILC work day and the comprehensiveness of discipline meant that interaction, if any, with other personnel in the British sector, as well as the French, was very limited.[20]

Political agendas and ethnic comparisons: coloured labour, Indian labour, coolie ethnicities

There were three registers for assessing the physiology, cultural traits, and work skills of the ILC in Europe. The first was the label 'coloured' or 'native' labour, which communicated new anxieties because of the notion that it could replace white manpower in the very heart of the metropolis.[21] The second was the term 'Indian labour', which carried a special terminological charge because, at the very moment that the British Empire needed this resource most acutely, there was a widespread campaign in India to end the system of indentured migration and to claim 'the coolie' as a national resource and the object of moral uplift.[22] The war had also stimulated interest in the industrial future of India, and with it debates about the health, efficiency, and skills of 'Indian labour', or rather the regrettable want of these qualities in this workforce.[23] These discussions reached the theatres of war, where Indian manpower was deployed. And, finally, there were ethnic labels such as 'Santhali', 'Pathan', or 'primitive hill-man' labour, which were shaped by the long history of generating workforces for British military and commercial projects in India, a history that had extended into Europe as a consequence of the Great War.[24]

---

[20] *The Catholic Herald of India*, 26 September 1917, p. 623; 24 October 1917, p. 714 (henceforth *TCHI*). The 23rd UP company located in a stretch of 'desolated, wild country-side' along the Somme saw very little of the French. Kashi Nath, *Indian Labourers in France*, pp. 9, 22.

[21] For an American surgeon, the throngs of 'coloured labour' in France prophesied the doom of European civilisation. Harvey Cushing, *From a Surgeon's Journal: 1915–1918*, Boston: Little, Brown and Company, 1936, pp. 143, 190.

[22] See Chapter 3.

[23] *Indian Industrial Commission Report, 1916–1918*, Calcutta: Government Printing, 1918, p. 170, paras 235–36.

[24] See Chapter 4. Also Kaushik Ghosh, 'A Market for Aboriginality: Primitivism and Race Classification in the Indentured Labour Market of Colonial India', in Gautam Bhadra, Gyan Prakash and Susie Tharu (eds), *Subaltern Studies No. 10: Writings on South Asian History and Society*, Delhi: Oxford University Press, 1999, pp. 8–48.

The Department of Labour in France had appointed advisors 'to study the peculiarities of, and the best way to handle different classes of Native Labour.'[25] The 'ethnicising' and 'tribalising' frames put around all coloured units allowed for the discussion of their physiology and culture in terms that justified a more comprehensive discipline, inferior treatment, longer work hours, and fewer rest days than was possible with British or Canadian labour companies. Comparisons between coloured corps reinforced the notion that a lower standard of institutional care was appropriate to all. If, for instance, the ILC men were inherently more fragile than South African or Egyptian labourers, then their death from respiratory disease could be discounted. Ethnicised dividing lines also allowed symptoms of assertiveness or discontent to be isolated within a particular company, and changes of units were used to step up work norms.[26] The cross-cutting imperative—that of standardising the use of all labour, white or coloured—was the weaker drive, though it gathered force in 1918.[27]

However, the vocabulary of ethnic comparison was rendered more complex by the variety of political agendas that shaped the mobilisation of each coloured unit. For instance, the co-option of Fijian chiefs gave a special gloss to accounts of the small labour contingent of 104 men from that colony. *The Times* cast the Fijians as 'aristocrats of the Pacific' whose willingness to work as stevedores was especially praiseworthy, for 'in his island home the Fijian is not a manual worker.'[28] This conceptual distance between the ethnically 'pure' Fijian and the 'real' coolie, the Indian placed on sugar plantations, made it easier for the Fiji Corps to winch itself up from the level of 'coloured labour' and to be lauded for its war service.[29]

---

[25] TNA WO/107/37, p. 11.

[26] TNA WO/107/37, p. 121.

[27] White manpower was fleetingly placed in the same frame of comparison to score points in conscription debates, or to suggest that military discipline would be as salutary for unruly trade unionists as it was for civilisationally 'backward' coloured labour. 'An Army of Labour', *The Times*, 27 December 1917, p. 8.

[28] Ibid.; 'The Fijian and his Ways', *The Times*, 21 April 1920.

[29] 'Indians and half-castes' had not been permitted to enlist. Sir Charles Lucas (ed.), *The Empire at War*, vol. 3, London: Oxford University Press, 1924, p. 395. If ethnic integrity was one consideration, the other was to ensure the retention of Indian labour on plantations, given the wartime boom in cane sugar prices and anxiety about the suspension of indentured migration. See 'Indian Labour', *Wairarapa Daily Times*, 20 January 1915, p. 5, http://paperspast.natlib.govt.nz, last accessed 15 November

Praise for the ILC was very faint in comparison to the plaudits received by the Fiji Corps, but it, too, benefitted from a more paternalist cast of representation than that which was the lot of the Chinese, Egyptians, and South Africans.[30] The need to conciliate political opinion in India in 1917–18, and the fraught situation along her borders at this time, meant that loyalty had to be looked for and found in the ILC.[31]

In its 'Report on the work of labour during the war' the Department of Labour accepted that Indians were motivated by a fidelity to 'their' King Emperor, so they 'could always be relied upon to turn out.'[32] The Chinese Labour Corps, by contrast, was described as rigidly adherent to contract and having come 'primarily for money'.[33] A special tone of loathing was reserved for Egyptian labourers because they had to be acknowledged as politically aware beings, but supporting the Turkish side.[34] But though harsh, racist terminology was applied quite freely to the men from South Africa and Egypt, they were also cast as splendid stevedores, with their stamina contrasted to the physical 'frailty' of the Indians.[35]

Recruitment and organisation: 'unsatisfactory terms of enrolment'[36]

Provincial officials tapped into existing structures of authority to meet quotas for the ILC. However, recruitment for France, as for Mesopotamia, had to

---

2019. Indian settlers were also kept out of the British West Indies Regiment; officials cited the closer familiarity of Afro-Caribbeans with the food and language of the metropolis, but the retention of Indian plantation labour was another consideration.

[30] An instructional pamphlet stated that undue familiarity between white personnel and the Chinese Labour Corps (CLC) subverted discipline. However, its advice for ILC officers was different: 'It is a great mistake to imagine that civility or good fellowship towards an Indian is likely to lower the white man in his eyes'. *Notes for the Guidance of Officers of the Labour Corps in France*, pamphlet in TNA WO 107/37 (henceforth *Notes*), pp. 73, 59. Lord Ampthill, advisor to the ILC, may have authored such passages.

[31] See Chapter 4.

[32] TNA WO 107/37, p. 42.

[33] *Notes*, p. 73.

[34] The 'Note on Egyptian Labour', 1917, contains observations such as: 'They are immoral, and do not confine themselves to ordinary forms of immorality.' Appendix, TNA WO 107/37.

[35] TNA WO 107/37, pp. 33, 39–42; Ampthill, 16 February 1918, IOR/L/MIL/5/738.

[36] TNA WO 107/37, p. 43.

take some account of longstanding patterns of waged work away from home.[37] This led to the modification of some of the suggestions put forward by the War Office. For instance, the War Office wanted 'duration of war' agreements but local governments felt this indefinite formulation would discourage labour recruitment, so the term was fixed at a year.[38] To secure more control over the men the War Office suggested the use of deferred payments, holding back some part of the wage until the end of service.[39] But a wage advance was the norm for migrant contract work, and its importance had probably increased in areas such as Chota Nagpur because of the suffering of families who had received no money or information from men sent earlier to Mesopotamia.[40] Eventually the men who enrolled for France were given a generous three-month advance on their wages to encourage creditors and families to let them go.[41]

Though the men were recruited for 'General Service', which meant in theory that they could be sent anywhere and changed around from one unit to another, recruits made it clear that they were offering themselves specifically for the European theatre. Pandit Kashi Nath described rustics from the United Provinces coming to the depot 'suspicious and careful', insisting the *sahib* understand that they wanted to go to *Phranch* (France), not *Bachchra* (Basra).[42] Some of the men in the ILC, as well as the Garhwali and Gurkha NCOs posted with them, had prior experience of work in other theatres and had realised that conditions would be better in Europe and there would be more acknowledgement for war service.[43]

---

[37] F&P, Internal, B, August 1917, nos 110–15.

[38] 'One year or the period of the war, whichever was less.' Ibid. In January 1918, when the War Office insisted on 'period of war' for fresh ILC drafts, the Nagas of Manipur refused to go to France. Home, Establishment, B, February 1918, nos 191–209.

[39] Army Department, 9 March 1917, IOR/R/2/513/215.

[40] See complaints in *TCHI*, 21 March 1917, p. 183.

[41] IOR/R/2/513/215; F&P, Internal, B, August 1917, nos 110–15. Local governments were authorised to make compulsory wage deductions for the labourer's family. Ibid.

[42] Kashi Nath, *Indian Labourers in France*, p. 5. *Bachchra*: Basra (but in Hindi, *Bachchra* is also a calf). See also Viceroy to India Office, 20 May 1917, IOR/L/MIL/7/18302.

[43] Some of the Lushais and Nagas in the ILC had gone as porters with the Abor expedition, 1911–12. *Mizo leh Vai*, February 1918. The 23rd UP company contained men who had served as followers in the South African War; the Kabul, Lushai, and Tibet expeditions; and more recently in Mesopotamia. Memo, Kashi Nath, IOL/L/MIL/5/738.

The Labour Corps in France, sent in units of 2,000, were reorganised in August 1917 into companies of 500, the Department of Labour concluding that this was the better size for the economical use of labour.[44] It also referred vaguely to the need to 'prevent tribal feuds'.[45] As a result of this reorganisation some companies were given a stronger ethnic designation, while others retained the broader provincial designation. For instance, two Burma companies from the Chin hills were given the ethnic label 'Chin', whereas two recruited from upper Burma retained the label 'Burmese'. The 'Kumaon' companies recruited from the central Himalayas were now distinguished from the rest of the 'United Provinces' companies. Ampthill hailed these changes as good for morale.[46] These ethnic labels papered over the actual diversity of elements within a particular company, a diversity effaced even further by the political charge which these ethnic labels acquired on the return of the men to India. However, cohesion also emerged from below due to recruitment from groups already bound by some shared experience, and by the reliance on each other for assistance.[47] This support system filled the gaps left by institutional care and made the men very resistant thereafter to any indiscriminate assignment in drafts.[48]

Confusion of command?

Much of the criticism on the arrival of the Corps in France—that its organisation was 'confused' or 'too elastic'—arose from the discomfort caused by the

---

[44] TNA WO 107/37. Each company was divided up into four platoons under a Lieutenant.

[45] Ibid. Interestingly, the 12th ILC in Mesopotamia was recruited from a variety of different communities in Assam, and though there were complaints about language problems there was no reference to 'tribal feuds'.

[46] Ampthill to General H. V. Cox, Military Secretary, India Office, 25 July 1917, IOR/L/MIL/5/738. The Belgian Jesuit mission used the labels 'Catholic' and 'Oraon' interchangeably, to take credit for the companies they had helped to raise in Chota Nagpur.

[47] Sainghinga joined the Lushai Labour Corps in the company of young men he grew up with. Writing decades later, he remembers those who brought water to and comforted the seasick on the outward voyage. See Sainghinga, *Indopui*.

[48] The DOL agreed that on recovery, casualties 'would be re-posted only to those companies of the same tribal designation as those in which they previously were serving.' 17 July 1917, TNA WO 95/83. The men in ILC companies stationed at Marseilles said that they would not extend their stay if they were separated and sent up in drafts. Ampthill, 16 February 1918, IOR/L/MIL/5/738.

racial and occupational hybridity of its upper command structure.[49] Unable to spare more than three British Commissioned Officers for each Labour Corps of 2,000 men, the Government of India added civilian supervisors, drawing upon Europeans, Eurasians, and educated Indians, some of the latter from the Provincial Civil Service.[50] Some 'Indianisation' of command had in fact taken place in the ILC, but the Government of India was reluctant to acknowledge this development.

In France, Brigadier General Evan Gibb, the Director of Labour, insisted that he would need five British Commissioned Officers per company.[51] Ampthill contended that the better solution was to give all the civilian supervisors an Indian Army Reserve Officer commission, thereby knitting the ILC together as a self-sufficient formation that could be treated as an extension of the Indian Army.[52] The ideal of pulling the different territorial components of empire together into one cohesive unit was one that Ampthill was pursuing in other forums as well.[53] However, the Government of India, which had accepted the idea of commissions for some aristocratic Indians, 'deprecated' the idea of giving commissioned rank to middle-class educated Indians.[54] Eventually the European and Eurasian supervisors were given a commission in the British Army or with the Indian Army Officer Reserve, and the Indians a commission in the Native Indian Land Forces, an experiment with a Territorial Force.[55] The War Office stated that ILC officers were to be regarded as part of the Indian Expeditionary Force in France.[56]

---

[49] TNA WO 107/37, pp. 38–39, 43–45.

[50] Minute, C. H. Selwyn, India Office, 11 May 1917, IOR/L/MIL/7/18302. Among the Europeans and Eurasians were serving and retired officials, planters, and missionaries. George Orwell's father Richard Walmsley Blair, an opium agent at Motihari, served with the 51st Ranchi labour company in France from November 1917 to May 1918. Appointments to the command structure were shaped by assistance rendered in recruitment, experience in 'managing coolies', and influence with targeted communities. Lower down, headmen, some of whom were 'tribal' chiefs, were appointed over sections of 240, and mates over gangs of thirty. IOR/L/MIL/7/18304. Men with some education were appointed as clerks, interpreters and mates.

[51] Gibb to Cox, 16 September 1917, IOR/L/MIL/7/18302.

[52] Ampthill to DOL, 25 August 1917, IOR/L/MIL/5/738, p. 214.

[53] W. D. Rubinstein, 'Henry Page Croft and the National Party, 1917–1922', *Journal of Contemporary History*, vol. 9, no. 1 (1974), pp. 129–48.

[54] IOR/L/MIL/7/18302.

[55] Ibid.

[56] WO to India Office, 24 November 1917, IOR/L/MIL/7/18574.

Another distinguishing feature of the ILC was its reliance, at lower levels of command, on Indian NCOs to drill and supervise recruits, in contrast to the South Africans and Chinese Corps where British NCOs were used more extensively. For instance, a Chinese labour company was assigned eight British sergeants and nine British corporals.[57] An Indian labour company had only four British staff sergeants as foremen, and these were attached only when specially authorised.[58] The presence instead of Indian NCOs—one Havildar Major, one Pay Havildar, one Havildar, and twenty-one Naiks—meant that the ILC was cast in a more military frame than some of the other coloured labour units, the propaganda value of which was mined in captions to war photographs: 'Members of an Indian Labour *Battalion* reading papers'; 'Contalmaison, Autumn 1917, Burmese *troops* receive their mail'.[59]

Making over into military labour

Along the long way: disorientations and reorientations

The first step in surrendering one's body to the army was the ritual of stripping naked and submitting to an invasive medical examination—an unfamiliar and shaming experience, and one recalled with discomfort by Sainghinga.[60] Peter Alderson recounted what his father William Hubert Alderson, Captain of the 42nd Ranchi company, witnessed when his men were

> all lined up ... for a rapid medical inspection (like I had when I registered for National Service) when you have to drop your trousers and have your privates inspected for signs of VD ... the men were shocked and horrified, because exposing themselves was only to give point to an intended mortal insult. A great cry of '*Nai!*' went up ... and it took some time to sort out a way ... without them all heading for home.[61]

For some Indian companies, medical intervention would be experienced as a gateway to entry and exit with little actual care in between.[62] However, a

---

[57] *Notes*, p. 60.

[58] *Notes*, p. 50. TNA WO 107/37, pp. 38–42.

[59] NAM.2001–01–277–6 and NAM.2001–01–277, National Army Museum, www. nam.ac.uk/online-collection, last accessed 17 November 2019. Emphasis added. Of course, photograph titles may not be contemporaneous.

[60] Sainghinga, *Indopui.*

[61] Email through Rachel Friedli, 13 February 2011. *Nai*: No!

[62] Ampthill critiqued the lack of medical care on 17 December 1917 for the Kumaon

European doctor came regularly to the Ranchi companies when they were working in the Ancre valley, and a Royal Army Medical Corps corporal was deputed to some other companies.[63]

Daryl Klein, a CLC commander, described how the 'village free-liver' from China was transformed into a numbered coolie whose 'wakeful hours are taken from him and transformed into bounden duties.'[64] The process of taking control of the labourer's time began with the daily roll call, which was a lengthy process at large labour depots in India.[65] Experience in Mesopotamia established that drilling reduced the time labourers took to get to work, and it checked the scattering of workmen when they came under fire. Sainghinga gives a humorous account of how this orientation of their bodies to command inaugurated their disorientation from a familiar landscape. '[A] Gorkha havildar of three stripes' taught the Lushais that when he said 'right turn' they had to look towards Vanlaiphai, and when he said 'left' they had to turn to Tlabung; but when they were brought to march before the Deputy Commissioner's bungalow, they turned in all directions.[66]

At the provincial labour depot, the men were issued the uniforms and kit that marked them as military property: 'blouse and pyjamas made of woolen material, one coat warm, of drill, lined with cotton blanketing ... one flannel vest ... one pair of mittens'.[67] Sainghinga writes that '[a] number to mark us was given ... to wear on our wrist.'[68] The quality of kit was an index of standing in the Indian Army: the Gurkhas received a British-style greatcoat, other sepoys 'serge overcoats, on the Indian pattern', and the followers a coat of such bad quality that men in the Mule Corps referred to it derisively as 'mehter ki

---

companies; 24 January 1918 for the 22nd Khasis at Doingt; and 4 March 1918 for work parties at Nancy. IOR/L/MIL/5/738. This was a routine experience for Indian labourers in Mesopotamia.

[63] *TCHI*, 28 November 1917, p. 803; Kashi Nath, *Indian Labourers in France*; Sainghinga, *Indopui*.

[64] Daryl Klein, *With the Chinks*, London: John Lane, 1919.

[65] 'Bombay Labour Corps. Visit to Camps at Poona', *Times of India* (*TOI*), 9 November 1918, p. 17.

[66] Sainghinga, *Indopui*.

[67] Adjutant-General India, 26 March 1917, Baroda Residency, War, W-24.

[68] Sainghinga, *Indopui*. Perhaps Sainghinga meant armbands, because the numbered wristlets riveted onto the CLC and SANLC were probably not used for the ILC.

brandi', or fit only for sweepers.[69] Some of the Indian officers in the lower command structure of the ILC preferred to shiver through the winter rather than accept the follower's service dress.[70]

Nevertheless, for hill-communities that had not hitherto entered the regular army, the spectacle of their young men standing in drilled formation was a novel one. Such displays were more typically associated with Gurkha units at the festival of *Dussehra*. In Sainghinga's memory, the sight of Lushai youths massed in formation on the parade ground of Aizawl was an augury of ethnic destiny.[71] The occasion was one which merited an official photograph as well.[72]

Men who had never seen the sea before

Railways and steam ships had made modern war a test of demographic strength, but getting manpower up to a railhead in India could involve a time-consuming journey by footpath, bridle path, cart-road, or river. Shortage of shipping caused by the heavy demand for freight to Basra was another problem.[73] For some labour companies, the staggered stages by which they were brought down from some remote village to Bombay, taken cautiously up the Red Sea, and then across the Mediterranean to Taranto for the rail journey to France, was a significant part of the war experience. The 66th Manipur Labour Corps assembled to drill at Imphal, then set off on 19 May 1917 to walk 210 km to the rail head at Dimapur. Taking the train to Gauhati and then through central India to Bombay, the men finally embarked for France on 6 June 1917. Thereafter, two cholera quarantines, one at Aden and the other near Taranto, would take them to the end of July 1917 before they took the overland train to France.[74] The Chin Labour Corps left Tiddim on 23 June 1917, and

---

[69] Major H. M. Alexander, *On Two Fronts, Being the Adventures of an Indian Mule Corps in France and Gallipoli*, London: W. Heinemann, 1917.

[70] 8 March 1918, WO 95/384. A conference of Labour Group commanders stated sympathetically that the officers ought to get clothing appropriate to their station, not 'coolie blouses'. Ibid.

[71] Sainghinga, *Indopui*.

[72] The photograph is hazily reproduced in Sainghinga, *Indopui*. For a photograph of the Burma Labour Corps, see 1917, Tonkinson Papers, Box 50, Centre for South Asian Studies, University of Cambridge.

[73] IOR/L/MIL/7/18302; TNA WO 95/43.

[74] Kanrei Shaiza, *Āpuk Āpaga Rairei Khare, France Khavā, 1917–18, Khala Republic Day, 1974, Delhi Kakā*, Imphal: City Press, 1974.

reached Marseilles on 8 September 1917. Some drafts sent for the ILC were detained for three to four months in Egypt while others worked for short periods on the Suez stretch of the passage home.[75]

H. A. Orton, a medical orderly, described the sleeping accommodations below deck for labourers on the SS *Berrima*: 'Two foot wide boards covered with straw palliasse packed very tightly side by side, two blankets each with instructions to use kit bags as pillows. They were allowed the freedom of the lower decks.'[76] His account is of passengers seen rather than heard, getting stronger with better sleep and food: 'their chatter became a clamour and their strange sing-song chants passed the time away.'[77] However, the sea journey, as recounted by Kanrei Shaiza, was an experience marked by violent bouts of seasickness and an outbreak of cholera.[78] Overcrowded labour depots and men packed like sardines on ships which were barely seaworthy created conditions for epidemic disease.[79] Some recruits were consigned to a watery grave, a disturbing experience for their companions.[80] Others were buried at Taranto.

Sainghinga describes the Lushais getting weaker due to seasickness and a monotonous diet of potatoes, onions, and ginger.[81] The tedium was broken by moments of fear, as during a submarine alarm, or of excitement, such as when the Lushais sighted Mount Sinai along the Red Sea and told each other that this was where Moses received the Ten Commandments.[82] Clearly, for some 'tribals' with a mission school background their movement through biblical

---

[75] Ampthill to DOL, 17 December 1917, IOR/L/MIL/5/738.

[76] H. A. Orton, 'A Piece of History for the Indians Who Now are Resident in this Country', Imperial War Museum, Document 11808.

[77] Ibid.

[78] Shaiza, *Āpuk Āpaga Rairei Khare, France Khavā, 1917–18*. The story still circulating in Manipur is that men concealed their sickness during the voyage for fear that they would be thrown into the sea before they were dead, or that the white men would eat the flesh from their bodies. Pamkhuila Shaiza and Kachuiwung Ronra Shimray, 'Did the White Soldiers Really Cannibalise Naga Labour Corps During World War I?', DailyO, 1 June 2017, https://www.dailyo.in/variety/cannibalism-tangkhul-naga-labour-corps-northeast-india-northeast/story/1/17564.html, last accessed 17 November 2019.

[79] See accounts of Fathers Floor and Ory, *TCHI*, 22 August 1917, p. 543; *TCHI*, 29 August 1917, p. 557.

[80] Sainghinga, *Indopui*.

[81] Ibid.

[82] Ibid.

landscapes and into a wider Christian ecumene was as significant an experience as their encounter with war in the metropolis.

Officers often assumed that for 'illiterate' personnel, the short, sharp shock rather than time-consuming instruction was the appropriate method for their introduction to new routines. Kashi Nath writes that after a man was dropped overboard at Port Said to demonstrate that his lifebelt would keep him afloat, the men developed a new understanding of this uncomfortable accessory.[83] Sainghinga, a knowing consumer of modern medicine who accepted the necessity of vaccination, recalled their being subjected without explanation to a chemical spray at Marseilles: 'We did not like it and we did not know why it was necessary.'[84]

Assessing and managing Indian labour

Unskilled, exotic, fragile

The Viceroy had warned that Indian labour was 'less adaptive than British to unaccustomed work.'[85] When they were put to work loading and unloading transports at Marseilles, the verdict was that the men's physique was inferior to that of Chinese and South African labourers, but that they compensated with their tractability.[86] Shifted out to the Third Army area, many Indian companies were put on battlefield clearance and salvage.[87] Some were detailed to road and railway construction, or to forestry work under the supervision of Canadian labour companies.[88] In October 1917, three Indian companies were transferred to the construction of an aerodrome complex for the Royal Flying Corps around Nancy.[89]

---

[83] Kashi Nath, *Indian Labourers in France*, pp. 6–7. The 1st Battalion Gurkhas sailing from Karachi in October 1914 found it difficult to understand why water had to be conserved, because they were surrounded by it. 'Subedar Gamirsing Pun stopped all waste … by making 12 selected men each drink one pint of sea water.' 6th Queen Elizabeth's Own Gurkha Rifles, https://www.6thgurkhas.org, last accessed 17 November 2019.

[84] Sainghinga, *Indopui*.

[85] Viceroy to India Office, 14 February 1917, IOR/L/MIL/7/18302.

[86] TNA WO 107/37, pp. 40–41.

[87] TNA WO 107/37, pp. 39–40; TNA WO 95/384.

[88] TNA WO 95/384.

[89] TNA WO 95/83; Baring, *R.F.C.H.Q., 1914–1918*, p. 255.

By this stage of the war, Mesopotamia and frontier military works had absorbed a lot of artisanal labour from India. Nevertheless, craft skills were discovered in the ILC, some deriving from the construction of border-roads and railways, forestry work, or the craft-training encouraged at missions to provide a livelihood for the laity and to demonstrate that converts did not develop an 'aversion' to manual labour.[90] A former Deputy Director of Labour remarked that the work in France involved little use of machinery 'and therefore gave scope to individual and collective contrivance to a degree not possible with machine production.'[91] The initiatives taken by some Indian labour companies to secure lighter craft-oriented work, or to make their daily existence more comfortable, brought skills and adaptability to light.[92] The Khasis working on a stone quarry at Peronne were probably taxed more heavily than the 150 members of a UP company who, 'with 50 looms constructed by themselves, were turning out 1000 mattresses a day.'[93] The Lushais, who were probably salvaging fuel for themselves, demonstrated that wooden revetments from abandoned trenches could be turned into charcoal, a fuel required for trench heaters and used in gas masks.[94] Yet one Forest Control Officer's explanation for why the 27th UP company was better at charcoal burning than German prisoners of war was that 'they stood the heat of opening a kiln better than white men.'[95] Ampthill declared that some lime-burners in the 50th NWFP company had 'nearly wept' at the sight of the kilns prepared by the Royal Engineers. These had not been hooded, so at the first rain the lime

---

[90] Transfrontier Pashtuns had a reputation for rock-cutting and tunnelling. IOR/P/Conf/56, G1514, 1920. The Welsh Calvinist Mission claimed it had disseminated skills in lime-burning and the use of the carpenter's saw among the Khasis. Nalini Natarajan, *The Missionary Among the Khasis*, New Delhi: Sterling, 1977, p. 64. A settlement of Bengali Christian artisans near Calcutta provided recruits for the Bengal Labour Corps. Anonymous, *Father Douglass of Behala, By Some of His Friends*, London: Oxford University Press, 1952.

[91] A. D. Lindsay, 'The Organisation of Labour in the Army in France during the War and its Lessons', *The Economic Journal*, vol. 34, no 133 (1924), pp. 69–82.

[92] 'The Indian labourers are of course, not so good as Europeans at digging ... but they beat both British and French troops at fascine-making'. Ampthill, tour diary, 20–21 November 1917, IOR/L/MIL/5/738.

[93] 18 December 1917, TNA WO 95/384.

[94] Ibid. India supplied huge quantities of forest produce such as lumber, fodder-grass, leather-tanning products and resin for the war.

[95] TNA WO 95/384.

swelled and slaked. Subsequently, they were allowed 'to do the job in their own way'.[96]

In the CLC, a higher pay bracket was conceded for skilled labour. This did not happen in the ILC, but certain skills, such as in rough carpentry and railway plate-laying, began to be acknowledged.[97] A Khasi company did rail-head work, learning 'such semi-skilled labour as the drilling of bolt-holes in rails ... as speedily as Europeans.'[98] The shift in descriptive phraseology is pal-pable by March 1918, when one Captain A. H. Holland described the 61st Chin company and 66th Manipur company working with 'keenness and intel-ligence', the latter beginning to provide checkers for road-work which might allow the release of more white labour.[99] The ILC's reputation for stevedore work also improved. The Department of Labour observed that at first there had been consternation at base depots when Indians had replaced 'Kaffir' labour (the South African Native Labour Contingent, or SANLC), but they had equalled and sometimes exceeded that performance.[100] In January 1918 Ampthill noted that at the forward supply base of Abancourt, the 'inferiority' of the Indian companies to British and South African companies was 'almost negligible'.[101] At Abancourt, this commendation came at a considerable physi-cal cost.

Time-work or task-work; segmentation or standardisation?

A. D. Lindsay, Deputy Director of Labour in France, recalled that treating the men in British labour companies as though they were 'living shovels' had had a disastrous effect on morale.[102] There was an even greater tendency to treat native labour as though it was just a factor of production, but with less concern for its wastage. A draft of Maratha Mahars had stoked the very ship

---

[96] Ampthill to DOL, 17 February 1917. IOR/L/MIL/5/738.

[97] As the 65th and 66th Manipur companies learnt to construct camps and make trench boards, Royal Engineers personnel were released for forward areas. TNA WO 107/37, p. 42. Kumaon labourers earned a reputation for railway-laying in the 5th Army area. 4 March 1917, TNA WO 95/83; *Notes*, p. 59.

[98] Ampthill, Notes, 5 August 1917, IOR/L/MIL/5/738, p. 240.

[99] Chelmsford, IOR Mss, vol. 15, p. 275.

[100] TNA WO 107/37, p. 42; 22 November 1917, TNA WO/95/83.

[101] Ampthill, 6 January 1918, IORL/MIL/5/738.

[102] Lindsay, 'The Organisation of Labour in the Army in France'.

they had sailed on, then at each halting spot from Taranto they had been seized upon for fatigues 'without the slightest show of decency at consideration'.[103] At Faenza they had constructed a tennis ground for officers; in St Germain they had loaded a train. Ampthill complained that even '[t]he order that the troops should have opportunity to obey the calls of nature was disregarded.'[104]

The agreement signed by the ILC said nothing about working hours or rest days, and in France these were debated largely above their heads. The Department of Labour was expected to raise and standardise the output for all units of unskilled labour, white or coloured. However, the danger it constantly warned against was that if coloured labour was worked in proximity to white labour, then standardisation would take place in a downward direction: 'the native working alongside has his ideas of the position of the white man disturbed in addition to the natural tendency to slacken to the white man's pace.'[105] The SANLC men had, for instance, dared to complain that the Canadians worked fewer hours and got Sunday off.[106]

It is also instructive to compare the DOL's prescriptions for improving the output of British labour with those for coloured labour. To alleviate their alienation from work, it was thought that British labourers ought to be assigned to familiar units, and given the sense of a task accomplished.[107] In contrast, when dealing with the CLC and SANLC, the stress was put not on *esprit de corps*, but on plumbing the depths of deception to arrive at their true capacity for work. Slackness of supervision 'reacted upon natives to an extent not appreciated by officers used only to European Labour.'[108] The supervision of the CLC 'should approximate as closely as possible to labour conditions in China.'[109] Employers had not realised 'the considerable moral

---

[103] Ampthill to DOL, 17 December 1917, IOR/L/MIL/5/738.

[104] Ibid.

[105] TNA WO 107/37, p. 28. Describing the skills his Ranchi labour company had acquired in trench-tunnelling and railway-laying, the Reverend A. T. Williams wrote, 'The type of British labour in these parts is just left standing cold on a job when these boys get to work and they know it, which is not altogether good for them.' *Chota Nagpur Diocesan Paper*, October 1918, Bishop's Lodge, Ranchi.

[106] 19 March 1917, TNA WO 95/83.

[107] *Notes*, pp. 6–7, 16.

[108] TNA WO 107/37, p. 27.

[109] Ibid., p. 72.

deterioration' that resulted from failure to get a full day's work from the South African native.[110]

However, the Department of Labour did sometimes bracket white prisoners of war with coloured labour, the assumption being that, in the absence of patriotism, other incentives and controls had to be devised.[111] By combining these two categories it could take the edge off prescriptions designed to intensify labour across the board. For instance, in advising a general shift from time-work to task-work, it added carefully that this would be especially advantageous for the CLC and prisoners of war, 'for whom there could be no interest in our winning the war.'[112]

Since piecework payment or the offer of a bonus were prohibited for military labour units in France, increases in work intensity were bargained for in the currency of rest.[113] The 'employers', for instance the Royal Engineers or the Controller of Salvage, would outline a fixed task and permit a cigarette break or an earlier knock-off time for speedy completion. The issue, then, was to set the task at the right level. However, there was always some uncertainty as to whether, in the case of coloured labour, the shift from time-work to task-work really left the balance of advantage with the employer. Some of the Chinese companies, by a creative reorganisation of their work, were held to have knocked off at scandalously early times.[114] With reference to the SANLC, the contention was that the correct management technique was simply tough supervision.[115]

The stereotype that circulated about Indian labourers was not so much that they were hiding their true capacity for work, but that they were physically incapable of intensifying the pace.[116] Indian labourers 'would plod along till [they] completed quite a good day's work'; they were capable of 'steady work

---

[110] Ibid., p. 27.

[111] Ibid., chapter II.

[112] Ibid., p. 117.

[113] *Notes*, p. 6; 13 September 1917, TNA WO 95/83. In May 1918 in Mesopotamia, payment for piecework over and above a daily task was introduced. F. D. Frost, *Report of the Labour Directorate, Mesopotamian Expeditionary Force from October, 1916 to October, 1918*, Baghdad, 1919, p. 13.

[114] 25 May 1918, TNA WO 95/384.

[115] TNA WO 107/37, pp. 27–28.

[116] See Assistant Director of Labour, 10 December 1917, TNA WO 95/384.

whether watched or not, in contrast to the Kaffir or Chinaman'; they had to be worked 'in large gangs under their own NCOs'.[117] Such statements hinted that work hours could stretch on until output reached the prescribed level. In India, employers used the same justification to oppose any reduction in factory hours—namely that Indian labourers were physiologically weak, and illiterate, and therefore incapable of concentrated work. They were also culturally predisposed to a dispersed work schedule, so reducing factory hours would not translate into higher per capita production.[118] Responding to the wartime interest in the topic of industrial fatigue and labour efficiency, one ILC officer concluded that for British labour a task requiring six hours a day was ample, but Indian labour was 'so constituted that it cannot put the same intensive effort into work.'[119]

Fathers Floor and Ory's newsletters describe a nine-hour workday for the Ranchi and Oraon companies, the men setting off at seven in the morning and working from eight to five with a break for lunch.[120] They claimed that the men of the Catholic-dominated companies from Chota Nagpur embraced a further extension of their hours in the form of daily Mass at five in the morning and rosary, catechism, or confession in the evening.[121] In August 1917 we find Ampthill pleading with the DOL for collective rest days for the ILC men, pointing out that promises had been made in India about Sunday observance for Christians.[122] Sundays off do seem to have been worked in for Ory

---

[117] TNA WO 107/37, pp. 42–43; E. Pearson (MP), 'Report on Labour Organisation in France', January/February 1918, TNA CAB 24/58.

[118] *Report of the Indian Factory Labour Commission*, 1908, vol. I, para. 84, also pp. 203–4, pp. 259–60; *Indian Industrial Commission Report*, p. 90.

[119] Lieutenant Colonel H. U. Perrot, 'Organised Labour: A Suggestion for India', *TOI*, 4 July 1919, p. 7. However, he conceded that the same principle might apply to 'certain aboriginal labour employed on certain tasks.' See also Afterword.

[120] *TCHI*, 26 September 1917, p. 623. In deep winter, working days were sometimes shortened. *TCHI*, 10 April 1918, p. 273.

[121] *TCHI*, 3 October 1917, p. 645; 24 October 1917, p. 713; 10 April 1918, p. 272. Floor and Ory clearly wanted to guard against any future relapse into 'paganism' given that a revivalist upsurge, the Tana Bhagat movement, was in full flow back in Chota Nagpur.

[122] 8 August 1917, IOR/L/MIL/5/728, p. 244. In the Khasi, Lushai, and Chin hills the struggle with chiefs over Sunday observance constituted a keystone of Christian community formation.

and Floor's Catholic companies, although rest days were also used to overhaul kit and clean the camp.[123]

However, at other sites, and perhaps everywhere during intense phases of the war, the pace of work could be relentless, with the limit sometimes only reached with physical breakdown. It was after April 1918 that the need to conserve all non-combatant labour, whether white or coloured, was finally recognised and the pace of work relaxed.[124] In February 1918, the 22nd Khasis were praised for having 'established a record for rapid loading of permanent way material' when the railway was being pushed up to Marcoing.[125] However, Ampthill complained that overexertion was leading to a deterioration in health, and the company had to be hurriedly repatriated on 1 March 1918 due to an outbreak of beriberi.[126] Among the reasons Ampthill gave for the refusal of Indian companies at the supply base of Abancourt to accept any formal extension of their service in France was that they were 'dead stale and tired'.[127]

Embodied experience: withstanding the cold

Bahut jara suru hua, lekin kapra bahut achha wala milta hai, koi hath ke chamra se lohu nikalta, lekin hoshiyar admi hamar moja hath men lagate hain.

(It has become very cold, but we get very good clothes. Sometimes our hands bleed [perhaps due to chilblains] but intelligent men use their socks to cover them.)[128]

The extracts selected by the censor from ILC letters to illustrate the morale of the men tended to confirm the picture he drew of uncomplicated beings, delighted with their food and clothes.[129] Significantly, none were from

---

[123] *TCHI*, 17 October 1917, p. 694; *TCHI*, 21 November 1917, p. 789. The ELC did not get Friday off for collective prayers.

[124] 13 May 1918, TNA WO 95/384.

[125] Labour Commandant, 5th Army, 26 February 1918, enclosure in Ampthill to Viceroy 6 April 1918, Chelmsford IOR Mss letter nos 183, 272.

[126] 24 January 1918, IOR/L/MIL/5/738; Senior Medical Officer, 4 March 1918, TNA WO 95/83.

[127] A while before they had been getting one day off for every seventeen and a half days, and by this point they received a day off once for every eight and a half days. Ampthill, 21 February 1918, IOR/L/MIL/5/738.

[128] Letter from Barla, n.d.; *TCHI*, 30 January 1918, p. 93.

[129] IOR/L/MIL/5/828, III, pp. 405–6. Ampthill had to ask sometimes for more rice or meat, but the continuous recitation of food items in letters sent by Indian sepoys

Abancourt, a major railway junction, supply base, and ordnance dump, where at one point the 40th Naga, 61st and 62nd Chin, 65th and 66th Manipur, and 69th Garos were concentrated.[130] It is the spare, repetitive entries of the Senior Medical Officer's diary that give us a chilling sense of the toll taken by respiratory disease at this site.[131] Ampthill's observations about Abancourt are a contradictory mix, registering simultaneously his desire to report that the ILC was performing well, his conviction that if the men were felled by pneumonia it was because of 'malarial germs' brought over from India, and, conversely, his obligation to note old huts, cold flooring, and the 'grind of relentless toil'.[132] Arriving at Abancourt on 6 January 1918, he observed that the men were withstanding the cold well.[133] This was the very day that the Senior Medical Officer recorded the deaths of three men of the 66th Manipur company from bronchial pneumonia.[134] Ampthill attributed respiratory infection to 'the germs of malaria', but he also recommended that once winter was over, other companies be given 'the exacting work of this great distributing centre'.[135] Certainly the extent of malnutrition in India was being exposed on the battlefields of World War One, but it was also easier to put the blame for physical breakdown on bodies that 'harboured' malarial fevers and beriberi than on the carelessness with which coloured labour was used.

---

and labourers does communicate a sense of wondrous plenty in the midst of war: 'Day by day we get bread and meat and many kinds of vegetables which we have never tasted in our lives. Even in the early morning we get vegetables with our chapattis'. Noronha Kanda, 43rd Ranchi company to Kushal Mia Murda, Chota Nagpur, 3 March 1918, IOR/L/MIL/5/828, I, p. 187.

[130] IOR/L/MIL/5/738.

[131] 23 October 1917 onwards, TNA WO 95/4007. See also WW1/182/H, casualty appendix to war diary, IEF, A, vol. 24, pt II, December 1917 to February 1918.

[132] 8 December 1917, TNA WO 95/4007; tour report, 6 January 1918, IOR/L/MIL/5/738.

[133] Ibid.

[134] 6 January 1918, Senior Medical Officer's diary, LOC, Abancourt, TNA WO 95/4007. A later parade time was discussed but rejected as unviable. Ibid.

[135] Tour report, 6 January 1918, IOR/L/MIL/5/738. Blargies Communal Cemetery Extension nearby has forty-six Indian graves. Indian companies working around Nancy suffered extensive sickness because of a long delay in getting adequate warm clothing and shelter. Ampthill, 20–21 November 1917, Cox, 4 March 1918, IOR/L/MIL/5/738.

Some of the essentialist comparisons made at the time between the vitality of different units of coloured labour might well break down if we could compare the toll on bodies in similar milieus. Significant frostbite injury was noted in an SANLC company at Abancourt and in a Lushai company working at Roisel dump, in both cases due to the insufficient issue of leather gloves.[136]

To keep the men on their feet over the winter of 1917–18, some Indian companies were given a dose of opium mixed with treacle twice a week.[137] 'Treacle' was the euphemism under which Indian Army officers could requisition opium from military stores to keep sepoys, followers, or porter columns going in conditions of cold, fatigue, and fear.[138] Some Christian supervisors complained that this practice might reintroduce an addiction which the missions had been discouraging.[139] Brigadier Gibb, the Director of Labour, insisted that with Indians opium worked better than quinine to ward off fever, but he added that the dose also secured better work, so clearly the drug was offered as an incentive.[140] General H. V. Cox, Military Secretary at the India Office, ruled obliquely that no exception could be taken to the use of opium 'under medical advice'.[141]

Discipline

Constraining experience

The regime of segregation that had closed around the SANLC and the CLC was extended to the ILC, but enforcement was more discreet.[142] Instead of the

---

[136] 2 January 1918, TNA WO 95/4007; Ampthill to DOL, 4 January 1918, IOR/L/MIL/5/738, p. 70.

[137] IOR/L/MIL/7/18302.

[138] Henry Edward Shortt, IOR Mss Eur. C435. For the Abor expedition 1911–12, see IOR Mss Eur. D 1024/3.

[139] Cox to Gibb, 19 November 1917, IOR/L/MIL/7/18302.

[140] Gibb to Cox, 1 December 1917 (personal), IOR/L/MIL/7/18302.

[141] Cox to DOL, 10 December 1917, IOR/L/MIL/7/18302.

[142] In response to newspaper criticism, the DOL drafted a statement defending the confinement of the CLC, ELC, and SANLC to enclosures: 'It would be obviously undesirable, and would show a want of consideration of ... the French population to allow them to wander about ... without restrictions.' 21 September 1917, TNA WO 95/83. Interestingly, there was no reference to the ILC. The language used for the CLC was more openly racist, as in a proposal 'to erect Group pounds into which all the Chinese strays will be put.' 4 May 1918, TNA WO 95/537.

galvanised iron sheets surrounding the SANLC compounds, or the barbed wire and armed guards circling Egyptian Labour Corps and CLC camps, separation may have been enforced by Indian NCOs.[143] The length of the workday and the remoteness of worksites probably did the rest.[144]

Passes were given rarely, and only to groups under the supervision of an officer or a YMCA worker. Coloured labourers were not only prohibited from entering French cafes, but their own canteens did not have permission to sell liquor.[145] Two 'wet' canteens that had been introduced for Indian companies were shut down.[146] The other norm was to permit coloured labourers to keep only a minimal amount of money in their possession to discourage gambling or the acquisition of tastes inappropriate to their station, and to ensure they returned home with savings.[147]

Military law

'[S]implicity in procedure, combined with promptness'[148]

A great deal of the discipline must have been left to the informal authority of headmen and mates of Indian labour companies, many of whom had helped in recruitment.[149] However, the Department of Labour's *Notes* has sections

---

[143] Ampthill noted, but with disapproval, that the ILC base depot at Les Olives, Marseilles, had no guard room and no guards. 10 February 1918, IOR/L/MIL/5/738.

[144] Appealing for help through a Welsh newspaper, one of the Commanding Officers of a Khasi company, the Presbyterian missionary David Stephen Davies, wrote that shortage of writing paper and envelopes made it difficult for his men to write to their loved ones. 'They are also obligated to keep within the confines of the camp, every place is "Out of Bounds" to them, so that they are unable to ... look for, and to purchase such comforts'. Lieutenant D. S. Davies, in *Y Cymro*, 25 July 1917, p. 14, in Welsh Newspapers, The National Library of Wales, https://newspapers.library.wales/view/3447857/3447871, last accessed 17 November 2019. My thanks to Lloyd Price for the translation.

[145] TNA WO 95/83. The French authorities prohibited the use of cafes by coloured labour. 3 August 1917, TNA WO 95/83.

[146] 22 October 1917, TNA WO 95/83.

[147] *Notes*, p. 53. The ILC men may have received 5 francs—that is, Rs. 3–2 out of their monthly pay of Rs. 20/–. *TCHI*, 28 November 1917, p. 803.

[148] TNA WO 107/37, p. 63.

[149] When a man of the 41st Ranchi company refused to go to work, the other members

relating to the formal mechanisms of discipline as well. Many of the COs of British labour companies did not have have sufficient seniority or experience, so the CO of the Labour Group, a higher level of command, could restrict their powers.[150] However, for coloured labour, the *Notes* stressed the need 'for simplicity in procedure, combined with promptness.'[151] For instance, the CLC fell under the British Army Act, but in its case the 'want of qualified officers and great urgency' was invoked to institute 'a summary form of Field General Court Martial'.[152]

As pointed out in Chapter Three, commanding officers of the ILC both in Mesopotamia and France discovered that, irksome as it was, 'coolies' enrolled under the Indian Army Act would have to be court-martialed before they could be sentenced to a flogging.[153] Ampthill asked for an ordinance which would permit commanding officers to order a summary flogging without this formality: 'The Indian, like the child or a dog, does not understand deferred punishment.'[154] The arguments he offered are very revealing of service conditions for the ILC. Rigorous imprisonment, Ampthill said, was meant only for serious cases, and labourers would welcome confinement to barracks.[155] Since labourers did not get certain institutional benefits such as 'good conduct pay' or 'acting rank', there was less that could be taken away.[156] Fines would not make an impact because the men had very little money and nowhere to spend it, and this would penalise their families.[157]

Ampthill was not given the special ordinance he asked for, but the *Notes* steered attention to the extensive powers given to COs of detachments under

---

of his gang pinned him down 'out of fright for the consequences of foolishness.' Father Ory had him tied to a post, perhaps in imitation of the British ritual of field punishment, until he asked for pardon. *TCHI*, 9 January 1918, p. 33.

[150] *Notes*, p. 29.

[151] TNA WO 107/37, p. 63.

[152] *Notes*, p. 68.

[153] Ampthill to DOL, 8 August 1917, IOR/L/MIL/5/738.

[154] Ibid.

[155] Ibid.

[156] Ibid.

[157] Ampthill to DOL, 31 August 1917. IOR/L/MIL/5/738. Deferred pay could not be withheld, because it was part of ILC service conditions. WO 95/43. Military authorities were cautious about cutting into the already low wages of Indian sepoys and labourers.

the Indian Army Act 'when they held a Summary Court Martial'.[158] This was a tribunal 'peculiar to the Indian Army' in which the CO, as sole judge, was able to deliver a wide range of punishments including a flogging of up to thirty lashes, which could be carried out immediately.[159] I do not have any records for ILC courts-martial in France, but the war diaries for Mesopotamia reveal that summary courts-martial and summary general courts-martial handed down sentences of corporal punishment and fines to the Indian Labour and Porter Corps, especially in jail-recruited units.[160] Indian labour companies were usually described as 'tractable and willing', but the situation changed as their contracts began to come to a close.

Transforming experience: engaging with environments and object-worlds

Battlefield salvage: the plentitude and waste of the 'European Great War'

From the spring of 1917, as the German submarine blockade began to make itself felt, salvage activity rose in importance. In July 1917 a Controller of Salvage was appointed, and fifteen Indian labour companies were allocated to battlefield clearance in the Third Army area.[161] Side by side with officially prescribed salvage work, soldiers of all ranks and nationalities searched for material to supplement food, fuel, clothing, and shelter, or to shape into souvenirs to be sold, exchanged, or gifted. British officers of the Indian Army prided themselves on 'resourceful' Pashtun orderlies, or batmen (soldier-servants), said to display a special talent for extending regimental comforts.[162] Race and rank determined whether acts of appropriation were categorised as amusing examples of pilferage, souvenir collection, loot, theft, or barbarity.[163]

---

158 *Notes*, pp. 54–55; TNA WO 107/37, p. 46.

159 *Manual of Indian Military Law*, Calcutta: Government Printing, 1922, pp. 13, 19. See Indian Army Act (Act VIII of 1911), section 64, cl. 1(a) and (b) and sections 74–76.

160 Home, Jails, B, January 1921, nos 9–11, 12, 15.

161 TNA WO 95/384.

162 Joatamon, *A Mug in Mesopotamia*, Poona, 1918, p. 34.

163 'We have become grossly selfish … When a man is killed we rush to him to see whether he's got any food in his haversack, or, that priceless possession, a safety-razor.' A. M. Burrage, *War is War*, New York: E. P. Dutton and Co., 1930. An American surgeon who was fascinated by Indian soldiers was also ready to believe that they were 'congenital thieves'. Cushing, *From a Surgeon's Journal*, pp. 62–63.

But because they worked upon the environments in which they were positioned, Indian labourers developed a particularly intimate relationship with natural and material resources, and landscapes of devastation could soften sometimes to take on other meanings.

An Indian cavalryman posted as NCO with a Lushai labour company complained bitterly about conditions, which were very different from those he had come to expect as his due in France. They were five miles from the nearest village. They never saw a newspaper and had no recreation. There was no medical care, so twenty men had come down with mumps, and yet there was no separation of the sick. 'The men are utterly filthy and take no care of their health.'[164] And yet this was probably the very same site of which Sainghinga would recall that '[w]e had good times together.'[165] His memoir describes how the 26th and 29th Lushai companies positioned at the ruins of Monchy-au-Bois used salvage material to create spaces and activities they could claim as their own. Sainghinga relates the men's rising apprehension as their train moved through ever more shattered landscapes towards the frontline, then the joy of waking up after the first night to discover an abandoned field with a growth of greens, something they missed terribly in their meals in France. Their first act of salvage was to create a sense of 'home' by boiling up a pot.[166] Well before the YMCA organised any recreation, the Lushais made their own arrangements:

> We looked around and collected corrugated iron sheets and other things, and we built a big recreation hall. The other room was made into a canteen. We pooled our money to buy and sell all kinds of things. The canteen began to make a profit. We bought a bioscope. Since many of us had not seen 'moving pictures' it brought us much joy. The recreation hall was used as a fellowship hall on Sundays.[167]

The tents of the 41st, 42nd, and 43rd Ranchi Company were pitched on both banks of the Ancre valley, an area that had been wrested back after prolonged German occupation with enormous loss of life on both sides. Father Ory

---

[164] Punjabi Muslim, Lancers, to Driver, General Hospital, Rouen, 19 October 1917, IOR/L/MIL/5/828, p. 362.

[165] Sainghinga, *Indopui*.

[166] Sainghinga, *Indopui*. The men posted seeds in their letters home so that their families could also taste *feren antem* [French greens].' Ibid.

[167] Ibid.

wrote of the ghastly scenes the men encountered as they stripped down dug-outs and filled in shell holes:

> every five yards we come across bones still wrapped up in their putties, arms and legs blown off by shell-fire. One of our old Ranchi boys had his heart full and stood by weeping ... The Park of Thiepval is littered with human remains ... British and German helmets lie in heaps.[168]

And yet the same men fished in flooded shell holes along the Ancre river, hunted down hares startled from the high grass by heavy shelling, and returned to camp decked out in odds and ends that had been abandoned on battlefields:

> German helmets have taken a hold on their fancy, when the steel pike has been knocked off, they stick field flowers in the hole. What with the airman's fur headgear and the Pomeranian blue ribboned cap, they make a most successful parody of the mighty War Lord's noble army.[169]

Other articles, 'eloquent if malodorous evidence of the life-and-death struggle' in which they had figured, found their way into the kit of coloured labourers—for instance, military coats found unfit for combatant use, which were dyed grey or black and kept for labourers or for prisoners of war.[170] Men crafted cigarette holders and pipes to smoke their allowance of 'ration' cigarettes and loose tobacco.[171] But the debris that surrounded them and that they worked upon could also be lethal, though there was a tendency to attribute 'accidents' to the naïveté of illiterate personnel.[172] When a man trying to make a cigarette holder out of a detonator had his hands ripped open, Father Ory concluded that this 'slight accident' would work as a warning, 'as it is in their

---

[168] *TCHI*, 26 September 1917, p. 623.

[169] *TCHI*, 16 January 1918, p. 48.

[170] Isaac F. Marcosson, *The Business of War*, London: John Lane, 1918, pp. 120, 123.

[171] *TCHI*, 7 November 1917, p. 742; 28 November 1917, p. 803. However, it was not such homely items but warlike objects fashioned by two Chang Nagas in France which were then sent back from the Naga hills to the Pitt Rivers Museum, Oxford—a *dao* (machete), and a German helmet fashioned into a warrior headdress with the addition of a pair of *mithan* horns. *Report of the Pitt-Rivers Museum*, 1921. Mithan: a semi-wild bovine.

[172] See *Notes*, p. 56 for safety instructions for Indian and Asiatic personnel on salvage work. There was a far more acute concern that the CLC would demand compensation for work injuries.

nature to take lessons from experience alone.'[173] However, even he had to admit that no human prudence could really keep the men safe from the unexploded bombs lurking everywhere around their worksites.[174]

Sainghinga recalled how they had also been cautioned not to eat the tinned beef, soda water, and sweets they found in German trenches, lest these had been poisoned.[175] The Ranchi companies had set out eagerly for the 'hidden treasures and fairy-like surprises' of German dugouts in Rossignol Wood. One Johan, opening what he thought was a brandy bottle, uncorked a tear gas bomb.[176] In this glimmer of riches found in trenches we get a sense of how men, for whom want and making do were so much a part of everyday existence, experienced the plentitude and waste of the 'European Great War'.[177] In his ethnography of the Lhota Nagas, J. P. Mills remarked in passing that '[t]he men who went to France with the Naga Corps thought our method of cleaning an animal and throwing away the offal most wasteful.'[178]

Suggestive equivalences: food, hospitality, entertainment

We were all Johnnies to them.[179]

The men in the ILC worked upon what they found in their kits, canteens, and environments not only to recreate what was comfortable and familiar, but also to forge connections with those around them. By striving to place themselves in a common frame of 'war service', they could claim some of the amenities which combatants demanded as their due. They were also taught how to position themselves in this frame, for British and Australian soldiers, as well as German prisoners of war, found some relief from fear and monotony in the exoticism of Indian personnel, and in assuming a pedagogical role. For one Australian soldier, William Henry Nicholson, the most eye-popping moment

[173] TCHI, 3 October 1917, p. 645. Sainghinga, the man of education, had the same attitude. Indopui.
[174] Three men of a Ranchi company were mortally injured when one put his foot on a Mills bomb. TCHI, 20 February 1918, p. 144. The number of near escapes is remarkable.
[175] Sainghinga, Indopui.
[176] TCHI, 26 June 1918, p. 494.
[177] Ibid.
[178] J. P. Mills, The Lhota Nagas, London: Macmillan, 1922, p. 78.
[179] Kashi Nath, Indian Labourers in France, p. 9.

of his service in France was his glimpse of an Indian labour company, perhaps a Naga one, at Mailly:

> There are some quaint subjects of the King on this front, Chinamen, Kaffirs, Negros, etc; but some natives of Kasmir, India, that I saw today take the biscuit. They look as if they had been cannibals in civil life, and stretch the lobes of their areas by boring them and wearing brass ornaments in the holes. One fellow I saw was wearing a large brass door knocker in his left ear and about 16 brass hooks in the other. He was a big chief I suppose.[180]

From the amused yet confident position of a different sort of colonial, Nicholson put himself in the same frame. On furlough in London he wrote of a 'comfortable class of English people', who thought that 'Australians were a savage tribe ... very fierce and cantankerous; and wore bones in their noses.'[181]

Race distinctions did not vanish, but the barriers were sometimes lowered to allow forms of subaltern cosmopolitanism to emerge. However, one hardly finds any references to friendly interaction between Indian and other 'coloured' units, even at sites where they camped or worked in proximity.[182] Yet there may have been some interaction for Indian labourers, and soldiers did note that the French paid their 'black' soldiers the same wages as white soldiers, at least in theory. It is also difficult to recover some account of relations between the ILC men and French residents, partly because of the remoteness of worksites. 'The Pathans are not happy,' wrote Ampthill. 'They had been told by the cavalry they would have access to large cities and a glorious time among *Houris*.'[183] Sainghinga's description of the effort it took to obtain a photograph recording their presence in France gives us a sense of the importance of the act and the isolation of their campsite:

---

[180] William Henry Nicholson, diary, 19 July 1917, pp. 60–61, in World War One Collection, State Library New South Wales, http://ww1.sl.nsw.gov.au/diaries, last accessed 17 November 2019.

[181] 19 August 1917, Ibid.

[182] Objecting strongly to the proximity of ILC and British West Indian camps at Fournier, Ampthill said it was 'not well to keep Indians and Negroes in close proximity' and that there had been 'disagreeable incidents'. 2 February 1918, IOR/L/MIL/5/738. British West Indian soldiers prided themselves on being combatants who received much the same pay as British soldiers, and therefore not the same as 'coloured' labourers in France. Howe, *Race, War and Nationalism*, pp. 121–22, 129.

[183] Tour report, 4 January 1918, IOR/L/MIL/5/738.

One day on 25.9.1917, with 2nd Lt G T Badeley we went to a place not too far away where there were only three French houses and we asked them to take a photograph. We gave 30 francs for the photo. Except for this one time, while we were at Monchy-au-Bois for about five months and after we shifted up to 24.2.1918, we did not see a single civilian again.[184]

The British censor of letters had an ambivalent attitude about the rather too rapturous accounts that sepoys gave of the kindness and graciousness of the French.[185] 'Although they are white they don't look down on dark people,' wrote one Lushai labourer, adding that African soldiers got the same salary, and the same rations, as the French.[186] Indian labour companies must have had some engagement with the French at Marseilles, but I could find no reference to this. Perhaps it was no coincidence that of the three companies—the 63rd and 64th Bengal and the 57th Oraon—sent to the French zone of Nancy, the 57th under Father Floor was made up of Oraon Catholics and the 64th, under Father Douglass of the Oxford mission, had a cluster of Bengali Christians. Billeted in barns and lofts, their interaction with the French had some propaganda value. British military authorities found occasion both to deplore the 'filth' of French villages and to revel in the impression that Father Floor created when his Oraon Catholics began to clean up the streets and sing in the parish church.[187] Father Floor reported proudly that local prejudices, which he attributed to the behavior of the French Moroccans who had preceded them, soon dissolved, and his men were invited to tea on their departure.[188]

The Department of Labour felt that too much fraternisation between British NCOs and the 'coloured' labour they supervised might erode discipline.[189] Ampthill warned against the tendency of British soldiers 'to treat the

---

[184] Sainghinga, *Indopui*. See image 14 for this photograph. Taking home a photograph of themselves in uniform was one of the ways in which labourers could recast themselves as soldiers, and, for those in other posts, as officers. A photograph of Kanrei Shaiza, interpreter with the 66th Manipur company in France, has him posing sternly with the swagger stick of an officer. See frontispiece of his travelogue: Shaiza, *Āpuk Āpaga Rairei Khare, France Khavā, 1917–18*. British Tommies also had photographs taken of themselves with a swagger stick when they went out in civilian clothes.

[185] IOR/L/MIL/5, III, p. 342.

[186] Kailuia, 'France ram', *Mizo leh Vai*, September 1918.

[187] Anpthill to DOL, 24 November 1917, IOR/L/MIL/5/738.

[188] *TCHI*, 5 June 1918, p. 428.

[189] TNA WO 107/37, p. 73.

Indians as Gollywogs.'[190] Yet some space for fraternisation among Indian, British, and Dominion personnel had to be allowed, for it was one of the themes of war propaganda. Kashi Nath gave a rapturous description of the 'few glorious days' when a host of Australians camped nearby:

> They would swarm into our barracks ... exchange cigarettes ... eat small bits of chapattis .... would teach our men how to darn socks, would ... drill them, ... bring their own football and start kicking it about. Once I found an Anzac soldier lathering and shaving one of our men ... two others were ... awaiting their turn.[191]

Turning conscientiously thereafter to extol the friendliness of 'Tommy Atkins', he wrote of British NCOs who sent postcards when they left, and of meals offered and hospitality returned in the form of '*dal chapati korma* and Indian sweets': 'Often at night I would find soldiers sitting snuggled in a corner talking, talking, with our men and often wondered what they could talk about when the others understood hardly a word.'[192]

Perhaps 'speech acts', rather than speech alone, built bridges across race that left a mark in the vocabulary of returning servicemen. For instance, the phrases a Ranchi company picked up in an instructional context from the British sappers who guided them into dugouts reappeared when the Ranchi men played football: 'Come here, you b***** fool'; 'Stick to it, Johnny'; 'Hang on, man'.[193]

Transnational circuits of congregational music provided a common point of reference for Christian Lushais and sailors on board the ship that took them to France.[194] It is with some disingenuousness that Sainghinga wonders why, in clashes with *vais* (Indians from the plains) over water supply, 'the *sap* (sahib) workers of the ship would always take our side ... they would give us the sticks of the brooms used to sweep the ships. If we had off-times together ... we would sing God's songs together.'[195] At Monchy-au-Bois, sap soldiers would visit the Lushais on Sundays:

---

[190] 5 August 1917, IOR/L/MIL/5/738.
[191] Kashi Nath, *Indian Labourers in France*, pp. 9–10.
[192] Ibid.
[193] *TCHI*, 28 November 1917, p. 504.
[194] There were Lushais who could follow the tonic solfa notation for hymns even if they could not read, and they would repeat the song after a lead singer. 'We had gone through Sankey's entire revised song-book with 1200 hymns ... We also loved to sing Alexander's hymns.' Sainghinga, *Indopui*.
[195] Ibid.

Sometimes we sang hymns together. Most of them knew 'Abide with me' and 'Nearer my God to thee.' We found very few who knew other hymns. However they knew songs that were not hymns, what we called *hla lenglawng* (sentimental songs).

Indian soldiers and labourers positioned in Europe were aware that they had to take on a certain public persona if they wanted to be placed on the same footing, at least notionally, as British and Dominion forces.[196] Kashi Nath writes that his men would warn each other not to indulge in unseemly behavior before 'these sahibs', namely the British and Australian soldiers who befriended them, 'men who though of a different nation were soldiers of the same Empire.'[197] Being able to give was a matter of pride, a demonstration of responsiveness to the ideals of sacrifice associated with war service. The 26th Lushais donated their canteen profits to charity, although the 1,200 francs was a substantial sum for them.[198] One Kumaon company used up their store of tea for an incoming party of British soldiers and allowed them to heat up bully beef in their cookhouse, explaining to their officer, 'Sahib, this is war time.'[199]

Food constituted a complex symbolic terrain. Kit, ration items, and canteen supplies were markers of status, elevating the Tommy far above the Indian sepoy, and the latter above the follower ranks. But an important part of imperial propaganda was the capacity of the British to bring supplies right up to the front line and to meet the dietary requirements of loyal 'ethnic' soldiers. For the Indian infantry and cavalry regiments in Europe, special arrangements had been made to ensure the availability of fresh meat, slaughtered in the appropriate way for Muslims, Hindus, and Sikhs. In contrast, fresh meat was a rarity for the ILC.[200] Assuming that the 'primitive' element in the ILC would accept just about any kind of flesh, Ampthill proposed that their rations be supplemented with horsemeat. However, he had to report that it had become 'a matter of dignity' with the hill-men to accept only the same meat as Europeans.[201]

---

[196] Padre Dinanath, Indian YMCA worker, wrote, '*Har chavani Hindustan ka namoona hai*'—every Indian encampment was like a sample of Hindustan. '*Ham Log France mein kis tarah rehte hain*', *Ladai ka Akhbar*, 29 August 1918.

[197] Kashi Nath, *Indian Labourers in France*, pp. 46–47.

[198] IOR/L/MIL/5/738.

[199] Ampthill to Cox, 17 December 1917, IOR/L/MIL/5/738.

[200] Cox, 12 September 1917, IOR/L/MIL/7/18304.

[201] Ampthill to DOL, 19 October 1917 and 23 October 1917, IOR/L/MIL/5/738. The Army was searching for ways to use animals slaughtered as unfit for use.

Although the men in the ILC wanted to reproduce 'home' in their meals, they felt they were entitled to the ration and canteen items dispensed to other soldiers, and which they too had come to enjoy. The 59th Burma Company wanted sesame oil for cooking, but they also asked for 'sprats and smelts as do the German prisoners'.[202] Cox noted with astonishment that the canteen items most in demand with the Manipur and Chin companies were 'note-books, sardines, sausages and soap'.[203]

Suggestive equivalences: leisure and organised sports for labourers

Ampthill had felt it was politically important to give the men in the ILC a sightseeing tour of England before they returned.[204] However, shopping and sightseeing trips, even within France, were only organised from March 1918, when the men had to be induced to extend their stay.[205] Nevertheless, the idea of organised recreation was acceptable within the military framework, whereas in India 'leisure' was still a disputed entitlement for labourers.[206] The *Indian Industrial Commission Report, 1916–1918* accepted that organised games would be good for the health of factory operatives but also remarked that until workers learnt to use their leisure advantageously, shorter hours might not be an 'unmixed benefit'.[207] However, in France there was just one officer, Captain Griffiths, who took the harsh view that if the men were being worked properly, they ought to be too tired for recreation.[208] Many ILC companies organised hockey and football for themselves well before any

[202] Ampthill to Cox, 4 January 1918, IOR/MIL/5/738.

[203] Cox, tour diary, 9 March 1918, IOR/L/MIL/5/738.

[204] Ampthill to C. S. Bayley, 15 October 1917, IOR/L/MIL/5/738, p. 152.

[205] Field Marshall Sir Douglas Haig to WO, 15 March 1918, IOR/L/MIL/7/18759; 27 February 1918, TNA WO 95/384.

[206] The argument was that leisure was in fact idleness: 'the more they can earn in a given time, the more frequent holidays they take.' *Report of the Indian Factory Labour Commission*, vol. I, p. 23, para. 31.

[207] *Indian Industrial Commission Report*, p. 190.

[208] Ampthill to DOL, 9 September 1917, IOR/L/MIL/5/738. Traditional sports, such as wrestling, were being supplemented in the Indian Army by modern organised games, such as football and hockey. E. D. Ushaw, 'Football at the Front', *The Windsor Magazine*, no. 48 (1917), pp. 69–75. In World War One it was the CO's responsibility to organise leisure, as it kept Indian personnel at camp and provided the entry point for war propaganda and 'improving' lectures.

YMCA assistance, to the surprise of Ampthill, who had not expected to discover this interest among labourers.[209] The joy of displaying his dexterity at football, a game learnt at his mission school in Ukhrul, shines through Kanrei Shaiza's memoir about his service as an interpreter with the 66th Manipur labour company:

> S. Kanrei was the most skillful player. He was swift and nimble footed whom nobody could chase down once a sprint with the ball was made. He was a proficient striker too as he would regularly score goals. Because of his skill and good spirit, everyone watching the game, including his officers, was very pleased with him and showered him with praise.... People would come in thousands to see these matches. It was like people from almost all the nations were there.[210]

The sphere of performance, like that of football, was also one which allowed exchanges between military personnel. The 39th Manipur company, for example, entertained by some neighbouring units, 'returned the compliment by giving exhibitions of Naga dances.'[211] However, the transfrontier Pashtuns, whom Ampthill cast as the one 'mercenary' element in the ILC, resisted the idea of regulated leisure. The CO of the 50th NWFP company said that the men wanted only 'a fire, cigarettes, smoking and talking', and the CO of the 48th NWFP company said that they did not take kindly to organised games.[212] In fact, there was a mysterious 'affair' in the 48th NWFP company in connection with an athletics day which resulted in an inconclusive enquiry and its supervisor, Khan Sahib Mohammad Gul Khan, being sent home under a cloud.[213]

Suggestive equivalences: in the flow of mass commodity circuits

The other way in which Indian labourers placed themselves in the same frame as other military personnel was by adding certain distinctive items to their kit. Sepoys and labourers found that military service could secure them the privilege of telling the time themselves, instead of only being told it. During the First World War mass commodity chains and military supply channels made

---

[209] Ibid.

[210] Shaiza, *Āpuk Āpaga Rairei Khare, France Khavā, 1917–18*.

[211] Ampthill to DOL, 14 October 1917, IOR/L/MIL/5/738. See image 13.

[212] Ampthill to DOL, 9 September 1917, IOR/L/MIL/5/738.

[213] IOR/L/PS/11/134, file 1232/18. Gul Khan may have demonstrated rather too conspicuously that he wielded more influence with the transfrontier Pashtuns than their British COs. Ibid.

the wristlet, an item of jewellery for women, into something available for the ordinary soldier. Army contractors began to issue cheap, reliable, mass-produced wristwatches.[214] The wristwatch, 'ration-cigarettes' (rather than snuff, chewing tobacco, or cheroots), and the safety razor (surfacing in Europe with the arrival of American troops) increasingly featured in the kit of Indian military personnel.[215] The possession of such objects and a familiarity with their use indicated someone who had been out in the world. When sepoys and labourers described their war experiences, these items provided rich descriptive references and analogies. For instance, expressing his scepticism about Kitchener's newly trained recruits, one Indian veteran wrote home: 'Manufacturers of watches in this country have made watches for the Kitchener Army ... only one or two are capable of going for a year or two ... I have no faith in these watches, the only reliable timekeepers among us are those which we brought from India.'[216]

Kashi Nath's account of the 'epidemic of watches' that overtook his labour company is interesting for the density of transactions taking place around this object:

> In the beginning it was hard to make the men understand the variation in the time of sunrise and sunset ... then commenced our epidemic of watches. Every man aspired to have at least one ... watches were very cheap. The most envied were those who possessed a *bijli ke ghari* which glowed in figures of fire, even at night. One of the men had... three watches, one purchased from the canteen, another bought from a chum 'Tommy,' and a third in a deal ... from an American. This ardour cooled, for watches stopped frequently, as they are apt to do when one is ... performing heavy manual labour. ... Some watches did however come out to India.[217]

---

[214] John E. Brozek, 'The History and Evolution of the Wristwatch', *International Watchman Magazine*, January 2004 http://www.qualitytyme.net/pages/rolex_articles/history_of_wristwatch.html, last accessed 10 November 2019.

[215] Padre Dinanath referred to sepoys shopping for watches. Dinanath, '*Ham log France mein kis tarah rehte hain*'. A Parsi traveller noted that sepoys in Mesopotamia were wearing watches, which were cheaper there than in India. Manockjee Cursetjee, *The Land of the Date: A Recent Voyage from Bombay to Basra and Back, 1916–1917*, Bombay: C. M. Cursetjee, 1918, p. 204.

[216] Sultan Mabarik Khan, Central Indian Horse, France to Gauhar Rahman, Bannu, 30 July 1917, IOR/L/MIL/5/827, IV, p. 516.

[217] Kashi Nath, *Indian Labourers in France*.

Kashi Nath implied that it was impractical for labourers to wear watches, but being able to tell time for themselves was an act of self-assertion by men whose work hours could stretch on indefinitely. In Mesopotamia, the Director of Labour inspecting the 6th Indian Porter Corps at Kut said that they were 'a fine body of men but appear to lack discipline ... At 11 o'clock when work is supposed to stop, they all point to their wristwatches, which many of them have and inform their Indian Officers that it is time to stop.'[218]

In the sound of the guns: auditory and other experiences of the front line

Indian and Chinese coolies at the front hear aeroplanes long before the British, and give valuable warning.[219]

Sikimanding Sap i lungmawl e, i lungmawl e,
German Rallian tawnin tir suh ka lungdi, chheih
Ka suihlung leng tur hi dawn ve la.

...

Ka Di tap ruaiin mi ring lo la, mi ring lo la,
German rallian kulhpui kan han tawn ni chuan e
A surin ngen mu a sur sung sung.

[Second Commanding Officer, you are thoughtless, O so thoughtless,
Do not send my Beloved to face the huge German troops,
Think of the loneliness I will have to endure.

...

Do not think I cried tears of terror, My Love,
The day we stormed the German fortress,
Bullets hailed like rain from the skies.][220]

The definition of 'danger zone' was a point of contention for coloured labour in Europe.[221] The CLC could not be worked less than sixteen kilome-

---

[218] 10 July 1918, TNA WO 95/4991.

[219] 'Did you know this', *Port Pirie Recorder*, 8 August 1918, p. 3, in Trove, National Library of Australia, http://trove.nla.gov.au/newspaper, last accessed 18 November 2019.

[220] 'German Ral Run' ('The Storming of the German Troops'), Mizo (Lushai) song, referred to variously as old, folk or classic. Trans. Cherrie Lalnunziri Chhangte, http://mizdaydreambeliever.blogspot.fr/2008_01_01_archive.html, last accessed 10 November 2019

[221] In September 1917 two Egyptian companies were fired upon for striking work after

tres from the front line, but the Department of Labour said that this did not exempt them from sites exposed to air raids.[222] The South African government's insistence on a high degree of segregation for the SANLC and a prohibition on its use near the front hampered its mobility.[223] Prisoners of war were not supposed to be deployed less than thirty kilometres from the front or in scattered parties.

The ILC agreement made no specification about distance from the front line, which suggests that it could be used more flexibly than these other formations.[224] Enquiries indicated that very varied assurances had been given to Indian companies, from the vague formulation that 'they would not be called upon to fight' to the promise that they would not be taken into the danger zone.[225] To an enquiry about whether Indians could be deployed up to six kilometres from the front line, Ampthill pointed out that billets above ground at this distance were often more exposed to shelling than trenches at the front, and that the spirit of their contract should not be violated.[226] However, there was little resistance in the ILC to deployment close to the front, although the men of one NWFP company protested that working under aerial bombardment was a violation of their agreement. Harrowing exposure to shelling and bombing along the Somme from mid-January 1918 certainly made the Ranchi companies long to return home.[227]

---

an air raid at Boulogne. 21 September 1917, TNA WO 95/83. After their camps in Dunkirk were bombed on 30 July 1918, the CLC had to be forced to return to work. Xu, *Strangers on the Western Front*, p. 86.

[222] 2 July 1917 and 5 September 1917, TNA WO 95/83.

[223] TNA WO 107/37, p. 25.

[224] This issue may have prompted the War Office to ask for the full number of Indians it had initially requested. No more white labour could be sent to France, and the Secretary of State for War said it was 'inadvisable' to raise the question of employing the Chinese within ten miles from the front. 2 July 1917, TNA WO 95/83. However, on 1 October 1917 the Commander-in-Chief, India, reported that labour recruitment was being compromised by rumours that steel helmets had been issued to the ILC, whereupon the War Office replied that there was no intention to deploy them near the front. 7 October 1917, TNA WO 95/83.

[225] 11 November 1917, TNA WO 95/83.

[226] Ampthill to Cox, 9 December 1917, and to DOL, 14 December 1917, IOR/L/MIL/5/738.

[227] *TCHI*, 15 May 1918, p. 368; 22 May 1918, p. 387; 10 July 1918, pp. 534–35; Ampthill to Cox, 4 January 1918, IOR/L/MIL/5/738. A map shows the ILC

Indian labour companies would get swept up in a moving front line on two terrifying occasions. During the Cambrai offensive launched in November–December 1917, some were working on roads at very forward points such as Bus, Fins, and Manancourt Wood.[228] The second time was during the series of attacks starting on 21 March 1918 which opened the German spring offensive:

> Since the 6th March our life has been a veritable hell. We have been shelled and bombed night and day ... The Germans being twice on us we had to run for dear life ... Three nights we ran, sleeping one hour along the road ... None of us could sleep though for the last month, as the shells went bang, bang, bang, every minute.[229]

Under fire, twelve men of the 44th UP company at Achiet were killed and seventeen wounded; ten went missing from the 46th UP company at Manancourt.[230] On 23 March 1918, the Commander of the 61st Labour Group was ordered to send away all coloured labour, but since no white labour was at hand, he kept the 26th Lushais to clear out ammunition dumps at Bray and Merignolles. The 59th British labour company was so exhausted when it reached Merignolles that the Lushais kept working until they were relieved by the 59th Burma labour company on the afternoon of 25 March.[231]

This brings us to 26 March 1918, when the Lushais retreated through Amiens, which was rocking under a heavy barrage, and to the stirring passage in Sainghinga's memoir where he relates how they suddenly wanted to turn around and fight:

> we could hear the rumble of houses falling down. People, women with babies, and children all filled with fear ... and in tears ... One called out to me as I was in the front ... 'Sainghing, Sainghing, tell our commander we don't want to go ahead.'
>
> 'Let him think of acquiring guns for us, we are returning to fire at the Germans.'
>
> The Commander said, 'I cannot give you guns, we have to march on.'[232]

---

bunched close to the frontline in February 1918: Pearson, 'Report on Labour Organisation in France', p. 13 and appendix 2.

[228] They were praised for a very orderly retreat. TNA WO 107/37, p. 80; 17 December 1917, TNA WO 95/384.

[229] Father Ory to Dr Moulman, Calcutta, 2 April 1918, IOR/L/MIL/5/828, pt. III.

[230] Ampthill to Cox, 31 March 1918, IOR/L/MIL/7/18510.

[231] Lieutenant Colonel A. O. Vaughan, 61st Labour Group, 14 April 1918, IOR/L/MIL/5/738.

[232] Sainghinga, *Indopui*. Sainghinga composed his memoir sometime during World

The spring offensive seemed to generate such sagas of labour companies turning around to join the stand against the Germans, or wanting to do so.[233] Equally, there were allegations that some units stampeded to get away.[234] Nevertheless, the Indian companies were acknowledged to have held up very steadily through all the fear and chaos of the retreat.[235]

'Thus far and no further'

Throughout this period, restiveness was also rising in Indian companies.[236] On 12 March 1918, Cox noted that over the following three months 20,000 men of the ILC would have to be repatriated, yet shipping was not available and their labour was badly needed.[237] The terms seemed to be good—a bonus of Rs. 25/–, with Rs. 10/– extra pay for the first three months and Rs. 15/– extra for every month thereafter. Yet on 22 February 1918, only three Indian companies were willing to extend their term.[238] Lord Ampthill tried to express what they felt: 'we are treated like animals. Nobody takes any notice of us, there is not recreation, or time for recreation, and we get no credit for the work we do.'[239]

On 18 March the 39th Manipur company suddenly refused to work, though it was not due to leave until 10 April. Ampthill hoped that they would see

---

War Two. However, writing from the Lushai hills in July 1918, when the men had just returned home, a Baptist missionary reported that, seeing old men and women swarming out from Amiens, 'there arose within their hearts such a chivalrous spirit that for the moment ... they could have gone back and forced the oncoming hosts ... if someone had given them guns and ammunition.' J. H. Lorrain to Mrs Lewin, 12 July 1918, MS 811/IV/66/1 (i), Lewin collection, University of London.

[233] See 'The Maurice letter', *TOI*, 14 May 1918, p. 7. For a report that CLC men had resisted 'the Huns' with picks and shovels, see Klein, *With the Chinks*, p. 247. Xu Guoqi contends that this did happen. Xu, *Strangers on the Western Front*, p. 93.

[234] Ampthill, who visited the Abancourt emergency labour camp on 29 March 1918, praised Indian companies for marching away steadily carrying their kit, which was 'more than can be said for many British units or for the Chinese and Italians who left everything behind.' Ampthill to Cox, 31 March 1918, IOR/L/MIL/7/18510; see also TNA WO 95/4007.

[235] IOR/MIL/L/7/18510.

[236] TNA WO 107/37, p. 41; 5–16 March 1918, TNA WO 95/384.

[237] Cox, 12 March 1918, IOR/L/Ml/5/738.

[238] IOR/L/MIL/5/738; TNA WO 95/4007.

[239] Ampthill to Adjutant General, 21 February 1918, IOR/L/MIL/5/738.

reason, 'as of course it is open mutiny on their part.'[240] The headmen of one Naga company declared they could hold the men for three weeks at most: 'If they aren't shifted they'll burn their camp.'[241] Hoping the men would stay on until October 1918, the War Office wanted them to sign a fresh contract with a new termination date. Ampthill was convinced that they would refuse to do so, but might be persuaded to treat the extension as 'overtime' until shipping could be arranged.[242] He wrote: 'This is not the time for niceties of legal contract, nor is it necessary to take power to compel the men to work when they will go on working voluntarily if only they are left alone ... The Indian labourers have had more than they bargained for.'[243]

On the one hand, the ILC men refused to allow what they felt was a breach of their agreement to be turned into a 'voluntary contract'.[244] If they had to go on working beyond the concluding date, they would cast it as a favour to their officers, to be reciprocated by the arrangement of their passage home. But the military authorities also behaved with circumspection. Though punitive measures were reviewed, there were no trials for mutiny.[245] Harsh action would have been embarrassing, especially after the spring offensive, during which the ILC companies had been praised for their constant readiness to turn back and keep working.[246] Companies whose contract had come to an end and who refused to carry on were separated from the others and sent to a 'rest camp' on their way out.[247] Those who went on working finally got some rest breaks and recreational trips, and the King reviewed some parties of ILC officers, NCOs, and headmen at Buckingham Palace, an event captured in newsreels.[248]

---

[240] IOR/L/MIL/7/18302.

[241] Lt —, native Christian, to Mrs —, n.d., IOR/L/MIL/5/828, p. 405. Significantly, three weeks would bring them up to the date they were due to leave.

[242] 17 March 1918, TNA WO 95/83; also Cox, 12 March 1918, IOR/L/MIL/5/738.

[243] Ampthill to Cox, 31 March 1918, IOR/L/MIL/7/18510.

[244] Similarly, Indian soldiers being treated for wounds in Britain felt that being asked to go back and risk death again was a breach of norms of service, and they refused to sign papers saying that they were returning to the front 'voluntarily'.

[245] TNA WO 95/384.

[246] TNA WO 107/37, p. 45. Coercion would have not gone down well in India, and in addition the Nagas, Chins and Lushais would be returning to a border still in the throes of insurgency.

[247] Sometimes reduced rations signalled official displeasure. 30 April 1918, TNA WO 95/537; 19 May 1918, TNA WO 95/83.

[248] IOR/L/MIL/7/18759; 31 May 1918, TNA WO 95/384.

At the threshold of war

The labels of 'coloured' or 'native' labour justified inferior care and a harsher work and disciplinary regime than that experienced by white labourers. The notion was that to 'work' natives properly, the managerial regimes peculiar to them also had to be imported into the metropolis. To see Indians labouring in these positions in Europe also served as a reassuring reminder that empire carried on serenely in areas far removed from scenes of industrial slaughter. As Fendle, the protagonist of *The Dripping Tamarinds*, watches the men of his Burmese company 'heaving at a huge mass of rusted German barbed wire ... their brown bodies beaded with sweat ... his memory recaptured hot, shimmering visions of the Irrawaddy valley; of black river steamers anchored in the glare, of paddy sacks being dumped on to lighters.'[249] The new discursive element was provided by the search for loyal ethnic groups such as the Nagas and Chins, who, it was hoped, would contribute to the postwar future of empire in India. However, the war also gave a fillip, both in India and in theatres of war overseas, to a more generalised discourse about 'Indian labour' and the degree to which its 'efficiency' could be improved, although stereotypes about the 'unskilled coolie mass' were difficult to displace.

Labourers entered the theatre of war often wary that they might be taken over the threshold into combat. The battles that had taken place were starkly visible in the damaged land they worked over, in the density of the bodies they stumbled across, and in the scatter of broken bayonets, abandoned ammunition and kit which they gathered up. Ongoing battles were ever present in a skyscape of observation balloons and aerial sorties, and the thunder and flash of heavy guns melded into the weather that assailed them. In March 1918, non-combatants of various sorts found themselves assimilated into a moving frontline with an inevitability they had dreaded for weeks.

But labourers also engaged with the material of war in a particularly visceral way. The sheer weight of the iron rails and girders they wrenched out of dugouts and heaved onto lorries; their daily exposure to danger 'along the trenches where

---

[249] Lowis, *The Dripping Tamarinds*, p. 153. A correspondent enthused about his glimpse of an Indian labour company cutting trees in French woodland: 'On the instant we breathed the atmosphere of Asia, and recalled distant scenes and half-forgotten memories.' 'The Army behind the Army', *The War Illustrated*, 15 December 1917. Writing in the same vein, Candler declared that 'the old type Indian servant' had 'increased his prestige in the war.' Edmund Candler, *The Sepoy*, London: John Murray, 1919, pp. 227–28.

Mills bombs lurk in the high grass and explode at a touch'; the pain of hands sticking to frozen metal and the bite of icy winds in sopping marshy tract.[250] This was the war as they experienced it through their bodies, an experience that brought some home disabled and others stronger in health and with a sense of consequence, and left many buried in cemeteries in France. By retrieving and recycling objects strewn about the battlefields, the men in the ILC renewed their life for military use, although the German offensive swept away many salvage piles. Indian labourers clearing up the Ancre valley also revived the hope that ravaged earth might be restored to productive farmland.[251]

However, if the fate of the highly publicised India Expeditionary Force of 1914–15 was to be damned by faint praise, this was even more the case for the less interesting coolie formations.[252] Two labour companies stayed on in France until well after the armistice, constituting, along with Indian artillery drivers, pockets of depletion and exhaustion at the edge of triumphalist displays of victory.[253] It was perhaps appropriate, then, that '[o]n armistice day India was represented in France by only artillery and A.S.C. drivers and by Indian Coolie Corps.'[254]

---

[250] *TCHI*, 3 January 1918, p. 7; *TCHI*, 9 January 1918, p. 33; Baring, *R.F.C.H.Q., 1914–1918*, p. 255. See Ampthill's description of the 26th Lushai company 'often crying with the pain of frozen hands' because they were handling metal without gloves. Ampthill to Cox, 4 January 1918, IOR/L/MIL/738, p. 70.

[251] Burial parties had preceded the Ranchi companies as they began their work, but ploughing parties began to follow them. *TCHI*, November 1917 and 15 May 1918, p. 368. The artist William Orpen remarked on the 'incredible' rapidity with which Indians had changed the whole face of this area. William Orpen, *An Onlooker in France, 1917–1919*, London: Williams and Norgate, 1921.

[252] IOR/L/MIL/7/18354.

[253] In August 1919 there were still 680 Indian labourers in northern France, along with 14,441 artillery drivers, remount personnel, and Accounts and Postal employees. Their presence, as the YMCA worker Reverend A. W. McMillan pointed out, permitted the earlier demobilisation of many a British soldier, yet the impression in England was that all the Indians had left France in 1915. McMillan, 'Indian Echoes from France', pp. 1–20. For the rising value of their services during the period of demobilisation, see TNA WO 95/43.

[254] Francis Younghusband, 'India', in Sir Charles Lucas (ed.), *The Empire at War*, vol. 5, London: Oxford University Press, 1926, p. 342.

6

THE ENDS OF WAR

HOMECOMING FOR THE INDIAN SOLDIER AND FOLLOWER, 1914–21

Bruno Cabanes suggests that the 'end of the war' should be understood as a transition taking place in fits and starts, with periods of simultaneous demobilisation and remobilisation. Yet, as he points out, '"1919" was also a moment, a coalescence of expectations.'[1] This useful formulation allows us to knit the war years closely to their aftermath while giving sufficient weight to the post-Armistice conjuncture. In Mesopotamia, the Labour Directorate complained of the difficulty of explaining to 'Asiatic labourers' that the signing of the Armistice meant a halt to fighting, not the actual end of the war.[2] But some British units in India were equally obtuse. Speaking 'man to man', a spokesman for disaffected British personnel told the Commanding Officer at Pune that six months had expired since the Armistice, so by law they were no longer soldiers and were therefore not obliged to leave for combat on the Afghan frontier.[3] The UK had passed a War Definition Act in 1918 (8&9

---

[1] Bruno Cabanes, '1919: Aftermath', in J. Winter (ed.), *The Cambridge History of the First World War*, Cambridge: Cambridge University Press, 2014, pp. 172–98.

[2] Commerce and Industry, Emigration, August 1919, nos 8–9. 'On various occasions when Asiatics ... have been kept under the stress of circumstances beyond their agreements, trouble has resulted.' GOC, Force D, 29 December 1918, in AD, ADG's Branch, Establishment, A, May 1919, nos 1869–73.

[3] Nigel Gresley Woodyatt, *Under Ten Viceroys: The Reminiscences of a Gurkha*, London:

Geo. V, c. 59) which gave government the power to determine 'what date is to be treated as the date of the termination of the present war' for certain purposes. The Government of India assumed similar powers in the Termination of the Present War (Definition) Act 1919. Under these acts the war was officially declared to have terminated on 31 August 1921 for the UK and on 1 September 1921 for India.[4]

The different power configurations, interventions and struggles through which war is terminated form a thriving subfield of War and Conflict Studies and International Relations. This chapter explores the 'termination of the war' using a variety of different timelines. By doing so, one gets a multifaceted sense of the way the Great War segued into postwar imperial militarism, and of the political consequences for India. Protests in 1919 against the Rowlatt Act, sometimes intertwining with the Khilafat movement against British and French aggrandisement in Ottoman territories, were interventions to arrest this segue.[5] To a longstanding campaign to control the deployment of Indian labour overseas was added a demand to have a say in the use of Indian military manpower, and to critique not only its fiscal costs but also the international order it kept in place.[6]

H. Jenkins, 1922, p. 272. For other such incidents in India see Julian Putkowski, 'Mutiny in India in 1919', https://www.marxists.org/history/etol/revhist/backiss/vol8/no2/putkowski2.html, *last accessed 10 November 2019*.

[4] Legislative Department, Legislative, B, June 1919, nos 8–9. The Public Prosecutor used this date to argue that the Khilafat leaders Muhammad Ali and Shaukat Ali were seducing Muslim soldiers from their obligation to serve 'for the duration of the war and six months after'. *The Historic Trial of the Ali Brothers*, part II, Karachi: New Times Office, 1921, p. 45.

[5] The 'Rowlatt Act' refers to the Revolutionary and Anarchical Crimes Act of 10 March 1919, which extended wartime emergency powers for arrest and detention without trial or judicial review.

[6] Jacobsen argues that in 1919 the War Office conceptualised the now extremely swollen Indian Army as an eastern extension of the British Army, to be used widely in the Middle East. However, this ambition was thwarted by the heavy cost of the Afghan war and the permanent occupation of Waziristan. Marc H. Jacobsen, 'The Third Afghan War and the External Position of India, 1919–1924', Naval Oceans Systems Centre, San Diego CA, pp. 37–38, http://www.dtic.mil/dtic/tr/fulltext/u2/a195401.pdf, last accessed 10 November 2019. However, the political backlash against this design should also be factored in.

Moving from macro- to microhistory, this chapter explores the way in which, through a series of seemingly apolitical actions, Indian combatants and non-combatants had also been changing the terms of their employment. The nature of their exit from the war, or more broadly their transition from military service to civilian life, was one such sphere of activity. In engaging with the theme of return, the chapter does not only focus on the concentrated point of demobilisation in 1920–21, but ranges over the weary length of the war. In this way, one can integrate the war years more closely with their tumultuous aftermath and examine homecoming as a part of the war experience of Indian personnel, and one they tried to shape.

Bombay and Karachi were not just gateways to theatres of war overseas. They were also turnstiles through which returning soldiers and followers were rerouted to hospitals, and to their depots for furlough, discharge or redeployment. The commemorative plaque put up by the Bombay Port Trust at Ballard Estate testifies that some 1,870,000 troops and personnel embarked and disembarked at the docks there over the course of World War One. Temporary followers, such as the men in the Indian Labour Corps, the Inland Water Transport and the Mesopotamian Railways, were particularly prominent in this back-and-forth movement.

Some military personnel made a compact with gods or spiritual figures, vowing to adhere to religious injunctions or to distribute charity to secure their safe return.[7] If service had necessitated some breach of caste norms, then homecoming involved a passage through some ritual portal as well.[8] However, this chapter focuses only on the negotiation of Indian soldiers and followers with the institutional portals which could secure furlough, an early discharge, or a passage home at the end of their contract. Significant numbers of temporary followers insisted at the very outset on enrolment for a limited term. Those followers and soldiers who were engaged for 'the duration of the war' felt burdened by this indefinite commitment. It was an obligation which took

---

[7] Two young men gave a *tamasukh* (commitment) to the Sacred Heart, promising to give Rs 5/– when they returned to France if everything was well and they had not fallen into sin. *The Catholic Herald of India*, 4 July 1917, p. 898.

[8] The ruler of Nepal sent Brahmin priests to Gurkha depots in India to put returning soldiers through the *pani patiya*, a ritual to cleanse them of the 'pollution' of having crossed the seas. Woodyatt, *Under Ten Viceroys*, p. 165. The aim perhaps was to deflect criticism about having sent them overseas in the first place, and to encourage them to return to Nepal. See below.

them through emotional journeys ranging from psychic turmoil about imminent death to anger, frustration or resignation about the endless deferral of
return. Some tried to ensure an exit route at the very outset. 'It is often found',
went the complaint in Army Order 416 of 1921, 'that Gurkhas on enlistment
describe themselves wrongly and give fictitious addresses'.[9]

These were not apolitical issues, for, as the literature on everyday soldiering
reminds us, military service is embedded in social and institutional hierarchies.[10] As Indian military and civilian personnel realised that the continuation of their postings overseas enabled the earlier demobilisation of British
and Dominion personnel, they challenged the 'naturalness' of the gap between
their service conditions and those for white personnel.[11] Requests once voiced
in the language of grace and favour acquired the timbre of entitlement. When
troops from Indian princely contingents and the Nepalese Army returned to
demand parity of service benefits with the Indian Army, the political and
financial cost to their rulers of rallying to the support of empire was
increased.[12] As departmental followers and regimental followers similarly
pressed for an equivalence of service benefits with the sepoy, the rationalisation of manpower use emerged as an issue for military debate.[13]

The combination in 1919–21 of extended military deployment with seething civil unrest also fostered the emergence of the 'veteran' as a political category. It was a form of self-representation deployed by military personnel in
their letters to the press and to community spokesmen.[14] It was also boosted

---

[9] This made it difficult to transmit money to their heirs if they died on service. *Indian Army Orders, His Excellency the Commander-in-Chief in India*, 1922, p. 494.

[10] Christoph Jahr, *Gewöhnliche Soldaten: Desertion und Deserteure im Deutschen und Britischen Heer 1914–1918*, Goettingen: Vandenhoeck und Ruprecht, 1998.

[11] Even the very pliable Ajaib Singh, a VCO given an honourary King's commission and nominated to the Imperial Legislative Council, asked why meat was not included in peace-rations for Indian troops. The C-in-C's irritable response was that if it was not included this was because meat 'was not a general article of consumption among Indian troops.' *Capital*, 15 March 1918, p. 627.

[12] For this complaint from Jodhpur state, see Foreign and Political (F&P) Internal, B, October 1920, nos 120–25.

[13] See 'Conditions of Service of "Followers"', *Report of the Committee Appointed by the Secretary of State for India to Enquire into the Administration and Organisation of the Army in India*, Cmd 943, 1920, II, pp. 97–98 (Esher Committee).

[14] There was a mushroom growth of periodicals which addressed a soldier or soldier-aspirant public in Punjab.

by the political leverage Punjabi notables such as Malik Umar Hayat Khan or the Jat leader Chhotu Ram acquired by highlighting the war service of their communities.[15] And, very crucially, it materialised from government's concern with managing the path home from military service, both to ensure the renewal of manpower supply and to foster loyal postwar constituencies.

Homecoming was an imaginative trope deployed not only for recruitment but also for a wider audience. Educated Indians, kept at arm's length from military affairs by the denial of commissioned rank, had to be convinced nevertheless that the very paths by which India's resources were being drawn out for the war were winding back triumphantly towards political advance, industrial development, rural uplift and improvement in the quality of Indian manpower. Returning soldiers and followers were cast as one of the vectors which would bring about this transformation.[16] However, the 'returnee' could also materialise in very undesirable avatars—in the form of the deserter, the prisoner of war who had traversed enemy territory, or one of the 'maimed' beings noticed around Bombay from 1915. If the recruit came from one of the contested border tracts of India, then his path home was attended by the anxiety that he might join Mahsud or Afridi insurgents across the North-West Frontier, or Kuki-Chin rebels along the Assam-Burma border.[17] It was imperative to deploy even such unpromising returnees to the ends of war.[18]

---

[15] Debate in the Imperial Legislative Council on the 'Indian Defence Force Bill', *The Times of India* (*TOI*), 22 February 1917, p. 7. The Indian National Congress pressed for higher pay for soldiers. *TOI*, 30 April 1919, p. 8. Indian legislators Srinivas Sastri, B. N. Sarma and Madan Mohan Malaviya played a role in the abolition of corporal punishment in the Indian Army Act. See Radhika Singha, 'The "Rare Infliction": The Abolition of Flogging in the Indian Army, circa 1835–1920', *Law and History Review*, vol. 34, no. 3 (2016), pp. 783–818.

[16] Pandit Kashi Nath, *Indian Labourers in France*, Bombay: Oxford University Press, 1919.

[17] From the Naga Hills district, Deputy Commissioner Hutton reported that Budano, former headman of the 37th Naga labour company, was going around Kohima saying the Germans were unbeatable. Hutton attributed this disloyalty to Budano's ethnic hybridity—'half-Angami, half-Assamese', and 'mission-spawned'. J. H. Hutton, tour diary, 15 July 1918, Naga Exploratour, http://himalaya.socanth.cam.ac.uk/collections/naga/coll/9/records/detail/all/from_400.html, last accessed 18 November 2019. This hybridity placed Budano at the centre of information networks, including those reaching into Kuki rebel zones.

[18] Indian prisoners of war were to be screened for deserters, then 'shown the sights and

Terminating the war?

From war emergency to imperial militarism

Britain emerged from the war fiscally very weak but at the height of her power in terms of territory and spheres of influence. To maintain her hold over Iraq, southern Persia, the Persian Gulf and the Aden coast, she required boots on the ground from India.[19] When the declaration of the Armistice came, Indian military personnel were spread about Northern Europe, Syria, Palestine, Egypt, Iraq, and Persia. Some 160,000 men would return from February 1920 to January 1921, leaving around 105,000 still overseas.[20] Back in India, the tides of war, lapping at the Pashtun borderlands from 1915, surged up in May 1919 as Afghanistan made its bid for autonomy. Peace was concluded with Afghanistan in August 1919, but by December a still more arduous campaign opened out in Waziristan, on the 'British' side of the borderland. Thirty-one Indian Labour Corps had to be kept in place to meet the logistical demands of the Afghan and Waziristan campaigns.[21] William Slim, posted with the 1/6th Gurkha Rifles, described his untranquil experience of studying for officer exams at Abbotabad in autumn 1920: 'On every village green in England monuments were rising which proclaimed the war was over, yet here I had only to raise my eyes to see once more the piled sandbags, the rough stone parapet, and writhing strands of barbed wire.'[22]

---

feted' in England before repatriation. Home, Political Deposit, June 1918, no. 2. British and Indian military personnel taken prisoner after the surrender at Kut, Mesopotamia, on 29 April 1915 were discouraged from publicising their suffering. However, after the Armistice, testimonies of brutal treatment were recorded to strengthen the British case for absorbing German East Africa and retaining control over Iraq. See GOC 'D' to CGS. 17 December 1918, WW1/1161/H, vol. 63, diary no. 100703. The Punjab government used soldiers who had returned from Turkish captivity to counter Khilafat propaganda. Home, Political, December 1920, no. 28.

[19] For an excellent account of imperial over-stretch, see Keith Jeffrey, *The British Army and the Crisis of Empire, 1918–22*, Manchester: Manchester University Press, 1984.

[20] *Council of State Debates*, vol. 1, 1 February 1921–10 March 1921, Delhi: Government Press, p. 298. The figures for February 1921 were 74,700 in Mesopotamia and Persia and 23,000 in Egypt and Palestine. Ibid., p. 310.

[21] AG, India to GOCs, 6 March 1920, Public Works Department, General, vol. 1064, 1918–20, Maharashtra State Archives, Mumbai (MSA).

[22] Field Marshal Sir William Slim, *Unofficial History*, London: Cassell, 1959, p. 101.

In spring 1920, even as the Indian Army was imposing a tighter line of control through the central belt of Waziristan, an Arab uprising against British occupation gathered force in Mesopotamia.[23] Not only were demobilisation orders suspended for Indian troops stationed there, but in autumn 1920 70,000 additional British and Indian troops had to be rushed to Mesopotamia to crush the uprising. Circling across to a belt of virtually autonomous territory along the Assam-Burma border, the armistice of November 1918 was the signal for a pincer movement by the Assam Military Police and the Burma Rifles to suppress the Kuki-Chin uprising. At a huge cost to Indian revenues, the Government of India emerged in 1920 with tighter control over two border 'Alsatias'. India offers a good illustration, therefore, of Erez Manela and Robert Gerwarth's contention that the 'end of the war' would look very different spatially and chronologically if 'ethnic minorities, imperial troops and East European or non-European theatres' figured more prominently.[24]

The result of this situation was that Punjab, the major recruiting ground for the Indian Army, continued to be conceptualised as an imperial home front. It therefore had to be insulated from militant anti-colonial propaganda flowing in from Bengal, or along the paths which took Punjabi migrants towards South-East Asia and onwards to the Pacific coast.[25] This imperative left its mark on the 1918 Sedition Committee Report headed by Justice Rowlatt, which recommended the extension into peacetime of wartime ordinances for summary detention without trial. Alarming rumours abounded about what the perpetuation of executive powers would mean in daily life, particularly in Punjab, where subordinate officials had forced the pace of recruitment and the collection of war funds.[26] Indians in public life pointed out that the Rowlatt Act put the brakes on the promise of political transformation at the very outset. Above all, it was the continued tax burden of imperial militarism which

---

[23] The previous year in Mesopotamia, Indian and British troops had battled with Kurdish insurgents.

[24] Robert Gerwarth and Erez Manela, 'Introduction', in *Empires at War, 1911–1923*, Oxford: Oxford University Press, 2014.

[25] *Sedition Committee Report*, Calcutta: Government Press, 1918, pp. 96–97, 210–211, and chapter XI. Its two sittings were held in Punjab and Bengal. External danger was apprehended primarily from Ghadar networks in South-East Asia and the USA. The report makes no mention of the Bolsheviks. The Russia it describes is one of anarchist cells and terrorist methods, not sweeping mass movements. Ibid.

[26] Home, Political, A, May 1919, nos 619–40.

drew fire from across the political spectrum. The first postwar budget, presented in March 1919, saw military expenditure soar upwards and the deficit increase due to the Afghan war and the Waziristan operations. Three more deficit budgets would follow:

Table 7: Revenue, Expenditure and Defence Expenditure of British India 1911–23 in crores of rupees.[27]

Year	Revenue	Expenditure	Surplus and Deficit				Defence Expenditure
1911	124.2	118.3	+5.9	–	–	–	29.3
1912	130.3	125.6	+4.6	–	–	–	29.3
1913	127.8	124.3	+3.5	–	–	–	29.8
1914	121.7	124.4	–3.7	–	–	–	30.7
1915	126.6	128.4	–1.8	–	–	–	33.4
1916	147.0	135.9	+11.2	–	–	–	37.5
1917	168.9	156.7	+12.2	–	–	–	43.6
1918	184.9	190.6	–5.7	–	–	–	66.7
1919	195.6	219.2	–23.6	–	–	–	87.0
1920	206.1	232.1	–26.0	–	–	–	87.4

Year	Central Revenue	Central Expenditure	Central Surplus and Deficit	Provincial Revenue	Provincial Expenditure	Provincial Surplus and Deficit	Defence Expenditure
1921	115.2	142.8	–27.6	70.4	79.2	–8.8	69.8
1922	121.44	136.4	–15.0	75.7	77.2	–1.5	65.3
1923	132.8	130.4	+2.4	78.9	76.1	+2.8	54.2

The 1919–20 Esher Committee Report on postwar military reorganisation confirmed fears in India that the War Office intended to tighten its control over the deployment of the Indian Army.[28] Nationalist opinion demanded

---

[27] Compiled from P. J. Thomas, *The Growth of Federal Finance in India: Being a Survey of India's Public Finances from 1833 to 1939*, London: Oxford University Press: 1939, table 3, 'Revenue and Expenditure of British India', p. 497, and table 6, 'Principal Heads of Expenditure', p. 502 (one crore: Rs 10,000,000).

[28] *Report of the Committee Appointed by the Secretary of State for India to Enquire into the Administration and Organisation of the Army in India.* For strong criticism, see

military retrenchment to make room for industrial and economic reconstruction, the reversal of wartime ordinances to allow for the expansion of political life, and a say in the use of the Indian Army.

The experience of delayed repatriation

The post-Armistice deployment and redeployment of significant numbers of Indian combatants and non-combatants left its mark on war diaries and regimental histories. On 5 September 1919 the Adjutant General's Branch noted that, far from being in a position to cut down numbers, the Indian Army was several Indian battalions short.[29] Troops were needed for the field army and the Waziristan Force, to relieve battalions posted overseas, and to control internal civil unrest.[30] Officers previously instructed to encourage soldiers to muster out found themselves negotiating to extend agreements.[31] Shifted from Palestine to Kantara after the Armistice, the men of the 58th Rifles (Frontier Force) expected to get leave in April 1919, but the uprising in Egypt meant their retention as part of the army of occupation:

> Marriages had been arranged and serious financial loss was anticipated ... The influenza epidemic which had ravished the Punjab ... had left many homes unprotected. Moreover, no letters were being received from India. This, perhaps, was as well as they would have told of riots in the Punjab ... Furlough had been sanctioned for ten per cent ... but owing to the Afghan attacks on the frontier posts the Indian Government was unable to send any reinforcements; so only a few very urgent cases could be allowed to leave the Battalion.[32]

The battalion finally disembarked on 10 February 1920 at Karachi, the port from which it had left for France five and a half years earlier.[33]

Report on Native Newspapers, Bombay Presidency, (RNPB), no. 40, 9 October 1920; no. 43, 23 October 1920; *The Servant of India*, 10 February 1921, p. 17.

[29] Note, ADG's Branch, 5 Sept 1919, AD, ADG's Branch, A, May 1922, No. 1784–1786 and appendix.

[30] In Punjab, recruitment was reopened in June 1919 and a 'moderate number of demobilised sepoys seemed ready to re-join, in spite of complaints of their treatment before, their compulsory disbandment, and the deprivation of the very uniform they had been wearing.' Home, Political, Deposit, August 1921, no. 50.

[31] AD, ADG's Branch, A, May 1922, nos 1784–86 and appendix.

[32] A. G. Lind, *A Record of the 58th Rifles F. F. in the Great War, 1914–1919*, Waziristan: Commercial Steam Press, 1933, pp. 116–21.

[33] Ibid., p. 128.

In May 1919 the 48th and 127th Pioneer Battalions, then working on the Persian road, received joyful tidings of return, but found themselves moving upcountry instead to deal with a Kurd insurgency. They were poised to leave from Basra on 4–5 December 1920, but their departure was delayed again due to 'trouble with Arabs'. The 121st Pioneers and the 2/107th Pioneers remained in Syria, working on roads until March 1920. The 2/128th Pioneers, raised in February 1918, confronted striking mill-hands in Bombay then sailed to join the Army of the Black Sea. In May 1922, all four Pioneer Battalions were finally 'relieved on grounds of expediency by British troops'.[34]

Military personnel returning home from active service felt they had earned a right to the safe expression of grievances. Some transport drivers who returned invalided to Bombay in 1916 refused to accept their allowance for civilian clothing when they found out that it was Rs 8/– as against the combatant scale of Rs 15/–.[35] The Maharaja of Bikaner complained bitterly that travelling back from Egypt after four and a half years of risking their lives for empire, his officers found themselves excluded from the British officers' mess on board the ship, 'even though they said they would dine in the European fashion'.[36] On their homecoming to India in 1920 the Jodhpur Lancers, a princely state unit, went on strike to demand a continuation of free rations in peacetime, and other concessions given to soldiers of the Indian Army.[37]

A key concern for combatants and non-combatants was to merge the war bonus granted on 31 July 1918 with the basic wage, and to press for the continuation into peacetime of benefits given to men on active service.[38] The *Jat*

---

[34] W. B. P. Tugwell, *History of the Bombay Pioneers*, London; Bedford: Sidney Press, 1938, pp. 302–46.

[35] They were given the combatant scale. Army Department, War, 1916–17, I, nos 10800–801, pp. 270–72.

[36] 29 October 1919, IOR/L/S/11/160, file 7767.

[37] F&P, Internal, B, October 1920, nos 120–25 They also protested plans to disband one section. Ibid. A year later unrest erupted again, and the British political resident suspected some link with a 'Young Rajput' society then in conflict with the Jodhpur ruler. F&P, Internal, B, file no. 66. As a special war measure, the Mysore princely state agreed to make service benefits for its soldiers equivalent to those of the Indian Army. Palace Papers, file 177 of 1918, Karnataka State Archives, Bengaluru (KSA).

[38] When the war bonus was sanctioned in July 1918, some newspapers complained that soldiers would have preferred a permanent increase of pay. 30 July 1918 in *Selections from the Native Newspapers of North-Western Provinces and Oudh*, no. 32, 10 August 1918; *Leader*, 29 July 1918.

Gazette is replete with news items from 1919–20 indicating that Indian personnel were pressing for a reduction of the gap between British soldiers' service conditions and their own. Where the War Office was the paymaster, they argued, Indian soldiers should be paid the same rates as British soldiers and receive the same rations, clothes and family allowances.[39] The *Jat Gazette* demanded better barracks and hospitals, a co-operative store, a bank and regimental schools.[40] It complained that, due to discrimination in medical care during the Afghan War, Indian soldiers had suffered a higher death rate than British soldiers.[41] It requested obliquely that that the harsher, more summary form of court-martial used for Indian soldiers be amended.[42] And it commented on the rudeness exhibited by British soldiers to Indian VCOs and NCOs.[43] A demand filtering through many newspapers was that if King's commissions were thrown open to educated Indians, then serving Indian officers (the VCOs) should also be promoted to this level.[44]

The most frequent complaint concerned continued deployment without leave.[45] Indian military clerks in Mesopotamia complained that their British counterparts were given leave, but if they asked for it they risked a court-martial.[46] The rushing of three British and seventeen Indian infantry battalions from India to Iraq to crush the Arab uprising in September 1920 seemed to confirm

---

[39] 24 March 1920 in *Punjab Press Abstracts* (*PPA*), no. 14, 3 April 1920. An 'Indian Officer in Mesopotamia' complained that Indians were not given the Army of Occupation allowance sanctioned for British soldiers. When rebellion broke out in Kurdistan, their demobilisation had been suspended, but not that of British soldiers. *Bombay Chronicle*, 25 October 1920 in *RNPB*, no. 44, 3 October 1920, pp. 26–27.

[40] *Jat Gazette*, 24 March 1920, *PPA*, no. 14, 3 April 1920.

[41] *Selections, NWP&O*, no. 35, 20 August 1919. Military authorities recommended that the station hospital system for British troops should be extended to Indian soldiers and followers, because having experienced excellent war hospitals their expectations had risen. Despatch to SSI, Military Department, 16 March 1917, AD, Medical, A, January 1918, nos 2684–88.

[42] Ibid.

[43] *Jat Gazette*, 24 March 1920, *PPA*, no. 14, 3 April 1920.

[44] The *Vijayi Maratha* said that there would be terrible discontent if commissions were given only to Brahmins (that is, to educated upper-castes), leaving out the Maratha rank and file soldier. *RNPB*, no. 53, 25 December 1920.

[45] For a complaint that after four years in Mesopotamia a unit had been sent to Persia without seeing their families, see *RNPB*, no. 30, 24 July 1920, p. 29.

[46] *Vakil*, in *PPA*, no. 8, 19 February 1921, p. 72.

the charge that, while the Dominions declined to help, India bore the burden of imperial military commitments.[47] The British General Staff had insisted on sending the three British battalions posted in India, despite the Viceroy's protests that this would compromise internal security. Its position was that '[t]he Indian troops in that country [Iraq] are reported to be suffering from a sense of injustice on account of their long detention overseas, and a feeling has arisen among them that they are being exploited for the advantage of British troops'.[48]

The period 1920–22 witnessed steady improvements in benefits, especially for the VCOs.[49] However, the bestowal of war rewards also acquired an authoritarian cast. In 1921 a general order warned that pensions could be revoked for disloyalty, and recipients of land grants in Punjab were required to display an active loyalty in times of trouble.[50] Officials scrutinised petitions for pensions, or other service claims, for marks of consultation with the dread figure of the lawyer.[51]

The management of return: life chances and afterlives

Sipāhī kī roṭī sir beche kī
[Proverb: The soldier gets his bread by selling his life.][52]

---

[47] *The New Times*, 10 September 1920, in *RNPB*, no. 38, 18 September 1920, p. 23; *Bande Mataram*, 22 December 1920, and *Vakil*, 22 December 1920 in *PPA*, no. 1, 1 January 1921, p. 5; Douglas E. Delaney, *The Imperial Army Project: Britain and the Land Forces of the Dominions and India, 1902–1945*, Oxford: Oxford University Press, 2018, p. 173.

[48] 'Reinforcements for Mesopotamia', Memorandum, by General Staff, War Office, 9 Sept 1920, Cabinet Papers, TNA CAB/24/111/44. 'We are anxious', wrote General Monro, C-in-C, India, in September 1918, 'to reduce the Army to pre-war standards, but so long as we have such commitments in Palestine and Mesopotamia, we are powerless.' Sir George Barrow, *The Life of Sir Charles Carmichael Monro*, London: Hutchinson,1931, p. 248.

[49] See 'Military Regulations', *TOI*, 16 Dec 1922, p. 12.

[50] Imran Ali, *The Punjab under Imperialism, 1885–1947*, Princeton: Princeton University Press, 1988, p. 99.

[51] *Coloured Victims of the Great War: Their Groans and Grievances at the Feet of the Crown and the Country* (anonymous pamphlet, n.d., c. 1930). I thank Stefan Tetzlaff for giving me this invaluable source for veteran mobilisation during the depression years.

[52] S. W. Fallon, *A New Hindustani–English Dictionary*, London: Trubner and Co., 1879, p. 736.

The likelihood of return was a crucial aspect of recruiting propaganda not only for non-combatants but also for soldiers.[53] One way to recruit in areas where there was no tradition of military employment was to draw upon the testimony of the 'returnee', a strategy long used to encourage 'chain migration' to plantations. Raajibhai Patel, a Baroda official, relied upon artisans and workers who had returned from Mesopotamia to overcome the reluctance of labourers to enlist.[54] In Mayurbhanj, where resistance to Labour Corps recruitment had set off an uprising, enlistment for railway work picked up with the return home of a man who had worked in Basra.[55]

As the fortunes of the Entente powers improved, war propaganda drew upon actuarial calculation to reassure soldiers that recruitment did not mean they were going to die. The *Ladai ka Akhbar* seized upon the London life insurance company Prudential's calculation that the odds of death for British soldiers were lower than those for infants: '*Ran bhumi ki upeksha palne mein adhik mrityu hoti hai*' ['there is a higher chance of death in the cradle than on the battlefield'].[56] The plague epidemic of 1918 in Punjab, coinciding with two deadly cycles of influenza, gifted recruiters with another argument. Not only was a man more likely to die at home than in the healthy environment of a military station, but his death in the first context would have no meaning, whereas on the battlefield it would bring glory and secure his family a pension.[57]

---

[53] Posters dwelt on the recruit turned recruiter, the rustic who returned to display his transformation into an upstanding soldier or a well-nourished labourer. Labourers, wrote one propaganda paper, did not set off to die, but to return *sukhshali, dhanvan, samajhdar*—as men of experience, happy and solvent. *Ladai ka Akhbar*, 29 August 1918, p. 14.

[54] Raajibhai Patel to Manager, English Office, Baroda, 6 February 1917, Baroda Residency, War W-91(A), MSA.

[55] *Report on the Administration of Mayurbhanj for 1917–1918*, Baripada: State Press, Mayurbhanj, 1918, pp. 55–56.

[56] *Ladai ka Akhbar*, 1 August 1918, p. 37.

[57] '[I]ndeed it is undoubtedly true ... that the war saved more lives in the Punjab owing to the collection of men in cantonments where the ravages of influenza in 1918 were met by efficient medical precautions and remedies than it wasted on the field of battle.' J. T. Marten, *Census of India, 1921*, vol. I, part 1, Calcutta: Government Printing, 1924, chapter 1. In fact, respiratory disease and relapsing fever found a congenial environment in crowded military barracks and labour depots, and troop movement spread it to the civilian population. In October 1919, influenza spread among labour

Pedagogies for the returning soldier and labourer

Once they were in service, recreational programmes for soldiers and labourers sought to foster the right kind of perspective about their own future, that of their community, and that of India in the postwar empire. Indian cavalry officers, and later a chosen few from the Indian Labour Corps, were treated to a tour of selected sites in England.[58] For the rest, the Indian YMCA used the media of lantern slide and lecture to take Indian soldiers and labourers once again through the sights they had glimpsed on their journey to Europe, and to give them a sense of how far they had come in their understanding of the world.[59] The aim was to impress upon them the geographical reach of empire, its industries and its resources, reassuring them at the same time that they— their particular community or home—were 'known' within this formation, and that they had a place in its landscape.[60] Reverend A. W. McMillan, who worked with the Indian YMCA, described this endeavour:

> There were imaginary trips around the British Empire, men re-embarked afresh on the voyage from Bombay to Europe, and saw once more the ports they had visited; naval and other war-pictures were shown ... One missionary pioneer from the Lushai Hills ... was able to conduct imaginary pictorial tours through the very villages and hills from which these men had come, and they were able to look upon chiefs and other men and women whom they recognised—and all this within four miles of the German trenches.[61]

---

units at Lahore, among them recruits from Madras Presidency in the 111th and 14th Labour Corps. J. Mackenzie, 'Influenza: Preliminary Note on a Fatal Pneumococcal Infection and its Suggested Spread from Sheep to Man', *Journal of the Royal Army Medical Corps*, vol. 35, no. 6 (1920), pp. 481–84.

[58] Lord Ampthill stressed that unless some of the Labour Corps men saw England before they returned, 'this splendid and phenomenal effort on the part of the most remote and least civilised of His Majesty's subjects will be wasted so far as India is concerned.' Ampthill to C. S. Bayley, 15 October 1917, IOR/L/Mil/5/73.

[59] In the four and a half months of the winter of 1917–18 in France, the Indian YMCA held 266 entertainments and lantern slide lectures, attended by audiences of between 200 and 500 men. A. W. McMillan, 'Indian Echoes from France', *The East and the West*, vol. XVIII (1920), pp. 1–20.

[60] Ibid. Kashi Nath claimed that working side by side with British, Australian, Canadian and American soldiers, the men of his labour company had acquired 'this sense of a vast unity, of belonging to a huge Empire with undreamt of immense resources.' Kashi Nath, *Indian Labourers in France*, p. 46.

[61] McMillan, 'Indian Echoes from France', p. 6.

However, very different ideas were also in circulation about the lessons which sepoys and labourers ought to take home. The conjuncture at which McMillan was writing was marked as well by General Dyer's order to fire volleys of bullets upon a civilian gathering at Jallianwalla Bagh. McMillan's criticism of the itinerary devised for the Indian Army contingent brought over in July 1919 for the Victory celebrations touched upon this event. Instead of philanthropic institutions such as Dr Barnardo's Homes or an Institute for the Blind, 'they were shown demonstrations in the art of bombing by a Handley-Page aeroplane!—as though they had not seen enough bombing demonstrations in every theatre of war ... and latterly even in the Punjab!'[62] McMillan was criticising the line of thought which held that the most important lesson for homeward-bound Indian personnel was a full understanding of the military and industrial might of empire. Officials hoped that Kukis and Chins returning from France would disseminate this understanding to dispel that 'millenarian' idea, so conducive to futile insurrection, that their homeland was at the centre of the world.[63]

Pandit Kashi Nath, commander of the 23rd United Provinces Labour Company, assured readers of his pamphlet, *Indian Labourers in France*, that his men were returning as capable and enlightened subjects of empire.[64] War service, he wrote, would send them back to their villages with a better sense of their place within the vast reaches of empire, and with bodily habits and dispositions which would transform their old habitus. His own role was that of the educated and enlightened Indian officer who could testify that this 'silent' transformation was indeed taking place, for such rustic beings did not have the capacity to articulate experience in any complex way: 'Perhaps if the men were themselves questioned they would only say that they had seen a few strange countries, that France was the land of intense cold and the sea the place where you got sea-sick, and that they had saved a few rupees—now all spent.'[65]

---

[62] Ibid., p. 18. McMillan was referring to the aerial bombing of a protest rally at Gujranwala, Punjab on 11 April 1919. He also noted that in London the contingent was confined behind 'lofty close-fitting iron hoarding topped with barbed wire, while a British sentry stood at each entrance.' Ibid., p. 13.

[63] William Shaw, *Notes on the Thadou Kukis*, Calcutta: Asiatic Society of Bengal, 1929, p. 50.

[64] Kashi Nath, *Indian Labourers in France*.

[65] Ibid.

And yet, as Kashi Nath assured his readers, these men now knew that sanitation would preserve their health, and that if they fell ill they might recover 'merely by the administration of a few tabloids.'[66] They would be readier to migrate and to cultivate 'the still vast desert places of India', using improved methods of agriculture.[67] The pamphlet made no reference at all to the political turmoil enveloping India. Its soothing conclusion was that the war had taught Indians how much, 'in these days of fierce competition', they still needed the shelter of empire. However, Kashi Nath's wholehearted endorsement of the social transformations he had witnessed in wartime Britain gives us a glimpse of his own yearning for change.[68] The West was now going to be 'a young man's world ... a world anxious for higher standards of efficiency, full of specialists.'[69] Where would the unchanging East be then, he asked wistfully? To paraphrase, would merit and efficiency be recognised on the other side of the globe as well?

Something to show for it: saving and spending

> How has the Kafir Government welcomed you home? Each sepoy when he returns is discharged and cast adrift. The Sircar takes from him his warm coat. Even his boots are taken from off his feet, and his body is searched like a thief's lest a single cartridge may be concealed on his person.[70]

In his novel *Abdication*, Edmund Candler puts these words in the mouth of Barkatullah, the demagogic Muslim editor, as he addresses a Khilafat meeting.[71] Having been repeatedly told that they would get 'free' clothes, soldiers and followers could feel humiliated by having the better items of their kit stripped from them at discharge.[72] Many had been induced to enlist by extrav-

---

[66] Ibid.

[67] Ibid., pp. 47–48.

[68] Ibid.

[69] Ibid., pp. 33–35.

[70] Edmund Candler, *Abdication*, Suffolk: Richard Clay and Sons, 1922, p. 252. As Director of Publicity in Punjab 1919–21, he would have had an ear to the ground.

[71] Ibid.

[72] Home, Political, Deposit, August 1921, no. 50. Yet one transfrontier Naga chief, Churangchu of Chisung, managed to smuggle back a Mauser rifle from France. J. H. Hutton, tour diary, 25 November 1921, Naga Exploratour, http://himalaya. socanth.cam.ac.uk/collections/naga/record/r72245.html, last accessed 18 November 2019.

agant promises that they would return home with a land grant and a pension, and some of the literature on demobilisation has tended to assume accordingly that these were widely distributed.[73] In fact, the rule was that a combatant had to serve for fifteen years to qualify for a pension. To soften the blow of retrenchment, a special mustering out pension based on ten years' service and above was introduced for a limited period.[74] Nevertheless, at the point the Armistice was declared many thousands of Indian soldiers and labourers might have served just for a year or a year and a half.[75] Most would therefore be discharged with just a gratuity.

Land grants and *jangi inams* (special pensions) were meant only for those put on a list for 'distinguished service'.[76] The land grant came with an exemption from the land tax for 'two lives', and the *jangi inam* was a monthly allowance given in addition to the retiring or invalid pension and was also payable for 'two lives'.[77] The phrase 'for two lives' had a particularly munificent ring. As the Adjutant General in India pointed out, it perpetuated 'the memory of Government's generosity throughout another generation.' However, he also added an actuarial justification, noting that the life expectancy of men who had served 'under the conditions pertaining to the greatest war in history, will be somewhat impaired'.[78] If a medical board decided that a soldier or labourer

---

[73] W. H. Vincent, Home member, 19 June 1919, Home, Political, Deposit, July 1919, no. 37.

[74] AD, Adjutant General's branch, A, December 1920, nos 2658–3663. The mustering out rules ceased to apply to those demobilised after 31 October 1920. Ibid.

[75] Some 211,000 men were recruited in the period from June 1918 to 11 November 1918, the Armistice. 'Recruiting in India Before and During the War, 1914–18', p. 26, IOR/L/MIL/17/5/2152.

[76] In 1916 the Adjutant General proposed that land grants be recommended for 4 per cent of the strength of the army. F&P, General, B, March 1919, no. 8. A 1919 pamphlet warned that land grants were meant to reward conspicuous merit, not to inaugurate a scheme of military colonisation. IOR/L/Mil/7/18492. However, Imran Ali calculates that about 20 per cent of the land available in the Bari Doab canal colony was put aside for war veterans. Ali, *The Punjab under Imperialism*, p. 114.

[77] The monthly allowance was Rs 10/- for VCOs, Rs 5/- for NCOs and Indian ranks, and Rs 2 ½ for non-combatants. A total of 14,100 *jangi inams* were given in World War One.

[78] Adjutant General, Note, 3 August 1916. F&P, General, B, March 1919, no. 8. When the monthly sum for the *jangi inams* of World War One and Two were raised to

had suffered a wound or injury 'attributable to military service', he would receive a pension for the period of recovery; if the damage was medically certified as permanent, he would receive it for the rest of his life.

Rewards which did not cost the state very much were more widely on offer, such as free schooling for children of deceased, disabled or impoverished soldiers and followers.[79] So was preferential employment at the lowest levels of the security establishment, in the police, the forest guard, and local militias— all of which were rising in significance due to civil unrest.[80] The bottom line, however, was that the men's own savings would constitute their primary gain from war service. Advice about what they could do with their savings was therefore an important aspect of war propaganda.[81]

To convince the soldier or labourer that he would return with accumulated wages, recruiting speeches cast food and clothing as 'free', rather than as something earned. All other expenditure was 'pocket money'—that is, a matter of pleasurable choice, not necessity.[82] Officers of

---

Rs 500/– in 2011, it resulted in a demand for the extension of Indian freedom fighter pensions into the second generation as well.

[79] There was a debate about whether the state ought to support higher-level education for 'soldier orphans' as well. The United Provinces government felt it might divert them from the army, but Montagu, Secretary of State for India, felt they should be allowed to move up. An Indian official of the education department pointed out vehemently that higher education fostered responsibility and initiative, crucial qualities in modern warfare. Department of Education, A, February 1919, nos 26–28.

[80] Home, Police, A, October 1919, nos 184–86.

[81] Soldier savings schemes catered only for British personnel. However, some Indian regiments set up their own saving and loan funds. For the 63rd Palamcottah Light Infantry, see Controller Defence Accounts, vol. 475, March–April 1916, and for the 58th Rifles, see Lind, *A Record of the 58th Rifles F. F.*, p. 130.

[82] Recruiting around Ranchi for the Labour Corps, the Jesuit missionary Father Molhant drew up an alluring balance sheet. Of his monthly wage of Rs 20/–, the recruit could keep Rs 2/– as 'pocket-money', send Rs 6/– for the *burhiya*, his wife, and deposit Rs 12/– with the Catholic Co-Operative Bank. Adding the bonus of Rs 60/–, he would return with Rs 200/– in hand: 'That will help you to buy a field— and in one year you are all *zemindars*!' *The Catholic Herald of India*, 27 June 1917, p. 410. *Zemindars*: landowners. The Belgian Jesuit mission encouraged members of the laity in the ILC to deposit their accumulated wages in the Catholic Co-Operative Bank, whose capital suddenly increased by Rs 450,000/–. *Report on the Administration of Bihar and Orissa, 1917–1918*, Patna, 1919, p. vii. Labourers enrolled through the

labour companies were expected to ensure that the men returned home with savings.[83]

McMillan described how in France, using a set of slides illustrative of English farming and fruit-growing, he reminded Indian soldiers and labourers that they were agriculturalists who lacked capital and were in debt. But now they were going home with money, he urged:

> rather than waste your money like irresponsible children ... invest in your land to improve your breed of cattle ... try new crops like tomatoes ... dig a new well or plant an orchard, and thus have something tangible to show ... for the time spent in the service of the Sarkar.[84]

Why were men, schooled in painstaking husbandry, being lectured on the need to improve their farms?[85] The war had given a stimulus to pedagogies of 'rural uplift'. India's agricultural exports balanced Britain's trade deficits, provisioned theatres of war, and met wheat shortfalls in Britain. The improvement and diversification of agricultural production in India was also a crucial component of discussions about instituting a system of imperial preference to restore Britain's commercial prosperity after the war.

Anglican mission at Ranchi were encouraged to withdraw their accumulated wages only for the redemption of land, the purchase of cattle and the repayment of debts. *Chota Nagpur Diocesan Paper*, August 1918; October 1918, Bishop's Lodge, Church of North India, Ranchi.

[83] Lord Ampthill pressed the Government of India to ensure that returning Indian labourers used their savings to clear their debts or buy a small shop or a cart, 'to derive permanent advantage from their service in France.' Ampthill to H. V. Cox, 6 April 1918, F&P, Internal, B, June 1918, nos 294–95. A Lhota Naga song celebrating the return of the labour companies from France begins with a joyful call asking women to meet them on the road home with drinks of 'madhu', but concludes with a sagacious warning:

> They have given us money
> as countless as the grains of ash on the hearth
> But he who gives thought to it,
> Only he will keep his money.

J. P. Mills, *The Lhota Nagas*, London: Macmillan, 1922, pp. 205–6.

[84] McMillan, 'Indian Echoes from France', pp. 6–7, 8.

[85] A Hindi propaganda paper had a regular feature titled 'The Importance of Agriculture in War Time'. *Ladai ka Akhbar*, 24 July 1918, p. 19.

The form of currency in which Indian soldiers and labourers were to receive their savings was a significant issue. In December 1917, due to wartime disruptions in specie supply, the government introduced small-denomination paper currency to supplement silver rupee coin, and posters and pamphlets tried to persuade Indians not to 'hoard' coin or melt it down.[86] However, when it came to Indian military personnel it was important not to push the 'modernisation' of financial attitudes too far. War posters picture the recruit being offered or returning home with coins, not notes.[87] In his memoir about the journey of the Lushai Labour Corps to France, Sainghinga Sailo gives a wonderful account of the stir they caused when they returned to their villages with accumulated wages in the form of silver rupees.[88] One man took his coins from him and, without saying a word, spread them out on a *thlangra* (a winnowing tray): 'He spread it all out and even took it out to the *likapui*. And everybody went about touching it. In those days except for Pu Zotawna, the son of Darphawka, it was considered a large amount to be having 60 coins.'[89] Shortly afterwards, the missionary Herbert Lorrain summoned Sainghinga and put his money into a five-year post office savings scheme. Sainghinga concludes his memoir rather flatly, as a consumer of modern finance: 'When I moved to Aizawl, in 1923, I was able to take out more than I had kept. It was a good thing that he had done.'[90]

One of the desires which spurred the search for off-farm work was to return with the means to marry, thereby securing the transition to adult masculinity and a place in the line of descent.[91] A story which circulated in the Chin Hills

[86] 'Hoarding Rupees. How it Helps the Germans', *TOI*, 21 June 1918, p. 5.

[87] Imperial War Museum poster, IWM PST 12563, 'Tamil text with image of a soldier holding a stack of coins', and IWM PST 12573, Urdu, 'Who will take this uniform, money and rifle'. A Sikh soldier advised his family not to accept the money he sent home via the Post Office in notes. Prem Singh, 15th Sikhs, 27 April 1915, letter no. 26, IOR/L/Mil/5/825, pt 3.

[88] Sainghinga Sailo, *Indopui 1914–18, Mizote France Ram Kal Thu*, Aizawl, n.d. (c. 1940s).

[89] Ibid. *Likapui*: a high platform outside a traditional Mizo house.

[90] Ibid.

[91] Indian soldiers and followers remained unpersuaded that masculinity could be valorised through male comradeship alone. They wanted to find a place in posterity through the generational cycle of marriage and reproduction. One Punjabi writer recalls that his two unmarried uncles were considered 'temporary entities', because their lands would pass to their married brothers. Gurnam Singh Sidhu Brard, *East of Indus: My Memories of Old Punjab*, New Delhi: Hemkunt Publishers, 2007, p. 28.

was that men who had served in the Labour Corps in France returned with money to pay for any bride they chose.[92] However, Indian military personnel also expressed an interest in the idea that by reducing ceremonial expenditure they might secure a better education for their children.[93] Missionaries in India hoped that returning lay members would support Christian community formation by donating to churches and schools, or opening accounts with denominational co-operative banks.[94] What had to be discouraged were intemperate celebrations which kept 'pagan' forms of community coherence alive. The response to such advice was, to put it succinctly, mixed. However, in Manipur the Baptist missionary William Pettigrew felt that the young men returning from France probably contributed to the erosion of interest in a festival he disapproved of—the *kathi-kasham*, or 'soul departure feast'.[95]

The returnee in his undesirable avatars

Desertion and fraudulent re-enlistment

In monitoring the path home from service, the Army Department also had to contend with unauthorised forms of self-discharge. Rewards for the arrest of

---

[92] Cited from Vumson, in Lian H. Sakhong, *In Search of Chin Identity: A Study in Religion, Politics and Ethnic Identity in Burma*, Copenhagen: NIAS Press, 2003, p. 134. However, as the price of food and cloth spiralled, so too did bride price. *Mizo leh Vai*, July 1919; and Reverend J. Bressers, 'New Marriage Laws', *The Catholic Herald of India*, 13 November 1918, p. 879.

[93] Indian soldiers were deeply struck by the literacy of men and women of humble orders in Europe. However, when two Sikh soldiers supported the idea of reducing ceremonial expenditure to spend more on their children's education, they invoked not European norms, but the ideal of a Sikh past 'uncorrupted' by Brahmanical influence. Teja Singh, 2nd Lancers, France to Ganga Singh, Sialkot, Punjab, 6 March 1918; Gurmukhi and Ishar Singh, 2nd Lancers, France to Jassu Singh, Ludhiana, 4 March 1918, IOR/L/Mil/5/827/6, pp. 854–55.

[94] Oraons from Gangpur, who had served with the ILC in France, gave Rs 10/– each towards the building of the Catholic church at Kesramal, making up a third of its cost. *Missions belges de la Compagnie de Jésus: Congo, Bengale, Ceylan*, 1922, p. 32. Christians of the 51st Ranchi company in France sent Rs 125/– for two altar crosses for the Anglican churches at Tapkara and Murhu. *Chota Nagpur Diocesan Paper*, October 1918.

[95] William Pettigrew, 'My Twenty-Five Years 1897–1922 at Ukhrul Mission School' in *Reverend William Pettigrew: A Pioneer Missionary of Manipur*, Imphal: Fraternal Green Cross, 1996, appendix 1, p. xix.

deserters went up in 1915 from Rs 5/– to Rs 20/– for a combatant and Rs 10/– for a follower, and in October 1917 the definition of desertion was broadened.[96] Transfrontier Pashtun desertion posed the danger of trained military men going over to insurgent ranks. It also raised the unwelcome issue of political sympathy for the Ottoman side.[97] However, we have to take account of the more numerous instances of reservists who did not report for duty, recruits who bolted during their training, and soldiers and labourers who went on leave and did not return. One index of the postwar imperative of maintaining India as the garrison of empire was the concern, continued into 1920, about high rates of desertion.

Unauthorised exits sometimes evolved into unauthorised re-entry—that is, re-enlistment under a different or assumed name.[98] In prewar days this episodic form of engagement with military service was treated somewhat leniently, particularly when it involved 'uncivilised' transfrontier recruits. But with the outbreak of war, army orders indicated that the full weight of military law would apply.[99] Nevertheless, the two amnesties announced for Indian Army deserters suggest that military authorities still took some account of the recruit's need to position military service within the frame of family and community obligations.

In World War One, Indian soldiers experienced an intensification of training schedules and a diversification of tasks. The difficulty of getting leave, and the sense of imminent death at certain conjunctures, gave an entirely different

---

[96] AD, letter no. 53086, 24 October 1917, General, 1917–18, no. 1284, MSA.

[97] The shock event in April 1919 was the mass defection of men from the North and South Waziristan militias, which contributed some 1,800 deserters to the Afghan side. *Operations in Waziristan, 1919–1920*, Calcutta: Government Printing, 1921, pp. 86, 97.

[98] See F&P, Internal, B, January 1919, no. 338. Some British soldiers, engaged on the prewar term of twelve years, tried to arrange an earlier exit by fraudulent re-enlistment on 'duration of war' terms. *Indian Army Orders, The Commander-in-Chief, India*, 1916, p. 484, para. 678.

[99] *Compendium of the More Important Orders of the Government of India, Army Department and Indian Army Orders, Issued from the 1st August 1914, to the 31st December 1917*, Calcutta: Government Printing, 1919 (henceforth *Compendium*). One explanation for unrest in the 130th Baluch regiment in 1915 was that from 1913 the CO had taken stricter action against transfrontier men who overstayed their leave. Home, Political, Deposit, November 1915, no. 16.

meaning to engagements to serve for 'the duration of the war'.[100] A man who returns, wrote a soldier of the 34th Sikh Pioneers posted in France, 'is one who has died and is born again.'[101] In the prewar era, members of the Indian ranks could take leave for up to sixty days annually, provided that not more than 20 per cent were absent at any one time.[102] However, leave allowance was always very tight for regimental and departmental followers.[103] Temporary followers, such as the men enrolled in 'Coolie Corps', were not entitled to any leave at all.[104]

British officers treated applications for leave or early discharge with routine scepticism. The author of a wartime sketch noted gaily that he loved the sepoy and looked after his welfare by refusing to grant him leave 'because of calamities which happen when his leave is due to expire … by doing so I also stemmed flow of telegrams … "Brother dangerously ill … grant extension 10 days"'.[105] Yet the censor in France let communications pass in which Indian soldiers dissuaded their brothers from joining the army or put together stories to secure a place in the leave quota. Of a letter in which a Punjabi Muslim reassured his sister that he would devise some way of returning but requested that she take care of their parents if he could not, the censor remarked:

> if it were not so familiar as to be altogether commonplace, it would be almost incredible that [this] extract … should on the whole be typical of sepoy sentiment, but so it is. They would like to get out of it if they could, but are prepared to go on enduring, if necessary.[106]

---

[100] For a textured sense of these shifts, see Roly Grimshaw, *Indian Cavalry Officer, 1914–1915*, eds Colonel J. Wakefield and Lieutenant Colonel J. M. Weippert, Tunbridge Wells: Costello, 1986.

[101] L. N. A. Manea Singh, 12 April 1915, IOR/L/Mil/5/825/3, letter no. 33.

[102] *Compendium*, paras 611–42.

[103] The difficulty of getting leave was blamed for prewar desertion in mule-drivers. AD, Quartermaster General's Branch, Transport, A, July 1914, nos 792–816.

[104] However, an order of 8 November 1916 offered temporary followers, such as the men of the Indian Labour and Porter Corps and those in the Inland Water Transport, leave on full pay for one-twelfth of the period they had served if they agreed to re-engage for further service. And if they did not get a gratuity or bonus on discharge they were also promised one month's leave on full pay. *Indian Army Orders, The Commander-in-Chief, India, 1916*, para. 876.

[105] Myuank, 'Indian Army Reflections', in C. Howard Turner (ed.), *Indian Ink, Being Splashes from Various Pens in Aid of the Imperial Indian War Fund*, Calcutta: T. H. Camp-Howes, 1918, pp. 5–6.

[106] Punjabi Muslim soldier to his sister, 31 August 1915, and n. 1 in Omissi, *Indian*

Narratives of domestic crisis could in fact be painfully real given that a plague epidemic beset Punjab in 1915, and drought, influenza and plague overtook large patches of India in the second half of 1918.[107] Subterfuge prevailed on both sides, for commanding officers tried to maintain the strength of their unit by delaying repatriation, denying leave, or offering it on condition that the applicant extended his term of engagement.[108]

Gajendra Singh gives an eloquent account of the contrast which Indian cavalrymen in France drew between their own prolonged separation from their families and the leave given to British personnel.[109] As their service in France began to reach three years, Indian cavalrymen let their expectations of leave or replacement reach the ears of their officers. The legal stipulation on which they relied was the rule that soldiers could ask for a discharge after serving for a minimum of three years. What they skirted was the qualifying clause which stated that they could not exercise this three-year option in wartime.[110] An Indian Army order of 12 May 1918 had to stress that the discharge of a soldier at his own request was 'not to be sanctioned merely because the applicant is likely to become troublesome if his request is not granted.'[111] The restiveness running through a unit when repatriation orders were delayed could make life difficult for Commanding Officers. Subordinate Indian staff at the Central Laboratory in Basra were so fed up about not getting leave after the Armistice that they conspired to murder their senior officer and set the

---

Voices of the Great War: Soldiers' Letters, 1914–18, letter 131, Basingstoke: Palgrave Macmillan, 1999, p. 94. However, letters were held back if the discussion of making an exit was too specific.

[107] The army began to arrange for information to be passed on to soldiers about the death of relatives due to influenza. Home, War, B, April 1919, no. 50.

[108] In July 1920, against the background of the crisis looming in Mesopotamia, the Adjutant General's Branch (ADG) reported that Commanding Officers, concerned to maintain unit strength, were resorting to the 'entirely illegal ... practice of requiring men to extend their service as a condition to the grant of furlough'. Note, 30 July 1920, AD, ADG's Branch, A, May 1922, nos 1784–86 and appendix.

[109] Gajendra Singh, *The Testimonies of Indian Soldiers and the Two World Wars: Between Self and Sepoy,* London: Bloomsbury, 2014, pp. 78, 89.

[110] '[I]t has apparently escaped their attention, that in the agreement which the soldier signs special exception is made for the case of war.' Captain Tweedy, censor, to H.V. Cox, 29 June 1917, IOR/L/Mil/5/827, III, p. 400.

[111] IA Order no. 227, 12 May 1918. *Compendium*, p. 171, para. 227.

building on fire. The plotters were overheard and sent back under arrest, achieving, as this officer remarked, part of their objective.[112]

Comparisons about leave could spiral into bitter political criticism, as illustrated by an anonymous petition 'in broken *Parbatia* [hill dialect]' directed to General Sir Baber Shumsher Jung from some soldiers of the Nepal contingent.[113] Convalescing in Dehradun after field service in Waziristan, they discovered they were to be sent back to their regiments, whereas Indian Army soldiers were being allowed to go home on leave:

> The English who fought with us got enlisted on Rs 50/–. We, your own subjects, are disposed of at Rs 11/–. We had to come away ... leaving our land to lie fallow ... these British look upon us as a mere trifle and care for us no better than pubes ... they say 'Gurkha has come under our control.'... The subjects of our Gurkha Government are exhausted. If the wish is to denude the country ... to whose house are we to go on our return ... Let fair justice be done to us, we beseech you with folded hands on our feet.[114]

The Gurkha of the archetypal narrative ran away from home to join the army, never in the reverse direction. In fact, anxieties about desertion from Gurkha units had surfaced as early as 1915, and by 1918 the strain of overlong absences was very evident.[115] In September 1918, the British Resident asked the

---

[112] Henry Edward Shortt, IMS, 'In the days of the Raj', typescript, IOR Mss Eur. C 435.

[113] See GOC Meerut Division, 29 January 1918, F&P, Internal, B, April 1918, nos 106–109.

[114] A note added insistently: 'We had got leave from Rawal Pindi. We ought to be allowed to go on leave. We also ... want to see the faces of our father and mother'. F&P, Internal, B, April 1918, nos 106–109. The British resident in Nepal reported that ex-soldiers of the Indian Army were complaining about inadequate pensions and unfair treatment. Resident, 24 October 1917 in F&P, Internal, B, January 1919, no. 338. One propaganda pamphlet declared that Nepal had provided 'more than one in six of the total male population belonging to the martial classes between the ages of 18 and 35'. *Blood and Treasure: India's War Effort*, Oxford: Oxford University Press, 1918, p. 5. The petition reveals the strains of this contribution. A critical Nepali press had emerged, as well as a fledgling political movement demanding civil liberties.

[115] When the British Resident asked the Nepal government for help in recalling reservists and men on furlough in January 1915, the latter described the difficulty of filling its own vacancies. F&P, External, B, April 1915, nos 171–203. In 1917, the Commanding Officer was empowered to give convalescent leave to men who

Prime Minister of Nepal to persuade some 1,100 men who had overstayed their leave to return.[116] Fifty desertions had also taken place from the 3rd–9th Gurkha Rifles posted in Kohat.[117] The Prime Minister, Chandra Shamsher Rana, agreed, but pointed out that his government was exposing itself to criticism for breaching the convention that once the deserter reached Nepal he was free from pursuit.[118] A six-week furlough was barely enough for the soldier to make it to his remote mountain village and back. The pursuit of deserters, he added, might lead to the harassment of men who were on authorised leave, and jeopardise recruitment.[119] He asked that those who surrendered be treated leniently, forfeiting only their past service and pay, and that they be sent back immediately at the termination of war.[120] The Army agreed, but phrased the promise of return very cautiously: 'they will be sent back with all possible speed'.[121]

Sometimes soldiers and followers who had been dismissed for some offence, overstayed their leave, or left without a proper discharge would change their name and re-enlist. The declaration which the soldier or labourer had to make at enrolment included no less than three questions asking whether he had testified truthfully about previous service:

> Do you now belong to His Majesty's forces, the reserve, or the Imperial Service Troops of any native state or the Nepal State army? Have you ever served in His Majesty's forces, the reserve, or the Imperial Service Troops of any native state, or in the Nepal state army? If so, state in which, and the cause of discharge.[122]

In the prewar period, enquiries were not very searching when the direction of unauthorised movement was from princely state units into the Indian Army.[123] Nepal's government complained continuously about men deserting its units in

---

returned from active service even if they had been certified as fit for duty. He could give a maximum of three months to Indian soldiers and four and a half months to Gurkha soldiers. *Compendium*, para. 640.

[116] These were soldiers home on leave after service in Egypt and Mesopotamia. F&P, Internal, B, January 1919, no. 338.

[117] Ibid.

[118] Legislative, 1918, no. 802.

[119] Ibid.

[120] Ibid.

[121] Ibid.

[122] See IOR/L/MIL/7/18354.

[123] An order of 26 May 1892 stated that soldiers discovered to be deserters from the 'native' forces would be dismissed. However, this applied only to those princely

order to enrol in the Indian Army as combatants or followers.[124] The introduction of a recruitment bonus of Rs 50/– for Indian soldiers in June 1917 increased the concern about 'fraudulent enlistment'. Pointing out that this offence had become very prevalent, an army order stressed that it would be dealt with invariably by court-martial and punished with severity.[125]

As pressure for manpower stepped up, revenue officials used harsher tactics to force villages to surrender their runaways.[126] Yet some civil and military officers felt that traditional recruiting zones needed time to absorb the higher rate of casualties, and the greater difficulty of getting leave. This may explain why in the opening phase of the war, when British deserters were given one to two months to surrender, the grace period granted to Indians eventually stretched to seven to eight months.[127] The Deputy Commissioner

---

forces which had been pulled up to a higher standard for incorporation into the Imperial Service Troops. F&P, Internal, B, January 1919, no. 338. In October 1918, due to a cited war emergency, the Udaipur state was asked to condone the desertion of two men from the Udaipur State Forces, who had enrolled in the 32nd Lancers. Ibid.

[124] F&P, Internal, B, September 1915, nos 151–53. The Punjab government proposed unsuccessfully that the deserter who had re-enlisted 'fraudulently' be treated as leniently as the one who had deserted and not re-enlisted. 29 August 1918, Legislative, October 1918, no. 802.

[125] IA Order 1402, 1917, *Compendium*, para. 752. However, dismissal wasn't invariable, as the order also provided for wage stoppages to recover the bonus. Ibid.

[126] See 'Congress Report on the Punjab Disorders', in *The Collected Works of Mahatma Gandhi*, vol. 17, 25 March 1920, pp. 114–292, https://www.gandhiservefoundation.org/about-mahatma-gandhi/collected-works-of-mahatma-gandhi/017–19200201–19200630/, last accessed 11 November 2019. In 1918 there were incidents in Punjab, the United Provinces and Bombay Presidency where crowds resisted the apprehension of deserters or liberated newly enrolled men. See *Pratap*, 6 May 1918.

[127] On 7 August 1914 a War Office order offered a pardon to British military personnel in a state of desertion if they surrendered on or by 4 September 1914 within the UK, or 4 October 1914 at a station outside the UK. An IA order of 19 December 1914 set out similar terms. Indian personnel could surrender on or before 15 January 1915, or 15 February 1915 at stations outside India. However, in May 1915 the grace period of one to two months was extended. The deserter could now surrender by 15 July 1915 within India, and 15 August 1915 outside India. IA order 209 of May 1915. See also F&P, War, A, August 1915, nos 7–9.

of Rawalpindi, a heavily recruited district, had argued for an extension of amnesty on the grounds that news of the offer had not percolated sufficiently and he expected 600 deserters to come in.[128]

Towards the close of 1917, the Punjab provincial recruiting board suggested a second amnesty. The Adjutant General approved, noting that most deserters were 'raw recruits, who had little or no sense of responsibility, were homesick, or found the intensive training inseparable from war conditions very arduous.' The majority, he added, were still at large, so amnesty would bring them 'back to the colours'.[129] And, indeed, the figures for desertions from 1 August 1914 to 31 March 1918 in Punjab, along with the numbers still 'not accounted for', indicate that some districts must have been awash with deserters.[130] Desertion was also a problem in Burma, where the government was trying, rather unsuccessfully, to build up local recruiting pools.[131]

---

[128] F&P, War A, August 1915, nos 7–9; F&P, War, B, February 1916, nos 7–11. Amnesty was withheld from soldiers who had deserted on active service or deserted to the enemy, and from those deserters who had 'enrolled themselves improperly in the same or any other corps or department'. F&P, War, A, August 1915, nos 7–9; Legislative, October 1918, no. 802. However, in 1920, by an amendment to the Indian Army Act, those guilty of desertion (other than desertion on active service) or of fraudulent enrolment would not be tried by court-martial if they had subsequently served 'in an exemplary manner' for not less than three years in Her Majesty's Forces. Act XXXVII of 1920, s. 67.

[129] Legislative, 1918, no. 802.

[130] Of 10,320 recruits in Ferozepur district, 2,131, that is 20.6 per cent, had deserted, of whom only 970 were accounted for. Of 770 recruits from Montgomery district, 523, that is 69.3 per cent, had deserted, of whom 284 were accounted for. Rawalpindi, a key recruiting zone which had provided 27,519 recruits, had 2,658 deserters, 9.6 per cent of the total, of whom 679 were unaccounted for. Elsewhere, the percentages were lower. Legislative, 1918, no. 802. As Ahuja points out, the number still at large indicates the level of rural sympathy for the deserter. Ravi Ahuja, 'The Corrosiveness of Comparison: Reverberations of Indian Wartime Experiences in German Prison Camps (1915–1919)', in Heike Liebau, Katrin Bromber, Katharina Lange, Dyala Hamzah and Ravi Ahuja (eds), *The World in World Wars: Experiences, Perceptions and Perspectives from Africa and Asia*, Brill: The Netherlands, 2010, pp. 131–66.

[131] GOC Burma division, 1 November 1918, Legislative, 1918, no. 801. Notices in Burmese 'nightly thrown on the screen at the chief bio-scopes' promised a free pardon to deserters. *TOI*, 14 October 1918, p. 11.

The announcement of the second amnesty was delayed due to a prolonged discussion about the legal form by which to include some 700–1,000 soldiers jailed for desertion or absence without leave.[132] Announced on 11 October 1918, it again came with a generous grace period.[133] Interestingly, transfrontier deserters, who were not allowed to rejoin the service, were permitted nevertheless to surrender and get a discharge certificate which protected them from arrest if they ventured into British territory.[134] Clearly, lines of political communication with recruiting pools in transfrontier territory were still being kept open.

The disabled soldier: terminating the war, conserving its trace

The debtor's agents cannot look into people's grievances with the Creditor's eye.[135]

Among the figures making their way home were those too incapacitated for further service, temporarily or permanently. Walter Lawrence, commissioner for the welfare of sick and wounded Indian soldiers in France and England, stressed that it was of the utmost political importance to ensure that invalids returned 'as regiments, armed and equipped ... the spectacle of wounded and sick men in Hospital clothes will have a very depressing effect in India, and a very bad effect on recruiting.'[136] Indeed, the *Times of India* had noted that it was the flow of shattered men from Mesopotamia in 1916 which alerted the Bombay public to logistical failures in this theatre.[137]

Medical officers engaged in a specialised form of 'war-salvage', sorting patients into those who could be speedily sent back to active service, those who needed a longer convalescence, and those who were to be discharged or pensioned off. Medical boards deciding on disability pensions assessed the degree of bodily damage 'attributable to war', whether it was permanent or

---

[132] Legislative, 1918, no. 802.

[133] Ibid.

[134] Adjutant General's Branch, 14 October 1918, F&P, Internal, B, January 1919, no. 338. In 1920, transfrontier soldiers and cavalrymen who had deserted from the Northern Waziristan Militia were told that they would not be considered outlaws if they handed over their rifles. *Operations in Waziristan*, appendix E, p. 159.

[135] *Coloured Victims of the Great War*, p. 30, para. 11.

[136] Lawrence to Kitchener, 5 August 1915. TNA WO 32/5110.

[137] In contrast, officials in the remote Himalayas viewed events 'through the distorting medium of a mass of paper.' *TOI*, 11 September 1916, p. 8.

temporary, and how far it affected capacity to earn a livelihood in civilian life. In general, medical expertise was expected to pare down the government's pensionary commitments.[138] Highlighting his war service, the Medical Officer of the Military Orthopaedic Hospital at Kanpur listed the number of malingerers he had weeded out, and the number of invalid pensions he had saved or scaled down by effecting a cure.[139]

One disciplinary issue which emerged was whether Indian soldiers and followers who refused to undergo surgery for some injury or physical problem which rendered them 'ineffective' should forfeit their service gratuity or disability pension. The point of perplexity was that their refusal was often couched in terms which equated bodily loss with spiritual loss, thereby extending it into the afterlife.[140] An American surgeon in France heard that Gurkha personnel rarely permitted an amputation because of their belief in transmigration: 'Can one imagine a future if on one leg, or ... on no legs at all.'[141]

In 1918 there was a discussion about Muslim soldiers who had to be discharged as medically unfit because of some 'slight deformities' which might have been overcome by the removal of a finger, or surgical treatment for ailments relating to genitals or the rectal passage, such as piles.[142] Some officers held that the soldiers refused surgery simply to secure an early discharge or a wound pension. Others accepted that the 'uneducated Mussalman' did have religious scruples about the inspection of his genitals and the surgical excision

---

[138] Frances Miley and Andrew Read, 'The Purgatorial Shadows of War: Accounting, Blame and Shell Shock Pensions, 1914–1923', *Accounting History*, vol. 22, no. 1 (2016), pp. 5–28.

[139] DGIMS, IMS, June 1920, no. 782. (DGIMS: Director General, Indian Medical Service).

[140] A Sikh soldier at Brighton hospital refused a skull surgery to treat his paralysis because his religion forbade him to shave his head. One writer concluded that '[i]n the Pavilion Hospital every patient is free—free to die if he prefers it to an operation.' Alfred Ollivant, 'The Indian Hospital', 1916, http://www.sikhmuseum.com/brighton/arts/ollivant/index.html, last accessed 10 November 2019. In 1917 the Punjab government allowed a time period of two months for the medical treatment of recruits rejected for some 'temporary or easily curable complaint', but hospitals were increasingly overburdened with men who were still unfit, and those who 'resolutely refused to be operated upon'. 'Recruiting in India', p. 32.

[141] Diary entry, 4 May 1915, in Harvey Cushing, *From a Surgeon's Journal: 1915–1918*, Boston: Little, Brown and Company, 1936, p. 63.

[142] AD, ADG's Branch, Pensions, A, March 1919, nos 3514–15 and appendix 2.

of tissue or body parts.[143] The Punjab government secured an opinion from thirteen *maulvis* (Islamic scholars) that in situations of exigency Muslims could allow an examination of private parts and accept surgery.[144] Nevertheless, no clear-cut decision emerged as to whether the refusal of surgery could be punished by the denial of gratuity or a wound pension.[145] As one official pointed out, the necessity of the surgical procedure in question was not always clear.[146] It was left to the Army Commander to decide whether or not a penalty would be imposed; this authority was subsequently delegated to the General Officer Commanding.[147]

In determining disability pensions, it was accepted that employment options for military personnel were far more limited in India than in Britain. The difficulty of constantly recalling soldiers and followers to determine whether the disability had decreased was also recognised.[148] But in fixing the pension there was also a presumption that 'unskilled work' required a lower degree of fitness.[149] Temporary followers, among them the large numbers in the Labour and Porter Corps, were not admitted to third-degree injury pensions—those in which the man was categorised as no longer fit for military service but capable of 'contributing materially towards his livelihood.'[150]

The loss of body parts due to frostbite was accepted as legitimate grounds for claiming an injury pension.[151] Exposure to this form of war injury was one basis on which Ampthill had pleaded unsuccessfully for the men of the ILC to be recategorised as soldiers.[152] Battlefield salvage and porterage could mean

---

[143] Molesworth, ADG's Branch, 29 January 1918, ibid.

[144] Ibid.

[145] Ibid.

[146] E. H. Payne, 14 January 1918, ibid. Nor, one might add, was the outcome of surgery always predictable.

[147] See Army Instruction (India), no. 55, 19 February 1918; superceded by no. 342 of 16 April 1918. *Army Instructions, India*, 1918.

[148] See discussion on the feasibility of applying the UK Ministry of Pensions schedule to the Indian Service. Defence, A, April 1923, nos 1903–8.

[149] For an inconclusive discussion about the classification of deafness caused by wounds or shell shock, see despatch from Secretary of State for India, Army Department, no. 47, July 1916.

[150] *Compendium*, pp. 404–405, para. 1456.

[151] *Compendium*, p. 403, para. 1454.

[152] They were 'doing the work of soldiers ... facing the risks of soldiers ... Many ... have had to have their hands or feet amputated in consequence of frost bite. Others have

deadly encounters with munitions, but accidents at construction sites could also leave non-combatants with crippling injuries. Bodily damage which was visible was more easily 'attributable to war' than morbidity arising from long hours in the cold and the wet, or exposure to bouts of malaria.[153]

The figure of the wounded Indian soldier was compelling enough to establish the Imperial Indian Relief Fund as the largest charity fund ever raised in India, and the line between official and charitable funds was often blurred to the government's advantage.[154] At first there was talk of setting up an asylum for disabled soldiers, but this was rejected due to arguments that many would stay away.[155] The proposal may have also seemed to associate military service with a state of penury.[156] A further issue was that an asylum meant a perma-

---

suffered mutilation on account of bombing by enemy air craft and in accidents with the shells and bombs which they have had to handle ... let them ... have the honour of being able to say they have served as soldiers.' Ampthill, to General H. V. Cox, 26 February 1918, IOR/L/Mil/5/738.

[153] About 83 per cent of the 520 Indians who died in the malarious swamps of Macedonia, mostly of disease, were non-combatants. Helen Abadzi, 'The Indian Cemetery in Salonica', 30 November 2006, https://elinepa.org/en/the-indian-cemetery-of-salonica/, last accessed 10 November 2019. Using blood samples he took in this theatre, Ludwik Hirszfeld contended that blood group B was most prevalent in India. Projit Bihar Mukharji, 'From Serosocial to Sanguinary Identities: Caste, Transnational Race Science and the Shifting Metonymies of Blood Group B, India c. 1918–1960', *The Indian Economic and Social History Review*, vol. 51, no. 2 (2014), pp. 143–76. Tuberculosis contracted on service was the other health hazard. '[M]en of our Native Labour Corps in France and Flanders', wrote one military doctor, contracted tuberculosis 'of a progressive and fatal kind, and doubtless many developed it later as a result of infection contracted during the war'. Col. S. Lyle Cummins, 'Tuberculosis as a Problem for the Royal Army Medical Corps', *Journal of the Royal Army Medical Corps*, vol. XLVI, no. 6 (1926), pp. 401–7.

[154] The announcement of an extra Rs 6/– from the Imperial Indian Relief fund for disabled soldiers who attended the Queen Mary's Technical School for trade training was carefully phrased to suggest it was a grant from the government while allowing room for deniability.

[155] ADG, 21 December 1916, IOR/L/Mil/7/18582.

[156] In 1919–20, there were fervent demands in the press for beggar homes to deal with the stream of human misery pouring into large towns due to drought and high prices. See *Report on Indian Newspapers and Periodicals in Bengal*, no. 7, 21 February 1920, pp. 115–17; *Tribune*, 27 February 1920; 'Bombay Beggar Problem', *The*

nent commitment of funds, whereas the official stance was that war charities had a finite life.[157] Nevertheless, the possibility that destitution might overtake the ex-soldier, or his widow and children, had to be acknowledged—for instance, through eligibility for one-time charitable grants.

In India, as elsewhere, bodily damage was sanitised in war publicity materials. We find no reference to those who had suffered terrible facial disfigurement, or those left with limited mobility.[158] An otherwise cheery account of Indian soldiers at Brighton hospital records the broken phrases in which an Indian ammunition driver who had lost both feet to frostbite summed up his future: 'My job horses. India-rubber leg.'[159] We do not glimpse the blind in any photograph. They were said to be few in number, and no effort was made to expand the painfully meagre provisions in India for retraining them.[160] Instead, St Dunstan's, a British charity for the blind, provided a grant which added Rs 5/– a month to the service pension of blind soldiers.

Nor was the light of publicity shed upon those soldiers or labourers admitted to lunatic asylums.[161] Annual reports for provincial asylums registered the

---

Pioneer Mail, 13 August 1920, p. 25; 'Professional Beggars', *The Pioneer Mail*, 15 October 1920, p. 22. In 1920 the Deputy Commissioner, Bombay took over the Dadar camp, once used to house the Indian Labour Corps, to lodge beggars swept off the streets.

[157] However, in 1928 government decided to continue its annual contribution to the Queen Mary's Technical School for disabled soldiers. IOR/L/Mil/7/12521.

[158] Pratyoush Onta, 'Dukha during the World War', *Himal*, 6 December 2016, http://himalmag.com/dukha-during-the-world-war, last accessed 18 November 2019.

[159] Ollivant, 'The Indian Hospital'.

[160] Blind personnel were directed to the Victoria Memorial School at Bombay but not many turned up. Viceroy to Secretary of State for India, Despatch, Army Department, no. 4, 10 January 1919. This was attributed to their fatalistic outlook. IOR/L/Mil/7/18481. St Dunstan's, the British charity for the blind, offered the same justification for not extending its training schemes to India. David Castleton, *In the Mind's Eye: The Blinded Veterans of St Dunstan's*, Barnsley: Pen and Sword Military, 2013 (not paginated).

[161] Hilary Buxton points out that neat ethnic distinctions in the medical assessment of mental breakdown had to be rethought in World War One, but in the postwar period there was a return to stereotypes about the 'martial races' and a reluctance to acknowledge that they had experienced mental trauma. Hilary Buxton, 'Imperial Amnesia: Race, Trauma and Indian Troops in the First World War', *Past and Present*, vol. 241, no. 1 (2018), pp. 221–58.

presence of 'military insanes', but the tendency, at least in Punjab, was to assert the 'temporary nature' of their 'mental aberrations' and to anticipate a rapid recovery.[162] The paternalist framing of the recruitment of 'primitive' populations for labour units made it particularly problematic to detect any signs of mental stress in the men. The comforting assumption was that the very depth of their backwardness had shielded them from trauma, or that a delight in archaic violence—a desire to 'take heads'—made them serviceable for modern warfare.[163] The introduction of 'modern and enlightened' attitudes to mental illness received some publicity only with the setting up of the Ranchi Mental Asylum for European patients in 1919.[164]

It was the soldier who was 'maimed', but not hopelessly so, who was foregrounded in Indian publicity about rehabilitation. The figure in a wheelchair glimpsed in a photograph or two from English hospitals disappears from sight, and so does the wheelchair itself.[165] In posters about rehabilitation in India what we see are rough and ready crutches, and even these appear as scenic rather than bodily props.[166] There is one disturbing exception—a photograph of the Prince of Wales inspecting a line of 'maimed' soldiers at Bombay during his 1921–22 tour. They stand with the support of their crutches, wearing rough drawers and looking poor, worn out, and dispirited.

Trade training in motor driving and motor and pump maintenance for disabled soldiers was formally inaugurated in March 1917 at the Queen Mary's Technical School (QMTS) in Bombay, and later at the Lahore Technical Institute.[167] A 1919 Red Cross poster for an exhibition in India displays two

---

[162] *Triennial Report on the Working of the Punjab Lunatic Asylum. For the Years 1918, 1919 and 1920*, Lahore: Government Press, 1921.

[163] See Chapter 4.

[164] This was reflected in Act VI of 1922, which amended the Indian Lunacy Act of 1912. The label 'mental hospital' was introduced, and the licence for such institutions could be revoked if there was no provision for 'curative treatment'.

[165] See 'The Four Worst Cases in the Brighton Hospital', 1915, British Library, Photo 24(19); also 'King George V decorates Havildar Gagna Singh with the Indian Order of Merit, 21 August 1915' in Hannah Midgley, 'Brighton Pavilion's Crowned Care for Wounded Soldiers', *Brighton Journal*, 15 March 2016, https://bjournal.co/brighton-pavilions-crowned-care-for-wounded-soldiers, last accessed 18 November 2019.

[166] See below.

[167] F&P, Internal, B, August 1918, 486–88. Paul Murphy, 'Queen Mary's Institute, Pune', *History Today*, vol. 45, no. 11 (1995).

related images.[168] In one, four men and their instructor are positioned around the open bonnet of a car.[169] In the other, three men seated on the floor, their leg amputations visible, busy themselves with simple carpentry, curls of wood surrounding them.[170] A book compiled by Douglas McMurtrie, the Director of the American Red Cross Institute for Crippled and Disabled Men, contains another illustration showing five men, four with amputated legs, operating hosiery-knitting machines at a table. The title reads: 'India's Men Go to School. At Queen Mary's Technical School Bombay, disabled soldiers of the Indian forces are taught to shun the beggar's calling and prepared for useful lives.'[171] Lest readers miss the particular significance of this victory, it is spelt it out for them. Teaching disabled Indian soldiers to be self-supporting 'must appear wonderful to us who have been accustomed to regard the hordes of mendicants in India as a natural element in that country's curious make-up.'[172]

One of the men operating a knitting machine seems to have a prosthetic leg of the simple pin-and-bucket type, but it is the rough aid to mobility, the crutch, which is more visible. The image is framed as a pedagogical scene, but war-damaged bodies have, reassuringly, almost already materialised as skilled workmen. The veneer of modernity served to sever the association between 'trades' and forms of livelihood associated with the 'menial' castes, and to augur the emergence of dynamic new sectors of the Indian economy.[173] 'It is

---

[168] 'India Restores her War Cripples to Self-Support', Library of Congress, 1919, https://www.loc.gov/item/00651704, last accessed 18 November 2019.

[169] 'Automobile mechanics is a popular trade...', ibid.

[170] 'The loss of limb does not prevent the injured soldiers of India's forces from becoming good carpenters', ibid.

[171] Douglas C. McMurtrie, *The Disabled Soldier*, New York: Macmillan, 1919, https://commons.wikimedia.org/wiki/File:The_disabled_soldier_(1919)_(14763611871).jpg, last accessed 10 November 2019.

[172] Ibid., p. 203. For the economist Vera Anstey, wartime Bombay illustrated the 'striking anachronisms' of India through the co-existence of the up-to-date operating theatre with the haunts of 'emaciated disabled beggars, who drag their possibly self-mutilated limbs through the noisome dust and dirt of the gutters.' Vera Anstey, *The Economic Development of India*, London: Longman, Green and Co., 1929, p. 1.

[173] Officers prided themselves on the ability of the Indian Army to attract recruits from substantial land-holding strata. They had a tendency, therefore, to disapprove of trades such as poultry-keeping or basket-weaving which might bring soldiers down to the level of low-caste 'menials'.

only within recent years that millions of Indians have begun to wear socks, but they wear them now,' reported the American journalist Eleanor Egan, indicating that hosiery was an increasingly profitable business.[174] Training in motor mechanics, the maintenance of pumps, machine-made hosiery, and tailoring and hosiery-making were also of immediate use to the army in workshops and the army clothing department.[175]

The label 'maimed' covered such a wide range of conditions that it facilitated optimistic conclusions about the success of trade training.[176] Nevertheless, the figures given for soldiers being fitted out for artificial limbs at Bombay or those being trained in some trade at QMTS or Lahore are very modest, and this despite reports of large numbers of Indian personnel being sent home severely injured or invalided at certain conjunctures in the war.[177] The figure given in March 1917 for the number of 'maimed' soldiers in hospital or discharged to pension was also quite high, at 8,873.[178] However, the Adjutant General responded irately to a suggestion about compiling their names and addresses:

> I am at a loss to see of what value some names and addresses are going to be to any one and must protest against what I consider will be the imposition of unnecessary labour on the depot staff, to say nothing of the possibility of raising false hopes in the 8000 odd maimed soldiers.[179]

---

[174] Eleanor Franklin Egan, *The War in the Cradle of the World: Mesopotamia*, New York; London: Harper and Brothers, 1918, pp. 65–66.

[175] 'Trained men are placed in Bombay and other industrial centres in workshops and factories; with regiments or the army clothing department as tailors; in the mechanical transport service as chauffeurs, in the government dockyards, ordnance factories, and arsenals as turners, fitters, machinemen, engine drivers, and ammunition box-makers.' McMurtrie, *The Disabled Soldier*, p. 203. The United Provinces government proposed to train soldiers who had lost an arm as field-men for demonstration farms and to run oil engines; the latter were expected to revolutionise irrigation. The Forest Department, then supplying huge quantities of war material, also offered to absorb some.

[176] Men with injuries of the first, second and third degree were eligible for admission to the Queen Mary's Technical School for disabled soldiers. Army Instruction (India), no. 43, 21 January 1919.

[177] Of the 1,100 Indians wounded at Gallipoli, 475 had been sent back to India 'in a permanently maimed condition'. 'Wounded Indians', *TOI*, 7 May 1915, p. 5.

[178] IOR/L/Mil/18582.

[179] General Sir Havelock Hudson, 4 April 1917, IOR/L/Mil/18582.

The information circulated about facilities for disabled soldiers was so rose-tinted as to verge on propaganda, but there was a reluctance to seek them out actively along their paths home from war.[180]

There is one intriguing discussion about the merits of the shaped leg versus the wooden pin-leg for Indian sepoys which reveals how an object could be valued less for its practical use than for its evidentiary value. On 17 September 1915, Walter Lawrence, commissioner for the care of welfare of Indian soldiers in Europe, suggested that the Government of India arrange the manufacture of artificial limbs, aiming for something 'between bucket and pin and the more elaborate description of artificial limb.' Assurances had been given, he pointed out, that 'maimed' men would receive 'first-class artificial limbs of a suitable and practical nature when they reached India.'[181] The conditions of life to which disabled Indian soldiers and labourers would return put a question mark over the durability and potential repair and replacement of their shaped limbs.[182] Nevertheless, they insisted on the more expensive articulated limbs, which could cost up to Rs 300/– apiece. Claude Hill, then on the Viceroy's Council, recalled that at first government supplied only the wooden limb, leaving it to private benevolence to pay for the superior variety, which soldiers referred to as 'rrubberr'. But 'to avoid jealousy it became necessary to give rubber limbs to all who asked for them ... In the majority of cases, as was discovered later in their homes, the proud possessors of these used them only as exhibition toys. And confined practical use to the ordinary wooden limbs.'[183] C. P. Lukis, Director General of Medical Services, pointed out that

---

[180] Imperial War Museum posters, no. 8, PRC 450, PST 12600 and PST 12601. The themes covered were 'Pensions, Teaching of Trades, Medical Aid. How discharged Soldiers can get their pensions. How families of Soldiers killed in action or who died on active service can get their pensions. How disabled Soldiers can learn a trade. How wounded Soldiers can receive treatment if their wounds give them trouble.' See also propaganda pamphlet, *Letter to the Loyal Women of India*, Oxford: Humphrey Milford, n.d. (c. 1919).

[181] Walter Lawrence to Sir Alfred Keogh, Director General, Army Medical Services, 17 September 1915, IOR, Walter Lawrence, Mss Eur. F 143/79, British Library.

[182] '[S]ooner or later the springs break ... and when the men return to Nepal there is no means there for having them repaired,' wrote a former CO of the Gurkha convalescent section at Dehradun on 20 September 1917. DGIMS, Stores, January 1917, no. 23.

[183] Claude H. Hill, *India-Stepmother*, Edinburgh: William Blackwood and Sons, 1929, p. 207. See *TOI*, 13 March 1915, p. 15.

while the shaped limb was 'too elaborate and too good' for Indian soldiers, promises had been made by the King and the Secretary of State for India at Brighton Hospital that they would receive the same kind of artificial limb as British personnel.[184] For the disabled soldier the 'rrubberr' leg was testimony to an injury 'attributable to the war', and a reminder of wartime promises.

A legacy of distrust from battlefields in France and Mesopotamia filtered into the debate about the point at which the soldier under medical treatment was to be pensioned off and released into civil life. The insistence on sending wounded sepoys back into battle once they had been declared fit for duty violated their understanding that, having done their bit, they should not have to suffer such fear again.[185] With war circling back to the North-West Frontier in 1919–20, soldiers invalided to India had reason to wonder whether recovery would mean their return to service.[186] A vernacular pamphlet issued by the Indian Soldiers' Board in September 1919 was still assuring those who entered the Lady Chelmsford Orthopaedic Hospital at Dehradun that they could leave when they chose and would not be asked to rejoin the army.[187] Another reason for distrust was this: would the recovery of bodily capacity or the learning of a trade under a military aegis lead to the downgrading of an injury or disability pension—even perhaps its withdrawal?[188] Of the proposal to provide orthopaedic treatment, Havelock Hudson, the Adjutant General, wrote: 'The Indian is suspicious by nature and though he may ... receive benefit from the treatment, [he] may fear to give it undue prominence by skill in a trade from fear it may affect his pension.'[189] Finally, would the government feel it was absolved of

---

[184] Director General, IMS, 6 February 1917, DGIMS, Stores, January 1917, no. 192. He pointed out that at the Marine Lines Hospital in Bombay, amputation cases were given both 'a shaped limb (lower) ... [and] a superior folding pin and bucket leg.' C. P. Lukis, 17 September 1917, IOR Walter Lawrence Mss Eur., file 43/79.

[185] David Omissi, *The Sepoy and the Raj, The Indian Army, 1860–1940*, London: Macmillan, 1994, p. 118.

[186] Whereas the new entrant received an enlistment bonus, the wounded man who was declared fit received no incentive for return to service.

[187] At the Lady Chelmsford Orthopaedic Hospital at Dehradun, soldiers under treatment could learn to operate oil- and electricity-driven engines and motor cars.

[188] Soldiers invalided from service on account of 'disability aggravated by field service' were given a pension for three years in the first instance, then re-examined; if the disability persisted the pension was made permanent. See *Compendium*, para. 1455.

[189] Home, Medical, A, October 1919, nos 21–57.

its obligation to scale pensions to some standard of respectability if it could persuade the disabled to learn 'demeaning' trades such as tailoring?[190]

Writing to Lady Willingdon, wife of the Bombay governor and a powerful patroness of war charities, Surgeon General Sir Charles Pardey Lukis suggested that men should be introduced to trade training after their pension had been settled and they had passed into civil life, or 'they may regard Your Excellency's philanthropic scheme as part of a dark and deadly scheme to either deprive them of their pensions or to lessen the amount.'[191] Others argued that disabled soldiers should be kept in service until they were fitted out with an artificial limb, or until orthopaedic treatment had improved limb functionality. The same disciplinary framework which had shaped them for military use would, it was felt, reshape them into self-sufficient, productive beings. It would aid that painful and often dispiriting process of restoring movement to a limb, or of manipulating the stump of an arm or a leg to fit an artificial limb, and it would encourage persistence in trade training. The receipt of full pay during this period was expected to compensate for their continued subjection to military discipline.[192]

The government's initial decision was that once men were fit enough to be transferred from hospital to the QMTS or another trade training institution, they would get full pay for only six months. If they did not persevere, they could be told to leave.[193] However, the War Office pointed out that it had proved difficult to keep British disabled soldiers under treatment once they were discharged from the army.[194] The Government of India accepted its suggestion that Indian soldiers be kept on full pay for the entire period required to fit them for an artificial limb, instead of discharging them after six months.[195]

---

[190] At first, soldiers waiting to be fitted out with limbs at a Bombay hospital were reluctant to learn tailoring, fearing it might lower them in the estimation of their caste-fellows, for whom respectability lay either in agriculture or soldiering. Major Hirsch to Director General IMS, 14 March 1917, in Home, Medical, A, October 1919, nos 21–57.

[191] 17 March 1917, in Home, Medical, A, October 1919, nos 21–57.

[192] Ibid.

[193] General Officer Commanding, Bombay Brigade to Director Medical Services, 31 August 1917.

[194] War Office to India Office, 20 June 1918, IOR/L/Mil/18582. The War Office offered to pay for the extra expense. Ibid.

[195] Army Instruction (India), no. 1403, 17 December 1919, in IOR/L/Mil/1858.

War rewards and the tremors of political change

In India, November 11th, 1918, is rivaled in importance by August 20th, 1917.[196]

On 20 August 1917, Edwin Montagu, the Secretary of State for India, announced that future policy would involve 'the increasing association of Indians in every branch of the administration, and the gradual development of self-governing institutions with a view to the progressive realisation of responsible government in India as an integral part of the British Empire.' The context was one in which war demands on India were escalating. In March 1917 government had launched the first Indian War Loan, and in June 1917 it set out to double the pace of recruitment. Scholarly work has focused so much on the constrained nature of the constitutional reforms actually conceded in 1919 that one loses sight of the electrifying effect of Montagu's announcement.[197] In his five-month-long progression around India, he would receive a bundle of petitions from spokesmen for 'low-caste', 'untouchable' and tribal communities, demanding in one way or another the right to represent themselves in legislative bodies, insisting that socially advantaged groups should not 'usurp' that power.[198] Some newspapers, otherwise strongly in favour of elected legislatures, asked with a twinge of anxiety whether democratisation, taken too far, might descend into anarchy. 'The advocacy of the right of self-determination by every element of the Indian population, has its

---

[196] *Seventy-Ninth Annual Report of the Wesleyan Mission in the Mysore Province*, Mysore: Wesleyan Mission Press, 1919, p. 1.

[197] The thrum of change can be heard in a chapter titled 'A Strange Event', in which B. R. Ambedkar explains why Congress suddenly passed a resolution in December 1917 urging the removal of the disabilities of the Depressed Classes. It was galvanised into action by the resolutions passed by leaders of the non-Brahmin movement asking government to 'grant to Untouchables their own representatives' in legislative bodies. 'What Congress and Gandhi have done to the Untouchables', 1945, reprinted in Vasant Moon (ed.), *Dr. Babasaheb Ambedkar: Writings and Speeches*, vol. 9, Education Department, Government of Maharashtra, 1991, pp. 1–12. For an insightful exploration of the emergence of a Dalit public sphere, see Anupama Rao, *The Caste Question: Dalits and the Politics of Modern India*, Berkeley: University of California Press, 2009.

[198] In November 1917, a tribal association in Ranchi, the Chota Nagpur Unnati Samaj, sent a representation along these lines. *Gharbandhu*, vol. 42, no. 2, 15 January 1918, Gossner Theological College Archives, Ranchi.

inevitable result in the present chaos in Russia,' pronounced the *Leader*, a prominent Allahabad paper founded by Madan Mohan Malaviya.[199] Spiralling inflation stoked fears of social upheaval. Newspapers were replete with complaints from the 'respectable' classes that they were being ground down, whereas domestic servants, barbers and labourers were raising their charges and war profiteers were flourishing.[200]

Recruitment propaganda began to conceptualise the return home in ways which evoked both hope and anxiety about the nature of the postwar order. A Madras recruiting officer told 'untouchable Paraiyans' that '[w]hen you wear the King Emperor's uniform, you will be able to walk through the Brahmin quarter and spit where you like.'[201] Higher castes were put on their mettle by descriptions of the bleak future they faced if they fell behind the lower castes in enlistment:

> Do you realise who are joining the armies? They are the Passies and Gujjars ... The rule of Nature is that the fittest will survive. If these low castes got armed and became powerful ... imagine how you would feel like in your own village if you have to salute a Passi Subedar even though you are a Maharaj or a Thakkur? How would you like that?[202]

At Multan, Michael O'Dwyer, the Punjab governor, reproached the Kharrals for lagging behind the Punjabi Christians: 'Most ... were formerly humble menials, the servants of the zamindars, but they have realised that service brings *izzat* [honour].'[203] Vernacular papers had begun to comment on

---

[199] *Leader*, 11–12 July 1918, in *Selections, NWP&O*, no. 28, 13 July 1918, p. 364. *The Oudh Punch* criticised the audacity of some Bengal *dhobis* in laying their grievances before the Secretary of State for India. *Selections, NWP&O*, no. 6, 6 February 1918, p. 110.

[200] See *Report on Indian Newspapers and Periodicals in Bengal*, no. 4, 24 January 1920; no. 5, 31 January 1920.

[201] Gilbert Slater, *Southern India: Its Political and Economic Problems*, London: George Allen and Unwin Ltd, 1936, p. 291.

[202] 'An appeal to the Brahmins and Rajputs of Aauadh', Urdu, n.d. (c. 1918), Imperial War Museum, poster, ART IWM PST 12575, www.iwm.org.uk/collections/item/object/31124, last accessed 18 November 2019.

[203] 16 February 1918, in *War Speeches of His Honour Sir Michael O'Dwyer*, Lahore: Government Printing, 1918, p. 102. At Gujranwala, on 8 August 1917, O'Dwyer reproached the Virak Sikhs for lagging behind their social inferiors the Labana and Mazhabi Sikhs. Ibid., p. 55. Pashtun policemen at Quetta beat up the 71st Punjab

the figures of the low-caste recruiter and the low-caste recruit, and not always with approval.[204] A poem in the *Bijnor Punch* ridiculed the airs of Chamar recruits: 'They who used to get husks and bran at house now get *ghi*, rice and gram in their rations, why then should not their martial ardour be kept up!'[205]

The expansion of military recruitment therefore added another layer of anxiety to the rapid politicisation of community identity generated by Montagu's announcement. It also set off some ripples in the army. Established 'martial castes' made disparaging remarks about the new communities being tapped for combatant service.[206] Soldiers in France commented on the growing presumption of regimental and hospital followers, some from the 'untouchable' castes. A Muslim cavalryman remarked that the 'civilisation and enlightenment' of France had not only taught some of his fellow Muslims 'to drink and be shameless', but also had a shocking effect on the regimental followers:

> I, and others, see as great a difference in the disposition of followers ... as there is between the earth and the sky. The sweeper of my troop said one day (may I be forgiven for repeating it), 'God has dealt very harshly with me in that while (at heart) I am a citizen of this country, he caused me to be born in Hindustan, and hence I have to pass my days in a contemptible occupation! These people consider everything as lawful for food—nothing is forbidden them—and I am the same. Therefore there is no difference between me and these people. They remove dirt with their own hands and so do I. Therefore I am in a very unfortunate position (because I was not born here) ...'[207]

Infantry, a Punjabi Christian regiment with a 'lower-caste' element. To avoid conflict, it was shifted to garrison duty in the Persian Gulf. GOC, 4th Quetta Division to Adjutant General, India, 14 April 1918, WW1/1019/H, vol. 461, diary no. 29644, p. 30.

204 *The Hindustani*, 11 July 1918, complained of the arrogance of low-caste recruiters once they donned a coat and boots. *Selections from Indian-Owned Newspapers, United Provinces*, no. 28, 13 July 1918, pp. 468–69.

205 *Selections, UP*, no. 42, 19 October 1918, p. 635. The CO of the 1/23rd Sikh Pioneers at Ambala said that his ('low-caste') Mazhabi Sikhs, whom service had made more assertive, would support government against the Akalis (who were predominantly Jat Sikhs). Some also pressed for a separate *rakh* (a grant of canal colony land). Home, Political, B, 1922, file 584.

206 A letter from Rawalpindi reported disapprovingly that the Kalliary (Kallars), 'a low and wholly savage caste', were being recruited. Mohomed Hayat, to Jemadar Mohomed Sher Khan, Tiwana, 9th Hodson's Horse, France, IOR/L/Mil/5/828, IV, p. 728.

207 Zabu Shah, 6th Cavalry, France, to Mahomed Manavar Zaman Khan, Farrukabad

A global war and some local emancipations

The drive to expand recruitment set off other small tremors. As pointed out in Chapter Four, in the Assam-Burma hill districts and the central Himalayas exemption from corvée—that is, sanctioned forms of labour tax—had been offered as an incentive in raising Labour Corps for France.[208] Returning soldiers and labourers sought to broaden the interpretation of this concession by bringing their children and other relatives under its umbrella. This increased the pressure on those still left on the corvée roster, a burden further increased by the trail of death left by the influenza pandemic of 1918–19. There is a complex link, therefore, between recruitment and the eruption of discrete postwar movements to end regimes of corvée along the central Himalayan belt.[209]

Push and pull around the interpretation of service rewards was also very visible in the Assam and Burma hill districts.[210] Officials had to stress that

---

district, UP, India, Urdu, 28 July 1917, IOR/L/Mil/5/827, pt 4, p. 519. It was likely the same cavalryman who wrote that the efforts of the YMCA to improve the character of sweepers and followers had produced the result that 'if they do not claim to have equal right with Europeans, [they] have got all the other Indians to acknowledge that they have equal right with them.' Sabur Shah, 6th Cavalry, France, to Mahomad Manavar Zaman Khan, Kaimganj, Farrukabad, United Provinces, Urdu, 12 August 1917. IOR/L/Mil/5/828, pt IV, p. 544.

[208] The Raja of Tehri Garhwal claimed that the 1,117 labourers who enrolled for a Kumaon Labour Corps for France were actually from his kingdom, and that he had given them a lifelong exemption from *bent* and *begar* (the compulsory provision of supplies and porterage). Report on services rendered by the Tehri Durbar, 31 August 1920, Political Agent for Tehri Garhwal State, File T-C/108/D, no. 702. In the Khasi hills, the exemption from labour tax was offered when drafts had to be sent for the companies already there. Assam Secretariat, Political, B, nos 315–26.

[209] At Kotgarh, Shimla, the American missionary Satyanand Stokes, who had assisted in recruitment, began to help returning soldiers to claim their dues, among them the promised exemption from labour tax. The result was that by 1920, 371 out of 715 households on the corvée list were exempted. Asha Sharma, *An American in Gandhi's India: The Biography of Satyanand Stokes*, Bloomington: Indiana University Press, 2008, pp. 89, 92, 105–7.

[210] Those returning from the Lushai Labour Corps asked for an exemption not only from *Kuli Pui*—that is, compulsory but paid labour for official projects—but also from *Kuli Te*—short-term porterage for chiefs. J. Zorema, *Indirect Rule in Mizoram, 1890–1954*, New Delhi: Mittal Publications, 2007, p. 93. They also tried to stretch their personal exemption from corvée to include family members as well. Some

only those actually working the lands of men who had enrolled in the Labour Corps were exempt from the labour tax, and only those actually resident in the recruit's household were exempt from the annual house tax.[211] The Assam and Burma governments were also very concerned to reassure chiefs and headmen that although government was giving up its own claims to labour tax, it was not encroaching on their 'customary' claims to the labour of a very dependent element of village society.[212] This element was referred to by various local names—for instance, by the designation *boi* in the Lushai hills. However, officials tried to avoid translating these terms as 'slave', using words such as 'orphan' or 'lodger' instead.[213] In low-population hill districts, it was this dependent stratum upon which chiefs and headmen could draw most flexibly when faced with a sudden spike in the government's demand for labour. Some chiefs also expected a share in the wages of those they sent.[214] However, in the Lushai hills the administration decided to let *bois* who had served in France retain their savings. In fact, this led to a modification of Lushai 'customary' law, with the following elliptical explanation for the shift:

> Some of these men were orphans or prior to going to France were living in the houses of people who were no relations of theirs ... It was obviously inequitable that ... the latter [the man supporting them] should be able to take the whole of

Khasis asked for licences for their muzzle-loading guns as a war reward, but their request was rejected. Assam Secretariat, Political, B, April 1918, nos 316–494, ASA.

[211] 'Order No. 3 of 1917–18', *Mizo leh Vai*, December 1918, pp. 180–81.

[212] In 1915, to prevent conflict around *boi* servitude in the Lushai hills during the war, the local administration called a halt to all efforts to mitigate it. F&P, External, 1923, file 522.

[213] Such semantic exercises, as Indrani Chatterjee points out, reveal the tension between official denials of the existence of servitude and the need to acknowledge its presence. Indrani Chatterjee, 'Slavery, Semantics and the Sound of Silence', in Indrani Chatterjee and Richard M. Eaton (eds), *Slavery and South Asian Society*, Bloomington: Indiana University Press, 2006, pp. 287–315.

[214] Some of the 'hill-men' enrolled in the Labour Corps for France had put down their chiefs as the heir to the gratuity given if they died on service, instead of nominating a close relative. J. H. Hutton, Deputy Commissioner in the Naga Hills, insisted on upholding this nomination, arguing that it was this understanding which 'undoubtedly contributed to inducing the chiefs to let their retainers enrol.' 1 January 1918, IOR/L/Mil/7/18302. His suggestion was implemented. See Army Instruction (India), no. 629, 18 June 1918.

the money that the lodger gained in France ... this led to modification of the custom by the courts to meet the needs of the special case.[215]

The strategy of using the authority structures of labour servitude to secure recruits but offering emancipation as a reward figured even more prominently in recruitment to the Jail Labour and Porter Corps. Prisoners were promised that satisfactory service in Mesopotamia would not only be rewarded by a remission of sentence, but also wipe out the 'convict stain'. What they hoped for was immunity from the harassing routines of police surveillance imposed on ex-convicts.[216] However, demobilisation orders stated that police and village officials were to be given advance notice of the release of men from the Jail Corps in order to ensure the safe absorption 'of this decidedly dangerous element into the civil population'.[217] The disbanding of this Corps gave the police a handy explanation for the wave of crime and unrest which swept certain towns in 1919–21.[218] Pandit Pearay Mohan, editor of the *Tribune*, blamed the unrest on harsh recruiting methods but added that the exercise of enlisting prisoners had sent them home with their 'propensities for mischief ... whetted rather than diminished by their sojourn in foreign lands.'[219]

The evanescence of war service: the labourer's lot

In the turbulent years 1919–21, the distribution of honours and rewards for war service was one of the means by which the government rallied notables to its side.[220] However, the capacity of empire to elevate those of middling or

---

[215] N. E. Parry, *A Monograph on Lushai Customs and Ceremonies*, 1928, Aizawl: Tribal Research Institute, 1974, pp. 63–65. This 'special case' applied thereafter to all cases in which the chief's dependants were recruited for a military expedition. Ibid.

[216] Some who had gone home on furlough protested against the continued imposition of the obligation to report to the police, and they were exempted. Home, Department note, 11 May 1917, Home, Jails, A, September 1917, nos 10–13.

[217] *Demobilisation Orders (India). Supplementary Instructions for Porter and Labour Corps, Enrolled Followers and Syce Corps*, Calcutta: Government Printing, 1919, paras 34, 74.

[218] The Calcutta police blamed a spurt in crime on the return of the Jail Corps. *The Pioneer Mail and Indian Weekly News*, 19 November 1920, p. 16.

[219] Pandit Pearay Mohan, *An Imaginary Rebellion and How it was Suppressed*, Lahore: Khosla Brothers, 1920, p. 31.

[220] Aravind Ganachari, 'First World War: Purchasing Indian Loyalties: Imperial Policy

humbler status who had rendered loyal service was also on display.[221] One strategy was to acknowledge the social ambitions of the Indian VCOs, pitting them conceptually against educated malcontents. In 1920 the Government of India agreed to increase VCO pensions, noting the influence that VCOs wielded and enabling them to maintain in retirement that gentlemanly status which they had acquired in the army.[222] The VCOs had overseen the rapid training of the vast number of new recruits taken on in 1917–18, and they made it very clear that they expected a substantial improvement in wages and opportunities.

However, when it came to rank and file Indian soldiers and followers the official position was that the pattern of war rewards ought to follow the line of rural hierarchy rather than disrupting it. The 'martial classes' would return to the ranks of the substantial peasantry, and followers to the stratum of the *kamin*, low-caste village artisans and labourers. This was a stance which offered many fiscal advantages. By casting the archetypal sepoy as a shareholder in the income of a family farm, government could argue that his disability pension, or the family pension if he died on service, did not have to conform to the 'living wage' which had been adopted as a norm in the UK.[223] The comparison between 'yeomen' sepoys and 'menial' followers also justified the perpetuation

---

of Recruitment and "Rewards"', *Economic and Political Weekly*, vol. 40, no. 8 (2005), pp. 779–88.

[221] 'The services of the martial classes, on whom the burden of sacrifice has fallen,' O'Dwyer thundered, 'are receiving and should continue to receive prior recognition from Government, and that as the so-called political concessions will be of less benefit to them than to other classes, we will have to look around for forms of recognition and reward which they regard as suitable and desirable.' Cited in 'Congress Report on the Punjab Disorders'. Ampthill recommended 'marked concessions' for returning Indian labourers to create a party of loyalty in every centre in India. Ampthill to General H. V. Cox, 19 April 1918, IOR/L/Mil/5/738.

[222] Viceroy to SSI, 31 March 1920, Defence, A, April 1923, nos 1903–8.

[223] The Viceroy argued that the principle of independent subsistence overlooked the sepoy's connection with the land and the 'corporate organisation of family life'. Service pensions of Rs 5/–, 6/– and 7/–, after fifteen or eighteen years, were enough for sepoys and Naiks (NCOs) because they returned to their farms at an early age. He added that too much wage variation across India made it impossible to determine the 'living wage'. Viceroy to SSI, 31 March 1920, Defence, A, April 1923, nos 1903–8.

of a class of 'lower followers'—those with wages below Rs 16/– a month, whose disability pension could be kept at three-fourths the combatant rate.[224]

The war years did see some shifts. Following discussion, it was accepted that assistant surgeons, regimental followers and the Army Bearer Corps could be considered for 'distinguished service' awards, but the size of the land grant or the *jangi inam* would be half of that provided for the combatant. 'There is a vast difference', pronounced India's Adjutant General, 'between the status of combatants and that of followers who are usually *kamins*. To treat both alike would be both unpopular and impolitic'.[225]

Government was particularly keen to avoid any long-term commitment in relation to temporary followers, among them the substantial numbers who had served in the Labour and Porter Corps. Not only were they ineligible for land grants or *jangi inams*, but if they died on service their families would receive only a one-time gratuity of Rs 300/– instead of the family pension given to permanent followers.[226] Their wound and injury pension was three-fourths the combatant rate, the same as that for permanent followers.[227] They were also excluded from third-degree injury pensions—that is, the pension

---

[224] The Adjutant General, India, wanted mule-drivers and the ambulance men of the Hospital Corps to receive the same wound and injury pensions as the sepoy, arguing that they were exposed to equal risk. 20 May 1921, Defence, A, April 1923, nos 1903–8. The decision taken was that non-combatants with a wage above Rs 16/– would get the same disability pension as combatants, and those with a wage below Rs 16/– would get a pension at three-fourths of the combatant scale. Ibid.

[225] Adjutant General, 3 August 1916, F&P, General, B, March 1919, no. 8. In Punjab, the measure of land awarded for distinguished service was two rectangles of canal colony land for a VCO, one rectangle for NCOs and rank and file soldiers, and half a rectangle for non-combatants. A rectangle was equivalent to twenty-five acres. Half a rectangle per family was also the standard allocation for certain 'untouchable' communities who had been granted some land to aid in their reclamation. This was the sole exception to the policy of never giving canal colony land grants to the *kamins*, the labouring and artisanal groups. Ali, *The Punjab Under Imperialism*, pp. 93–94.

[226] The gratuity was reduced to Rs 150/– if the recruit was enrolled but died before entry into active service.

[227] *Compendium*, pp. 404–5, para. 1456. At first the men being recruited to the ILC for France were offered a wound and injury pension at half the combatant rate, but the terms outlined on 9 March 1917 put it at three-fourths. See Assam Secretariat, Political Department, Political, B, April 1918, nos 316–499, ASA.

given in cases where the wound or injury rendered the person unfit for military service but did not prevent him 'from contributing materially towards his livelihood.'[228] Perhaps the understanding was that 'unskilled' labourers did not require a high standard of health or dexterity to make ends meet.

In general, non-combatants were more likely to profit from war rewards if they lived in areas where combatant recruitment had also clustered and where benefits were of the collective sort, such as a general remission of revenue.[229] However, recruitment for the Indian Labour and Porter Corps had taken place over a wider geographical area than combatant recruitment, so connections with officialdom were more tenuous. This is evident in the spatial distribution of soldier boards—advisory committees composed of officials and retired Indian VCOs, set up in January 1919 to investigate veteran grievances and to disburse charitable grants.[230]

Interestingly, local governments had not responded enthusiastically when proposals to set up such bodies were first floated, fearing that these would undermine the authority of the subordinate revenue bureaucracy.[231] Some retired Indian officers and ex-soldiers set up their own associations, which were later absorbed into the official soldier boards.[232] However, the Bengal government refused to set up soldier boards, even though the army's technical departments had drawn significantly upon this province. There was a reluctance to acknowledge the war services of a province associated in the official mind with a 'seditious' literati.[233] The Bihar and Orissa government decided that for 'the aboriginal tribes' so prominent in the Labour Corps, the headmen in the Santhal Parganas and missionaries in Ranchi and other districts of Chota Nagpur would suffice as an official link.[234] On much the same grounds,

---

[228] *Compendium*, p. 405, para. 1456. Also Home, Political, B, June 1917, no. 430.

[229] One reason for compiling district war histories was to locate individuals and villages who had to be acknowledged for their services. The Punjab government took control of a lot of the largesse on offer. For revenue remissions in Punjab, Delhi, and the United Provinces see Home, Political, Deposit, July 1919, no. 37.

[230] IOR/L/Mil/7/18492.

[231] Ibid.

[232] For the Saran association, see L. S. S. O'Malley, *Bihar and Orissa District Gazetteers, Saran* (revised edition, ed. A. P. Middleton), Patna: Government Printing, 1930, p. 43.

[233] IOR/L/Mil/7/18492. Despite public protests, the 49th Bengal Infantry, which had drawn upon educated Bengalis, was disbanded in August 1920.

[234] IOR/L/Mil/7/18492.

the Assam and Burma governments decided that there would be no soldier boards for the 'primitive hill-men' who had served in Labour Corps.[235] These governments, as well as that of the North-West Frontier Province, were also resistant to the introduction of the constitutional changes being contemplated for the rest of India.[236]

A nation of coolies? A nation of mercenaries?

'What has India to gain by sending her sons to fight the sordid squabbles of international financiers?'[237]

The discussion about postwar service benefits and rewards was taking place against the backdrop of sharp criticism in political forums about the continued burden of military expenditure and the use of Indian troops in Egypt and Mesopotamia to suppress uprisings against British occupation, and internally to suppress labour strikes and protests against the Rowlatt Act.[238] Many Indian newspapers pointed out that the deployment of Indian soldiers had not secured settler rights for Indians in East Africa, South Africa, or, more recently, in Mesopotamia.[239] They rejected the contention that Indian troops

---

[235] The North-West Frontier Province government was initially opposed to the constitution of a soldier board, but relented on the grounds of the 'good behavior' of the province during the Third Afghan War and the Waziristan campaign. The NWFP was also excluded from the 1919 Government of India Act, on the basis that it was too turbulent an area and that the *jirga*, a council of tribal elders, was the more appropriate form of representation.

[236] However, some subordinate Naga employees embraced a modern form of associational life by setting up a 'club' at Kohima, possibly in January 1918. Members would submit a statement to the Simon Commission in 1929 asking for the Nagas to be left alone to shape their own destiny rather than be included in the new constitution being formulated.

[237] *The Bombay Chronicle*, 30 June 1920, in *RNPB*, no. 27, 3 July 1920.

[238] For sharp criticism, see *Abhudaya*, 7–8 March 1919, in *Selections, UP*, no. 11, 15 March 1919; and *Shakti*, 11 March 1919, in *Selections, UP*, no. 12, 22 March 1919. '[H]as not the sepoy been used to murder innocent people at Jallianwala Bagh ... at Chandpur ... to subjugate the proud Arab or Mesopotamia ... to crush the Egyptian?' M. K. Gandhi, 'Tampering with Loyalty', *Young India*, 29 September 1921, in Home, Political, 1921, no. 303.

[239] *RNPB*, no. 27, 3 July 1920, p. 26; *RNPB*, no. 31, 2 October 1921. The *Vakil* pronounced it disgraceful that Indian troops were employed in Mesopotamia and

were stationed in Persia and Mesopotamia to ensure the safety of routes to India. 'Why should Indians die in these lands,' editorialised the *Mahratta*, 'earning dividends for oil-speculators and dishonour for their country men?'[240] Punching hard, it pronounced, 'The use of our soldiers to trample down freedom in the Near and Middle East brands us as a nation of mercenaries in the eyes of our Asiatic fellow-brethren as we have already been branded now as a nation of coolies by the British colonies.'[241] From Lahore, the *Zamindar* wrote: 'judging from estimated military expenditure India appears to be at war with the whole world.' War posters, it noted, said every rupee contributed to the war loan would be turned into a bullet with which to strike the Germans. However, it predicted that '[o]ur money will now be showered on our own heads in the form of bullets.'[242]

Hopes of Wilsonian internationalism withered rapidly, and vernacular papers denounced the League of Nations mandate system as a mere front for British and French imperialism.[243] Pamphlets urging Indian soldiers to rally to the cause of preserving the Sultan's sovereignty over Islamic lands were found in far-flung outposts of empire. Muslim soldiers and labourers returning home in 1920–21 would be reproached by figures in the Khilafat movement for aiding in the transfer of Arabia and Mesopotamia to 'Christian' rule.[244] We also catch the occasional glimpse of an Indian officer or soldier raising subscriptions for the Khilafat fund—an activity government was loath to punish, because it was presented as the right of loyal Muslims to petition for the redress of a religious grievance.[245]

Egypt. 'They had conquered East Africa, but today there is very little difference between [the] condition of Indians there and that of animals.' *PPA*, no. 5, 29 January 1921 p. 54.

[240] *Mahratta*, 15 August 1920, in *RNPB*, no. 31, 31 July 1920, p. 22; and 7 July 1920, in *RNPB*, no. 28, 10 July 1920, p. 9. The *Bombay Chronicle* called insistently for the recall of Indian soldiers from Turkey, Mesopotamia and Persia. *RNPB*, no. 31, 31 July 1920; and no. 36, 4 September 1920.

[241] Home, Political, A, August 1920, no. 112.

[242] *Zamindar*, 9 March 1921, *PPA*, no. 11, 12 March 1921, p. 113.

[243] A 'League of Thugs', declared the *Bande Mataram*, *PPA*, no. 8, 19 February 1921.

[244] In September 1920, returning from overseas service, men of the 127th Baluch Infantry found some family members had responded to the Khilafat call to migrate to Afghanistan. Orders posting this regiment to the North-West Frontier were hurriedly cancelled. Woodyatt, *Under Ten Viceroys*, p. 284.

[245] A Muslim officer of the Mysore princely state contingent who publicly auctioned

Gandhi and other Indian leaders were realising that India's aspirations to self-government had to find a place on the anti-imperialist platforms emerging the world over. 'Asia' became the geographic label under which they aligned their quest for self-government with struggles for autonomy in Persia, Iraq, Egypt and Afghanistan.[246] It was in this context that leaders of the Khilafat movement and Gandhi invited military and police personnel to think about the politics of their deployment.[247] In demanding the restoration of Ottoman rule over Islamic holy sites and Muslim-majority populations, many Khilafat leaders accepted that constitutional changes would have to be introduced to give Arab provinces greater autonomy.[248] Gandhi pointed out that Arab aspi-

---

his watch for the Khilafat fund was given a personal warning. Palace Papers, file 67 of 1920, SL, nos 1–5, KSA. More problematically, a few ex-servicemen were sighted drilling volunteers for the Khilafat and non-cooperation movements. Shahid Amin gives a vivid sketch of Bhagwan Ahir, who had served as a follower in Mesopotamia, began to drill Congress volunteers, and would be sent to the gallows for a clash in February 1922 which led to the burning alive of twenty-one policemen at Chauri Chaura, Gorakhpur. Shahid Amin, *Event, Metaphor, Memory: Chauri Chaura, 1922–1992*, Berkeley: University of California Press, 1995, pp. 80–81.

[246] See Carolien Stolte and Harald Fischer-Tiné's insightful assessment of the Khilafat movement as a postwar form of Pan-Asianism, conceptualised around the idea of an Asia in which India could link her aspirations to self-determination with West Asia and Central Asia. Carolien Stolte and Harald Fischer-Tiné, 'Imagining Asia in India: Nationalism and Internationalism (ca. 1905–1940)', *Comparative Studies in Society and History*, vol. 54, no. 1 (2012), pp. 65–92.

[247] 'Apart from the question of the Khilafat', wrote Gandhi, 'and from the point of abstract justice, the English have no right to hold Mesopotamia.' Indians, he argued, ought to see that the source of their livelihood was not tainted. *Young India*, 30 June 1920. The Nagpur session of the Indian National Congress of December 1920 called upon 'military, clerical and labour classes' not to offer themselves for service in Mesopotamia, but it did not call upon serving personnel to resign.

[248] See appeal of the Muslim League deputation to the British Premier in *Muslim India and Islamic Review*, vol. VII, no. 10 (1919), pp. 370–73. Historians such as A. C. Niemeijer note such pronouncements but assess them as a contradiction in terms. A Khilafat meeting of 20 March 1920 in Madras hoped that peace terms would ensure the suzerainty of the Sultan-Khalifa over the 'federated autonomous Muslim states' of Arabia, Syria, Palestine and Mesopotamia. At Paris, the Khilafat leader, Muhammad Ali, stated that in calling for *status quo ante bellum*, he was not ruling out political changes to secure autonomous development for non-Turkish races, Muslims, Christians or Jews. Muhammad Ali, 'India's Message to France',

rations to self-government were compatible with the continuation of Ottoman suzerainty, just as Indian demands for self-government were compatible with continued membership of the British Empire.[249] However, for Gandhi, the most important reason for supporting the Khilafat cause was the nature of the nation state which was to be brought into being. Since Muslims of India were stricken by the fate befalling the holy places of Islam, Hindus were bound to rally to their support. Empathy would forge that affective bond between the two major cohabitants of the space of the nation, which would infuse the demand for self-government with irresistible strength. Therefore, when the Central Khilafat Committee decided on 23–24 November 1919 to boycott the peace celebrations planned for December 1919, Gandhi supported the decision.[250]

Nevertheless, some Congress leaders were ambivalent about what the mobilisation of transnational Muslim publics would mean for the political balance of power in postwar India. Lala Lajpat Rai held that 'any further extension of the British empire in Asia is detrimental to the interests of India and fatal to the liberties of the human race.' However, the reasons he gave for this were different from Gandhi's. Lajpat Rai's argument was that while the deployment of non-European troops in Europe 'had abolished an invidious bar', it had also widened the scope of British militarism. If Britain used Indian troops in Egypt, Persia, Arabia, Syria and Central Asia, it could also use soldiers from these territories in India, with the result that '[t]he Hindu Muslim problem will become ten times more troublesome'. Secondly, if Muslim populations in these territories continued to resist British occupation, the Indian Army would be in constant use, draining India's human and economic resources.[251]

---

21 March 1920, in A. C. Niemeijer, *The Khilafat Movement in India, 1919–1924*, The Hague: Nijhoff, 1972, pp. 97–98 and p. 216, n. 87.

[249] *TOI*, 10 April 1920 and 12 April 1920.

[250] To underline this, Gandhi held that the 'Punjab atrocities' should not be linked to the Khilafat issue as a reason for the decision. Speech at Khilafat Conference, Delhi, 24 November 1919, *Bombay Chronicle*, 6 December 1919, pp. 136–42. However, the two issues did merge in his subsequent speeches and in Congress resolutions. Home, Political, file no. 303/1921.

[251] Presidential address, Indian National Congress, Calcutta, 4 September 1920, in *Lala Lajpat Rai: Writings and Speeches*, ed. Vijaya Chandra Joshi, vol. II, Delhi: University Publishers, 1966, pp. 38–41.

It was in India's interests, therefore, that the Muslim countries of West Asia remained independent.[252]

Commemoration and counter-commemoration

Following the signing of the Treaty of Versailles on 28 June 1919, Peace Celebration Day was fixed for 19 July 1919 in the UK. With the Jallianwala Bagh massacre and official atrocity still fresh in public memory, the Government of India used the excuse of the hot weather to postpone celebrations until December 1919. The felicitation of officials who had raised men and resources for the war in a very high-handed way had already become a contentious issue.[253] In addition, the fact that drought and influenza were afflicting India gave an edge to criticisms of the peace celebration.[254] Officials made it clear to Indian notables that they were expected to make the celebrations a success, but the programme also took on a sober, pious cast, with religious gatherings, the distribution of charity, and the collection of contributions for disabled soldiers figuring prominently.[255] What followed were battles within many municipal committees over the allocation of funds for the event.[256] Congress and Khilafat leaders pressured the public not to participate, asking beggars, for instance, not to accept the food being distributed. In a pamphlet titled *Loyal Efforts Made Celebrations a Success*, one municipal

---

[252] Ibid.

[253] A mass gathering at Bombay Town Hall on 11 December 1918 obstructed the Municipal Committee from felicitating the outgoing governor, Lord Willingdon, on the grounds of his discourtesy to the nationalist icon Bal Gangadhar Tilak. Muhammad Ali Jinnah was honoured for his role in this protest by the construction of Memorial Hall in the Congress complex at Bombay. In Punjab, the vernacular press criticised the collection of a memorial fund in 1919 to honour the Punjab governor Michael O'Dwyer, who had turned the province into a war machine. The following year, a Jallianwala Bagh Trust was set up to preserve, as a national memorial, the site where the military fired on civilians during his governorship.

[254] See *RNPB*, no. 1, 3 January 1920, pp. 5–7.

[255] Home, Public, B, March 1920, nos 58–59.

[256] M. Naeem Qureshi, *Pan-Islam in British Indian Politics: A Study of the Khilafat Movement, 1918–1924*, Leiden: Brill, 1999, pp. 131–33. The Secretary of State for India complained of receiving virtually no information about peace celebrations in India. Home, Political, Deposit, January 1920, no. 42.

councillor declared triumphantly that he had nevertheless managed to give alms to 1,100 beggars.[257]

The transformation of imperial civic rituals into national ones, as explored by Douglas E. Haynes, left its trace on many autobiographies.[258] Recalling his schoolboy years, Prakash Tandon spoke of his enjoyment of events such as Victory Day—that is, Peace Celebration Day—and the visit of the Duke of Connaught in 1921. However, he felt that there was a lack of meaning to such events, whereas Gandhi's invocation of *Bharat Mata* and Muslim leaders' references to *Madar-i-Hind* and the Khilafat tapped into a deep emotional seam.[259] Of the boycott of the Prince of Wales's visit to India in 1921, the Bombay correspondent of the *Manchester Guardian* wrote: 'The days are gone by when a royal visit to India was merely a delightful ceremony. In every municipality, the exact measure of hospitality to be shown has been hotly debated. Every act of homage is a real bending of the political will.'[260]

In 1916–17, Congress and Muslim League leaders had lauded the sacrifices of Indian soldiers for making Britain readier to negotiate with demands for self-government within empire.[261] Over 1920–21, the conflict over the use of India's military manpower resulted in the narrowing down of war commemoration to a 'soldier's ceremony'. This was the phrase used by the Duke of Connaught when he laid the foundation stone for the All India War Memorial

---

[257] Kazi Fakhurdin, *Loyal Efforts Made Celebrations Success*, Hyderabad, Sindh: Standard Printing Works, 1920, British Library pamphlets. The distribution of grants from the Imperial Indian Relief Fund to injured soldiers and destitute soldier families was made a conspicuous feature of Peace Celebration Day. *India's Services in the War*, Bengal, vol. IV, Lucknow: Newul Kishore Press, 1922, p. 22.

[258] Douglas E. Haynes, *Rhetoric and Ritual in Colonial India: The Shaping of a Public Culture in Surat City, 1852–1928*, Berkeley: University of California Press, 1991, pp. 213–14.

[259] Prakash Tandon, *Punjabi Century, 1857–1947*, Berkeley; Los Angeles: University of California Press, 1968, pp. 19–21.

[260] Cited in Evelyn Roy, 'The Crisis in Indian Nationalism', in *The Labour Monthly*, vol. 2, no. 2 (1922), pp. 146–57, 149.

[261] 'The Indian soldiers have saved the lives of the British soldier on the French battlefield ... Those who once considered us slaves have begun to call us brothers ... We must push our demand while this notion of brotherhood is existing'. Bal Gangadhar Tilak, leader of the Home Rule movement, Nasik Conference, 1917, *Bal Gangadhar Tilak: His Writings and Speeches*, Madras: Ganesh and Co., 1922, p. 241.

in Delhi on 10 February 1921.[262] The tour programme of the Prince of Wales in 1921–22, boycotted by Congress and the Khilafat committee, included at every point public meetings with ex-soldiers and pensioners, with special mention made of the disabled among them.[263]

Even so, as Jay Winter points out, the history of commemoration plays out at many levels, and the national is not necessarily the most significant or the most enduring.[264] It was the kindness of one of their officers, Maynard Mansfield Knight, which the men of the 1st Madras Labour Corps honoured when they paid for a memorial plaque to him in St Bartholomew's Church, Bobbing.[265] Knight's entries in this unit's war diary give us a tangible sense of the suffering imposed on his men by work conditions on the Khanikin railway. Yet just eleven days before his death from influenza at Mirgana he had noted, 'in all my experience have not met so willing a lot of labour.'[266]

Most Indian labourers melted away from official attention on their return home. Transfrontier Pashtun labourers who had served in France returned to India under a cloud of suspicion because of turbulence on the North-West Frontier.[267] In the Assam hill districts the local administration made a conspicuous effort to celebrate the return of the Labour Corps from France. However, commemorative activity only resonated over time if it found a local niche. At Tura in the Garo hills, the date chosen for the celebration of Labour Corps Day

[262] *India's Contribution to the Great War*, Calcutta: Superintendent Government Printing Press, 1923, p. 261.

[263] M. O'Mealey (ed.), *His Royal Highness the Prince of Wales' Tour in India, 1921–1922*, Delhi: Foreign and Political Department, Government of India, 1923, pp. 37, 95, 115, 413, 423.

[264] Jay Winter, 'Remembrance and Redemption', *Harvard Design Magazine*, no. 9 (1999), http://www.harvarddesignmagazine.org/issues/9/remembrance-and-redemption, last accessed 10 November 2019.

[265] 'Memorials located within the Borough of Swale, Kent', Historical Research Group of Sittingbourne, http://www.hrgs.co.uk/wp-content/uploads/2017/10/Swale-memorials-list-as-at-2.3.2017.pdf, last accessed 10 November 2019.

[266] TNA WO 95/5277.

[267] Ampthill had resisted the suggestion that the Pashtuns in the Indian Labour Corps be 'surreptitiously detained in France' to check accounts of the spring offensive spreading along the North-West Frontier. He pointed out that the men were consumed with anxiety about their families and property and that government had promised repatriation at the end of their contract. Ampthill to H. V. Cox, 24 April 1918, IOR/L/Mil/5/738l.

is 16 July, the day the men of the Garo labour company returned to the town from which they had set out. It is a date of local and not imperial significance.[268] For the missionary Robert Johnson, a pond at Haka, constructed through punitive labour after the crushing of the Chin uprising, was a 'tangible memorial to justice'. But the villagers who pointed it out to him said: 'This is our lake, and it was made by the villages from Sakta and other places when they fought the British.'[269] A mark of retribution had been appropriated as a memorial to resistance. Johnson suggested a third, more conciliatory location for it in memory: 'Its chief glory may be that it was the site of baptismal service in 1949, the 50th anniversary of Christian mission among the Chin.'[270]

In western India, the Maharaja of Kolhapur, one of the iconic figures of a peasant-pastoralist-based movement for political and social advance, prevailed upon the Prince of Wales to inaugurate on 19 November 1921 not only the official Maratha War Memorial at Pune, but also the Chhatrapati Shivaji Maharaj Memorial, a statue of the seventeenth-century hero positioned within a student dormitory complex.[271] Welcoming the Prince, the Maharaja declared that it was the British Raj which had opened the doors of learning for Marathas. Now that Marathas had proven themselves in the field, they had to fit themselves for the Council Chamber.[272]

Conclusion

This chapter has drawn upon the literature which assesses demobilisation not as an event but as a process shaped by a variety of different interven-

---

[268] Garo Labour Corps Day remained on the official calendar. 'Garo Labour Corps Recruits Remembered on 100th Anniversary', *The Shillong Times*, 16 July 2018, www.theshillongtimes.com/2018/07/16/garo-labour-corps-recruits-remembered-on-100th-anniversary/, last accessed 17 November 2019.

[269] Robert G. Johnson, *History of the American Baptist Chin Mission*, vol. 1, Valley Forge, PA: R. G. Johnson, 1988, p. 408.

[270] Ibid.

[271] A. B. Latthe, *Memoirs of His Highness Shri Shahu Chhatrapati Maharaja of Kolhapur*, vol. II, Bombay: Times Press, 1924. During the siege at Kut al-Amara, Mesopotamia, when Indian soldiers had to be persuaded to eat horse or mule flesh, the Maratha regiments, which included 'not merely the Mahratta caste, but allied castes such as the Dhangars, Parits, Dhobis &c., would listen only [to] their social leader the Chhatrapati of Kohlapur.' Ibid., pp. 400–4.

[272] *His Royal Highness the Prince of Wales' Tour in India, 1921–22*, p. 14.

tions.[273] Within the fiction of a clear periodisation of World War One, shorter and longer phases which shaped the war experience of many participants are discernible. In India, a clear transition to peace was muddied by the longue durée of imperial militarism. Nevertheless, conserving the traces of their encounter with the 'European Great War' was of crucial significance for those who hoped to have something to show for it.

Military accounts trailed behind the hectic expansion of the Indian Army, and files were misplaced during the closure of many recruiting depots in 1922.[274] Temporary followers were particularly disadvantaged, because in the early stages of the war many had been sent off to Mesopotamia without being enrolled. Turning out wearing a medal and some item of military clothing or securing an officer's testimonial were ways of getting a hearing.[275] To contain

---

[273] Adam R. Seipp, *The Ordeal of Peace: Demobilization and the Urban Experience in Britain and Germany, 1917–1921*, Farnham: Ashgate, 2009.

[274] Units were instructed to compile a register of pensioners to curtail the great delay in settling claims. Army Instruction (India), no. 346 of 1922, in *Indian Army Orders, His Excellency the Commander-in-Chief in India*, 1922, p. 393. An Indian Army Reserve Officer commented on the inadequacy of the casualty record in regimental diaries, particularly of those who died in hospital of wounds or disease. 'Preface' in W. S. Thatcher, *The Fourth Battalion Duke of Connaught's Own Tenth Baluch Regiment in the Great War*, Naval and Military Press, 2009, pp. xviii-xix. In distributing one-time charitable grants to soldiers' families, district officers used the casualty list forwarded by the Indian Soldier's Board, but they also accepted cases brought to their notice in other ways. *India's Services in the War*, Madras, vol. IV, Lucknow: Newal Kishore Press, 1922, p. 23.

[275] F. O. Fowler, the Deputy Commissioner who went with the Chin Labour companies to France, composed the following testimonial: 'This Certificate is given to _____ who enrolled voluntarily as a mate in the Burma Labour Corps and worked in France for the British Government during the great war. He worked loyally and well in all; whether by night as well as by day and every advance and often dangerous condition and willingly and cheerfully bore his share of the burdens of the day. This fact should ever be remembered to his credit by those who have any dealings with him and may all officials deal with him and his family in a liberal way for he who placed his service at the disposed of the empire in its hour of stress may he and his family never be forgotten'. Salai Van Cung Lian, 'Chin Involvement in World War 1', *Burma News International*, 15 November 2014, https://www.bnionline.net/en/chin-world/item/17872-chin-involvement-in-world-war-1-the-great-war.html, last accessed 11 November 2019.

its financial commitments, the government set a timeline for the making of pensionary or other claims. To extend these dates, soldiers and their families cited the 'unknowability' of the effects of a uniquely terrible war and the injustice of shifting the burden of proof to their shoulders.[276]

The scenes projected by the Reverend McMillan's magic lantern had taken labourers and soldiers from their homes and cultural environments into the expanse of empire, cultivating a new imagination of the world and their place in it. Now, for subordinate Indian personnel carrying on in post-Armistice Mesopotamia, empire materialised in the infrastructures of occupation that they had helped to put in place. Some threatened a strike in 1921 because when they went on leave to India, the increased pay for extending their service in Mesopotamia was withheld. Rattling off a list of acronyms, their anonymous petition threw out a challenge: 'What considerations have you given for our welfare, we who have worked so hard through fair and foul weather, without [whom] some directorates (especially WD, E&M, and IWT) would not now be existing?'[277] War propaganda had invited Indian subjects to embrace the 'we' of empire.[278] This 'we' now demanded proper compensation for lives distributed between sites of familial habitation and imperial service.

The question recurrently posed in assessments of demobilisation is whether the war experience of colonial soldiers and labourers sent them home with an outlook receptive to nationalist agendas.[279] Scholars have nuanced their

---

[276] 'How far is a Nation justified in taking men of a Foreign Nation to a fierce and scientific war, like the European Great War, get them disabled, and when they ask for some pension, to State to escape their liability the simple plea of time-limit.' *Coloured Victims of the Great War*, p. 13, para. 36, and p. 28, para. 92.

[277] 'The poor sufferers of Mesopotamia', anonymous petition, n.d., Home, Political, 1922, file 51/2. The Works Department, the Electrical and Mechanical Department, and the Inland Water Transport.

[278] The appropriation by Indians of the 'we' of empire was noted in other contexts, but with amusement. A British officer on board a hospital ship commented on 'that surprising change in the Indian vernacular whereby their speech is no longer of "Gooralog" and "Sahib-log" but of "we" which fraternal pronoun is significant of so much.' John Hartman Morgan, *Leaves From a Field Note-Book*, London: Macmillan, 1916, p. 39.

[279] For a fresh approach see Richard S. Fogarty and David Killingray, 'Demobilization in British and French Africa at the End of the First World War', *Journal of Contemporary History*, vol. 50, no. 1 (2014), pp. 100–23.

answer by pointing out that anti-imperialist perspectives crystallised not only in national frames, but from regional and transnational positions as well.[280] Among the diverse political publics emerging in India, there were also those which did not take a directly oppositional attitude to the colonial regime.

Indian notables drew upon the services of soldiers from their community to advance their agendas, but they also had to take up veteran issues.[281] Government officials began to address veterans as a political constituency, one which had to be shaped as a force for order and loyalty. The government decided to give all ex-soldiers the franchise, overriding the property criteria of the new constitution of 1919.[282] Instead of assuming that military personnel were indifferent to politics, it tried to shape their opinion. Indian soldiers who formed part of the army of occupation in Egypt were given an opportunity to learn to read and write, and parties of Muslim soldiers were sent to Mecca to dispel rumours that the holy city was under British occupation.[283] The Punjab government deployed British and Indian officers to hold discussions in recruiting districts with village headmen and ex-soldiers, reassuring them that the Rowlatt Act was meant to protect faithful employees against vindictive reprisals, that the Afghan war was going well, and that the harsh terms imposed on Turkey had no religious implications.[284] However, while the

---

[280] Sugata Bose, 'Nation, Reason and Religion: India's Independence in International Perspective', *Economic and Political Weekly*, vol. 33, no. 31 (1998), pp. 2090–97.

[281] Sikh notables leveraged the war services of Sikh soldiers to get reserved seats for Sikhs in the Punjab Provincial Assembly. The Montagu-Chelmsford report said that it disapproved of communal electorates, but these had to be continued for Muslims, who had remained loyal in difficult circumstances; and they had to be given to the Sikhs of Punjab, 'a distinct and important people; they supply a gallant and valuable element to the Indian army; but they are everywhere in a minority, and experience has shown that they virtually go unrepresented.' *Report on Indian Constitutional Reform*, London: HMSO, 1918, p. 189.

[282] J. S. Meston, Finance Member to Military Secretary, to Commander-in-Chief, India, 7 December 1918, J. S. Meston, Mss, 4/3, pt II, Cambridge South Asia Archives. Tan Tai Yong, *The Garrison State: Military, Government and Society in Colonial Punjab, 1849–1947*, New Delhi: Sage, 2005, p. 259.

[283] Lind, *A Record of the 58th Rifles F. F.*, p. 116. *The Pioneer Mail and Indian Weekly News*, 1 October 1920, p. 2; IOR/L/Mil/6/18610.

[284] Home, Political, A, May 1919, nos 619–40; Home, Political, Deposit, January 1920, no. 76; Home, Political, Deposit, December 1920, no. 28.

government reached down to shape veteran opinion, aspirations and grievances also percolated upwards.[285]

The interface between regimental identities and the new political publics
emerging in India put the postwar government under immense pressure in two
instances—the Akali movement to take over *gurdwaras* (shrines) for a purist
order of Sikhism, and the Khilafat movement. The Punjab government was
eventually compelled to negotiate with the Akali movement in 1925 because
of the support it gathered among Sikh soldiers and in Sikh recruiting districts.[286] For somewhat similar reasons, but with less room for manoeuvre,
Viceroys Chelmsford and Reading felt they had to plead with Whitehall in
1919–20 to soften the harsh treaty terms emerging for the Ottoman Sultan.
Wartime propaganda had often made the point that, going by the number of
Muslims in its fold, Britain was the 'largest Mohammedan empire in the world',
larger by far than Turkey.[287] Now Khilafat spokesmen used the same rhetoric
of 'composite empire' to appeal for the restoration of the Sultan-Caliph's suzerainty over holy sites in Arabia, Mesopotamia and Constantinople. They said
that Muslim soldiers had fought for empire because they had been assured
that holy landscapes would remain safe for Muslim ecumenae. Would their
deaths in these territories now be rendered unholy?[288] Anxious not to 'create
martyrs' among Muslim soldiers, the Home Department restrained the Army
Department from harsh action, even when it reported that Indian troops as

---

[285] Thus one army officer reported back that 'the masses' felt government had been
'grossly ungrateful' in not announcing some general war boon. Home, Political,
Deposit, July 1919, no. 37. See also Home, Political, Deposit, January 1920, no. 76;
Home, Political, Deposit, December 1920, no. 28.

[286] Tan Tai Yong, 'Assuaging the Sikhs: Government Responses to the Akali Movement,
1920–1925', *Modern Asian Studies*, vol. 29, no. 3 (1995), pp. 655–703. 'Akali
Trouble: Pensioners' Representation', *TOI*, 11 November 1922, p. 13.

[287] See the startling visual illustration 1 comparing the demographic heft of
'Mohammedans' in the British, Ottoman and French empires. From G. A. Natesan
(ed.), *All About the War: The Indian Review War Book*, Madras: Natesan and Co.,
1915, p. 208.

[288] Some Khilafat speakers said that the bodies of those who had died fighting the Turks
had turned into the 'unclean' pig. *The Historic Trial of the Ali Brothers*, part I,
Karachi: New Times Office, 1921, exhibit 48, pp. 11–13; also Maulvi Hamid, at
Kahnaur, on 7 July 1921, in Home, Political, 1921, nos 1–303, appendix. A Muslim
soldier returning from Mesopotamia was refused a burial when he died in Bombay.
Some pensioned officers were called *kafirs* (infidels) for wearing medals. Ibid.

far afield as China had received Khilafat pamphlets and posters.[289] So insistent was Montagu that Muslim subjects had to be mollified that Lloyd George declared his attitude was not so much that of a member of the British cabinet as that 'of a successor on the throne of Aurangzeb!'[290]

* * *

Histories moving through the milestones of the Indian nationalist movement often skim over the war years to dwell at length upon the 'postwar' upheavals of 1919–21. The discontent of demobilised soldiers is added to the mix, but almost as a presumptive factor.[291] This book has tried to recapture the war as it was experienced by those who had been recruited in the follower ranks, reshaped for military use, and repositioned at worksites within India and overseas. The logistical management of war, and the compulsion which emerged to use different categories of colonial manpower in a more rational way, did not overthrow race and status segmentation in military work, but it unsettled hierarchies. War service left its mark on minds, bodies and families, but it also emerged as a resource which was tapped by Indian notables and community spokesmen to stake their claims on the postwar order. However, returning soldiers and followers also sought, not always successfully, something to show for their war service. This could take the form of coins to be turned into marriage ornaments, savings to be used for a bride price, a 'rubber' leg which testified to a war injury, a testimonial which spoke of faithful service by a cook or valet, or a discharge certificate to leverage an exemption from

---

[289] From Basra, a Muslim transport driver had been sharing his forebodings about the Christianisation of Jazirat-al-Arab with the charismatic Khilafat leader Shaukat Ali. Home, Political, A, February 1921, nos 341–54. The susceptibility of Indian soldiers posted at Egypt, Arabia, or Istanbul to local anti-British sentiment was also a source of concern.

[290] Timothy J. Paris, *Britain, the Hashemites and Arab Rule, 1920–1925: The Sherifian Solution*, London: Frank Cass, 2003, p. 461.

[291] Among the reasons given by the 1918 Sedition Committee report for postwar measures to prevent 'anarchical and revolutionary conspiracies' in India was the speculation that 'there will, especially in the Punjab, be a large number of disbanded soldiers, among whom it may be possible to stir up discontent.' *Sedition Committee Report*, 1918, p. 195. Madan Mohan Malaviya criticised this hypothesis for devaluing the sacrifices of the Punjabi soldier. H. N. Mittra (ed.), *Punjab Unrest, Before and After*, Calcutta: N. N. Mitter, 1920, p. 30.

forced labour. But the story of the war as experienced by muleteers, stretcher-bearers, 'menial' followers, and the men of the Labour and Porter Corps was also linked in subtle ways to larger visions of the nature of the postwar order.

AFTERWORD

LABOUR INSIDE AND OUTSIDE THE ARMY

This book has explored the exercises of power and the representations of the natural and social world through which bodies materialised as white and coloured soldiers, white and coloured labourers, martial races and menial followers. The exigencies of the war destabilised these representations—so, too, did the lived experience of those who engaged in 'war work', thereby bringing other identities and expectations into play. The mental and physical capacities of these different bodies were measured against each other, and in the process new imaginaries of 'military efficiency' and 'labour efficiency' emerged. I am not suggesting that clear parallels were being drawn between the domains of military work and industrial work, only that there was an ongoing discussion in both spheres about the need to conserve labour and improve its efficiency, along with a growing confidence that advances in scientific knowledge about physiology, nutrition, sanitation, and fatigue would allow deficiencies of race and climate in 'coloured' manpower to be reduced, if never quite overcome.

One of the key tenets of war propaganda was the assertion that the ruling race had the ability to make use of different races and castes, at different levels of civilisation, with different skills and dispositions, and then to send them back as assets to the society from which they had been drawn. The military frame offered 'order, continuity, routine', disciplining unruly British workers, turning 'raw coolies and bazaar scum' into efficient auxiliary units, and teaching backward races the use of better technologies, even if the actual working of these technologies was held to be beyond their understanding.[1] Britain herself would benefit: she had in her dependent colonies

---

[1] Edmund Candler, *The Sepoy*, London: John Murray, 1919, p. 233; Radhika Singha,

latent powers of human productivity and resources of agricultural, forest and mineral wealth which, scientifically used, would restore Britain's postwar commercial standing. At play was both a racialised discourse about comparative 'labour efficiency' and a sense that recalibrations were possible.

Labour efficiency in industry

For a striking illustration of this, we turn to Younghusband's appraisal of India's contribution to the war in *The Empire at War*, a multi-volume compilation sponsored by the Royal Colonial Institute to record 'the effort made in the late war by every unit of the overseas Empire'.[2] Britain, claimed Younghusband, had not enjoyed any advantage over Germany through the possession of India's human and natural resources: 'The Indian peoples, though numerous, have not the physical or mental energy of the Central Europeans and they lack too the initiative and resource as well as organising capacity.' India was essentially agricultural; labour of the quality required for the production of war material hardly existed outside a few establishments; and the average workman was 'of a low education standard' and possessed only 'a primitive knowledge of his craft', with no ambition to acquire knowledge of modern workshop methods and practices. Out of a population of 320 million, India put hardly 1 million into the field. 'Still', he concluded kindly, 'for India it was magnificent.'[3]

However, when Younghusband speculated about what prewar India might have looked like as seen through the covetous eyes of Germany, he described an underdeveloped country where agriculture was inefficient, communications were insufficient, and minerals and forest inadequately exploited. The foe might therefore reach the conclusion that the replacement of a 'sluggish British administration' would increase production in every way.[4] In short, even those who held that India's war contribution was unsatisfactory were

---

'Front Lines and Status Lines: Sepoy and "Menial" in the Great War, 1916–1920', in Heike Liebau, Katrin Bromber, Katharina Lange, Dyala Hamzah and Ravi Ahuja (eds), *The World in World Wars: Experiences, Perceptions and Perspectives from Africa and Asia*, Leiden: Brill, 2010, pp. 55–106, 62, 79, 80–83, 101–105. 'An Army of Labour', *The Times*, 27 December 1917, p. 8.

[2] Francis Younghusband, 'India', in Sir Charles Lucas (ed.), *The Empire at War*, vol. 5, London: Oxford University Press, 1926, p. 193.

[3] Ibid.

[4] Ibid., pp. 154–55.

pushed into the embarrassing admission that much more could have been done to develop her usefulness to empire. At Shimla, the summer capital of the Raj, Edwin Montagu, the Secretary of State for India, noted in his diary, 'it is so jolly to see daffodils, lilac, wisteria, pansies, banksia, roses, but oh, the rickshaws, I hate them more and more.'[5] And, again, 'when I see rickshaws and coolies showing that the water power has never been used, how neglectful we have been of the industrial improvement of India.'[6]

Indian political figures and newspapers did not let such admissions lurk in the background.[7] Even staunch loyalists did not hold back. If the industrial sector had not been suppressed, and if spending on education and public health had not been dwarfed by military expenditure, then India would have been able to give much more assistance during the war. After all, remarked the Aga Khan, the landless labourer who was 'little more than skin and bones' could not be sent to fight.[8] A point made repeatedly was that the Government of India's refusal to give up on 'Manchester principles' and assist Indian industry with tariff protection was responsible for the critical shortfall in munitions and other war material when imports from Britain were disrupted.

In Younghusband's comments there is an echo of the deliberations of the Indian Industrial Commission, which was set up in 1916 to offer suggestions on how government might best encourage industrial expansion in India.[9] Its report, submitted in 1918, conceded that 'the deficiencies in her [India's] industrial system ... render her liable to foreign penetration in time of peace and to serious dangers in time of war.'[10] However, it distributed the blame: 'Her labour is inefficient ... her intelligentsia have yet to develop a right tradition of industrialism. Her stores of money lie inert and idle.'[11]

---

[5] Entries of 19 April 1918 and 22 April 1918, in E. S. Montagu, *An Indian Diary* (ed. Venetia Montagu), London: W. Heinemann, 1930, p. 368.

[6] Ibid.

[7] 'Bureaucratic inefficiency', *The Tribune*, 8 January 1918, p. 2.

[8] The Aga Khan, *India in Transition: A Study in Political Evolution*, London: Philip Lee Warner, 1918, p. 289.

[9] *Indian Industrial Commission Report, 1916–1918*, Calcutta: Government Printing, 1918. The appointment of one of the members of the commission, Sir Thomas Holland, to the Munitions Board to deal with the shortfall in war material gave weight to its deliberations.

[10] *Indian Industrial Commission Report*, p. 4.

[11] Ibid.

The report had a short section on 'labour efficiency', which began with the statement that if the efficiency of Indian labourers was much lower than that of their western counterparts, it was partly due to 'inferior physique and tropical conditions'.[12] However, there was room for improvement. Higher wages, it went on, were not the answer. Labourers' standard of comfort was so low, their aspirations so limited to the desire to return to their village, that higher wages, far from improving their productivity, would increase instability at the workplace.[13] The report clearly subscribed to the prevailing notion that the Indian mill-hand was insufficiently committed to industrial and urban life.[14] Having reassured employers that it was not going to recommend higher wages, the Commission advocated shorter working hours, better sanitation, and measures against 'preventable disease' to raise labour productivity.[15] Its support for shorter work hours was clearly influenced by the interest being taken by the British and Indian press in the topic of 'industrial fatigue'—namely, the idea that the body's ability to turn energy into work was measurable, and that beyond a certain point fatigue resulted in diminished output.[16] A reduction in factory hours could therefore be recommended from a position of seeming objectivity—the vitality of the worker would be preserved and output would increase.[17] The point of debate was, of course, whether the same criteria which

---

[12] Ibid., p. 179, paras 235–36.

[13] Ibid. For instance, not having to pay house-rent back in the village, labourers did not look on rent for decent accommodation as a 'just and necessary expenditure'. Ibid.

[14] Ibid.

[15] Ibid.

[16] I draw upon Rabinbach's wonderful exposition of the turn-of-the-century reimaging of bodies as machines which transformed physical energy into productive power, thereby providing seemingly objective justifications for improving the conditions of labour. Anson Rabinbach, *The Human Motor: Energy, Fatigue and the Origins of Modernity*, New York: Basic Books, 1990. Fatigue was externalised, comments Steffan Blayney, and the body was understood as 'a cog in the industrial machine, far removed from the embodied experience of work.' Steffan Blayney, 'Industrial Fatigue and the Productive Body: The Science of Work in Britain, c. 1900–1918', *Social History of Medicine*, vol. 32, no. 2 (2019), pp. 310–28.

[17] For discussions in the *Times of India* on the theme of labour efficiency, see 'Industrial Commission: Efficiency of Labour', *TOI*, 13 November 1916, p. 11; 'Efficiency in Factories', *TOI*, 27 April 1917; 'Efficiency and Fatigue', *TOI*, 1 June 1918 and 15 June 1918. Describing the investigations into industrial fatigue then underway at muni-

decided the point of maximum productivity for the British worker could be applied to the Indian worker, who was described as physically weak, illiterate, and working in a tropical climate.

Did the Indian Industrial Commission's recommendations for reshaping the milieu of work leave any room for the volition of Indian mill-hands themselves? The report advocated programmes for the 'social uplift' of the labouring classes, to teach them to aspire to a better standard of living. Such programmes would induce them to work steadily at one site in order to achieve this goal. In addition, social work would encourage workers to co-operate in schemes for improving public health and sanitation.[18] The discussion concluded with the reassuring statement that the margin for improving the efficiency of the Indian mill-hand was so great that if the problem of low productivity was solved it would be of marked advantage to Indian industry.[19]

Ravi Ahuja points out that prewar bottlenecks in the supply of labour to certain industries pushed some employers to acknowledge that dismal health conditions led to such a poor level of labour efficiency that low wages could not make up for it.[20] For certain industries, and sometimes for limited periods, the lack of labour welfare measures was finally 'identified as a competitive handicap'.[21] World War One made the problem of labour supply more acute, and the surge of postwar labour unrest 'added the desideratum of "social harmony" to that of "efficiency".[22] Some cracks, Ahuja concludes, finally appeared

---

tions factories in England, a Calcutta business journal said that Indian manufacturers had to 'ascertain the best length of the working day', because such reforms would pay. 'The Working Day', *Capital*, 22 March 1918, vol. LX, no. 1498, p. 657.

[18] *Indian Industrial Commission Report*, pp. 179–85.

[19] Ibid., p. 180.

[20] Ravi Ahuja, 'A Beveridge Plan for India? Social Insurance and the Making of the "Formal Sector"', *International Review of Social History*, vol. 64, no. 2 (2019), pp. 1–42, 8–10. Aditya Sarkar gives a rich description of the way in which the plague epidemic of 1897–98 in Bombay created an acute labour shortage, providing labourers with a novel degree of bargaining power. Employers' new preoccupation with securing a reliable work force transformed into a debate about 'labour welfare measures' to stabilise social reproduction in the city. Aditya Sarkar, 'The Tie That Snapped: Bubonic Plague and Mill Labour in Bombay, 1896–1898', *International Review of Social History*, vol. 59, no. 2 (2014), pp. 181–214. I have benefitted from the comments of both these scholars.

[21] Ahuja, 'A Beveridge Plan for India?', pp. 8–10.

[22] The idea that some outlay would have to be expended on 'labour welfare' was accepted only in limited sectors of industry, and for limited periods. Ibid.

in the prewar consensus that India's young industrial sector could not afford labour welfare.[23]

To this scenario, one may add that two issues came together in mid-1918 to underline the importance of conserving labour. After the German spring offensive, the Government of India had decided to recruit another half-million men over the months following June 1918. June–July 1918 would also witness the first of three devastating attacks of influenza to hit India. The warning bell had sounded. India's labour resources were not as unlimited as they seemed. The *Times of India* reported that '[o]ne lesson of the epidemic is that the United Kingdom is not the only country where an active reconstructive social policy is imperative. The vigorous prosecution of a sanitary campaign is urgent in India which cannot stand these drains on its manpower.'[24]

Finally, the wartime tapping of India's resources had also widened the 'horizon of possibility' regarding the benefits of applying medical science and hygienist principles to the task of increasing labour productivity. This is vividly illustrated in an article with the intriguing title 'The Hook Worm and the War Loan', published in the *Indian Medical Gazette* in 1917.[25] The author, Lieutenant Clayton Lane MD, said he would put aside any reference to humanitarianism or the moral obligations of the employer and use an entirely economic argument to convince tea-planters at Darjeeling to construct latrines in their coolie lines.[26] Hookworm infections led to a lower labour output, whereas healthy labour would increase profits exponentially.[27] To raise the stakes of his claim, Lane stated that the additional income would be enough to pay off the Indian War Loan in three years. He was referring to the

---

[23] Ibid.

[24] 'India scourged by influenza', *TOI*, 2 December 1918, p. 7. See also *Hindustan*, 30 June 1918, in *Selections from the Native Newspapers of North-Western Provinces and Oudh*, no. 27, 6 June 1918.

[25] Lieutenant Colonel Clayton Lane, 'The Hook Worm and the War Loan', *Indian Medical Gazette*, vol. 52 (1917), pp. 161–64. Planters would rather have their workforce ingest thymol than spend on latrines. Nandini Bhattacharya's excellent assessment of Lane's enquiry into Ankylostomiasis in Darjeeling district concludes that research into tropical medicine did not effectively restructure public health in India. Nandini Bhattacharya, *Contagion and Enclaves: Tropical Medicine in Colonial India*, Liverpool: Liverpool University Press, 2013, pp. 177, 13.

[26] 'The Hook Worm and the War Loan'.

[27] Ibid.

loan floated in 1917 to help raise the sum of 100 million pounds 'gifted' by the Government of India for Britain's war expenditure.[28] The British press argued that this sum had given an entirely different picture of the financial capacity of India.

Military efficiency and manpower rationalisation

We have seen that from the turn of the century, follower shortages resulted in a shift from the policy of recruiting most stretcher-bearers and mule-drivers only when the need arose, to the creation of standing medical and transport follower units. The 1916–17 crisis in follower supply led to the increase of their benefits to a level just below that of the combatant. It was widely held by this time that departmental followers should form an integral part of the army. However, this process of formalisation took place in a more uneven way among the attached followers.[29] The belief that the Indian follower ranks had 'inherent' race- and caste-based skills was not abandoned, but there was a new conviction that small technological changes would give a gloss to these qualities and lead to a significant improvement in 'efficiency'. Pride in the ability to do this marks the journalist Edmund Candler's account of 'The Care of the Sepoy' at the Royal Pavilion Hospital in Brighton:

> In this miniature city the immemorial uses of the East continue ... But in the more mechanised world the West is impinging. The cook has adopted a rolling pin and no longer flattens out his food with the palm of his hand. He cooks on a gas-stove and has learnt not to blow out the jet when his work is done; the dhobi sadly manipulates an up-to-date laundry plant and sighs for the flat stone by the village tank; and the sepoy changes his clothes when he goes to bed.[30]

---

[28] Radhika Singha, 'India's Silver Bullets: War Loans and War Propaganda, 1917–18', in Maartje Abbenhuis, Neill Atkinson, Kingsley Baird and Gail Romano (eds), *The Myriad Legacies of 1917: A Year of War and Revolution*, Cham: Palgrave Macmillan, 2018, pp. 77–102.

[29] See Chapter 2 for a discussion on the uncertain line between public and private followers.

[30] Edmund Candler, *Year of Chivalry*, London: Simpkin, Marshall, Hamilton, Kent & Co., Ltd, 1916, pp. 280–81. See image 21 and the caption to H. D. Girdwood's photograph: 'The Gurkha kitchen: showing chappaties cooking on the clean and beautiful gas stoves provided for the various castes at the Hospitals. Our men appreciate the quickness and cleanliness of this fire compared with the slow lighting cow dung

Where caste prejudices seemed to pose a barrier to manpower rationalisation, the hope was that modifications of terminology and a change of tools would destigmatise certain kinds of work.[31] The sepoy might thereby be used more flexibly, and the disabled veteran motivated to take up new trades.[32] If the soldier could be persuaded to diversify his work, then followers could also be introduced to the use of arms to defend themselves.[33]

Interestingly, in a report titled 'Recruiting in India Before and During the War of 1914–18' the discussion about military efficiency takes on a more 'essentialist' quality in relation to the Indian combatant ranks than it does in relation to the non-combatant ranks.[34] According to the report, the principle that 'military efficiency' in the Indian Army rested on 'class efficiency' was recognised from the 1890s onwards. It prompted a reduction in the number of regiments raised in eastern and southern India 'and the elimination of less efficient classes wherever found'.[35] By the time 'the principle of military efficiency … reached a temporary limit—in 1914—it had definitely transferred the recruiting balance to a concentrated area of Northern India.'[36] To paraphrase, military efficiency was to be achieved by restricting recruitment to certain territories and communities, but the implementation of this principle was arrested by the wartime pressure to expand recruitment. The report recognised that rapid expansion of the army in any future emergency would rest on a wide representation of different communities, but it did not repudiate the relationship between military efficiency and 'class efficiency'.[37]

---

fires.' Photo 24(5), Photographic Record of the Indian Army in Europe during the First World War, British Library. One Medical Officer was convinced that incinerators could replace trenching systems for the disposal of waste in cantonments if their design was simple enough to suit the 'low intelligence' and conservatism of the 'sweeper class'. Major C. F. Wanhill, 'Incineration and Incinerators as Applied to Cantonments in India', *Journal of the Royal Army Medical Corps*, vol. 23, no. 6 (1914), pp. 600–14, 602.

[31] Chapter 2.

[32] Chapters 2 and 6.

[33] Ibid. *Report of the Committee Appointed by the Secretary of State for India to Enquire into the Administration and Organisation of the Army in India*, Cmd 943, 1920, II, pp. 97–98 (Esher Committee).

[34] 'Recruiting in India Before and During the War, 1914–18', IOR/L/Mil/17/5/2152. The report was meant to serve as a guide for any future war emergency.

[35] 'Recruiting in India', p. 5.

[36] Ibid.

[37] Ibid. By holding onto the ideology of 'martial castes', officials could formalise fol-

There is a different tonality to the discussion about the quality and performance of non-combatant manpower. As with Indian combatants, the quality of skilled and unskilled labour was said to depend considerably on territorial origin, although the reasons given for this opinion were more mixed.[38] However, the report concedes that 'careful selection' of labour could neutralise 'disadvantages of race and climate'.[39] Its guiding principle for the future was that it was 'possible to take men of the village artisan class and train them in a comparatively short time to European standards.'[40] It hailed the railway training camps set up in India during the war as a great success:

> In the Training Camps, men are thoroughly grounded in the use of all tools connected with the laying and maintenance of permanent-way, are taught discipline, and drill, are trained physically, are taught habits of personal cleanliness and encouraged to take part in games ... It is estimated that the value of such men is increased some 50 per cent by this training.[41]

The previous chapter explored the army's claims about the rehabilitation of disabled soldiers—namely that medical treatment in a disciplined military frame, followed by trade training sponsored by a prestigious war charity, had transformed them into skilled labourers ready to be placed in modern sectors of the Indian economy. Colonel Leland's description of the Motor Transport Department in Mesopotamia took the same kind of pride in the idea that trade training under a military aegis would return Asiatic drivers 'to India, Burma, Mauritius, and possibly Ceylon—Arabs, Jews and Armenians', all as 'useful members of a civilised society'.[42] Indian drivers, he declared, simply could not understand mechanics, but 'instruction was the key-note; they were taught to drive despite themselves'.[43] In other words, it was imperative not to pitch the level at which Indians could be expected to engage with technology too high. And yet, slightly later, we discover that 'native fitters' were in fact advancing so rapidly in their understanding of the internal combustion engine

---

lower labour and admit it to a system of graded benefits while continuing to keep the follower a step behind the sepoy.

[38] 'Recruiting in India', appendix XXII, p. 90.

[39] Ibid., p. 52.

[40] Ibid.

[41] Ibid., p. 47

[42] F.W. Leland, *With the M. T. in Mesopotamia*, London: F. Groom and Co., 1920, pp. 19–20.

[43] Ibid.

that they began to desert for better wages. Thereafter they were trained only for one particular job, the aim now being to prevent them from emerging as all-round mechanics.[44]

War propaganda and the dignity of labour

To sum up, then, Indian labour was being constituted in both civilian and military frames as an object of trade training, hygienist intervention and 'social uplift', but also as a resource whose value was rising due to the laws of supply and demand. To this we can add that the crisis of follower supply meant that war propaganda began, if belatedly, to cast non-combatant labour in a light which gave it some public standing.[45] Over 1917–18, the Indian Labour Corps began to figure in photographs, war journals and film footage.[46] The intended audience was not only humbler orders, but also educated Indians; such publications sought to convey the point that war service gave dignity to labour. A pamphlet composed for Indian schoolboys stated: 'This War has differed from other wars in this, that there has been so much work for those who were not fighters. Thus the Indian Labour Corps helped very much by building roads, by unloading waggons, and in many other ways.'[47] It also referred to the role of the lascars, Indian seamen, in merchant shipping.[48]

---

[44] Ibid., p. 55.

[45] What also gave the 'labourer' more standing, at least in public discourse, was the idea that the seizure of his or her person to enforce work, either by the employer or by the state, was not appropriate in modern conditions. The campaign against indentured migration contributed to the delegitimisation of legal provisions which made labour liable to criminal penalties for breach of contract. The Worker's Breach of Contract Amendment Act (Act XII of 1920) relaxed the severity of these penalties. In addition, by a convoluted path, wartime recruitment simultaneously enhanced and destabilised some forms of state-sanctioned impressment of labour. In the 1920s, enactments and executive orders allowing the impressment of labour and supplies were regularly assailed in legislative assemblies.

[46] In September 1918, film footage showing combatants and non-combatants working in Mesopotamia was handed over to the Central Publicity Board. 'Recruiting in India', p. 34.

[47] P. Charlier, *The Empire at War 1914–1918, A Short History for Indian Students*, Bombay: Oxford University press, 1920, pp. 29–30.

[48] Ibid., p. 131. A pamphlet titled 'Hoarding Rupees: How it Helps the Germans' also referred to the 'great services' of the Labour Corps and lascars. *TOI*, 21 June 1918, p. 5.

The idea that even those recruited to temporary labour units, such as the men in the Labour and Porter Corps, would wear a uniform and receive 'free food', medical care, and some compensation for injury or death at the worksite suggested that something more than mere subsistence was on offer.[49] The fact that Indian 'coolies' would have a presence in France, and that the wage on offer was higher than the sepoy's, inspired a burst of eloquence from one district officer of Surat:

> Labour is coming by its own; and the taint attached to manual, and menial, work is being obliterated by a little gold wash! The romance and glory of the 'Line' will remain; but tempered by the realisation that the War requires 'men' as well as 'arms'. And the Labourer for France must be a man; and may become a hero![50]

'Labour welfare': social reconstruction for postwar political reconstruction

Spiralling inflation in 1918–19 led to food and cloth riots in urban centres and set off a wave of strikes by mill-hands, as well as by postal, mint and other state employees, which lasted until 1922. This, combined with the Bolshevik revolution and the backdrop of industrial unrest in Britain, convinced both government and Indians in public life that agendas for postwar political reconstruction would have legitimacy only if some social reconstruction was also factored in. Some space would have to be created for discussion about 'labour welfare' and the 'uplift of the depressed classes'. But to what extent were labourers, or those they selected as their representatives, to be allowed a political voice in this process?[51]

---

[49] Compensation for injury and death for non-combatants was admitted in the frame of military service before it was introduced for labour in civilian life by the Workman's Compensation Act (Act VIII of 1923). One lascar's life story describes a work milieu which made men very vulnerable to crippling or fatal injury, but offered no compensation. See Amir Haider Khan, *Chains to Lose, Life and Struggle of a Revolutionary: Memoirs of Dada Amir Haider Khan*, ed. Hasan N. Gardezi, vols 1 and 2, Karachi: Pakistan Study Centre, University of Karachi, 2007, pp. 78–81, 86. Through strikes and refusal to re-engage, Indian lascars secured war-risk compensation in World War One, but delay and difficulty marked its actual realisation. G. Balachandran, *Globalizing Labour? Indian Seafarers and World Shipping, c. 1870–1945*, New Delhi: Oxford University Press, 2012, pp. 202–5.

[50] 'Note on Labour Corps for France', IOR/R/2/513/215.

[51] For the extreme difficulty textile labourers in Madras Presidency faced in getting any

The expansion of the state's own role as employer in wartime probably encouraged the idea that some form of paternalist state intervention might contain industrial unrest and trade unionism. This was the solution offered by one Lieutenant Colonel H. U. Perrot, who had raised a Santhal labour company and commanded a Labour Group in France. In a two-part essay in the *Times of India*, Perrot argued that in a newly industrial country like India labour and capital could not be left to battle it out. He proposed that the state take over the responsibility for supplying all unskilled labour to industry: 'Government should be the only trade-union'.[52] Labour Officers in France, he said, decided how much labour was going to be allocated to the 'employer'—that is, the engineer overseeing a particular project—and how it was going to be deployed. The men of the labour companies looked upon the Labour Officer as their protector and representative, but he also insisted on a high standard of discipline. 'It was fully recognised by all concerned that Labour was a technical branch of the Service and there was a total absence of any tendency to regard the labourer as a mere beast of burden.'[53]

This was, of course, just a single kite flying in the air. Some employers were now receptive to the idea that shorter hours and provision for housing might aid 'labour efficiency'. Many still held to the position that Indian industry could not afford any outlay on 'welfare' or shorter working hours if it was to stay competitive internationally. British and Indian business also felt that government ought to give them the ready assistance of the police and the military to suppress strike action.[54] In June 1920, the General Officer Commanding in Madras loaned some artisans from the Madras Labour Corps to run a private concern, the Electricity Supply Corporation, whose men were on

---

form of trade union leadership recognised over 1918–22, see Eamon Murphy, *Unions in Conflict: A Comparative Study of Four South Indian Textile Centres, 1918–1939*, New Delhi: Manohar, 1981, chapters 4 and 5.

[52] 'Organised Labour: A Suggestion for India', *TOI*, 4 July 1919, p. 7, and 5 July 1919. The Labour Group was made up of six to twelve labour companies. In October 1917 joint standing industrial councils had been set up in the UK on the grounds that the war had shown the need for consultation between government and representatives of employers and workmen, and that they would aid in the task of economic reconstruction.

[53] *TOI*, 4 July 1919, p. 7.

[54] See, for instance, 'Sholapur Situation: The Dispute Analysed. Need of Military Guards', *TOI*, 9 April 1920, pp. 9–10.

strike.[55] The Madras Labour Union protested the use of military labour to break strikes, but the Madras Chamber of Commerce insisted that this was an entirely legitimate exercise, 'essential in the public interest'.[56]

A certain mirroring of protocols of disciplining and negotiating with labour, and constant comparisons between time-work and task-work, monthly wage and piecework, can be observed across the military labour complex and the industrial complex. Even in wartime, we have seen that there were occasions on which the army chose to negotiate with discontented stretcher-bearers, or with Indian labour units in France, rather than employ very harsh militarist repression.[57] On the other hand, in peacetime India there was a tendency to recourse very rapidly to use of the army and police to suppress strike action.

Nationalising labour, nationalising the Indian Army

We have seen that 'labour welfare' had to be taken on board as part of the nationalist programme for postwar social reconstruction. But as far as the Indian Army was concerned, the Indian intelligentsia had every reason to want the 'coolie' and the 'menial' to dissolve into the hypermasculine persona of the Indian soldier. Here was a figure, it seemed, which could go anywhere in the war and find a welcome—to France and Belgium and even to colour-hostile Australia.[58] Educated Indians were remarkably ready to offer the

---

[55] *The Pioneer Mail and Indian Weekly News*, vol. 47, 9 July 1920, p. 24.

[56] Telegram, Madras Chamber of Commerce to Secretary GOI, Home, 30 June 1920. The Army Department said that when military interests were involved, as on this occasion, there was no objection. Deputy Secretary, AD to ADG, 5 August 1920. Home, Political, B, August 1920, no. 298. The first meeting of the All India Trade Union Congress, held in November 1920, also protested the 'employment of military, armed police, boy scouts and Pathan hooligans during strikes'. *TOI*, 2 November 1920, p. 9.

[57] Ruthlessly militaristic methods were, however, used to punish the brief strike of the Bombay Jail Labour Corps. See Chapter 3.

[58] Hardinge had been apprehensive about sending an Indian Army escort with German internees to Australia given the opposition of white labour there to the admission of Indians, but the soldiers were received with great enthusiasm. Hardinge to Governor General Australia, 28 August 1915, Hardinge correspondence, vol. 3, letter nos 75 and 108, CUL.

'blood' of Indian soldiers in order to prove the fitness of India to take her place among the self-governing colonies of empire. Amar Singh, an officer in the Imperial Cadet Corps who was in little danger of dying himself, wrote that he would 'much rather that every one of the Indians in France were killed than sent back', for later it would be 'flung in our teeth that we were not good enough for the Germans.'[59] And again, in October 1915, he noted: 'they must see it through ... It is on them that the honour of India rests. India will get tremendous concessions after the war.'[60]

Some Indian political figures also differentiated between manpower resources, which empire might ask for freely, and financial help, which would press heavily on the poor or on India's capital resources.[61] Gandhi's reasoning for arguing that Congress should support the call to raise half a million men from June 1918 onwards was that:

> We have not the economic strength to help it [empire] by munificent donations. Besides ... It is stupendous man-power which turns the scale. And India alone can create an impregnable wall of men against the German onslaught. If the Empire wins principally through the Indian army, it is clear that we can gain whatever rights we demand.[62]

Gandhi also had a dark premonition about the consequences of staying aloof from this exercise. Indian soldiers, he wrote, fought only to 'maintain their families and to prove themselves worth their salt.' If those who wanted *swaraj* (self-government) helped with recruitment, they could turn a mercenary army into a national army. If they did not participate, then this army could be used to crush the national movement.[63]

Gandhi failed signally as a recruiter, and the signing of the Armistice brought an end to this vista of an even more extended army. The 'nationalisation' of the army was going to be a long battle.[64] However, the need to replace

---

[59] DeWitt C. Ellinwood, *Between Two Worlds: A Rajput Officer in the Indian Army, 1905–21: Based on the Diary of Amar Singh of Jaipur*, Lanham: Hamilton Books, 2005, p. 381.

[60] Ibid., p. 392.

[61] See 'post-scriptum', in Lala Lajpat Rai, *England's Debt to India: A Historical Narrative of England's Fiscal Policy Towards India*, New York: B. W. Huebsch, 1917, p. xii.

[62] M. K. Gandhi, 'A Recruiting Appeal', bulletin no. 1, Nadiad, 22 June 1918, in Mahadev Desai, *Day to Day with Gandhi*, vol. I (November 1917–March 1919), Varanasi: Sarva Seva Sangh, 1968, p. 350.

[63] Ibid., pp. 350–51.

[64] See Chapter 6.

the word 'native' with the word 'Indian' in 'deference to popular sentiment' was recognised in the military sphere, as it had been in others. An amendment to the Indian Army Act in 1918 substituted 'Indian' for 'native' wherever it was used.[65] The word 'native' was also dropped from the 'Native Indian Land Forces', the Indian branch of the local defence units.[66] Finally, the 'native' princely states, who had helped so fulsomely in the war, were to be referred to now as the 'Indian states'.

Terminological changes and the 'horizon of possibility'

> The tendency among civilised peoples is for the status of the follower to be assimilated to that of the fighting man: and the Indian Army has now reached a stage of development at which further steps in this direction may reasonably be expected.[67]

We have seen that in Mesopotamia, the army had an extended role as employer of temporary labour units. Nevertheless, retrenchment began to kick in from 1920. The Adjutant General of India had wanted to retain some Labour and Porter Corps as part of the permanent establishment. He pointed out that stable bodies of labour became increasingly efficient, and that with the demand for labour going up it was difficult to get workers in sufficient quantity and for continuous work at officially sanctioned rates.[68] However, he acknowledged that such units required a paid supervisory staff, and this meant extra expenditure.[69] A still more limited proposal in 1923 to retain a skeletal establishment which would allow the speedy mobilisation of labour units in any future war also came to nothing, due to financial constraints and the reluctance of the princely states to support the scheme.[70]

However, in relation to the permanent follower establishment the short two-page section of the Esher Committee Report which deals with followers has some interesting insights to offer. It proposed various terminological changes to signal, quite forcefully, a modernising and rationalising drive in

---

[65] Indian Army Amendment Act (Act XI of 1918), F&P, Internal, B, June 1918, no. 5.

[66] Gazette notification, 16 March 1918, AD, Appointments, B, January 1919, nos 179–82.

[67] 'Recruiting in India'.

[68] ADG to GOCs, Northern and Southern Command, 6 March 1920, PWD (General), vol. 1064, 1918–20, MSA. Ibid.

[69] Ibid.

[70] F&P, Internal, file 354/1926.

manpower deployment.[71] Labour historians have pointed out that the forces of integration and segmentation, working simultaneously to shape the emergence of transnational labour markets under capitalism, leave their mark upon the terminology used for 'coloured' or colonised workforces. The use of the word 'coolie' rather than worker, 'sepoy' rather than soldier, and 'lascar' rather than seaman implies inferior capacity.[72] Historians have therefore explored the vernacular terminologies chosen by the men themselves, or their investment in English words.[73] World War One witnessed the coming into circulation of the word *jawan* for the Indian sepoy, a flattering colloquialism suggestive of vigorous and youthful masculinity.[74] Did Indian NCOs training large num-

---

[71] *Report of the Committee Appointed by the Secretary of State for India to Enquire into the Administration and Organisation of the Army in India*, pp. 97–98. In the report titled 'Recruiting in India', followers are described as a feature of armies in the Middle Ages which was retained in 'Oriental' armies, with the implication that the Indian Army had moved beyond this description. 'Recruiting in India', chapter 2, p. 35.

[72] Ravi Ahuja, 'Networks of Subordination—Networks of the Subordinated: The Ordered Spaces of South Asian Maritime Labour in an Age of Imperialism (c. 1890–1947)', in Ashwini Tambe and Harald Fischer-Tiné, *The Limits of British Colonial Control in South Asia: Spaces of Disorder in the Indian Ocean Region*, New York: Routledge, 2009, pp. 13–48, 24. Lascars preferred the words *khalasi* or *jehazi*. Ibid.; Jan Breman and E. V. Daniel, 'Conclusion: The Making of a Coolie', *The Journal of Peasant Studies*, vol. 19, nos 3–4 (1992), pp. 268–95.

[73] *Mazdoor*, rather than 'coolie', was the word which Indian mill-hands preferred to use. Chitra Joshi, *Lost Worlds: Indian Labour and its Forgotten Histories*, Delhi: Permanent Black, 2005, p. 74. In 1915 the word 'coolie' was officially prohibited in Fiji, one of the colonies which drew upon Indian indentured labour. In India the word persisted for many categories of 'unskilled' labour, the term railway 'coolie', or porter, being replaced by the label railway *sahayaks* (helpers) only in 2006. Jason Rodrigues, 'Indian Railway "Coolies" to be Renamed in Bid to Improve their Status', *The Guardian*, 2 March 2016, https://www.theguardian.com/world/2016/mar/02/indian-railway-coolies-renamed-improve-status, last accessed 10 November 2019.

[74] We encounter the word *jawan* many times in the trench diary of cavalry officer Roly Grimshaw, and in his novella about the war as seen through the eyes of Ram Singh, a cavalry NCO. Captain Roly Grimshaw, *Indian Cavalry Officer, 1914–1915*, eds Colonel J. Wakefield and Lieutenant Colonel J. M. Weippert, Tunbridge Wells: Costello, 1986, pp. 25, 145. The word *jawan* was also used by the Punjab governor in his recruiting speeches. *War Speeches of His Honour Sir Michael O'Dwyer*, Lahore: Government Printing, 1918, pp. 39, 110, 111, 131.

bers of young recruits, have something to do with its emergence? We have seen that use of the label 'Coolie Corps' continued along the frontiers of India, but units sent overseas were labelled the Indian Labour and Porter Corps.[75] In public speeches, Viceroy Lord Chelmsford even referred to them sometimes as labour battalions. However, the phrase 'menial servant' remained embedded in one of the provisions of the Indian Army Act.[76]

The section relating to 'Conditions of Service of "Followers"' in the Esher Committee Report begins by declaring that 'the term "follower" should disappear'.[77] It pronounces that the 'departmental followers' are, 'properly speaking, the subordinate Indian personnel of various departments and services.'[78] 'Regimental followers' should be enlisted, and attested men trained to defend themselves.[79] 'The term "sweeper" should be abolished. The necessary personnel for sanitary duties should be enlisted from low-caste men and trained as soldiers.'[80] With the introduction of piped water, Indian soldiers should be trained to draw their own water and convey it in buckets.[81] *Dhobis* (washermen) should be eliminated from unit establishments.[82]

---

[75] A Hindi petition asking for the payment of gratuity for a deceased son enrolled in a railway construction company uses the term '*sarkari* labourer', seeking the dignity both of official employment and an English designation. Petition of mother of Abraham Topno, n.d., in GELCA_001–0386, Gossner Evangelical Lutheran Mission Records, Ranchi.

[76] This provision, s. 22(1) (b) of the Indian Army Act (Act VIII of 1911), sanctioned the summary use of the rattan to discipline the follower of the 'menial kind', meaning perhaps the unenrolled servant. See also IAA s. 24. In 1920, corporal punishment had been abolished for all enrolled Indian followers and soldiers.

[77] *Report of the Committee Appointed by the Secretary of State for India to Enquire into the Administration and Organisation of the Army in India*, pp. 97–98.

[78] Ibid.

[79] Ibid.

[80] Ibid.

[81] Ibid. The elimination of the goatskin *massakh* (the bhisti's water-sack), which high-caste soldiers could not be expected to touch, seemed to clear the way. Medical officers were also beginning to condemn the *massakh* as unhygienic. Report of Colonel P. Hehir, 4 February 1917, IOR/L/Mil/7/18281.

[82] *Report of the Committee Appointed by the Secretary of State for India to Enquire into the Administration and Organisation of the Army in India*, p. 98. They could be kept in peacetime, but not at the expense of the state. Ibid.

Such suggestions indicate that the army was also claiming more of the sepoy's off-duty time. The Esher Committee suggested that the 'Hindustani' clothing worn by sepoys as off-duty dress and for fatigue duties be replaced by a 'fatigue order of dress, the khaki shirt and shorts, at Government cost', which, it pointed out, had become so common during the war.[83] With respect to British soldiers, the report underlined the need to give them more domestic comforts, stating that their barracks could not be regarded 'simply as dormitories.'[84] However, it also suggested that in hill stations they could perform some of the barrack duties which they performed in the UK.[85] Race and caste were still in the picture. Nevertheless, the Esher Report explored the possibility of using the designation 'soldier' as a unifying homology through which tasks could be restructured to facilitate the economical and trained use of manpower for the military machine.

[83] Ibid., p. 86.
[84] Ibid., p. 76.
[85] Ibid.

SELECT BIBLIOGRAPHY

ARCHIVES

India

Bhubaneshwar, Odisha

Odisha State Archives.

Bengaluru, Karnataka

Karnataka State Archives.

Chennai

Tamil Nadu State Archives.

Delhi

Delhi State Archives.
National Archives of India.
The Nehru Memorial Museum and Library.
The United Services Institution, Delhi.
Vidya Jyoti College of Theology, Library.

Haryana

Haryana Academy of History and Culture, Kurukshetra.

Mumbai

Asiatic Society of Mumbai, Library.
Maharashtra State Archives.

Ranchi, Jharkhand

Bishop's Lodge Records.
Gossner Theological College, Library and Archives.

SELECT BIBLIOGRAPHY

United Kingdom

Cambridge

Cambridge University Library, Cambridge.
Centre for South Asian Studies, University of Cambridge.

London

Imperial War Museum London.
India Office Records and Library, British Library.
The National Archives, Kew, London.
University of London Archives, Senate House Library, London.

NEWSPAPERS AND PERIODICALS

These are in addition to extracts from *Reports on Native Newspapers 1880–1921*.

The Behar Herald (microfilm, NMML, New Delhi).
Bombay Chronicle.
Capital.
The Catholic Herald of India.
Chota Nagpur Diocesan Paper (Bishop's Lodge, Ranchi).
Gharbandhu (Gossner Theological College Library, Ranchi).
Jangi Akhbar.
Ladai ka Akhbar.
The Leader.
The London Gazette.
Missions belges de la Compagnie de Jésus: Congo, Bengale, Ceylan, 1922.
Mizo leh Vai.
Modern Review.
Muslim India and Islamic Review.
The Pioneer Mail and Indian Weekly News.
The Servant of India.
The Singapore Free Post and Mercantile Advertiser.
The Times (UK).
The Times of India.
The Tribune.
The War Cry.
The War Illustrated.
Young India.

PRIVATE PAPERS

Cambridge University Library, Cambridge

Papers of Charles, first Baron Hardinge of Penshurst (1858–1944).

SELECT BIBLIOGRAPHY

Cambridge South Asia Archives

Papers of Sir James S. Meston (first Baron Meston), Indian Civil Service.
Thatcher Collection.
Tonkinson Papers, Box 50.

India Office Records

Barnes, Margarita, typescript, 'S. K. Datta and his people', Mss Eur C576/89/74.
Bentinck, A. H. W., Mss Eur D1024/3.
Chelmsford, 1st Viscount as Viceroy of India 1916–21, Mss Eur E264.
Hailey, Malcolm, Mss Eur E220/2.
Lawrence, Walter Roper, commissioner for sick and wounded Indian soldiers in France and England 1914–16, Mss Eur F143.
Milroy, A. J. W., diary, Abor expedition, Mss Eur D1054.
Peckham, Arthur Nyton, Mss Eur D078.
Roos-Keppel, George, Mss Eur D613.
Shakespear, Colonel John, Mss Eur E361/14.
Shortt, Henry Edward, Indian Medical Service, Mss Eur C435.

University of London, Senate House Library, London

Lewin Family Papers, Ms 811, Lieutenant Colonel Thomas Herbert Lewin, 1839–1916.

School of Oriental and African Studies, London

Mills, J. P., photographic collection.

Imperial War Museum London

Cashmore, Thomas Herbert, sound recording, no. 4912.
Orton, H. A., document 11808.

PUBLISHED PRIMARY SOURCES

Official Publications

127th Annual Report of the Baptist Missionary Society, 1918–19, London: Carey Press, 1919.
Report on Indian Newspapers and Periodicals in Bengal.
Administrative Report, Bombay Jail Department, 1916.
Administrative Report, Bombay Jail Department, 1917.
Administrative Reports of the Chin Hills and the North Eastern Frontier of Burma for the Year Ended 30 June 1917, Government of India, 1917.
Army Instructions, India, 1918.
Assam Baptist Missionary Conference Report, Calcutta: American Baptist Mission Press, 1913.

SELECT BIBLIOGRAPHY

Bell, Gertrude, *Review of the Civil Administration of Mesopotamia*, 1920.

Compendium of the More Important Orders of the Government of India, Army Department, and Indian Army Orders, Issued from the 1ˢᵗ August 1914, to the 31ˢᵗ December 1917, Calcutta: Government Printing, 1919.

Council of State Debates, vol. 1, 1 February 1921–10 March 1921, Delhi: Government Press, 1921.

Demobilisation Orders (India). Supplementary Instructions for Porter and Labour Corps, Enrolled Followers and Syce Corps, Calcutta: Government Printing, 1919.

Financial Statement of the Government of India for 1919–20, Bombay: Government Central Press.

Frost, F. D., *Report of the Labour Directorate, Mesopotamian Expeditionary Force from October, 1916 to October, 1918*, Baghdad, 1919.

India's Contribution to the Great War, Calcutta: Superintendent Government Printing Press, 1923.

Indian Army Orders, The Commander-in-Chief, India, 1916.

Indian Army Orders, His Excellency the Commander-in-Chief in India, 1922.

Indian Industrial Commission Report, 1916–1918, Calcutta: Government Printing, 1918.

Indian Jails Committee, vol. I, Report and Appendices, 1919–1920, Government Printing, 1920.

Johnston, J. Wilston, *The History of the Great War, Rawalpindi District*, Lahore, 1920.

Manual of Indian Military Law, Calcutta: Government Printing, 1922.

Marten, J. T., *Census of India, 1921*, vol. I, part 1, Calcutta: Government Printing, 1924.

O'Malley, L. S. S., *Bihar and Orissa District Gazetteers, Saran* (revised edition, ed. A. P. Middleton), Patna: Government Printing, 1930.

Operations in Waziristan, 1919–1920, Calcutta: Government Printing, 1921.

Our Indian Empire, General Staff India, 1940.

Parry, N. E., *A Monograph on Lushai Customs and Ceremonies*, 1928, Aizawl: Tribal Research Institute, 1974.

The Persian Gulf Administration Reports, 1873–1947 (Archive Edition 1986), vol. VII (1912–20); vol. VIII (1921–30).

Record of War Work in the Gurgaon District, Poona: Scottish Mission Industries, 1923.

Report on the Administration of Assam for 1918–19, Government of India, 1919.

Report on the Administration of Bihar and Orissa, 1917–18, Patna, 1919.

Report on the Administration of Criminal Tribes in the Punjab for the year ending December 1918, Lahore: Government Printing, 1919.

Report on the Administration of Mayurbhanj for 1917–1918, Baripada: State Press, Mayurbhanj, 1918.

Reports of Administration for 1918 of Divisions and Districts of the Occupied Territories in Mesopotamia, vol. 1.

Reports of Baptist Missionary Society (B.M.S.), 1901–1938, Mizoram: Baptist Church of Mizoram, 1993.

Report of the Commission Appointed by Act of Parliament to Enquire into the Operations of War in Mesopotamia, House of Commons, Cmd 8610, 1917.

Report of the Committee Appointed by the Government of India to Examine the Question of the Re-Organisation of the Medical Services in India, April 1919, HMSO: Parliamentary Papers, Cmd 946, 1920.

Report of the Committee Appointed by the Secretary of State for India to Enquire into the Administration and Organisation of the Army in India, Cmd 943, 1920 (Esher Report).

Report of the Committee on Emigration from India to Crown Colonies and Protectorates, June 1910, London: Eyre and Spottiswode, 1910.

Report of the Departments of the Civil Administration, Mesopotamia, 1917.

Report on Indian Constitutional Reform, London: HMSO, 1918.

Report of the Indian Factory Labour Commission, 1908, vol. I.

Report of the Pitt-Rivers Museum, 1921

Sedition Committee Report, Calcutta: Government Press, 1918.

Selections from Indian-Owned Newspapers, United Provinces.

Selections from the Native Newspapers of North-Western Provinces and Oudh.

Selections from the Native Newspapers for Punjab.

Statistical Abstract of Information Regarding the Armies at Home and Abroad, 1914–1920, London: War Office, 1920.

Triennial Report on the Working of the Punjab Lunatic Asylum. For the Years 1918, 1919 and 1920, Lahore: Government Press, 1921.

War Office: Statistics of the Military Effort of the British Empire during the Great War, 1914–1920, London: HMSO, 1922.

War Speeches of His Honour Sir Michael O'Dwyer, Lahore: Government Printing, 1918.

Non-Official Publications

Acts and Achievements of Hau Cin Khup, Chief of Kamhau Clan, Chin Hills, Tedim, 1927, in Khup Za Go, *Zo Chronicles: A Documentary Study of History and Culture of the Kuki Chin Lushai Tribe*, New Delhi: Mittal, 2008.

Aga Khan, The, *India in Transition: A Study in Political Evolution*, London: Philip Lee Warner, 1918.

Alexander, Major H. M., *On Two Fronts, Being the Adventures of an Indian Mule Corps in France and Gallipoli*, London: W. Heinemann, 1917.

Ambedkar, B. R., 'What Congress and Gandhi have done to the Untouchables', 1945, reprinted in Vasant Moon (ed.), *Dr. Babasaheb Ambedkar: Writings and Speeches*, vol. 9, Education Department, Government of Maharashtra, 1991.

Anand, Mulk Raj, *Across the Black Waters*, Delhi: Orient Longman, 1940.

———, *Untouchable*, London: Penguin, 2014.

Andrews, C. F., *Report on Indentured Labour in Fiji: An Independent Enquiry*, Allahabad: C. Y. Chintamani, 1917.

Anstey, Vera, *The Economic Development of India*, London: Longman, Green and Co., 1929.

Ao, W. Chubanungba, *Havildar Watingangshi Ao Longkhum: Off the Coast of Tunis 1917*, Shillong: Galaxy Book Centre, 2017.

Bachchan, Harivansh Rai, *In the Afternoon of Time: An Autobiography*, trans. and ed. Rupert Snell, Delhi: Penguin, 2001.

Balfour, Henry, 'The Welfare of Primitive Peoples', *Folklore*, vol. 34, no. 1 (1923), pp. 12–24.

Baptists in World Service, Boston: American Baptist Foreign Mission Society, 1918.

Baring, Maurice, *R.F.C.H.Q., 1914–1918*, London: G. Bell and Sons, 1920.

Barrow, Sir George, *The Life of General Sir Charles Carmichael Monro*, London: Hutchinson, 1931.

Bastavala, Dinoo S., *Stray Thoughts on the War*, Bombay: Commercial Press, 1918.

Bellers, Brigadier E. V. R., *The History of the 1ˢᵗ King George the V's Own Gurkha Rifles*, vol. II, 1920–47, Aldershot: The Wellington Press, 1956.

Bentinck, A., 'The Abor Expedition: Geographical Results', *The Geographical Journal*, vol. 41, no. 2 (1913), pp. 97–109.

Bingley, A. H., 'Rajputs, A Brief Account of their Origin, Religious Customs, and History, with Notes Regarding their Fitness for Modern Military Service', *United Services Institute Journal*, vol. XXIV (1895), pp. 135–61.

Birdwood, Field Marshal Lord, *Khaki and Gown: An Autobiography*, London; Melbourne: Ward Lock, 1941.

Blood and Treasure: India's War Effort, Oxford: Oxford University Press, 1918.

Bradley-Birt, Francis B., *Chota Nagpore: A Little-Known Province of the Empire*, London: Smith, Elder, & Co., 1903.

Brard, Gurnam Singh Sidhu, *East of Indus: My Memories of Old Punjab*, New Delhi: Hemkunt Publishers, 2007.

Bruce, C. G. and W. Brook Northey, 'Nepal', *The Geographical Journal*, vol. 65, no. 4 (1925), pp. 281–98.

Buchanan, George, *The Tragedy of Mesopotamia*, Edinburgh: William Blackwood and Sons, 1938.

Burrage, A. M., *War is War*, New York: E. P. Dutton & Co., 1930.

Candler, Edmund, *Abdication*, Suffolk: Richard Clay and Sons, 1922.

———, *The Long Road to Baghdad*, London: Cassell, 1919.

———, *The Sepoy*, London: John Murray, 1919.

———, *Year of Chivalry*, London: Simpkin, Marshall, Hamilton, Kent & Co., Ltd, 1916.

Carson, Laura, *Pioneer Trails: Trials and Triumph*, New York: Baptist Board Publication, 1927.

Casserly, Gordon, *The Land of the Boxers: Or, China under the Allies*, New York; Bombay: Longmans, Green and Co., 1903.

Castleton, David, *In the Mind's Eye: The Blinded Veterans of St Dunstan's*, Barnsley: Pen and Sword Military, 2013.

Charlier, P., *The Empire at War 1914–18: A Short History for Indian Students*, Bombay: Oxford University Press, 1920.

Chick, Noah Alfred, *Annals of the Indian Rebellion 1857–58*, Calcutta: Sanders, Cones and Company, 1859.

Clark, Mary Mead, *A Corner in India*, Philadelphia: American Baptist Publishing Society, 1907.

Coloured Victims of the Great War: Their Groans and Grievances at the Feet of the Crown and the Country, anonymous pamphlet, n.d. (c. 1930).

Creagh, Garrett O'Moore, *Indian Studies*, London: Hutchinson, 1919.

Cummins, Colonel S. Lyle, 'Tuberculosis as a Problem for the Royal Army Medical Corps', *Journal of the Royal Army Medical Corps*, vol. XLVI, no. 6 (1926), pp. 401–7.

Cursetjee, Manockjee, *The Land of the Date: A Recent Voyage from Bombay to Basra and Back, 1916–1917*, Bombay: C. M. Cursetjee, 1918.

Cushing, Harvey, *From a Surgeon's Journal: 1915–1918*, Boston: Little, Brown and Company, 1936.

Datta, V. N., *New Light on the Punjab Disturbances in 1919*, Shimla: Indian Institute of Advanced Study, 1975.

Deepchand, Pandit, '*Bharti hole re, kyun bahar khade rangroot*', in Rajaram Shastri, *Haryana ka Lok Manch*, no. 15, Kurukshetra: Haryana Academy of History and Culture, n.d..

Desai, Mahadev, *Day to Day with Gandhi*, vol. I (November 1917–March 1919), Varanasi: Sarva Seva Sangh, 1968.

Doke, Reverend Joseph J., *M. K. Gandhi: An Indian Patriot in South Africa*, London: London Indian Chronicle, 1909.

Downing, W. H., *Digger Dialects*, Melbourne; Sydney: Lothian Book Publishing Co., 1919.

Dunsterville, L. C., *Stalky's Reminiscences*, London: Jonathan Cape, 1928.

Egan, Eleanor Franklin, *The War in the Cradle of the World: Mesopotamia*, New York; London: Harper and Brothers, 1918.

Evans, Roger, *A Brief Outline of the Campaign in Mesopotamia*, London: Sifton, Praed, and Co., 1926.

Evatt, J. T., *Historical Record of the 39th Royal Garhwal Rifles*, vol. 1, 1887–1922, Aldershot: Gale and Polden Ltd, 1923.

Ewing, Ruth Grimes, *Our Life with the Garos of Assam, India*, Philadelphia: Dorrance and Company, 1971.

Fakhurdin, Kazi, *Loyal Efforts Made Celebrations Success*, Hyderabad, Sindh: Standard Printing Works, 1920 (British Library pamphlets).

Fallon, S. W., *A New Hindustani–English Dictionary*, London: Trubner and Co., 1879.

Forbes, Major General A., *A History of the Army Ordnance Services*, vol. 3, London: The Medici Society, Ltd., 1929.

Friedberg, Aaron, *The Weary Titan: Britain and the Experience of Relative Decline*, Princeton: Princeton University Press, 1989.

Gait, Sir E., *Census of India, 1911*, vol. 1, part 1, Calcutta: Government Printing, 1912.

Gandhi, M. K., *The Collected Works of Mahatama Gandhi*, Ahmedabad: Government of India, 1965.

Ghosh, Kali, *The Autobiography of a Revolutionary in British India*, Delhi: Social Science Press, 2013.

Goodrice, Caspar Frederick, *Report of the British Naval and Military Operations in Egypt 1882*, Washington: Bureau of Navigation, 1885.

Graham, General C. A. L., *The History of the Indian Mountain Artillery*, Aldershot: Gale and Polden Ltd, 1957.

Graves, Philip, *The Life of Sir Percy Cox*, London: Hutchinson, 1941.

Grimshaw, Captain Roly, *Indian Cavalry Officer, 1914–1915*, eds Colonel J. Wakefield and Lieutenant Colonel J. M. Weippart, Tunbridge Wells: Costello, 1986.

Gurdon, P. R. T., *The Khasis*, 1907, London: Macmillan, 1914.

Haldane, Aylmer, *The Insurrection in Mesopotamia, 1920*, London: Blackwood, 1922.

Hall, Lieutenant Colonel L. J., *The Inland Water Transport in Mesopotamia*, London: Constable and Co., 1921.

Hazari, *I Was an Outcaste: The Autobiography of an 'Untouchable' in India*, New Delhi: The Hindustan Times, 1951.

Herbert, Aubrey, *Mons, Anzac, Kut: By an MP*, London: Edward Arnold, 1919.

Hill, Sir Claude H., *India-Stepmother*, Edinburgh: William Blackwood and Sons Ltd, 1929.

The Historic Trial of the Ali Brothers, parts I and II, Karachi: New Times Office, 1921.

History of the Corps of Royal Engineers, vol. VII, Chatham: The Institute of Royal Engineers, 1952.

Hough, W., *Precedents in military law: including the practice of courts martial, the mode of conducting trials, the duties of officers at military courts of inquests, courts of inquiry, courts of requests, etc., etc.*, London: W. H. Allen, 1855.

How Gul Mahomed Joined the King's Army, Simla: G. M. Press, n.d. (c. 1918).

Hudson, General Sir Havelock, *History of the 19th King George's Own Lancers, 1858–1921*, Aldershot: Gale and Polden Ltd, 1937.

Hutchinson, Colonel H. D., *The Campaign in Tirah 1897–1898: An Account of the Expedition Against the Orakzais & Afridis under Gen. Sir. William Lockhart*, London: Macmillan, 1898.

Hutton, J. H., *The Angami Nagas*, London: Macmillan, 1921.

————, *Problems of Reconstruction in the Assam Hills: Presidential Address for 1945*, Royal Anthropological Institute of Great Britain and Ireland, 1945.

————, *The Sema Nagas*, London: Macmillan, 1921.

India's Services in the War, vols II, III, and IV, Lucknow: Newal Kishore Press, 1922.

India's War Finance and Post-War Problems, Poona, 1919.

Joatamon, *A Mug in Mesopotamia*, Poona, 1918.

Johnson, Robert G., *History of the American Baptist Chin Mission*, vol. 1, Valley Forge, PA: R. G. Johnson, 1988.

Kala, Govind Ram, *Memoir of the Raj*, New Delhi: Mukul Prakashan, 1974.

Kashi Nath, Pandit, *Indian Labourers in France*, Bombay: Oxford University Press, 1919.

Keen, J. W., *The N.W.F. Province and the War*, n.d..

Khan, Amir Haider, *Chains to Lose, Life and Struggle of a Revolutionary: Memoirs of Dada Amir Haider Khan*, ed. Hasan N. Gardezi, vols 1 and 2, Karachi: Pakistan Study Centre, University of Karachi, 2007.

Kingdon-Ward, F., 'The Assam-Burma Frontier: Discussion', *The Geographical Journal*, vol. 67, no. 4 (1926), pp. 299–301.

Klein, Daryl, *With the Chinks*, London: John Lane, 1919.

Kyles, Reverend David, *Lorrain of the Lushais: Romance and Realism on the North-East Frontier of India*, Stirling: Stirling Tract Enterprise, 1944.

Lajpat Rai, Lala, *England's Debt to India: A Historical Narrative of England's Fiscal Policy Towards India*, New York: B. W. Huebsch, 1917.

————, *Lala Lajpat Rai: Writings and Speeches*, ed. Vijaya Chandra Joshi, vol. II, Delhi: University Publishers, 1966.

Lambert, E. T. D., 'From the Brahmaputra to the Chindwin', *The Geographical Journal*, vol. 89, no. 4 (1937), pp. 309–23.

Lane, Lieutenant Colonel Clayton, 'The Hook Worm and the War Loan', *Indian Medical Gazette*, vol. 52 (1917), pp. 161–64.

Latthe, A. B., *Memoirs of His Highness Shri Shahu Chhatrapati Maharaja of Kolhapur*, vol. II, Bombay: Times Press, 1924.

Leigh, M. S. *The Punjab and the War*, 1922, Lahore: Government Printing, 1997.

Leland, F. W., *With the M. T. in Mesopotamia*, London: F. Groom and Co., 1920.

Letter to the Loyal Women of India, Oxford: Humphrey Milford, n.d. (c. 1919).

Lind, Colonel A. G., *A Record of the 58th Rifles F. F. in the Great War 1914–1919*, Waziristan: Commercial Steam Press, 1933.

Lindsay, A. D., 'The Organisation of Labour in the Army in France during the War and its Lessons', *Economic Journal*, vol. 34, no. 133 (1924), pp. 69–82.

Lucas, Charles (ed.), *The Empire at War*, vol. 3, London: Oxford Universitry Press, 1924.

————, *The Empire at War*, vol. 5, London: Oxford University Press, 1926.

Mackarness, F. C., *The Methods of the Indian Police in the Twentieth Century*, San Francisco: The Hindustan Gadar Office, 1915.

Mackenzie, J., 'Influenza: Preliminary Note on a Fatal Pneumococcal Infection and its Suggested Spread from Sheep to Man', *Journal of the Royal Army Medical Corps*, vol. 35, no. 6 (1920), pp. 481–84.

MacMunn, George F., *The Armies of India*, London: Adam and Charles Black, 1911.

———, *The Martial Races of India*, London: Sampson Low, 1933.

———, *The Underworld of India*, London: Jarrolds, 1933.

Macpherson, Major General Sir W. G. and Major T. J. Mitchell, *Medical Services, General History*, vol. 1, London: HMSO, 1924.

Madras War Fund: Report of Transactions to 31 March 1917.

Marcosson, Isaac F., *The Business of War*, London: John Lane, 1918.

McCall, Anthony Gilchrist, *Lushai Chrysalis*, London: Luzac and Co., 1949.

McMaster, Lieutenant Colonel Andrew Cook, *A Catechism on Act No. V of 1869, the Indian Articles of War*, Madras: Higginbotham and Company, 1869.

McMillan, A. W., 'Indian Echoes from France', *The East and the West*, vol. XVIII (1920), pp. 1–20.

McMurtrie, Douglas, *The Disabled Soldier*, New York: Macmillan, 1919.

Merewether, Lieutenant Colonel J. W. B. and Sir Frederick Smith, *The Indian Corps in France*, London: John Murray, 1918.

Mills, J. P., *The Ao Nagas*, London: Macmillan, 1926.

———, 'The Assam-Burma Frontier', *The Geographical Journal*, vol. 67, no. 4 (1926), pp. 289–99.

———, *The Lhota Nagas*, London: Macmillan, 1922.

Milner, A. E., 'The Army Bearer Corps', *Journal of the Royal Army Medical Corps*, vol. 6, no. 6 (1906), pp. 685–89.

Mittra, H. N. (ed.), *Punjab Unrest, Before and After*, Calcutta: N. N. Mitter, 1920.

Moberly, F. J., *History of the Great War Based on Official Documents: The Campaign in Mesopotamia, 1914–1918*, London: HMSO, 1923.

Modak, Captain G. V., *Indian Defence Problem*, Poona: G. V. Modak, 1938.

Montagu, E. S., *An Indian Diary*, ed. Venetia Montagu, London: W. Heinemann, 1930.

Morgan, John Hartman, *Leaves From a Field Note-Book*, London: Macmillan, 1916.

Myuank, 'Indian Army Reflections', in C. Howard Turner (ed.), *Indian Ink: Being Splashes from Various Pens in Aid of the Imperial Indian War Fund*, Calcutta: T. H. Camp-Howes, 1918.

Natesan, G. A. (ed.), *All About the War: The Indian Review War Book*, Madras: G. A. Natesan, 1915.

Nehru, Krishna, *With No Regrets: An Autobiography*, New York: The John Day Company, 1945.

Newland, A. G. E., *The Image of War, or Service on the Chin Hills*, Calcutta: Thacker, Spink and Co., 1894.

Nightingale, Florence, *Florence Nightingale on Social Change in India: Collected Works of Florence Nightingale*, ed. Gérard Vallée, Waterloo, ON: Wilfrid Laurier University Press, 2007.

'Note on the Physical Estimate of Malaria Disability', *The Journal of Tropical Medicine and Hygiene*, London: Blackwell Scientific Publications, 1922.

O'Mealey, M. (ed.), *His Royal Highness the Prince of Wales' Tour in India, 1921–1922*, Delhi: Foreign and Political Department, Government of India, 1923.

Omissi, David, *Indian Voices of the Great War: Soldiers' Letters, 1914–1918*, Basingstoke: Palgrave Macmillan, 1999.

Pant, Govind Ballabh, *Selected Works of Govind Ballabh Pant*, ed. B. R. Nanda, vol. 1, Delhi: Oxford University Press, 1993.

Patiala and the Great War: A Brief History of the Services of the Premier Punjab State, London: Medici Society, 1923.

Pearay Mohan, Pandit, *An Imaginary Rebellion and How it was Suppressed*, Lahore: Khosla Brothers, 1920.

Pettigrew, William, 'Manipur State 1891–1932', *The Baptist Missionary Review*, vol. XXXVIII, no. II (1932).

———, 'My Twenty-Five Years 1897–1922 at Ukhrul Mission School', *Reverend William Pettigrew: A Pioneer Missionary of Manipur*, Imphal: Fraternal Green Cross, 1996.

Phillips, Sir Percival, *The 'Prince of Wales' Eastern Book: A Pictorial Record of the Voyages of the H.M.S. Renown, 1921–22*, London: Hodder and Stoughton, 1922.

Playfair, Alan, *The Garos*, London: Nutt, 1909.

Playne, Somerset (ed.), *Indian States: A Bibliographical, Historical and Administrative Survey*, London: Foreign and Colonial Compiling and Pub. Co., 1921–22.

Proceedings of the Legislative Council of the Lieutenant-Governor of Bihar and Orissa Legislative Council, 1918.

Reid, A. S., *Chin-Lushai Land*, Calcutta: Thacker, Spink and Co., 1893.

Reid, Robert, *History of the Frontier Areas Bordering on Assam from 1883–1941*, Delhi: Eastern Publishing House, 1942.

Report of the Bombay Chamber of Commerce for the Year 1917, Bombay, 1918.

Reports by Missionaries of Baptist Missionary Society (B.M.S.) 1901–1938, Baptist Church of Mizoram, 1993.

Richards, Frank, *Old Soldier Sahib*, New York: Harrison Smith and Robert Haas, 1936.

Risley, H. H. and E. A. Gait, *Census of India, 1901*, vol. 1, part 1, Calcutta: Government Printing, 1903.

Roy, Evelyn, 'The Crisis in Indian Nationalism', *The Labour Monthly*, vol. 2, no. 2 (1922), pp. 146–57.

Rudolph, Suzanne H. and L. I. Rudolph with Mohan Singh Kanota, *Reversing the Gaze: Amar Singh's Diary. A Colonial Subject's Narrative of Imperial India*, Oxford: Westminster Press, 2002.

Russell, R. V., 'Review of Sarat Chandra Roy's *The Oraons of Chota Nagpur*', in *Folklore*, vol. 27, no. 1 (1916), pp. 107–9.

Sailo, Sainghinga, *Indopui 1914–1918: Mizote France Ram Kal Thu*, Aizawl, n.d. (c. 1940s).

Sandes, E. W. S., *In Kut and Captivity: With the Sixth Indian Division*, London: John Murray, 1919.

Sarkar, Sailendra Nath, *Biography of the Maharaja Sri Ram Chandra Bhanj Deo, Feudatory Chief of Mayurbhanj*, Calcutta: Mayurbhanj Estate, 1918.

Schwabe, Major G. Salis, 'Carrier Corps and Coolies on Active Service in China, India, and Africa, 1860–1879', in *Journal of the Royal United Services Institution*, vol. 24, no. 108 (1881), pp. 815–48.

Seventy-Eighth Annual Report of the Wesleyan Mission in the Mysore Province, Mysore: Wesleyan Mission Press, 1918.

Seventy-Ninth Annual Report of the Wesleyan Mission in the Mysore Province, Mysore: Wesleyan Mission Press, 1919.

Shaiza, Kanrei, *Āpuk Āpaga Rairei Khare, France Khavā, 1917–18, Khala Republic Day, 1974, Delhi Kakā*, Imphal: City Press, 1974.

Shakespear, L. W., *History of the Assam Rifles*, 1929, Aizawl: Firma KLM, Tribal Research Institute, 1977.

———, *History of Upper Assam, Upper Burmah and North-Eastern Frontier*, London: Macmillan, 1914.

Shaw, William, *Notes on the Thadou Kukis*, Calcutta: Asiatic Society of Bengal, 1929.

Singh, Khushwant and Satindar Singh, *Ghadar, 1915*, New Delhi: R and K Publishing House, 1966.

Singh, St Nihal, 'India's Man-Power', *The Contemporary Review*, vol. CXIII (1918), pp. 665–70.

Slater, Gilbert, *Southern India: Its Political and Economic Problems*, London: George Allen and Unwin Ltd, 1936.

Sommers, Cecil, *Temporary Crusaders*, London: John Lane, 1919.

Stevenson, E. S. B., *The Station House Officers' Vade-Mecum*, Madras, 1879.

Stockdale, Francis, *Walk Warily in Waziristan*, Devon: Arthur H. Stockwell Ltd, 1982.

Swayne, Martin (Maurice Nicoll), *In Mesopotamia*, London: Hodder and Stoughton, 1917.

Tandon, Prakash, *Punjabi Century, 1857–1947*, Berkeley; Los Angeles: University of California Press, 1968.

Teja Singh Khalsa Joins the Army, 1918 (British Library pamphlet).

Thatcher, W. S., *The Fourth Battalion Duke of Connaught's Own Tenth Baluch Regiment in the Great War*, Naval and Military Press, 2009.

Tilak, Bal Gangadhar, *Bal Gangadhar Tilak: His Writings and Speeches*, Madras: Ganesh and Co., 1922.

Travers, John (Eva Mary Bell), *Sahib-Log*, London: Duckworth and Co., 1910.

Tugwell, W. B. P., *History of the Bombay Pioneers*, London; Bedford: Sidney Press, 1938.

Ushaw, E. D., 'Football at the Front', *The Windsor Magazine*, no. 48 (1917), pp. 69–75.

Vaman, Govind Kale, *India's War Finance and Post-War Problems*, Poona: Aryabhushan Press, 1919.

Van Der Schueren, Father T., *Moral and Intellectual Uplift of the Aboriginal Races of Chota Nagpur, India*, London: East and West, 1928.

Vaughan, Lieutenant Colonel H. B., *St George and the Chinese Dragon*, 1902, Dartford, Kent: The Alexius Press, 2000.

Vermeire, M., *History of Barway Mission*, Katkahi, n.d..

Voices from India, Calcutta, 1922.

Wanhill, C.F., 'Incineration and Incinerators as Applied to Cantonments in India', *Journal of the Royal Army Medical Corps*, vol. 23, no. 6 (1914), pp. 600–14.

Wardle, Captain F. M., *Barrow's Sepoy Officer's Manual*, Calcutta: Thacker, Spink and Co., 1922.

Waters, Major R. S., *History of the 5ᵗʰ Battalion (Pathans) 14ᵗʰ Punjab Regiment*, London: James Bain, 1936.

The Wesleyan Methodist Church: The Twenty-Sixth Report of the South India Provincial Synod, Madras, 1919.

Willcocks, James, 'India's Military Potentialities', *The Indian Review* (1917), p. 374.

———, *With the Indians in France*, London: Constable and Company, 1920.

Willcocks, William, *Sixty Years in the East*, London: W. Blackwood and Sons, 1935.

Willcox, W. H., 'The Treatment and Management of Diseases Due to Deficiency of Diet: Scurvy and Beri-beri', *The British Journal of Medicine*, vol. 1, no. 3081 (1920), pp. 73–77.

Williams, L. F. Rushbrook, *India in the Years 1917–1918*, Calcutta: Government Printing, 1919.

Wilson, Alban, *Sport and Service in Assam and Elsewhere*, London: Hutchinson and Co., 1924.

Wilson, Arnold, *Loyalties; Mesopotamia, 1914–1917: A Personal and Historical Record*, London: Oxford University Press, 1930.

Wilson, Arnold, *Mesopotamia 1917–1920: A Clash of Loyalties*, London: Oxford University Press, 1930.

Wolseley, Garnet, 'The Native Army of India', *The North American Review*, vol. 127, no. 263 (1878), pp. 132–56.

Wood, F. T. H., 'Civil Sanitary Work in Mesopotamia', *Public Health*, vol. 33, no. 10 (1920), pp. 159–64.

Woodyatt, Nigel Gresley, *Under Ten Viceroys: The Reminiscences of a Gurkha*, London: H. Jenkins, 1922.

Wratislaw, Albert Charles, *A Consul in the East*, London: Blackwood, 1924.

Wright, Arnold, *Southern India: Its History, People, Commerce and Industrial Resources*, London: The Foreign and Colonial Compiling and Publishing Co., 1914–15.

Yagnik, Indulal Kanaiyalal, *The Autobiography of Indulal Yagnik*, trans. Devavrat N. Pathak, Howard Spodek and John R. Wood, vol. 1, Manohar: Gujarat Vidyapith, 2011.

Yeats-Brown, Francis C. C., *The Lives of a Bengal Lancer*, New York: The Viking Press, 1930.

Younghusband, Francis, 'India', in Charles Lucas (ed.), *The Empire at War*, vol. 5, London: Oxford University Press, 1926, pp. 151–352.

SECONDARY SOURCES

Books

Ali, Imran, *The Punjab under Imperialism, 1885–1947*, Princeton: Princeton University Press, 1988.

Amin, Shahid, *Event, Metaphor, Memory: Chauri Chaura, 1922–1992*, Berkeley: University of California Press, 1995.

Anand, Mulk Raj, *Across the Black Waters*, 1940, Delhi: Orient Paperbacks, 2000.

———, *Untouchable*, 1935, London: Penguin, 1940.

Anonymous, Father Douglass of Behala, *By Some of His Friends*, London: Oxford University Press, 1952.

Arnold, David, *Colonizing the Body: State Medicine and Epidemic Disease in Nineteenth-Century India*, Berkeley; Los Angeles; London: University of California Press, 1993.

Balachandran, G., *Globalising Labour? Indian Seafarers and World Shipping, c. 1870–1945*, New Delhi: Oxford University Press, 2012.

Bayly, C. A., *The Birth of the Modern World, 1780–1914*, Oxford: Blackwell Publishing, 2004.

Bhattacharya, Nandini, *Contagion and Enclaves: Tropical Medicine in Colonial India*, Liverpool: Liverpool University Press, 2013.

Blackham, Robert J., *Scalpel, Sword and Stretcher*, London: Sampson Low, 1931.

Blyth, Robert J., *Empire of the Raj: India, Eastern Africa and the Middle East, 1858–1947*, Basingstoke; New York: Palgrave Macmillan, 2003.

Boyd, William, *An Ice-Cream War*, 1982, London: Penguin, 2014.

Bristow, R. C. B., *Memories of the British Raj*, London: Johnson, 1974.

Busch, Briton Cooper, *Britain, India, and the Arabs, 1914–1921*, Berkeley: University of California Press, 1971.

Caplan, Lionel, *Warrior Gentlemen: 'Gurkhas' in the Western Imagination*, Oxford: Berghahn, 1995.

Clifford, James and George Marcus (eds), *Writing Culture: The Poetics and Politics of Ethnography*, Berkeley: University of California Press, 1986.

Corbett, Jim, *My India*, Delhi: Oxford University Press, 1952.

———, *The Temple Tiger and More Man-Eaters of Kumaon*, New York: Oxford University Press, 1955.

Corrigan, Gordon, *Sepoys in the Trenches: The Indian Corps on the Western Front, 1914–1915*, Staplehurst: Spellmount, 1999.

Das, Santanu, *India, Empire, and First World War Culture: Writings, Images, and Songs*, Cambridge: Cambridge University Press, 2018.

Das, Santanu (ed.), *Race, Empire and First World War Writing*, Cambridge: Cambridge University Press, 2013.

Delaney, Douglas E., *The Imperial Army Project: Britain and the Land Forces of the Dominions and India, 1902–1945*, Oxford: Oxford University Press, 2018.

Dena, Lal, *History of Modern Manipur, 1826–1949*, Manipur: Orbit Publishers, 1991.

Dendooven, Dominiek and Piet Chielens, *World War I: Five Continents in Flanders*, Ypres Lannoo, 2008.

Digre, Brian, *Imperialism's New Clothes: The Repartition of Tropical Africa, 1914–1919*, New York: Peter Lang, 1990.

Ellinwood, DeWitt C., *Between Two Worlds: A Rajput Officer in the Indian Army, 1905–21, Based on the Diary of Amar Singh of Jaipur*, Lanham: Hamilton Books, 2005.

Ellinwood, DeWitt C. and S. D. Pradhan (eds), *India and World War I*, New Delhi: South Asia Books, 1978.

French, Patrick, *Younghusband: The Last Great Imperial Adventurer*, London: Harper Collins, 1994.

Gardner, Nikolas, *Trial by Fire: Command in the British Expeditionary Force in 1914*, Westport: Praeger, 2003.

Gerwarth, Robert and Erez Manela (eds), *Empires at War, 1911–1923*, Oxford: Oxford University Press, 2014.

Ghosh, Colonel A., *History of the Armed Forces Medical Services, India*, Orient Longman: New Delhi, 1988.

Grundlingh, Albert, *Fighting Their Own War*, Johannesburg: Ravan Press, 1987.

———, *War and Society: Participation and Remembrance: South African Black and Coloured Troops in the First World War, 1914–18*, Stellenbosch: SUN Media, 2014.

Guite, Jangkhomang and Thongkholal Haokip, *The Anglo-Kuki War, 1917–1919: A Frontier Uprising Against Imperialism During the First World War*, London; New York: Routledge, 2019 (South Asia Edition).

Haynes, Douglas E., *Rhetoric and Ritual in Colonial India: The Shaping of a Public Culture in Surat City, 1852–1928*, Berkeley: University of California Press, 1991.

Heathcote, T. A., *The Indian Army: The Garrison of British Imperial India, 1822–1922*, West Vancouver: David and Charles, 1974.

———, *The Military in British India: The Development of British Land Forces in South Asia, 1600–1947*, Manchester: Manchester University Press, 1995.

Hevia, James L., *Animal Labor and Colonial Warfare*, Chicago: Chicago University Press, 2018.

Holmes, T. R. E., *A History of the Indian Mutiny*, London: Allen and Co., 1888.

Howe, Glenford Deroy, *Race, War and Nationalism: A Social History of West Indians in the First World War*, Oxford: James Currey, 2002.

Jahr, Christoph, *Gewöhnliche Soldaten: Desertion und Deserteure im Deutschen und Britischen Heer 1914–1918*, Goettingen: Vandenhoeck und Ruprecht, 1998.

Jeffrey, Keith, *The British Army and the Crisis of Empire, 1918–22*, Manchester: Manchester University Press, 1984.

Johnston, Hugh J. M., *The Voyage of the Komagata Maru: The Sikh Challenge to Canada's Colour Bar* (revised and expanded 2nd edition), Vancouver: University of British Columbia Press, 2014.

Joshi, Chitra, *Lost Worlds: Indian Labour and its Forgotten Histories*, Delhi: Permanent Black, 2005.

Kant, Vedica, *'If I Die Here, Who Will Remember Me?': India and the First World War*, Delhi: Roli Books, 2014.

Kapur, B. K., *Yester Years, Ramblings and Reflections of a Former Indian Ambassador*, New Delhi: Siddharth Publications, 1994.

Kaul, Chandrika, *Reporting the Raj: The British Press and India, c. 1880–1920*, Manchester: Manchester University Press, 2003.

Kelly, John D., *A Politics of Virtue: Hinduism, Sexuality, and Countercolonial Discourse in Fiji*, Chicago; London: University of Chicago Press, 1992.

Kerr, Ian J., *Building the Railways of the Raj, 1850–1900*, Delhi: Oxford University Press, 1995.

Kitchen, James, *The British Imperial Army in the Middle East: Morale and Military Identity in the Sinai and Palestine Campaigns, 1916–18*, London: Bloomsbury 2015.

Lamare, Sylvanus, *The Role of the Khasi Labour Corps in World War I*, Shillong: Eses Plus Publications, 2017.

Liebau, Heike, Katrin Bromber, Dyala Hamza, Katharina Lange, and Ravi Ahuja (eds), *The World in World Wars: Experiences, Perceptions and Perspectives from Africa and Asia*, Leiden: Brill, 2010.

Lowis, Cecil Champain, *The Dripping Tamarinds*, London: Laurie, 1933.

Mawani, Renisa, *Across Oceans of Law: The Komagata Maru and Jurisdiction in the Time of Empire*, Durham; London: Duke University Press, 2018.

Mazumder, Rajit K., *The Indian Army and the Making of Punjab*, Delhi: Permanent Black, 2011Metcalf.

Thomas, *Imperial Connections: India in the Indian Ocean Arena 1860–1920*, Ranikhet: Permanent Black, 2007.

Morton-Jack, George, *The Indian Army on the Western Front: India's Expeditionary Force to France and Belgium in the First World War*, Cambridge: Cambridge University Press, 2014.

———, *The Indian Empire at War: From Jihad to Victory, The Untold Story of the Indian Army in the First World War*, London: Little, Brown and Company, 2018.

Murphy, Eamon, *Unions in Conflict: A Comparative Study of Four South Indian Textile Centres, 1918–1939*, New Delhi: Manohar, 1981.

Natarajan, Nalini, *The Missionary Among the Khasis*, New Delhi: Sterling, 1977.

Niemeijer, A. C., *The Khilafat Movement in India, 1919–1924*, The Hague: Nijhoff, 1972.

Offer, Avner, *The First World War: An Agrarian Interpretation*, Oxford: Oxford University Press, 1989.

Omissi, David, *The Sepoy and the Raj: The Indian Army, 1860–1940*, London: Macmillan, 1994.

Onley, James, *The Arabian Frontier of the British Raj: Merchants, Rulers and the British in the Nineteenth-Century Gulf*, Oxford: Oxford University Press, 2007.

Orpen, William, *An Onlooker in France, 1917–1919*, London: Williams and Norgate, 1921.

Pachuau, Joy L. K. and William Schendel, *The Camera as Witness: A Social History of Mizoram, Northeast India*, Delhi: Cambridge University Press, 2015.

Page, Melvin E. and Andy McKinlay (eds), *Africa and the First World War*, London: Palgrave Macmillan, 1987.

Palit, Major General D. K., *Major General A. A. Rudra: His Service in Three Armies and Two World Wars*, New Delhi: Reliance Publishing House, 1997.

Paris, Timothy J., *Britain, the Hashemites and Arab Rule, 1920–1925: The Sherifian Solution*, London: Frank Cass, 2003.

Pernau, Margrit, *The Passing of Patrimonialism: Politics and Political Culture in Hyderabad 1911–1948*, Delhi: Manohar, 2000.

Pierce, Steven and Anupama Rao (eds), *Discipline and the Other Body*, Durham; London: Duke University Press, 2006.

Prasad, Ritika, *Tracks of Change: Railways and Everyday Life in Colonial India*, Cambridge: Cambridge University Press, 2015.

Prashad, Vijay, *Untouchable Freedom: A Social History of a Dalit Community*, Delhi: Oxford University Press, 2000.

Qureshi, M. Naeem, *Pan-Islam in British Indian Politics: A Study of the Khilafat Movement, 1918–1924*, Leiden: Brill, 1999.

Rabinbach, Anson, The Human Motor: Energy, Fatigue and the Origins of Modernity, New York: Basic Books, 1990.

Radhakrishna, Meena, *Dishonoured by History: 'Criminal Tribes' and British Colonial Policy*, Delhi: Oxford University Press, 2001.

Ramnath, Maia, *Haj to Utopia: How the Ghadar Movement Charted Global Radicalism and Attempted to Overthrow the British Empire*, Berkeley: University of California University Press, 2011.

Rao, Anupama, *The Caste Question: Dalits and the Politics of Modern India*, Berkeley: University of California Press, 2009.

Rawat, Ramnarayan S., *Reconsidering Untouchability: Chamars and Dalit History in North India*, Bloomington; Indianapolis: Indiana University Press, 2011.

Roy, Franziska, Heike Liebau, and Ravi Ahuja (eds), *'When the War Began We Heard of Several Kings': South Asian Prisoners in World War I Germany*, Delhi: Social Sciences Press, 2011.

Roy, Kaushik, *Indian Army and the First World War: 1914–18*, Delhi: Oxford University Press, 2018.

Roy, Kaushik (ed.), *The Indian Army in Two World Wars*, Leiden: Brill, 2012.

Roy, Tirthankar, and Anand V. Swamy, *Law and the Economy in Colonial India*, Chicago; London: University of Chicago, 2016.

Ruivanao, Ringkahao, *Biography of RS Ruichumhao/Haopa (1896–1933)*, Somdal, 2008.

Sarkar, Sumit, *Modern India 1885–1947*, Delhi: Macmillan, 1983.

Sakhong, Lian H., *In Search of Chin Identity: A Study in Religion, Politics and Ethnic Identity in Burma*, Copenhagen: NIAS Press, 2003.

Seipp, Adam R., *The Ordeal of Peace: Demobilization and the Urban Experience in Britain and Germany, 1917–1921*, Farnham: Ashgate, 2009.

Sharma, Asha, *An American in Gandhi's India: The Biography of Satyanand Stokes*, Bloomington: Indiana University Press, 2008.

Singh, Gajendra, *The Testimonies of Indian Soldiers and the Two World Wars: Between Self and Sepoy*, London: Bloomsbury, 2014.

Singha, Radhika, *A Despotism of Law: Crime and Justice in Early Colonial India*, Delhi: Oxford University Press, 1998.

Slim, Field Marshal Sir William, *Unofficial History*, London: Cassell, 1959.

Starling, John and Ivor Lee, *No Labour, No Battle: Military Labour during the First World War*, Stroud: Spellmount, 2009.

Strachan, Hew, *The First World War*, New York: Viking, 2005.

———, *The First World War: To Arms*, Oxford: Oxford University Press, 2011.

Streets, Heather, *Martial Races: The Military, Race and Masculinity in British Imperial Culture, 1857–1914*, Manchester: Manchester University Press, 2004.

Summerskill, Michael, *China on the Western Front: Britain's Chinese Work Force in the First World War*, London: Michael Summerskill, 1982.

Sumner, Ian, *The Indian Army, 1914–1947*, Oxford: Osprey, 2001.

Tan, Tai Yong, *The Garrison State: Military, Government and Society in Colonial Punjab, 1849–1947*, New Delhi: Sage, 2005.

Tarazi Fawaz, Leila, *Land of Aching Hearts: The Middle East in the Great War*, Cambridge, MA: Harvard University Press, 2014.

Tete, Peter, *A Missionary Social Worker in India; The Chota Nagpur Tenancy Act and the Catholic Cooperatives (1893–1928)*, Ranchi: Satya Bharatchi Press, 1986.

Thomas, P. J., *The Growth of Federal Finance in India: Being a Survey of India's Public Finances from 1833 to 1939*, London: Oxford University Press, 1939.

Tinker, Hugh, *A New System of Slavery: The Export of Indian Labour Overseas, 1830–1920*, Oxford: Oxford University Press, 1974.

Trench, Charles Chenevix, *The Indian Army and the King's Enemies, 1900–1947*, London: Thames and Hudson, 1988.

Ulrichsen, Kristian Coates, *The First World War in the Middle East*, London: Hurst and Company, 2014.

———, *The Logistics and Politics of the British Campaigns in the Middle East, 1914–22*, Basingstoke: Palgrave Macmillan, 2011.

Vanlalchhuanawma, *Christianity and Subaltern Culture: Revival Movement as a Cultural Response to Westernisation in Mizoram*, Mizoram: ISPCK, 2007.

Xu, Guoqi, *Strangers on the Western Front: Chinese Workers in the Great War*, Cambridge, MA: Harvard University Press, 2011.

Zorema, J., *Indirect Rule in Mizoram, 1890–1954*, New Delhi: Mittal Publications, 2007.

Zürcher, Erik-Jan (ed.), *Fighting for a Living: A Comparative History of Military Labour 1500–2000*, Amsterdam: Amsterdam University Press, 2013.

Chapters in Edited Books

Ahuja, Ravi, 'The Corrosiveness of Comparison', in Heike Liebau, Katrin Bromber, Dyala Hamza, Katharina Lange and Ravi Ahuja (eds), *The World in World Wars: Experiences, Perceptions and Perspectives from Africa and Asia*, Leiden: Brill, 2010, pp. 131–66.

———, 'Networks of Subordination—Networks of the Subordinated: The Ordered Spaces of South Asian Maritime Labour in an Age of Imperialism (c. 1890–1947)', in Ashwini Tambe and Harald Fischer-Tiné (eds), *The Limits of British Colonial Control in South Asia: Spaces of Disorder in the Indian Ocean Region*, New York: Routledge, 2009, pp. 13–48.

Bhattacharya, Shahana, 'Rotting Hides and Runaway Labour: Labour Control and Workers' Resistance in the Indian Leather Industry, c. 1860–1960', in Ravi Ahuja (ed.), *Working Lives and Worker Militancy: The Politics of Labour in Colonial India*, Delhi: Tulika, 2013.

Cabanes, Bruno, '1919: Aftermath', in Jay Winter (ed.), *The Cambridge History of the First World War*, Cambridge: Cambridge University Press, 2014, pp. 172–98.

Chatterjee, Indrani, 'Slavery, Semantics and the Sound of Silence', in Indrani Chatterjee and Richard M. Eaton (eds), *Slavery and South Asian Society*, Bloomington: Indiana University Press, 2006, pp. 287–315.

Chhina, Rana, 'Their Mercenary Calling: The Indian Army on Gallipoli 1915', in Ashley Ekins (ed.), *Gallipoli: A Ridge Too Far*, Wollomb: Exisle Publishing, 2013, pp. 233–53.

Dixon, Conrad, 'Lascars: the forgotten sea-men', in R. Ommer and G. Panting (eds), *Working Men Who Got Wet*, St John's: Memorial University of Newfoundland, 1980, pp. 265–81.

Ghosh, Kaushik, 'A Market for Aboriginality: Primitivism and Race Classification in the Indentured Labour Market of Colonial India', in Gautam Bhadra, Gyan Prakash and Susie Tharu (eds), *Subaltern Studies No. 10: Writings on South Asian History and Society*, Delhi: Oxford University Press, 1999, pp. 8–48.

Guite, Jangkhomang, '"Fighting the White Men till the Last Bullet": The General Course of the Anglo-Kuki War', in Jangkhomang Guite and Thongkholal Haokip (eds), *The Anglo-Kuki War, 1917–1919: A Frontier Uprising Against Imperialism During the First World War*, London; New York: Routledge, 2019, pp. 37–77.

Harrison, Mark, 'Disease, Discipline and Dissent: The Indian Army in France and England, 1914–1915', in Roger Cooter, Mark Harrison and Steve Sturdy (eds), *Medicine and Modern Warfare*, Amsterdam: Atlanta, 1999, pp. 185–203.

Kitchen, James, 'The Indianization of the Egyptian Expeditionary Force: Palestine 1918', in Kaushik Roy (ed.), *The Indian Army in the Two World Wars*, Leiden: Brill, 2012, pp. 165–90.

Mahato, Pashupati Prasad, 'Assertion and Reassertion as Jharkhandi: A History of Indigenous People of 1763–2007', in Asha Mishra and Chittaranjan Kumar Paty (eds), *Tribal Movements in Jharkhand, 1857–2007*, New Delhi: Concept Publishing, 2010.

Markovits, Claude, 'Indian Soldiers' Experiences in France during World War I: Seeing Europe from the Rear of the Front', in Heike Liebau, Katrin Bromber, Katharina Lange, Dyala Hamzah and Ravi Ahuja (eds), *The World in World Wars: Experiences, Perceptions and Perspectives from Africa and Asia*, Leiden: Brill, 2010, pp. 29–54.

Mohapatra, Prabhu P., 'Assam and the West Indies, 1860–1920: Immobilising Plantation Labour', in Douglas Hay and Paul Craven (eds), *Masters, Servants and Magistrates in Britain and Empire, 1562–1955*, Chapel Hill: University of North Carolina Press, 2004, pp. 455–80.

Mycock, Andrew, 'The First World War Centenary in the UK: "A truly national commemoration"?', in Ashley Jackson (ed.), *The British Empire and the First World War*, London; New York: Routledge, 2016, pp. 429–39.

Ningmuanching, '"As Men of One Country": Rethinking the History of the Anglo-Kuki War', in Jangkhomang Guite and Thongkholal Haokip (eds), *The Anglo-Kuki War, 1917–1919: A Frontier Uprising Against Imperialism During the First World War*, London; New York: Routledge, 2019, pp. 168–97.

Peers, Douglas M., 'The Raj's Other Great Game: Policing the Sexual Frontiers of the Indian Army in the First Half of the Nineteenth Century', in Steven Pierce and Anupama Rao (eds), *Discipline and the Other Body*, Durham; London: Duke University Press, 2006, pp. 115–50.

Schofield, John, 'Message and Materiality in Mesopotamia, 1916–1917', in Nicholas J. Saunders and Paul Cornish (eds), *Contested Objects: Material Memories of the Great War*, London: Routledge, 2009, pp. 203–36.

Searle, Geoffrey, 'The Politics of National Efficiency and of War, 1900–1918', in Chris Wrigley (ed.), *A Companion to Early Twentieth-Century Britain*, Malden, MA: Wiley-Blackwell, 2003, pp. 56–71.

Singha, Radhika, 'Front Lines and Status Lines: Sepoy and "Menial" in the Great War, 1916–1920', in Heike Liebau, Katrin Bromber, Katharina Lange, Dyala Hamzah and Ravi Ahuja (eds), *The World in World Wars: Experiences, Perceptions and Perspectives from Africa and Asia*, Leiden: Brill, 2010, pp. 55–106.

——, 'India's Silver Bullets: War Loans and War Propaganda, 1917–18', in Maartje Abbenhuis, Neill Atkinson, Kingsley Baird and Gail Romano (eds), *The Myriad Legacies of 1917: A Year of War and Revolution*, Cham: Palgrave Macmillan, 2018, pp. 77–102.

——, 'Passport, Ticket, and India-Rubber Stamp: "The Problem of the Pauper Pilgrim" in Colonial India c. 1882–1925', in Ashwini Tambe and Harald Fischer-Tiné (eds), *The Limits of British Colonial Control in South Asia: Spaces of Disorder in the Indian Ocean Region*, New York: Routledge, 2009, pp. 49–83.

——, 'The Recruiter's Eye on "The Primitive": To France—and Back—in the Indian Labour Corps', in James E. Kitchen, Alisa Miller and Laura Rowe (eds), *Other Combatants, Other Fronts*, Newcastle-upon-Tyne: Cambridge Scholars, 2011, pp. 199–224.

Tamir, Dan, 'Something New under the Fog of War', in Richard P. Tucker, Tait Keller, J. R. McNeill and Martin Schmid (eds), *Environmental Histories of the First World War*, Cambridge: Cambridge University Press, 2018, pp. 117–35.

Vumlallian Zou, David, 'Patriots and Utilitarians in the Anglo-Kuki War: The Case of Southern Manipur, 1917–1919', in Jangkhomang Guite and Thongkholal Haokip (eds), *The Anglo-Kuki War, 1917–1919: A Frontier Uprising Against Imperialism During the First World War*, London; New York: Routledge, 2019, pp. 157–67.

Journal Articles

Ahuja, Ravi, 'A Beveridge Plan for India? Social Insurance and the Making of the "Formal Sector"', *International Review of Social History*, vol. 64, no. 2 (2019), pp. 1–42.

Arnold, David, 'The "Discovery" of Malnutrition and Diet in Colonial India', *The Indian Economic & Social History Review*, vol. 31, no. 1 (1994), pp. 1–26.

Atabaki, Touraj, 'Far from Home, but at Home: Indian Migrant Workers in the Iranian Oil Industry', *Studies in History*, vol. 31, no. 1 (2015), pp. 85–114.

Bailkin, Jordanna, 'The Boot and the Spleen: When Was Murder Possible in British India?', *Comparative Studies in Society and History*, vol. 48, no. 2 (2006), pp. 462–93.

Bhadra, Gautam, 'The Kuki (?) Uprising (1917–1919): Its Causes and Nature', *Man in India*, vol. 55, no. 1 (1975), pp. 10–56.

Blayney, Steffan, 'Industrial Fatigue and the Productive Body: The Science of Work in Britain, c. 1900–1918', *Social History of Medicine*, vol. 32, no. 2 (2019), pp. 310–28.

Bose, Sugata, 'Nation, Reason and Religion: India's Independence in International Perspective', *Economic and Political Weekly*, vol. 33, no. 31 (1998), pp. 2090–97.

Breman, Jan and E. Valentine Daniel, 'Conclusion: The Making of a Coolie', *The Journal of Peasant Studies*, vol. 19, nos 3–4 (1992), pp. 268–95.

Buxton, Hilary, 'Imperial Amnesia: Race, Trauma and Indian Troops in the First World War', *Past and Present*, vol. 241, no. 1 (2018), pp. 221–58.

Chandra, Siddhartha, Goran Kuljanin and Jennifer Wray, 'Mortality from the Influenza Pandemic of 1918–1919: The Case of India', *Demography*, vol. 49, no. 3 (2012), pp. 857–65.

Cherian, Neema, 'Spaces for Races: Ordering of Camp Followers in the Military Cantonments, Madras Presidency, c. 1800–64', *Social Scientist*, vol. 32, no. 5/6 (2004), pp. 32–50.

Cooper, Frederick, 'What is the Concept of Globalization Good For? An African Historian's Perspective', *African Affairs*, vol. 100, no. 399 (2001), pp. 189–213.

Dasgupta, Sangeeta, 'Reordering a World: The Tana Bhagat Movement, 1914–1919', *Studies in History*, vol. 15, no. 1 (1999), pp. 1–41.

Deringil, Selim, '"They Live in a State of Nomadism and Savagery": The Late Ottoman Empire and the Post-Colonial Debate', *Comparative Studies in Society and History*, vol. 45, no. 2 (2003), pp. 311–42.

Dzuvichu, Lipokmar, 'Empire on their Backs: Coolies in the Eastern Borderlands of the British Raj', *International Review of Social History*, vol. 59, no. 22 (2014), pp. 89–112.

———, 'Roads and the Raj: The Politics of Road Building in Colonial Naga Hills, 1860s–1910s', *Indian Economic Social History Review*, vol. 50, no. 4 (2013), pp. 473–94.

Fischer-Tiné, Harald, '"Unparalleled Opportunities": The Indian Y.M.C.A.'s Army Work Schemes for Imperial Troops During the Great War (1914–1920)', *The Journal of Imperial and Commonwealth History*, vol. 47, no. 1 (2019), pp. 100–37.

Fogarty, Richard S., and David Killingray, 'Demobilization in British and French Africa at the End of the First World War', *Journal of Contemporary History*, vol. 50, no. 1 (2014), pp. 100–23.

Ganachari, Aravind, 'First World War: Purchasing Indian Loyalties: Imperial Policy of Recruitment and "Rewards"', *Economic and Political Weekly*, vol. 40, no. 8 (2005), pp. 779–88.

Greenhut, Jeffrey, 'The Imperial Reserve: The Indian Corps on the Western Front, 1914–15', *The Journal of Imperial and Commonwealth History*, vol. 12, no. 1 (1983), pp. 54–73.

Griffin, Nicholas J., 'Britain's Chinese Labour Corps in World War I', *Military Affairs*, vol. 40, no. 3 (1976), pp. 102–8.

Hopkins, A., 'Back to the Future: From National History to Imperial History', *Past and Present*, vol. 164, no. 1 (1999), pp. 198–243.

Hyson, S. and A. Lester, 'British India on Trial: Brighton Military Hospitals and the Politics of Empire in World War I', *Journal of Historical Geography*, vol. 38, no. 1 (2001), pp. 18–34.

Jackson, Kyle, 'Globalizing an Indian Borderland Environment: Aijal, Mizoram, 1890–1919', *Studies in History*, vol. 32, no. 1 (2016), pp. 39–71.

Johnson, R. A., '"Russians at the Gates of India"? Planning the Defence of India, 1885–1900', *Journal of Military History*, vol. 67, no. 3 (2003), pp. 697–743.

Johnston, Hugh, 'Group Identity in an Emigrant Worker Community: The Example of Sikhs in Twentieth-Century British Columbia', *British Columbia Studies*, no. 148 (2005/6), pp. 1–21.

Kamat, Manjiri N., 'The War Years and the Sholapur Cotton Textile Industry', *Social Scientist*, vol. 26, nos 11–12 (1998), pp. 67–82.

Killingray, David and James Matthews, 'Beasts of Burden: British West African Carriers in the First World War', *Canadian Journal of African Studies*, vol. 13, nos 1–2 (1979), pp. 5–23.

MacDonald, Kenneth Iain, 'Push and Shove: Spatial History and the Construction of a Portering Economy in Northern Pakistan', *Comparative Studies in Society and History*, vol. 40, no. 2 (1998), pp. 287–317.

Mawani, Renisa, 'Law As Temporality: Colonial Politics and Indian Settlers', *UC Irvine Law Review*, vol. 4, no. 1 (2014), pp. 65–95.

Mayer, Peter, 'Inventing Village Tradition: The Late 19th Century Origins of the North Indian "Jajmani System"', *Modern Asian Studies*, vol. 27, no. 2 (1993), pp. 357–95.

McKeown, Adam, 'Global Migration: 1846–1940', *Journal of World History*, vol. 15, no. 2 (2004), pp. 155–89.

Miley, Frances and Andrew Read, 'The Purgatorial Shadows of War: Accounting, Blame and Shell Shock Pensions, 1914–1923', *Accounting History*, vol. 22, no. 1 (2016), pp. 5–28.

Moyd, Michelle, 'Making the Household, Making the State: Colonial Military Communities and Labour in German East Africa', *International Journal of Labour and Working Class History*, vol. 80, no. 1 (2011), pp. 53–76.

Mukharji, Projit Bihar, 'From Serosocial to Sanguinary Identities: Caste, Transnational Race Science and the Shifting Metonymies of Blood Group B, India c. 1918–1960', *The Indian Economic and Social History Review*, vol. 51, no. 2 (2014), pp. 143–76.

Murphy, Paul, 'Queen Mary's Institute, Pune', *History Today*, vol. 45, no. 11 (1995).

Pachuau, Joy L. K., 'Sainghinga and his Times: Codifying Mizo Attire', *MZU Journal of Literature and Cultural Studies*, vol. 2, no. 2 (2015), pp. 272–93.

Ramnath, Maia, 'Two Revolutions: The Ghadar Movement and India's Radical Diaspora, 1913–1918', *Radical History Review*, vol. 92 (2005), pp. 7–30.

Rothwell, V. H., 'Mesopotamia in British War Aims, 1914–1918', *The Historical Journal*, vol. 13, no. 2 (1970), pp. 273–94.

Rubinstein, W. D., 'Henry Page Croft and the National Party, 1917–1922', *Journal of Contemporary History*, vol. 9, no. 1 (1974), pp. 129–48.

Sarkar, Aditya, 'The Tie That Snapped: Bubonic Plague and Mill Labour in Bombay,

1896–1898', *International Review of Social History*, vol. 59, no. 2 (2014), pp. 181–214.

Satia, Priya, 'Developing Iraq: Britain, India and the Redemption of Empire and Technology in the First World War', *Past and Present*, vol. 197, no. 1 (2007), pp. 211–25.

Singha, Radhika, 'Finding Labor from India for the War in Iraq: The Jail Porter and Labor Corps, 1916–1920', *Comparative Studies in Society and History*, vol. 49, no. 2 (2007), pp. 412–45.

———, 'The Great War and a "Proper" Passport for the Colony: Border-Crossing in British India, c. 1882–1922', *Indian Economic and Social History Review*, vol. 50, no. 3 (2013), pp. 289–315.

———, 'The "Rare Infliction": The Abolition of Flogging in the Indian Army, circa 1835–1920', *Law and History Review*, vol. 34, no. 3 (2016), pp. 783–818.

Stolte, Carolien and Harald Fischer-Tiné, 'Imagining Asia in India: Nationalism and Internationalism (ca. 1905–1940)', *Comparative Studies in Society and History*, vol. 54, no. 1 (2012), pp. 65–92.

Strachan, Hew, 'The First World War as a Global War', *First World War Studies*, vol. 1, no. 1 (2010), pp. 3–14.

Sundar, Nandini, 'Interning Insurgent Populations: The Buried Histories of Indian Democracy', *Economic and Political Weekly*, vol. 46, no. 6 (2011), pp. 47–57.

Tabili, Laura, 'The Construction of Racial Difference in Twentieth-Century Britain: The Special Restriction (Coloured Alien Seamen) Order, 1925', *Journal of British Studies*, vol. 33, no. 1 (1994), pp. 54–98.

Tan, Tai Yong, 'Assuaging the Sikhs: Government Responses to the Akali Movement, 1920–1925', *Modern Asian Studies*, vol. 29, no. 3 (1995), pp. 655–703.

Tetzlaff, Stefan, 'The Turn of the Gulf Tide: Empire, Nationalism and South Asian Labor Migration to Iraq, c. 1900–1935', *International Labor and Working Class History*, vol. 79, no. 1 (2011), pp. 7–27.

Tinker, Hugh, 'India in the First World War and After', *Journal of Contemporary History*, vol. 3, no. 4 (1968), pp. 89–107.

Wald, Erica, 'Health, Discipline and Appropriate Behavior: The Body of the Soldier and the Shape of the Cantonment', *Modern Asian Studies*, vol. 46, no. 4 (2012), pp. 815–56.

Winter, Jay, 'Remembrance and Redemption', *Harvard Design Magazine*, no. 9 (1999), http://www.harvarddesignmagazine.org/issues/9/remembrance-and-redemption, last accessed 10 November 2019.

Zou, David Vumlallian, 'Raiding the Dreaded Past: Representations of Headhunting and Human Sacrifice in North-East India', *Contributions to Indian Sociology*, vol. 39, no. 1, (2005), pp. 75–105.

SELECT BIBLIOGRAPHY

Online Sources

1914–1918-online: International Encyclopedia of the First World War, ed. Ute Daniel, Peter Gatrell, Oliver Janz, Heather Jones, Jennifer Keene, Alan Kramer and Bill Nasson, Berlin: Freie Universität Berlin, http://www.1914–1918-online.net/index. html, last accessed 10 November 2019.

6th Queen Elizabeth's Own Gurkha Rifles, https://www.6thgurkhas.org, last accessed 17 November 2019.

Abadzi, Helen, 'The Indian Cemetery in Salonica', 30 November 2006, https:// elinepa.org/en/the-indian-cemetery-of-salonica, last accessed 10 November 2019.

'Ambulance', *Encyclopaedia Britannica*, 1911, https://en.wikisource.org/wiki/1911_ Encyclopædia_Britannica/Ambulance, last accessed 10 November 2019.

Brozek, John E., 'The History and Evolution of the Wristwatch', *International Watchman Magazine*, January 2004, https://www.qualitytyme.net/pages/rolex_ articles/history_of_wristwatch.html, last accessed 10 November 2019.

Fecitt, Harry, 'The Indian Railway Corps, East African Expeditionary Force 1914– 1919', April 2015, http://gweaa.com/wp-content/uploads/2012/02/The-Indian-Railway-Corps-East-African-Expeditionary-Force_1.pdf, last accessed 10 November 2019.

'Fighting the Marris and the Khetrans', The Soldier's Burden, http://www.kaiserscross. com/304501/478822.html, last accessed 15 November 2019.

'First Despatch on Indian Constitutional Reforms', Calcutta, Government of India, 1928, https://archive.org/details/firstdespatchoni029261mbp, last accessed 10 November 2019.

'"France li Kata Ko": Mao Naga Labour Corps in First World War', *The Morung Express*, 30 December 2018, http://www.manipur.org/news/2018/12/30/france-li-kata-ko-mao-naga-labour-corps-in-first-world-war-morung-express/, last accessed 10 November 2019.

Gandhi, Mahatma, *The Collected Works of Mahatma Gandhi*, Mahatma Gandhi Media and Research Service, https://www.gandhiservefoundation.org/about-mahatma-gandhi/collected-works-of-mahatma-gandhi, last accessed 11 November 2019.

'Garo Labour Corps Recruits Remembered on 100th Anniversary', *The Shillong Times*, 16 July 2018, www.theshillongtimes.com/2018/07/16/garo-labour-corps-recruits-remembered-on-100th-anniversary/, last accessed 17 November 2019.

'German Ral Run' ('The Storming of the German Troops'), Mizo (Lushai) song, trans. Cherrie Lalnunziri Chhangte, http://mizdaydreambeliever.blogspot.fr/2008_ 01_01_archive.html, last accessed 10 November 2019.

Grant, David, 'Silver or Bronze Medals to Public Followers and Others', https://www. angloboerwar.com/forum/15-important-decisions-book/641-bronze-or-silver, last accessed 10 November 2019.

'A Guide to British Campaign Medals of WW1', The Great War 1914–1918, http:// www.greatwar.co.uk/medals/ww1-campaign-medals.htm, last accessed 11 November 2019.

Hausing, Kham Khan Suan, 'Unmindful of History: On Biren Singh and Manipur', *The Hindu*, 29 December 2017, https://www.thehindu.com/opinion/op-ed/unmindful-of-history/article22320391.ece, last accessed 10 November 2019.

House of Commons, Hansard Archives, http://hansard.millbanksystems.com, last accessed 10 November 2019.

Imperial War Museum, https://www.iwm.org.uk/, last accessed 10 November 2019.

'India Restores her War Cripples to Self-Support', Library of Congress, 1919, https://www.loc.gov/item/00651704, last accessed 18 November 2019.

'Indian Army Order by His Excellency the Commander-in-Chief in India', 1916, https://archive.org/stream/in.ernet.dli.2015.108822/2015.108822, last accessed 10 November 2019.

'Indian Military Transport Units in Macedonia', The Soldier's Burden, http://www.kaiserscross.com/304501/534401.html, last accessed 10 November 2019.

Jacobsen, Marc H., 'The Third Afghan War and the External Position of India, 1919–1924', Naval Oceans Systems Centre, San Diego, CA, http://www.dtic.mil/dtic/tr/fulltext/u2/a195401, last accessed 10 November 2019.

Jewish Virtual Library, http://www.jewishvirtuallibrary.org, last accessed 15 November 2019.

'J. P. Mills and the Chittagong Hill Tracts, 1926/27: Tour Diary, Reports, Photographs', ed. Wolfgang Mey, http://crossasia-repository.ub.uni-heidelberg.de/548/1/J.P._Mills_and_the_Chittagong_Hill_Tracts.pdf, last accessed 15 November 2019.

'King George V decorates Havildar Gagna Singh with the Indian Order of Merit, 21 August 1915' in Hannah Midgley, 'Brighton Pavilion's Crowned Care for Wounded Soldiers', *Brighton Journal*, 15 March 2016, https://bjournal.co/brighton-pavilions-crowned-care-for-wounded-soldiers, last accessed 18 November 2019.

Lian, Salai Van Cung, 'Chin Involvement in World War 1', *Burma News International*, 15 November 2014, https://www.bnionline.net/en/chin-world/item/17872-chin-involvement-in-world-war-1-the-great-war.html, last accessed 11 November 2019.

Lyons, Rupert, 'Audio memoirs of Major L. W. A. Lyons', https://www.bbc.co.uk/history/ww2peopleswar/user/91/u2169891.shtml, last accessed 10 November 2019.

MacMunn, George F., 'Mesopotamia: The Land Between the Rivers', *The Cornhill Magazine*, 7 December 1918, https://jfredmacdonald.com/worldwarone1914-1918/ottoman-18mesopotamia.html, last accessed 10 November 2019.

McMurtrie, Douglas C., *The Disabled Soldier*, Macmillan: New York, 1919, https://commons.wikimedia.org/wiki/File:The_disabled_soldier_(1919)_(14763611871).jpg, last accessed 10 November 2019.

'Memorials located within the Borough of Swale, Kent', Historical Research Group of Sittingbourne, http://www.hrgs.co.uk/wp-content/uploads/2017/10/Swale-memorials-list-as-at-2.3.2017.pdf, last accessed 10 November 2019.

'Menial', *Encyclopaedia Britannica*, 1911, https://theodora.com/encyclopedia/m/menial.html, last accessed 10 November 2019.

Moyd, Michelle, 'Extra-European Theatres of War', *1914–1918-online: International Encyclopedia of the First World War*, https://encyclopedia.1914–1918-online.net/article/extra-european_theatres_of_war, last accessed 10 November 2019.

Naga Exploratour, http://himalaya.socanth.cam.ac.uk/collections/naga/coll/4/xcontents/detail/all/index.html, last accessed 10 November 2019.

National Army Museum, www.nam.ac.uk/online-collection, last accessed 17 November 2019.

'New Zealand Memorial Brockenhurst', https://www.ypressalient.co.uk/New%20Zealand%20Memorial%20brockenhurst.htm, last accessed 10 November 2019.

Ngakang, Tuisem, 'Forgotten heroes of World War I: The Tangkhul Naga Labour Corps' Morung Express, 26 March 2017, https://issuu.com/morung_express/docs/march_26th__2017/10, last accessed 10 November 2019.

Ollivant, Alfred, 'The Indian Hospital', 1916, http://www.sikhmuseum.com/brighton/arts/ollivant/index.html, last accessed 10 November 2019.

Onta, Pratyoush, 'Dukha during the World War', *Himal*, 6 December 2016, http://himalmag.com/dukha-during-the-world-war, last accessed 18 November 2019.

Pandey, Sunir, '100 Years of Platitudes', *Nepali Times*, 3–9 January 2014, http://archive.nepalitimes.com/article/nation/100-years-of-platitudes,1025, last accessed 10 November 2019.

Papers Past, National Library of New Zealand, paperspast.natlib.govt.nz, last accessed 15 November 2019.

Putkowski, Julian, 'Mutiny in India in 1919', https://www.marxists.org/history/etol/revhist/backiss/vol8/no2/putkowski2.html, last accessed 10 November 2019.

Qatar Digital Library, https://www.qdl.qa/en, last accessed 10 November 2019.

'Real Dogs of War: England Will Send a Force to Act in Expedition Against the Abors', *New York Times*, 20 August 1911, https://www.nytimes.com/1911/08/20/archives/real-dogs-of-war-england-will-send-a-force-to-act-in-expedition.html, last accessed 10 November 2019.

Reddy, E. S., 'India and the Anglo-Boer War', 29 July 1999, http://www.mkgandhi.org/articles/boer_war.htm, last accessed 10 November 2019.

Rodrigues, Jason, 'Indian Railway "Coolies" to be Renamed in Bid to Improve their Status', *The Guardian*, 2 March 2016, https://www.theguardian.com/world/2016/mar/02/indian-railway-coolies-renamed-improve-status, last accessed 10 November 2019.

'Sahayaks in Army not to be Employed for Menial Tasks: Govt', *The Economic Times*, 12 June 2018, https://economictimes.indiatimes.com/news/defence/sahayaks-in-army-not-to-be-employed-for-menial-tasks-govt/articleshow/57756206.cms?from=mdr, last accessed 10 November 2019.

Shaiza, Pamkhuila and Kachuiwung Ronra Shimray, 'Did the White Soldiers Really Cannibalise Naga Labour Corps During World War I?', DailyO, 1 June 2017, https://www.dailyo.in/variety/cannibalism-tangkhul-naga-labour-corps-northeast-india-northeast/story/1/17564.html, last accessed 17 November 2019.

Singh, Sushant, 'Simply put: Why Sahayak is 'Buddy" for Army, Servant for Critics', *Indian Express*, 16 March 2017, https://indianexpress.com/article/explained/lance-naik-roy-mathew-sindhav-jogidas-simply-put-why-sahayak-is-buddy-for-army-servant-for-critics-4560889/, last accessed 13 November 2019.

Singha, Radhika, 'Indian Labour Corps', *1914–1918-online: International Encyclopedia of the First World War*, https://encyclopedia.1914–1918-online.net/article/indian_labour_corps, last accessed 10 November 2019.

———, 'Iraq: on duty once again?', *The Hindu*, 21 March 2004, https://www.the-hindu.com/todays-paper/tp-features/tp-sundaymagazine/iraq-on-duty-once-again/article28526093.ece, last accessed 26 September 2019.

———, 'Labour (India)', *1914–1918-online: International Encyclopedia of the First World War*, https://encyclopedia.1914–1918-online.net/article/labour_india, last accessed 10 November 2019.

'The Story of India Tea 1917–1918', British Pathé, https://www.youtube.com/watch?v=v5merLaAw4A, last accessed 10 November 2019.

Strachan, Hew, 'Pre-War Military Planning (Great Britain)', *1914–1918-online: International Encyclopedia of the First World War*, https://encyclopedia.1914–1918-online.net/article/pre-war_military_planning_great_britain, last accessed 10 November 2019.

Trove, National Library of Australia, http://trove.nla.gov.au/newspaper, last accessed 18 November 2019.

'Tura Remembers Garo Recruits to France during WWI', *The Shillong Times*, 17 July 2012, http://theshillongtimes.com/2012/07/17/tura-remembers-garo-recruits-to-france-during-ww-i/, last accessed 10 November 2019.

Vahed, Goolam, 'End of a dehumanising system', *The Mercury*, 20 April 2017, www.pressreader.com/south-africa/the-mercury/20170420/281724089428371, last accessed 10 November 2019.

Wadman, Ashleigh, 'Nursing for the British Raj', Australian War Memorial, 28 October 2014, https://www.awm.gov.au/articles/blog/nursing-british-raj, last accessed 13 November 2019.

Welsh Newspapers, The National Library of Wales, https://newspapers.library.wales, last accessed 17 November 2019.

World War One Collection, State Library New South Wales, http://ww1.sl.nsw.gov.au/diaries, last accessed 17 November 2019.

'WW1 memorial to India—an Indian soldier is remembered at Brockenhurst', https://www.newforest-life.com/WW1-memorial-India.html, last accessed 10 November 2019.

SELECT BIBLIOGRAPHY

Unpublished Texts

Kilson, Robin Wallace, 'Calling Up the Empire: The British Military Use of Non-White Labor in France, 1916–1920', Ph.D. dissertation, Harvard University, 1990.

Panandikar, Satyashraya Gopal, *The Economic Consequences of the War for India*, University of London thesis, 1921.

Panmei, Sodolakpou, 'State and Indigenous Intermediaries: Aspects of Administrative Arrangement in British India's Naga Hills, 1881–1945', Nehru Memorial Museum and Library, New Delhi, 2016.

Tetzlaff, Stefan, 'Entangled Boundaries: British India and the Persian Gulf Region During the Transition from Empires to Nation States, c. 1880–1935', MA thesis, Magisterarbeit, Humboldt University, 2009.

Verma, Sonali, 'Criminality, Mobility and Filth: Rewriting Magahiya Doms of Bihar and United Provinces c. 1866–1947', M.Phil. thesis, Centre for Historical Studies, Jawaharlal Nehru University, 2016.

Violett, Edward A., 'Faith Based Development: The Social Development Perspective in Catholic Social Teaching, With an Illustrative Case Study of the Ranchi Archdiocese', Ph.D. thesis, University of London, 2003.

'World War One Folk Songs', unpublished collection, Haryana Academy of History and Culture, Kurukshetra.

INDEX

INDEX

ABOUT THE AUTHOR

Radhika Singha is Professor of Modern Indian History at Jawaharlal Nehru University, New Delhi. Her research interests focus on the social history of crime and criminal law, identification practices, governmentality, borders and border-crossing.

1 — 18 : corrée, lascars. contracts
14 - 16
35 - 6" indentured labour

184
235
80